Spirits and Letters

Spirits and Letters
Reading, Writing and Charisma in African Christianity

Thomas G. Kirsch

Berghahn Books
New York • Oxford

First published in 2008 by

Berghahn Books
www.berghahnbooks.com

©2008 Thomas G. Kirsch

All rights reserved. Except for the quotation of short passages for the purposes of criticism and review, no part of this book may be reproduced in any form or by any means, electronic or mechanical, including photocopying, recording, or any information storage and retrieval system now known or to be invented, without written permission of the publisher.

Library of Congress Cataloging-in-Publication Data

Kirsch, Thomas G., 1966-
 Spirits and letters : reading, writing, and charisma in African Christianity / Thomas G. Kirsch.
   p. cm.
 Includes bibliographical references and index.
 ISBN 978-1-84545-483-8 (hardback : alk. paper)
 1. Christianity--Africa. I. Title.

BR1360.K565 2008
289.9'4096894--dc22

2008014704

British Library Cataloguing in Publication Data

A catalogue record for this book is available from the British Library

Printed in the United States on acid-free paper.

ISBN: 978-1-84545-483-8 (hardback)

*Dedicated to the nine passengers
who died in the car accident
near Siamungala, Zambia, on 14 June 1999*

Contents

List of Illustrations	x
Acknowledgements	xi
Notes on Language	xii
Introduction	**1**
Charisma – Institution	4
Charisma/Spirit/Orality – Institution/Letter/Literacy	8
African Literate Religion	10
'Spirit' and 'Letter' in African Christianity	15
Examining Literacy Practices	18
The Fieldwork	21
Outline of the Book	22

PART I HISTORIES AND ETHNOGRAPHIES

1 Colonial Literacies	**33**
Mission, School and Printing Press	34
Steps towards Secularization	37
Counterforce in Writing	39
What is a School?	41
Resistance and Non-religious Literacies	44
Colonial Bureaucracy	45
Evangelists as Administrators	48
2 Passages, Configurations, Traces	**53**
At the Edge of the Road	53
On the Road	55
Early Evangelisations	57
Christianity in the 1990s	60
Religious Intersections	65
3 Schooled Literacy, Schooled Religion	**71**
Enrolment in School	72
After the Ringing of the Bell	74
Recitations of Syllabi	75
Experiences with Mission Schools	77
Contemporary Religious Education	79

PART II LITERATE RELIGION

4   Literate Cultures in a Material World — 85
   The Bible as an Everyday Object — 86
   Literacy in Times of Paper Shortage — 87
   Getting Hold of Christian Publications — 89
   Publications as Property — 91

5   Indices to the Scriptural — 95
   Bible Talks — 95
   Programmatic Visibility — 99
   References to the Book — 102

6   The Fringes of Christianity — 105
   Blurrings and Criteria — 106
   Turning Letters Upside Down — 110

7   Thoughts about 'Religions of the Book' — 117
   Book People — 117
   Scriptural Inerrancy and Authority — 118
   Canonization and the Bridging of Realms — 120

PART III WAYS OF READING

8   Texts, Readers, Spirit — 125
   Bibles, Versions, Origins — 125
   Pamphlets and Eclecticism — 128
   Selections and Combinations — 130
   Private Readings, Implicit Influences — 131
   Bible Studies — 134

9   Evanescence and the Necessity of Intermediation — 137
   The Impossibility of Storing the Holy Spirit — 137
   Objects, Bodies and Spiritual Evanescence — 141

10   Setting Texts in Motion — 145
   Deciphering and Preaching — 146
   Sediments of the Spirit — 150

11   Missions in Writing — 155
   Literacy Networking — 157
   The Jehovah's Witnesses: Questions and Answers — 159
   The New Apostolic Church: Mediation via Circulars — 160

Supplements as 'Obligatory Passage Points'	162
Enablement through Denominational Publications	165

12 Enablements to Literacy — **169**
Rumination and Scholarship	170
Scripture and Enablement	173
Enabling Supplements	175

PART IV BUREAUCRACY IN THE PENTECOSTAL-CHARISMATIC MODE

13 Offices and the Dispersion of Charisma — **183**
Bureaucracy as Social Practice	184
Organizational Formalization as a Founding Myth	188
Dispersing Charisma, Allocating Offices	190
Charisma, Hierarchies, Variations	193
Ignorance and Mutual Recognition	195

14 Positions of Writers, Positions in Writings — **201**
Certifications of Authority	202
God's Secretaries	204
Identifications and Registries	207
Fixing Polyvalent Rites of Passage	208
Portrayals of the Momentary	210

15 Outlines for the Future, Documents of the Immediate — **213**
Agendas as Revelations	213
Reports of the Unpredictable	216
Agendas, Reports, and the Holy Spirit	221
Re-spiritualizing Bureaucracy	224

16 Bureaucracy In-between — **227**
Flows and Facades	227
African Christianity and the State	230
Formalizing Social Relations	231
Imagining the State	233
Legacies and Isomorphism	236
Presentations and Concealments	237
Bureaucracy as Pentecostal-charismatic Empowerment	239

17 Epilogue — **247**

Bibliography	267
Index	

List of Illustrations

1. Thatching the roof of a new church building, Nanyenda village, 1993. 57
2. Baptism ritual at a river, Simanzi village, 1999. 62
3. Spiritual healing, Simanzi village, 1999. 107
4. Preachers preparing for Sunday service, Mazwange village, 1999. 132
5. Certificate for officeholders, Spirit Apostolic Church, 1999. 203
6. Church Secretary, Siamujulu village, 1995. 205
7. Identity card, Spirit Apostolic Church, 1999. 207

All photographs © Thomas G. Kirsch.

Acknowledgements

The research that forms the basis of this book was conducted over a total of seventeen months' fieldwork in Zambia (April–June 1993; March–June 1995; April–October 1999; April–June 2001), and includes archival research in the National Archives of Zambia (NAZ). My research was generously supported by grants from the Free University Berlin (1993), the German Academic Exchange Service (1999) and the German Research Foundation (2001).

In Zambia my greatest debt of gratitude is to my hosts, the members of the Spirit Apostolic Church and my research assistants. Their hospitality and readiness to share their time with me was a constant source of encouragement. I still find my decision to leave their identities anonymous somewhat distressing in view of my wish to express my sincere gratitude to them.

In the academic world thanks are due to Ute Luig for having introduced me to the Gwembe Valley and for supervising my first field research in 1993. I am particularly grateful to Werner Schiffauer, Richard Rottenburg and my wife, Franziska Becker, for their support and thoughtful advice, as well as for creating an intellectually stimulating atmosphere that made anthropology a challenge in the most positive sense of the word. Finally, I would like to thank Robert Parkin for his revision of my English text.

The author and publisher gratefully acknowledge permission to use adapted versions of the following previously published works:

Kirsch, T. 2003. 'Church, Bureaucracy and the State. Bureaucratic Formalization in a Pentecostal Church of Zambia', *Zeitschrift für Ethnologie* 128(2): 213–31.

Kirsch, T. 2007. 'Ways of Reading as Religious Power in Print Globalization', *American Ethnologist* 34(3): 509–20.

Notes on Language

Some remarks should be made concerning language-use. First, verbatim quotations from texts will not be corrected orthographically and 'mistakes' will not be indicated, since this would mean submitting indigenous writings a posteriori to orthographic standardisation. Secondly, although my study mainly deals with contemporary African Christianity, my ethnographic descriptions are written in the past tense. This represents an attempt to account for the particularities of a socio-religious setting that I experienced as extremely dynamic. Thirdly, all quotations from the Bible are taken from the New International Version (South African Edition, 1978).

Most of the villages and individuals I mention have been made anonymous. The designation 'Spirit Apostolic Church' is also a pseudonym. Wim van Binsbergen (1993) has pointed out how the nomenclature of African Independent Churches in Botswana exhibits an 'endless permutation of always the same few elements, such as "in Zion" and "Apostolic"'. He thus cautions against analysing a given church name as some sort of deliberate theological statement since it 'is often ornamental'. Similarly here, the substitute name 'Spirit Apostolic Church' should not be read as a theological message of any kind.

Introduction

It had already got dark when the senior leaders of the Spirit Apostolic Church assembled at a fireplace outside the ceremonial grounds. Even though the Good Friday services were not yet finished, the leaders wanted to draw up an administrative schedule for the coming year. The General Secretary put a rough-hewn table near the fire and took a pen, a school exercise book and a ruler to the table. As if they were in an office, the other senior leaders took seats opposite him. In the background choir hymns alternating with sermons and periods of communal dancing could be heard – it was the first church meeting that year and most of the congregations were there. The General Secretary had just subdivided the first page precisely into lines when suddenly a pastor approached and asked him to come and help in the ceremonial grounds. One of the young women was showing signs of possession by evil spirits and none of the junior leaders had succeeded in exorcising them. Casually putting his writing implements on the table and excusing himself to the others for the interruption, the General Secretary joined the pastor. He prayed for the woman while laying on hands and started to speak in tongues. After all, he was one of the prominent spiritual healers and prophets of the church. By the time he returned to his desk shortly afterwards the woman had stopped rolling around on the ground. Having cast out the demons the General Secretary now resumed his bureaucratic paperwork.

This episode in a Pentecostal-charismatic church in Zambia in March 1999 touches on the main theme of this book which addresses a long-standing question in the history of ideas and which reconsiders influential conceptual dichotomies in the social sciences and the humanities by way of an examination of reading and writing practices in African Christianity.

In recent years there have been increasing calls for the development of an anthropology of Christianity in which anthropologists 'who study Christian societies formulate common problems' (Robbins 2007: 5). While there is no unanimity among scholars with regard to the achievability of a comprehensive definition of Christianity, it is becoming clear from the emerging body of research that Christian discourses and practices can fruitfully be examined with reference to a set of configurations which – in 'glocalized' variations (cf. Robertson 1995) – are characteristic of Christianities around the world.

This set of configurations entails varied and interrelated dualities such as body/spirit, immanence/transcendence, materiality/immateriality, visibility/invisibility, presence/absence, this-worldliness/other-worldliness and immediacy/eternity. This list is certainly not exhaustive and some dualities can be construed differently. Nonetheless, the dualisms have in common the fact that they reflect categorical distinctions pertaining to the idea of a foundational gap between human beings and the Divine which is significant for practitioners of Christianity, yet also precarious because it involves dilemmas and paradoxes (Cannell 2006a).

Broadly speaking two different modes for dealing with this gap can be discerned. In one mode Christian dualisms can be approached by privileging one pole of the duality over the other. Matthew Engelke, for example, in a series of recent publications presents the case of an African church in Zimbabwe, the Masowe weChishanu Church, whose members are committed to the 'enactment of an immaterial faith' (2007: 8) and for whom materiality is 'the single most important obstacle in developing a spiritual relationship with God' (2005: 119). Due to its material qualities this approach even affects how Masowe weChishanu apostolics relate to the Bible. Calling themselves 'the Christians who don't read the Bible', they dismiss the Scriptures as irrelevant and unnecessary, and instead strive to attain a materially unmediated 'live and direct' relationship with God.

The other common mode for dealing with the Christian dualisms listed above consists in reconciling them by, for example, emphasizing – as in contemporary Mormonism – that there is *no* 'opposition between this world and the next world – the material and the spiritual' (Cannell 2005: 338). This approach involves an attempt to bridge the gap between human beings and the Divine through the coalescence of the poles of dualities.

This book deals with the latter approach by examining a duality that has thus far almost completely been left untouched by anthropologists and which is, however, crucial to Christianity as a 'religion of the book' whose Trinitarian order encompasses the Holy Spirit: the dichotomy of 'the Letter' and 'the Spirit' as expressed in St Paul's dictum that 'the letter kills, but the spirit gives life' (2 Corinthians 3:6). Pursuing an anthropology of Christianity with regard to this prominent 'Pauline pair' (Caspary 1979) can help us gain insights into how religious practitioners try to come to grips with some of the 'central dilemmas of Christianity' (Cannell 2006b: 12).

This is particularly true for the examination of Pentecostal-charismatic movements. As David Maxwell has persuasively demonstrated in his recent study of the origin and development of Pentecostalism in southern Africa, these movements not only share an emphasis on the 'pneumatic practices of speaking in tongues, prophecy, divine healing and exorcism' (2006: 15) – their worldwide expansion since the turn of the twentieth century was made possible through 'advances in print technology and universal postage [which made Pentecostal publications] cheap and easy to print and dispatch around the world' (2006: 29). In these movements, it therefore seems, adherents did not (entirely) subscribe to the idea of an opposition between 'the Letter' and 'the Spirit' but were moved by both spirits *and* letters.

But since, in conceptual terms, 'Christianity has given rise to key discourses ... that persist even where their religious support have fallen away' (Keane 2006: 310), I also try to show in this book that certain facets of social-scientific thinking implicitly

– and yet in a momentous and at times problematic way – resound with the Christian dualist idea of 'the Letter' and 'the Spirit'. During my fieldwork in Zambia, for instance, what astonished and fascinated me in episodes like that described above was that they contradicted what I had read in the scholarly literature on religious charisma and what I thus expected to find when I started my fieldwork. In the above incident there was no personal division of labour between spiritual healing and prophecy, on the one hand, and bureaucratic administration, on the other. Instead, this was a case of a prophet-healer who also served the function of secretary in the form of a personal union. In addition, this was not an example of what Max Weber has called the 'charisma of the office', nor of the 'institutionalization of charisma' in the usual sense of the expression. In this church, the office of 'general secretary' was not ascribed any extraordinary power in and by itself. Moreover, during the eight years of my repeated visits to this church between 1993 and 2001, there was no increase in the emphasis put on church administration at the expense of Pentecostal-charismatic activities. Rather, as I came to realize, these dimensions were continuously kept in balance and, most importantly for my argument in this book, *coalesced*. With regard to the episode above, for example, local discourses maintained that secretarial work requires the assistance of the Holy Spirit, since only a spiritually endowed secretary would know how to administer a church in a divinely ordained way. Spirituality was seen as a precondition for bureaucratic work.

The aim of this book is, therefore, to challenge prevailing scholarly notions of the relationship between 'charisma' and 'institution' by examining reading and writing practices in Pentecostal-charismatic Christianity in contemporary Africa. Taking up the continuing scholarly interest in Pentecostal-charismatic churches in Africa (Meyer 2004a), and focusing on religious 'literacy practices' – that is, 'behaviour and conceptualisations related to the use of reading and/or writing' (Street 1984: 12) – I show how charismatically authorized church elders in rural Zambia refer to the Bible and other Christian literature, and how their bureaucratic writing practices are related to the Holy Spirit, which my interlocutors regarded as an evanescent spiritual being.[1] Thus, by analysing the social processes, conflicts and negotiations that revolve around the conjunction of Pentecostal-charismatic and literacy practices – or, in other words, around the use of writings by religious practitioners who are ascribed extraordinary spiritual powers – this book attempts to fill a significant gap in social science research.

Why is it that literacy practices among contemporary African Christians have been so widely ignored up to now? And, more generally, what makes the focus of this inquiry – 'Pentecostal-charismatic religions of the book' – seem at first sight like a contradiction in terms? As regards the first question, it appears that the problematic but still quite common association of Africa with 'orality' and of African Christianity with expressive and emotive styles of worship has led to a situation in which the empirical phenomenon of a literate African Christianity has for the most part been disregarded in scholarly circles.[2] As regards the second question, I suggest that the difficulties in thinking about 'Pentecostal-charismatic religions of the book' result from a set of conceptually questionable chains of association that, in the social sciences, are linked to Max Weber's work on types of authority, but which can also be demonstrated to resonate with other more general tenets in the Western history of ideas. In general these chains of associations attribute evanescent utterances to the unstable phenomenon of charisma while objectifying writings are accredited to institutionalized types of authority. In order to problematize this perspective let me, in what follows, start with a brief account of how the problem has been framed up to now, before introducing some findings from studies of African-initiated churches that conflict with dominant ideas regarding 'charismatic routinization' and the incompatibility between 'charisma' and 'institution'.

Charisma – Institution

Of all the contributions Max Weber made to the social sciences (Swedberg 2003) his work on types of legitimate authority, and particularly his notion of charisma, is certainly amongst the most important for anthropology (Keyes 2002: 248–49; see also Schnepel 1987) and has influenced scholars who do not otherwise subscribe to Weberian approaches. In Weber's well known definition, 'charisma' is specified as:

> a certain quality of an individual's personality by virtue of which he is set apart from ordinary men and treated as endowed with supernatural, superhuman, or at least specifically exceptional powers or qualities. These are such as are not accessible to the ordinary person, but are regarded as of divine origin or as exemplary, and on the basis of them the individual concerned is treated as a leader (1968a: 48).

Charisma is, here, situated beyond 'the ordinary'; it is 'exceptional' and 'extraordinary', because it differs from the 'impersonal' and 'stable' routinized realms. As a 'residual category' (Fabian 1979: 19) charismatic authority accordingly becomes defined by what it is *not*: traditional and rational-legal types of authority. On the whole Weber thus distinguishes between three 'pure types of legitimate authority', based respectively on:

> (1) Rational grounds – resting on a belief in the 'legality' of patterns of normative rules and the right of those elevated to authority under such rules to issue commands (legal authority); (2) Traditional grounds – resting on an established belief in the sanctity of immemorial traditions and the legitimacy of the status of those exercising authority under them (traditional authority); or, finally, (3) Charismatic grounds – resting on devotion to the specific and exceptional sanctity, heroism or exemplary character of an individual person, and of the normative patterns or order revealed or ordained by him (charismatic authority) (1968b: 46).

As concerns charisma, Weber's discussion is heavily influenced by Rudolf Sohm's *Kirchenrecht* (1892), in which Sohm depicts early Christianity as an inherently charismatic and divinely guided organization, while later developments in Catholicism represent, for him, a problematic lapse into ecclesiastical legalism. Yet whereas Sohm sees charisma as having a certain historical continuity and as being embedded in the communal structures of *ecclesia*, Weber modifies Sohm's formulation by emphasising the charismatic leader's innovative, even revolutionary, position.[3] According to Weber, the extraordinariness ascribed to charismatic leaders is intimately linked to an anti-traditionalistic and anti-institutional orientation that rejects preceding certainties and given structures by proclaiming a new vision of the world. In what has become an extensively cited quotation, he asserts:

> Charisma knows only inner determination and inner restraint. The holder of charisma seizes the task that is adequate for him and demands obedience and a following by virtue of his mission. His success determines whether he finds them. His charismatic claim breaks down if his mission is not recognised by those to whom he feels he has been sent. If they recognise him, he is their master – so long as he knows how to maintain recognition through 'proving himself' (1968c: 20).

The main steps in the emergence of charismatic leaders are the pursuit of the mission's inner goals, evidential proof and public recognition. All three elements combine with the gesture of a certain immediate instantaneousness, which turns its back on any form of structured *longue durée*.

Given this idea of charismatic leaders as innovators, Weber and innumerable subsequent scholars have depicted 'pure charisma' as being antagonistic to 'stable' social forms. Hans H. Gerth and C. Wright Mills, for example, assert that: 'Charisma is opposed to all institutional routines, those of tradition and those subject to rational management' (1948: 52). And Shmuel N. Eisenstadt describes charisma as having 'inherent antinomian and anti-institutional predispositions', which involve a 'revolutionary disdain of formal procedures' and 'strong tendencies toward the destruction and decomposition of institutions' (1968: xix).

In analytical terms, 'charisma' and 'institution' therefore seem to be characterized by fundamental contradictions. These appear most evident when charisma is compared to what represents the key symbol of formally organized institutions: bureaucracy. Here Weber points out:

> In contrast to any kind of bureaucratic organization of offices, the charismatic structure knows nothing of a form or of an ordered procedure of appointment or dismissal. It knows no regulate 'career', 'advancement', 'salary', or regulated and expert training of the holder of charisma or of his aids. It knows no agency of control or appeal, no local bailiwicks or exclusive functional jurisdictions; nor does it embrace permanent institutions like our bureaucratic 'departments', which are independent of persons and of purely personal charisma (1968c: 19–20).

The ideal type of bureaucracy stands for highly structured, regulated and impersonal social structures, which, once fully established, are 'the hardest to destroy' (Weber 1968d: 75). It devises authoritative formal inscriptions that, in bureaucratic capitalism, participate in constituting an 'iron cage' and in subduing those social realities that try to resist bureaucratic logic.

The word 'inscription' can be taken here in a very plain sense: bureaucracy means paperwork. Among the main characteristics of Weber's ideal type of bureaucracy, management by 'written documents' (1968d: 67; cf. Goody 1977: 15–16) is one of the first mentioned. If there are no files, there is no bureaucracy. The bureaucratic logic evolves by means of recording and registering. Thus, what bureaucracy is to formally organized institutions, writing is to bureaucracy – a symbol of the practice of fixing, objectifying and institutionalizing social realities (see also Davis 1982: 5).

Certainly the foregoing account of some Weberian concepts only deals with synthesized and abstract 'ideal types'. But it is theoretical frameworks of this kind that inform much scholarly work in the social sciences in general and in the anthropology of religion in particular. In these works several problems can be discerned which, up to now, I argue, have had detrimental effects on the conceptualization of research and the interpretation of empirical cases.[4]

The first problem concerns the widespread inclination among scholars to effectively treat Weberian ideal types not as heuristic analytical tools, but as reality. Despite claims to the contrary, empirical phenomena are then measured against what, from an ideal-typical point of view, is conceptualized as, for example, 'pure charisma'. On the one hand, this makes many empirical phenomena look somehow deficient – they are not quite how it ideal-typically could (should?) be. On the other hand, by somehow taking ideal types for reality and at the same time subscribing to the idea of an opposition between 'charisma' and 'institution', an 'either – or' logic is introduced into the analysis. Empirical findings are subsumed either under the category 'charisma' or under that of 'institution'. What follows from this is that the conceptual space between the ideal types – the composites, mixtures and hybrids that Max Weber was so aware of and that are the primary focus of this book – have thus far remained largely unattended to in empirical research. There certainly exist studies dealing with 'divisions of labour' within one and the same religious community between what has variously been referred to as 'priest and prophet' (Weber 1963; Firth 1970), 'bishop and prophet' (West 1975) or 'preacher and prophet' (Kiernan 1976). But, as will be discussed below, these studies commonly stress role complementarity, not the combination of roles in the form of personal unions. In the empirical cases analysed in this book, by contrast, personal unions were the rule rather than the exception. Here, religious authority usually relied on the idea of a Pentecostal-charismatic 'extraordinariness', namely on the notion that certain people can act authoritatively because of their association with powerful spiritual entities. At the same time, however, many of these charismatically authorized persons were also elected officeholders who committed themselves to regulated procedures and engaged in bureaucratic practices. They accordingly combined in their religious practice what in the social science literature has usually been categorically separated.

Secondly, and related to the foregoing, categorical distinctions that have been developed for application in diachronic studies are often employed unreflectively in synchronic analyses. Weber's suggestion that charisma 'cannot remain stable, but becomes either traditionalized or rationalized, or a combination of both' (1968a: 54) has been highly influential in the social sciences. For many scholars it has in fact provided a research programme: in their analyses, the study of charisma is more or less equated with the examination of processes of charismatic routinization. Here, charismatic authority is treated as a phenomenon that is always on the verge of obliteration; institutionalization, on the other hand, is what it all unavoidably leads to.

Yet, given the idea of an antagonism with an inevitable transition from one to the other – from charismatic to traditional or rational-legal types of authority – the (synchronic) existence of features ascribed to the category 'institution' in a particular 'charismatic' setting in many studies is almost mechanically interpreted as an indication of the routinization of charisma. Some inquiries, for example, already take the mere existence of writing in a 'charismatic' setting as evidence that this setting is beginning to be affected by a process of institutionalization. The question of how writings are actually used in this empirical setting then seems to require no further elucidation in this approach. In the final analysis this transposition of diachronic categories into synchronic settings therefore produces a problematic categorical asymmetry in which 'institution' appears always to outweigh 'charisma'.

Thirdly, the idea of an antagonism between 'charisma' and 'institution' is usually premised on the contrast between 'fluidity' and 'fixity'. Here, it is particularly the latter term which has become debatable when one takes 'traditional' and 'rational-legal' types of authority as instances of 'institutionalized authority'. After all, how can the idea of 'fixity' be reconciled with the prevailing contemporary view that social realities are multifarious and characterized by unremitting processuality? Inspired by Eric Hobsbawm's and Terence Ranger's *The Invention of Tradition* (1986), it has been amply demonstrated in recent decades, for example, that 'tradition' is not static, but rather the object of constant social negotiations, conflicts, redefinitions and inventions. Likewise, according to prominent approaches in the field of organization studies, 'formal organization' – that is, the organizational form that Weber calls 'rational-legal' – should not be treated as a regulated, formalized and structured outcome, but as an ongoing process in which social actors strive to regularize, formalize and give structure to what, in the final analysis, remains contingent and ambiguous (Weick 1979). And lastly, as regards the use of writings as a hallmark of 'formal institutions', it is all too clear that the meaning of a text – whether religious scriptures, laws in writing, or administrative documents – does not reside in the text itself (Fish 1980; Iser 2000). Admittedly, writings are characterized by physical materiality and therefore lend themselves to contrapositions between 'immaterial spirit and material text' (Keane 2007: 2) and the impression of the objective fixity of texts. But, nonetheless, writings only become relevant when they are embedded, used and interpreted in situated social practices. Furthermore, it is within practice and its concomitant discourses that the attribution of a text as authoritatively fixed is socially constructed. This quality is not inherent to the writings themselves.

None of these considerations is meant for one moment to suggest that recognizing the strained nature of the relationship between the ideal types of 'charisma' and 'institution' deprives it of all analytical value; this is undoubtedly not the case. Yet I argue that the perspectives outlined above have limitations when the issue of literacy is introduced: the emphasis on role complementarity acknowledges instances of the coexistence of charisma with institutions, yet it nevertheless reflects a typology that treats the difference between these dimensions as unbridgeable. Literacy practices are generally situated on the institutional side of this dichotomy. The focus on routinization, on the other hand, which frequently has a modernist aspect to it, sees literacy as a factor that effects an institutionalizing transformation of charisma. Therefore, since in both perspectives literacy is associated with the notion of an 'institution', they both generate problems of their own when it comes to accounting for the literacy practices of Pentecostal-charismatic communities.

How, then, can we try to avoid the above conceptual problems? In this book, the heuristic value of Weberian ideal types is acknowledged, but the focus is on how the dimensions of 'charisma' and 'institution' are synchronically related to each other and coalesce in a particular religious setting in Zambia. This perspective implies, first, approaching these dimensions symmetrically by rejecting the idea that there is an inevitable transition from one to the other. Secondly, although 'charisma' and 'institution' as ideal-typical categories tend to differ, among other things, in how authorizing reference points are constructed, what types of resources are employed, and their respective discursive formations, they are here translated into a research design in which both are examined as situated social practices. The present book accordingly deals with ways of doing, and more particularly with the social construction of charisma (Csordas 1997; Kirsch 1998, 2002; Wallis 1982) and its synchronic relations with 'institutionalization', the latter term being used as a verbal noun referring to the activity of institutionalizing. In general, this approach allows us to obtain a better understanding of what happens empirically in the space between what is ideal-typically categorized as 'charisma' and 'institution'.

Charisma/Spirit/Orality – Institution/Letter/Literacy

That the notion of a 'Pentecostal-charismatic religion of the book' appeared to many social scientists I spoke with to involve a contradiction in terms arguably has to do with the fact that the Weberian categories mentioned above are paralleled by two other influential dichotomies found within the Western history of ideas.

First, as mentioned above, certain facets of social-scientific thinking implicitly resound with the Pauline dichotomy between 'the Letter' and 'the Spirit' as expressed in Paul's dictum that 'the letter kills, but the spirit gives life' (2 Corinthians 3:6; see Chau 1995). In the parlance of the social sciences, 'the Letter' is a paradigm of law, literalism, objectification, orthodoxy and a diachronic *longue durée*; 'the Spirit', on the other hand, is an epitome of revelation, allegory, subjectivity, heterodoxy and synchronicity. Thus the ongoing debates about the relationship between 'structure' and 'agency' – still one of the 'unresolved core enigmata in social science and social theory' (Fuchs 2001: 24) – can to a certain extent be understood as a social science version of certain theological debates concerning the strained relationship between 'the Letter and the Spirit'.

Secondly, the Weberian dichotomy between 'charisma' and 'institution' is paralleled by common ideas concerning the contrast between the 'spoken word' and the 'written text' (cf. Goody and Watt 1963: 342–43). Here it is notable that proponents of what Brian Street has called the 'autonomous' model of literacy (1984: 1) also take recourse to ideal-typical constructs when, for example, talking about 'primary orality' (Ong 1982) or the 'full technical possibilities' (Goody 2000: 4) of literacy. These scholars have examined the cognitive and socio-cultural implications of literacy in previously oral cultures when, for instance, they address the 'consequences of literacy per se in African religion' (Janzen 1985). Yet, although the idea of a 'great divide' between 'orality' and 'literacy' has convincingly been criticized for several decades, it remains influential and is still used as a conceptual framework for shorthand and yet far-reaching interpretations.[5] Many of these interpretations are thus based on the well known formula *vox audita perit, littera scripta manet* ('the voice heard perishes, the written letter endures').[6] By categorically separating 'orality' and 'literacy' and associating 'orality' with 'evanescence' and 'literacy' with 'fixity', the oral–literate typology in these studies resonates with the dichotomy between 'charisma' and 'institution' outlined above.

Taken together the dichotomies 'charisma versus institution', 'spirit versus letter' and 'orality versus literacy' are characterized by partly overlapping semantic fields. By suggesting specific chains of associations, furthermore, this overlap creates a situation in which certain empirical phenomena disappear from view or become difficult to grasp conceptually. With regard to this overlap in semantic fields, for example, it is notable that Max Weber's 'iron cage' – which is intricately linked to bureaucratic inscriptions – collimates the Pauline notion of the 'killing letter'. In both cases, writings are equated with the static objectification of otherwise unstable and transient phenomena: 'By isolating thought on a written surface, detached from any interlocutor, making utterance in this sense autonomous and indifferent to attack, writing presents utterance and thought as uninvolved in all else, somehow self-contained, complete' (Ong 1982: 132). Here, writings are depicted as a means of objectification, the latter, in its turn, representing an important prerequisite for institutionalization (Berger and Luckmann 1966). Charisma, on the other hand, 'may be said to *exist only in the process of originating*. It cannot remain stable, but becomes either traditionalized or rationalized, or a combination of both' (Weber 1968a: 54, my italics). In this crucial aspect of Weber's definition, 'charisma' corresponds to what is frequently specified as a fundamental principle of 'oral culture': 'Words come into being through time, and *exist only so long as they are going out of existence* ... [W]hen I pronounce "reflect", by the time I get to the "flect" the "re" is gone, and necessarily and irretrievably gone' (Ong 1967: 40, my italics). When an utterance is submitted to writing, however, it 'ceases to be evanescent and becomes fixed, linear, reversible or retraceable, so that our beloved "re" remains intact ages after we have crossed "flect"' (Biakolo 1999: 43–44).

Generally speaking, this parallelism attributes evanescent utterances to the unstable phenomenon of charisma, while objectifying writings are allocated to particular institutionalized types of authority. In this mode of reasoning, which admits 'literacy into some analytical areas but [excludes] it from others' (Hofmeyr 1995a: 22), to contemplate the co-occurrence of charisma and writing appears problematic or even typologically impossible. And, indeed, there are many instances in the history of religion indicating that writing can restrict and transform charisma. Spiritual revelations have frequently been turned into dogmas after they have been written down. Yet, all the same, to talk of an intrinsic antagonism between charisma and writing would be misleading, since the history of religion also abounds with cases where charismatic leaders deliberately refer to and make use of writings. According to Fenella Cannell, for example, American Mormons see 'no necessary contradiction between the bureaucratic and the spiritual, but feel a strong pull towards both' (2005: 347). The Bahá'i Faith, on the other hand, emphasises that its prophet founder, Bahá'u'lláh (1817–92), wrote down his spiritual revelations by himself, in contrast to Jesus Christ who is also accepted as a divine manifestation by this religious community. A West African prophet of the twentieth century asserted that he was spiritually told to publish his teachings: 'Print it in books, effect complete circulation, and I will make you a holy Apostle for the whole world' (cited in Peel 1968: 115). Similarly, Joseph Smith, the founder of the American Church of Jesus Christ of Latter-day Saints, was said to have received a 'charismatic prerogative' to translate the Book of Mormon (White and White 1996: 96), a book that was originally inscribed in concealed golden plates of divine origin and that later became the sacred scripture of Mormonism. Conversely, cases like the Zimbabwean church founder Johane Masowe who in the early twentieth century 'encouraged his followers to throw away their Bible' (Dillon-Malone 1978: 58), or a contemporary branch of his church, the Masowe weChishanu apostolics, who refer to themselves as 'the Christians who don't read the Bible' (Engelke 2004, 2007), are illuminating and fascinating but in the final analysis quite exceptional.[7] As Adrian Hastings has pointed out in his book *The Church in Africa, 1450–1950*, 'Christianity was potentially everywhere a reading community' (1996: 457).

Against the background of these findings, it is necessary to re-examine the relationship between the dichotomies outlined above. The following sections embark on such an inquiry by briefly reviewing social science and, in particular, anthropological literature on reading and writing practices in African Christianity.

African Literate Religion

It has repeatedly been pointed out that in the early colonial period in southern Africa literacy was widely considered to be a means of empowerment. Among Western missionaries, reading skills were first and foremost understood as a precondition for access to the Word of God as contained in the Bible – the 'Magna Charta of all the rights and privileges of modern civilization' (Livingstone 1857: 579). The indigenous population, on the other hand, often saw literacy as a prominent constituent of the 'hidden power of the whites' (Turner 1979: 41). Part of the attraction of the early missions therefore lay in their implicit promise to facilitate the appropriation of this power. Yet the effects of this attraction did not always correspond to what the missionaries had anticipated. As David Barrett (1968) has shown, for example, the separation of indigenous Christian movements from Western missions frequently coincided with the publication of vernacular translations of the Bible. The appropriation of literacy thus contained within it its own subversive potential.

In recent years the double gesture of 'incorporation' and 'resistance' in the context of colonialism has most clearly been elaborated in a series of seminal works by Jean and John Comaroff (1989, 1991, 1997). In their analysis of the colonial encounter between the Tswana of South Africa and British Nonconformist missionaries – whom they regard as the spearhead of colonial hegemony in this part of southern Africa – they point out that the reactions of the Tswana 'consisted in a complex admixture of tacit (even uncomprehending) accommodation to the hegemonic order at one level and diverse expressions of symbolic and practical resistance at another' (1991: 26). They emphasise that: 'The most curious feature of the process, however, is that, notwithstanding the rejection and transformation of many elements of 'the' European worldview, its *forms* became authoritatively inscribed on the African landscape' (ibid.: 18). According to the Comaroffs, these 'forms' came to bear on the consciousness and practices of the colonized through, for example, the internalization of 'modes of rational debate, positivist knowledge, and empirical reason' (ibid.: 213), as well as the standardization of language and literary genres (1989: 282–89). The last point is a reference to their assessment that literacy played a crucial role in the missionaries' attempts to reform the consciousness of the Africans since, for Nonconformist missionaries, reading and writing skills promised 'the ascendance of the reflective, inner-directed self: a self, long enshrined in Protestant personhood, now secularized and generalized as bourgeois ideology' (1991: 63).

Two aspects are noteworthy in this context. First, although the Comaroffs and many other scholars rightly stress the role of literacy in the missionary enterprise, the actual scope of the impact of literacy on the consciousness and practices of the colonized has long remained rather hypothetical. It is only in recent years that detailed accounts of reading and writing practices in colonial Africa have become available through a number of historical studies (see, for example, Barber 2006; Draper 2003a; Hawkins 2002; Krüger 2006; Newell 2002; Peterson 2004). Surprisingly, however, situated literacy practices in contemporary sub-Saharan Africa have hitherto only rarely been made the object of anthropological investigation.[8] Indeed, it seems that there are more studies nowadays on audiovisual media (like television, film, video and the radio) in Africa than investigations into the practical use of what is still today the dominant media in many parts of Africa: the written word.

Secondly, it has often been claimed that literacy played a part in the formation of new subjectivities in Africa. Given the ethnographic findings presented in the present book, however, it appears debatable to me whether this reformation should be described generally as a move towards 'reflective, inner-directed' selves. After all, in most African-initiated churches the working of spiritual entities is ascribed an important role. In addition, many of them take it for granted that spiritual entities can take possession of a human being by, for example, entering his or her body. This idea of a spiritual permeability of the body implies that 'personhood' (Jackson and Karp 1990) might not (only) enshrine a human self but also, temporarily, spiritual entities.[9] Thus, on the one hand, spirits can become part of a person's identity, a process that in many cases forms the basis for processes of charismatic legitimation. On the other hand, as I demonstrate in the present book, the notion of a spiritual permeability of the body imbues literacy practices with epistemological premises (cf. Street 2003: 1) that in significant ways differ from those projected by the early Protestant missionaries. 'Spirituality' – that is, a person's privileged association with the Holy Spirit – in the Pentecostal-charismatic churches examined in this book represented something desired and aimed for, but most importantly spirituality was also seen as a means by which a whole range of religious activities such as healing and prophecy could be successfully accomplished as well as a divinely ordained reading of the Bible and secretarial work.

Similar to what has been stated above for literacy practices in contemporary sub-Saharan Africa in general, there is also a peculiar reluctance to engage with literacy practices in present day African Christianity (cf. Maxwell 2001: 502).[10] African Christian writings have so far mostly been dealt with in anthologies and editions (see, for example, Gunner 2002; Hexham 1994; Hexham and Papini 2002; Janzen and MacGaffey 1974). Yet up to now, apart from a very few publications, the ethnographic analysis of reading and writing practices among contemporary African Christians has not figured as prominently as might have been expected in light of the importance ascribed to the conjunction of Christianity and literacy.[11] This is all the more astonishing since the literature on African-initiated churches provides ample evidence – though it is scattered and often treated perfunctorily – of the existence of a great variety of African literacy practices in relation to, for example, Bible reading, the documentation of religious practice and indigenous religious writings. In the mid-1920s, for instance, the Christian witch-finder Tomo Nyrienda, who acquired dubious fame because he had killed several hundred alleged witches, devised the 'outlines of a literate administration' (Ranger 1975: 50-51) by writing letters to distant villages as well as baptismal lists (ibid.: 50), some of which were 'in "pretend-writing", obviously compiled by young men able to impress a congregation with their scrawling imitations but not, in fact, able to write' (ibid.: 63). But Nyrienda also claimed that 'a book of revelation had come down to him from heaven and that the book, when placed by the baptismal stream, could reveal witches' (ibid.: 72). Moreover, one of his pastors had collected a 'long typed and duplicated collection of texts in English' which Nyrienda used beside the Bible as the 'basis of his preaching' (ibid.: 52); indeed, when he was finally arrested, the police found him reading one of his 'beloved papers' (ibid.: 51). This prominent example of the history of Christianity in Zambia not only exemplifies the significance assigned to reading and writing in many African-initiated churches, it also indicates the great variety of forms in which they have appropriated literacy as trope and practice, such as the following.

On the one hand, as in Tomo Nyrienda's case, books always figured prominently in the religious imaginary of African indigenous Christians. Carol Muller, for example, demonstrates that a group of female members of the South African Church of the Nazarites (Ibandla lamaNazaretha) 'transferred the power and value attached to a central tenet of mission Christian ideology – that Truth is contained in the written word – onto traditional Zulu ritual performance and attire', this being an attempt to inscribe their selves 'into the heavenly Book with spiritual song and religious dance' (1997: 4). Similarly the Zambian prophetess Alice Lenshina, who founded the Lumpa Church in the 1950s, claimed to have been given a divine Book of Life. After a temporal death experience:

> Lenshina returned to life and recounted that she had seen God; she had been given three books by him and ordered to return to earth, in order to deliver the Africans from fortune tellers and magicians and all kinds of evil doers. As she showed some reluctance, God took back two books. ... The remaining one was written in an unknown tongue and could be read only by Lenshina. ... Anyone trying to read it would find in it either water or fire; he would become blind or sick or go mad (Oger 1960: 2).

When Dorothea Lehmann and John Taylor visited the Lumpa Church one of the local leaders told them that 'one day soon Mama Lenshina will give us our own Bible' (1961: 261). In this latter case and many comparable ones in African-initiated Christianity, 'the Bible' symbolically stands for divine revelation as attained or hoped for.

On the other hand, since the early decades of the twentieth century, a number of indigenous Christians have begun to set down religious experiences, visions and doctrines in written form. Among the best known of these documents is the script of Josiah Olunowo Oshitelu, the founder of the West African Aladura movement (cf. Peel 1968). Composed mainly between 1925 and 1934, the scripture comprises six volumes of cryptic symbols, which Oshitelu considered to be a manifestation of his revelatory visions (Turner 1967b; Probst 1989). Besides such writings with a particular spiritual language and script, which are also known from other churches (see, for example, Adams 1947; Hau 1961), writings in the Latin alphabet were authored and partly published by church leaders such as Ezekiel Guti (Maxwell 2006), George Khambule (Draper 2003b; Sundkler 1961a: 356, 1976: 119–60), Johane Maranke (Daneel 1971: 316, 321; Daneel 1987: 56–58), Simon Mpadi (Andersson 1958: 195–96; MacGaffey 1983, 1986: 113–16) and Josiah Olunowo Oshitelu (Mbiti 1987: 41; Turner 1967b, 1967c). In some cases it was the disciples and descendants of African church founders and prophets who were responsible for putting their particular life histories, prophetic sayings, liturgies or hymns down in writing. In the former Belgian Congo, for example, two adherents of the Christian prophet Simon Kimbangu set out to record the religious activities of their prophet in 1921 (Pemberton 1993; Raymaekers 1971). In southern Africa a similar collection of texts compiled by disciples and descendants emerged from the very first recorded indigenous Christian movement, initiated by the Xhosa prophet Ntsikana (Hodgson 1980). In 1932 followers of Johane Masowe published an account of the life history and visionary experiences of their religious leader (Dillon-Malone 1978: 50–58,

153–55). And finally, the South African Church of the Nazarites has been described as 'a church of narratives, dreams, and prophecies, many of which were recorded by Isaiah Shembe [the prophet-founder of the church] and his young amanuenses. Writing was always an important part of church life, and the documents gathered by the founder were selectively used by his successor to print the first published combined hymn and prayer book' (Gunner 2006: 156). In 1949 the son and successor of Isaiah Shembe even appointed an archivist to collect oral testimonies of the work of his father (Hexham and Oosthuizen 1996: xi–xiv).

In several of these cases the act of composing and/or dealing with religious texts was linked to spiritual entities. In her book *Alice Lakwena and the Holy Spirits War in Northern Uganda 1986–97*, for example, Heike Behrend points out that, in Lakwena's Holy Spirit Mobile Forces, it 'was the spirits who demanded that their speeches be put in writing and ... referred in their speeches to things already said and written down. They would call on the chief clerk to cite their speech of such-and-such a date, and scolded him if he could not find the passage' (1999: 152–53). Nevertheless, the text thus produced was not canonized and was 'never completed, because, right up to the end, the spirits continued speaking and producing new texts to be added to the old' (ibid.: 154). With regard to the scriptures of the Church of the Nazarites, on the other hand, Irving Hexham notes that the translation from Zulu into English by the prophet-founder's son, Londa Shembe, was seen as 'an inspired work with spiritual significance that was only possible through the gift of prophecy. No ordinary man could have translated this text the way Londa Shembe did, because in translating the original Zulu he was guided in a unique way by God and his Ancestor' (1994: xxii). The translation was therefore considered to represent a revelation.

Besides the foregoing, the literature on African-initiated Christianity also exhibits the existence of a wide range of administrative literacy practices that can be seen as exemplifying the transnational diffusion of organizational models of Christianity. Like Tomo Nyrienda's 'outlines of a literate administration' mentioned above, African Christians issued, for example, membership and congregation cards,[12] preacher certificates,[13] and 'passports to heaven' (Andersson 1958: 160–61). They put the laws of their church into writing,[14] produced minutes of committee meetings as well as programmes for, and records of, church services,[15] compiled membership registers and statistics,[16] and recorded dreams and confessions in notebooks.[17] In doing so some of them used typewriters (Hexham and Oosthuizen 1996: xii) and authorized documents by using church stamps (Behrend 1999: 154; Dillon-Malone 1978: 34). Such administrative writing activities can even be found in the work of African Christian prophets. As John Janzen and Wyatt MacGaffey remark for Congolese prophets:

> Modern prophets use secretaries mostly to write down their utterances, to keep minutes of seances, and to issue authorizations and convocations. In some prophetic groups the messages of the spirit, communicated through the prophet in ecstasy, are preserved in writing. Seances may be written up, partly

for the prophet's own future reference, partly to safeguard him if litigation should ensue; it is believed that a record of the divination will testify to what he really said. When a prophet wants members of a client's family to be present he issues a 'convocation', modeled on those of the government courts, typed in the manner of an official form, and enhanced with the inevitable rubber stamp (Janzen and MacGaffey 1974: 19).

Lastly, African-initiated churches usually refer to and make use of a great variety of religious writings, some of them being popular religious publications, others being printed and distributed by the churches themselves, while yet others are issued by Western evangelizing churches. Besides the Bible in different versions, these writings include a vast range of 'esoteric' or 'secret' literature like *The Sixth and Seventh Book of Moses*, well known in West Africa (Field 1960: 41). European and American denominations place emphasis on the distribution of books, tracts, pamphlets, magazines and circulars (Etherington 2005; Hofmeyr 2004, 2005; Kirsch 2007). Their publications have a wide currency and may be found in the remotest village, where they are on occasion even read by people who do not belong to the respective denomination. Some of the books that circulate are religious writings by Europeans. Among the most famous of these are John Bunyan's *The Pilgrim's Progress* (Hofmeyr 2002, 2004), which has been translated into eighty African languages, and Placide Tempels' *La philosophie bantoue* (1945), which was highly influential in the Jamaa movement (Fabian 1971). Others were written by Africans who had spent some time in Europe and, after returning, began to set down their religious ideas. An example is Prince Birinda de Boudieguy whose *La Bible secrète des noirs* (1952) had an impact on the Gabonese Bwiti movement (Fernandez 1982).

'Spirit' and 'Letter' in African Christianity

Bengt Sundkler once remarked briefly, concerning African-initiated churches, that 'in the midst of spontaneity [there] is in fact much more of printed or written forms of worship than one would possibly expect' (1978: 548). This observation has been supported and substantiated by the foregoing tour de force which indicated the existence of a great variety of literacy practices, even among African-initiated churches of a Pentecostal-charismatic type.

Studies of indigenous African Christianity can therefore help to problematize the dichotomies relating charisma/spirit/orality with institution/letter/literacy. As regards the issue of charismatic routinization, for example, Johannes Fabian points out, with reference to the Congolese Jamaa movement:

> Until the 1970s the movement functioned without bylaws, membership roles, or even written material for instruction. Networks of spiritual kinship and orally transmitted teachings were considered sufficient to safeguard the identity of the Jamaa. This changed when the decisive confrontation with the

church hierarchy came. For different reasons, loyal as well as dissident Jamaa groups were forced to adopt a complicated bureaucratic organization and to codify the doctrine in written manuals (Fabian 1994: 261).

For Fabian this development initially suggested that 'charisma was transformed into bureaucratic structures' (ibid.: 262; cf. Fabian 1971, 1991). Yet, in later decades, spiritual practices again became increasingly important in the Jamaa movement. Thus, Fabian suggests, in the long run 'change was not so much from enthusiasm to routinization, from charisma to a more formal *Herrschaftsform*, but from a concentration of charismatic authority to its dispersal or diversification' (ibid.: 269).

As regards the scholarly pattern of focusing on complementary 'divisions of labour', on the other hand, Jim Kiernan remarks in an intriguing article on Zulu Zionist churches: 'We are now faced with the paradox that a religion, whose fundamental expression lies in free and uninhibited sensory experience, utterance and movement, should be overstaffed with officials whose function it is to order, arrange, manage and control various aspects of that experience' (Kiernan 1982: 170). According to Kiernan this paradox is partly resolved by means of a complementary division of labour between ordained ministers and charismatic prophets:

> At meetings which are the concern of a single band, there is a partial separation of the spheres of authority and enthusiasm, so that the meeting is divided into two quite distinctive parts, with a definite break between them. The first part is a prayer and bible service under the direct control of the leader of the group, usually a minister or occasionally a preacher. The latter part of the meeting is given over to a healing session, of which a prophet takes charge or, in the absence of a prophet, some other healing specialist. This arrangement ensures that, as far as possible, neither the minister nor the prophet transgresses upon the competence of the other (ibid.: 171; see also Kiernan 1976).

In contrast to many other accounts, however, Kiernan not only acknowledges the combination of 'charisma' and 'institution' within one and the same religious community, he also stresses the blurring of boundaries between them. Concerning the relationship between prophets and ministers, therefore, Kiernan summarizes his argument as follows:

> The real differences between prophet and minister in this respect are that, firstly, ministerial control proceeds from an institutional endowment of the spirit acquired by rite of ordination from the acknowledged head of the church, while prophetic power is a personal infusion of the same spirit without human mediation, and secondly, the ultimate control is vested in the institutional authority of the minister. Nevertheless, there is a definite fusion and interpenetration of the roles of minister and prophet and to that extent a blurring of the distinction between the spheres of authority and enthusiasm

in Zionist religious experience at the band level. This blurring effect is further compounded in those instances in which the minister and leading prophet were one and the same person. ... Here the same individual stepped from one role to the other and back again and, in the course of doing so, combined the exercise of both sets of control in the management of the religious experience (ibid.: 173–74).[18]

This finding contradicts dominant scholarly discourses on charismatic routinization and the incompatibility of 'charisma' and 'institution'. However, it is astonishing that the above insights have not yet stimulated any in depth ethnographic examinations of how such 'personal unions' are practically enacted.

An indication of why such 'blurrings' are possible in principle can be found in Clive Dillon-Malone's book *The Korsten Basketmakers* where he states that, among the Masowe Apostles, prophets and preachers:

place a different emphasis on the source of their knowledge during Sabbath prayer services. Whereas the prophets refer to the word of God as contained in the Bible (as do the preachers), they also attribute their knowledge to the direct working of the spirit of God within them. *No contradiction, however, is seen in the two channels of knowledge, for the source of both is the same.* It is Jehovah himself who is communicating with his people through the medium of his word in the Bible and through the action of his spirit in the prophets (Dillon-Malone 1978: 88; my italics).

In Dillon-Malone's case, the two roles were complementary and nonetheless connected to each other through their shared source of knowledge. I suggest that the same principle holds true in cases, such as those examined in this book, where personal unions between 'preachers', 'administrators' and 'prophets' prevail. These functions are linked to each other by – and are understood to be different manifestations of – what is claimed to be the ultimate source of divinely ordained authority: the Holy Spirit.

Various ethnographic studies of African Christianity suggest that the African-initiated churches analysed here might not be anything out of the ordinary in this respect. In the Oberi Okaime Christian Mission in Nigeria, for example:

the movement's emphasis on the Holy Spirit and speaking in tongues implied that strange utterances and eventually words occurred early in the experiences of the spirit men during 'spirit seizure', or visions. Quite early too, some spirit men reputedly wrote these words down in strange characters on sheets of paper, leaves or bark of trees without comprehending their meanings. Only later – probably from 1931 onwards – did Seminant [the Holy Spirit] begin to 'reveal' to several of the leaders the meanings of the words and scripts. Eventually, probably in early 1933, two spirit men – Michael Ukpong and Akpan Akpan Udofu – at the bidding of Seminant went into seclusion ... in order to perfect the 'spirit language' and writing. [...] Ukpong 'received' the language from Seminant while Udofia wrote it down. Apparently both men also formulated some of the movement's doctrines, liturgy and hymns while in this seclusion (Abasiattai 1989: 505).

Here spiritual revelation and empowerment, textual meaning, secretarial work and an 'objectification' of doctrines through writing do not seem to have represented an insoluble contradiction in themselves. Similar findings are presented in an article by Peter Probst (1989), who up to now has dealt with the issue of 'the Letter and the Spirit' more explicitly than anyone else in anthropology. His re-analysis of studies of the Aladura movement in western Nigeria focuses on the religious appropriation of literacy in a colonial and postcolonial context. As already mentioned, the Aladura churches made use of a variety of Christian literature, amongst which was a sacred scripture that had been devised by the prophetic founder of the movement. Yet in contrast to prevailing scholarly ideas on the 'consequences of literacy', Probst concludes his article by pointing out that 'the increase of the use of writing within the congregations did not in fact lead to the disappearance of prophets. ... Rather, writing and print have become incorporated into the indigenous forms of religious experience' (1989: 492).

In the examples above, therefore, the Pentecostal-charismatic attributes of these various African-initiated churches can be demonstrated as being merged with features of an 'institutionalized' and literate organization. Yet, as already noted, in typologically separating Pentecostal-charismatic practices from the literacy practices of organizational formalization, the interface between these poles has long been neglected. In addition, due to the historical character of the data used in most of the studies referred to above, it has only rarely been possible for them to do what the present book tries to achieve, namely to investigate ethnographically how the blurring of Pentecostal charisma and literacy is produced in the situated practices and tangible social interactions of contemporary African Christians.

Before providing information on my fieldwork and presenting the outline of the book, I shall close this introduction by briefly situating my approach within certain of the major dimensions of recent anthropological debates on literacy.

Examining Literacy Practices

In his seminal book on literacy practices Brian Street criticizes the 'autonomous model of literacy' which he mainly sees represented in the early works of the anthropologist Jack Goody. Since the early 1960s Goody has authored a prolific series of studies (1963, 1968a, 1977, 1986, 1987, 2000), which for the most part deal with the implications of literacy in previously oral cultures. Street argues:

> that Goody overstates the significance that can be attributed to literacy in itself; [he] understates the qualities of oral communication; sets up unhelpful and often untestable polarities between, for instance, the 'potentialities' of

literacy and 'restricted' literacy; [he] lends authority to a language for describing literacy practices that often contradicts his own stated disclaimers of the 'strong' or determinist case; and polarizes the difference between oral and literate modes of communication in a way that gives insufficient credit to the reality of 'mixed' and interacting modes. Despite the density and complexity of social detail in Goody's descriptions of literacy practice, there is a peculiar lack of sociological imagination in his determination to attribute to literacy per se characteristics which are clearly those of the social order in which it is found (Street 1984: 5–6).

According to Street the 'autonomous model' tends 'to generalise broadly from what is in fact a narrow, culture-specific literacy practice' (1984: 1). In the form of a 'literacy myth' (Graff 1979: 3), literacy is thus depicted as a culturally neutral technology and goes along with connotations of progress, civilization, individual freedom and social mobility.

In contrast to this approach Street advocates an 'ideological' model which attempts 'to understand literacy in terms of *concrete social practices* and to theorize it in terms of the ideologies in which different literacies are embedded' (1984: 95; my italics; see also, for example, Ahearn 2001; Barton 1994; Baynham 1995; Besnier 1995; Street 1993; Wogan 2004). Concerning literacy as social practice, Street thus concurs with Shirley Brice Heath's interest in 'literacy events' which she defines as 'any occasion in which a piece of writing is integral to the nature of participants' interactions and the interpretive processes' (1982: 93). In the present book I shall adopt Heath's and Street's approach which, I am convinced, makes it necessary to use a rather 'agnostic' definition of literacy that takes a broad view without, however, falling back on the Western metaphorical usage of the term.[19] My notion of 'literacy' accordingly refers to all social practices that devise, make use of or relate to a piece of alphabetical writing.

I do not intend to resume the whole debate on literacy here which, in all its complexities, already crams library shelves and has recently been thoroughly reviewed by James Collins and Richard K. Blot (2003: 9–66). Yet four aspects of this debate are of particular relevance for the perspective and arguments presented in this book.

The first significant aspect is that it shifts the perspective from 'literacy' in the singular to a discussion of heterogeneous 'literacies' in the plural:

> When one focuses on culturally sensitive accounts of reading and writing practices, the concept of literacy as a single trait does not seem very feasible. A multiplicity of literacy practices can be distinguished, which are related to specific cultural contexts and associated with relations of power and ideology. As such, literacy can be seen as a lifelong context-bound set of practices in which an individual's needs vary with time and place (Verhoeven 1996: 1).

Literacies thus not only evince a plurality in cross-cultural comparison, they also display a high degree of variation within one and the same socio-cultural setting (see also, for example, Barton, Hamilton and Ivanič 2000; Collins 1995; Graff 1995; Heath 1982, 1983).

Secondly, this shift of focus is accomplished by examining specific socio-cultural practices. Thus, an attempt is made to determine the particularities of literacies with a view to in depth ethnographic case studies. This leads Jack Goody to call Brian Street a 'cultural relativist' (2000: 3) and to insist that 'we must distinguish the analysis of a particular social situation ... with another perfectly reputable form of social inquiry, namely, the attempt to examine the influence of one or more factors ... upon social life, either in a particular context or in a general one' (Goody 2000: 7–8).

In contrast to Street, Goody sympathizes with the latter form of analysis. His distinction between 'particularism' and 'generalization' is clearly an important one and should not be summarily dismissed (see also Street 2003: 3–4). Yet the problems start when previous 'generalizations' come to inform the examination of particular case studies to such an extent that the respective 'particularities' eventually become invisible. This happens when the scholarly generalizations concerning the potentiality of literacy are used as blueprints in assessing specific literacy practices. 'Literacy can...' is then mistaken for 'literacy is...' (see also Bloch 1998a; Halverson 1992).

Thirdly, it is evident that scholarly debates on literacy partly revolve around questions of agency.[20] In recent decades, proponents of the so-called 'autonomous model of literacy' have been accused of privileging the agency of literacy over that of actual readers and writers. Since my theoretical perspective in this book is informed by practice theories, the notion of 'agency' will also be important in what follows. On the one hand, 'agency' thus refers to the ability of people 'to act on their own behalf, influence other people and events, and maintain some kind of control in their own lives' (Ortner 2001: 78). On the other hand, my analysis also deals with people's ascription of agency and how this relates to their notions of personhood. It is notable, for example, that many Western missionaries in colonial Africa considered reading and writing skills to have an agency in and by themselves. Similarly, because of the spiritualistic outlook of the Pentecostal-charismatic churches examined in this book, 'agency' for them does not always mean 'human agency'. An assessment will therefore be made of the role that spiritual agency is assumed to play where literacy practices are concerned.

Lastly, hitherto the debate has for the most part been framed in terms of the relationship between 'orality' and 'literacy' (Collins and Blot 2003: 27). While recognizing that this analytical framework is important and that it has produced significant findings, I would also share Rosalind Shaw's (1990: 341) doubts concerning the appropriateness of categorical distinctions between 'oral' and 'literate' religions. The present book thus takes a partially different route by starting from the assumption that there exist other conceptual notions – such as 'the Letter and the Spirit' – which can productively be employed in ethnographic inquiries into literacy practices among Pentecostal-charismatic churches in Africa.

Introduction

The Fieldwork

My research on African Christianity in southern Zambia started in the Gwembe Valley in 1993, with an ethnographic study of a congregation of the *mutumwa* movement, the St Moses God's Holy Spirit Church (Kirsch 1998, 2002). In order to situate this church in its wider context, I made an extensive survey of churches in the Sinazeze area. The spatial range of this survey took Sinazeze, a small rural township with some shops and a health centre, as its starting point and covered all churches within an hour's walk. This roughly represented the maximum distance covered by local churchgoers on a Sunday. For reasons of comparison, my later fieldwork in the Gwembe Valley used the same spatial range.

During subsequent fieldwork in 1995, 1999 and 2001 I was therefore able to build on my contacts with a total of eighteen churches. Besides participant observation and numerous informal conversations, I conducted several hundred hours of interviews with leaders and members of these churches. The interviews were recorded on audiotape, which I subsequently transcribed and translated with the help of local research assistants, who also accompanied me during visits to churches and 'traditional' religious specialists. Whenever my Chitonga did not suffice to understand more complicated issues, my research assistants acted as interpreters.

Being visited by a white person (*mukuwa*) was generally considered prestigious. In the remoter villages my presence during church meetings raised curiosity and was accorded a certain entertainment value. My presence was also frequently linked to the expectation of material support. Some church elders therefore attempted to control my movements, though this did not represent a severe impediment to my research. On the one hand, this was due to the fact that I had, in the course of my survey in 1993, established contacts with lay members before I got to know the church leadership. These contacts had their own interactional dynamic, which the top echelons of the church hierarchy could do nothing about. On the other hand, my research assistants, with whom I had worked since 1993, were of great help in expanding my range of activities.

All the same there were undoubtedly social restrictions on my fieldwork. Being male, conducting interviews with female church members was not always easy to arrange, and it was out of the question even to consider conducting participant observation among women's associations. Another restriction on my research concerned the treatment of the history of the Spirit Apostolic Church. The elders of this church did not oppose my contacts with other religious communities except for the denomination from which their own Church originally derived, in the case of which their expectation of my solidarity with them rather than this denomination was made very clear to me. As a result, I never even tried to contact the latter.

During my different periods of fieldwork, most of the time I lived in the homesteads of various church elders. This permitted the participant observation of everyday practices, negotiations and conflicts, of Sunday services, choir rehearsals and Sunday schools, and of the preparation, practice and retrospective 'ritual criticism' (Grimes 1990) of congregational and administrative meetings. It also made possible the observation of everyday interactions between family members, neighbours and friends who belonged to different denominations or pursued non-Christian religious practices.

My contact with the Spirit Apostolic Church (SAC) also resulted from the survey of 1993. After talking to members of the SAC's Nanyenda congregation in the Gwembe Valley, I was invited to visit the denomination's headquarters in Siamujulu village on the Plateau. My periods of research in 1995, 1999 and 2001 were therefore conducted both in the Gwembe Valley and on the Plateau. In 1999, I spent some time with each SAC congregation. During this small-scale 'multi-sited ethnography' I became aware not only of organizational difficulties and local discrepancies in religious practice, but also of intra- and inter-congregational conflicts. Besides the comparative dimension of my research, it was this changing perspective on the multifarious, highly pluralistic and conflictual composition of the SAC that informed much of my analytical approach.

Outline of the Book

The book is divided into four parts within which theoretical reflections are integrated into the examination of contextualized ethnographic case studies from contemporary southern Zambia.

Part I introduces several dimensions of the historical and ethnographic setting that are important for the overall argument of the book. By analysing archival documents and reviewing the anthropological and historical literature, Chapter 2 deals with religious, educational and administrative literacies in colonial southern Africa, particularly in Northern Rhodesia (now Zambia). I demonstrate, for instance, that several of the practices of Western missionaries and their African partners were characterized by a blurring of functional differentiations, like the practice of acting as both a spiritual advisor and a religious administrator. The coalescence of 'religious literacy' and 'bureaucratic literacy' that is characteristic of many contemporary Pentecostal-charismatic churches in the area of my research is accordingly not a newly invented practice but to some extent had colonial precursors. In Chapter 3, the groundwork for the analysis of literacy practices among contemporary African Christians is laid by outlining the ethnographic, historical and geographic background of the area of my research. Here I treat first elementary features of the socio-cultural background, secondly the history of Christianity in southern Zambia, and thirdly the main characteristics of the contemporary 'religious field' in the area of my research. Chapter 4 examines how literacy and religion is promoted and dealt with in schools in this area. In thus assessing how present day members of Pentecostal-charismatic churches experience 'schooled literacy' and 'schooled religion', it is argued that the limitations and specificities of formal school education leave ample space for alternative literacies outside school.

Part II of the book presents some basic phenomena, contexts and social practices that crucially informed the uses of reading and writing in my area of research. The descriptions and arguments of this and the following chapters (except Chapter 8) are based on fieldwork data collected between 1993 and 2001. Chapter 5 starts with the observation that an examination of literacy practices must take into account the availability, affordability and local accessibility of writings. The chapter therefore describes the factors that have influenced the literacy practices found in my research area, such as paper shortages and the scarcity of reading materials. Here it is demonstrated, for example, that, despite the marked scarcity of written materials, people did not even treat copies of the Bible with exceptional respect, obedience or caution in their everyday lives. Thus, there was no 'fetishization' of the Bible or of literacy in general. Chapter 6 discusses how the Bible was made present in everyday discourses and practices in my research area. It is shown how citations of Biblical phrases served, among other things, the formation of group identities. A proper Christian, however, was not only expected to 'talk Bible' but also to handle it physically and use it as a visible emblem of identity. Public display of the Bible, the central basis of Christian worship, created a contrast with the rather secret paraphernalia of 'traditional' herbalists and witches. The view that treating Christianity as 'mere talking' was questionable also had another implication, though. It was assumed that if this was not backed up by recurrent consultation with the Bible, Christian talk might easily be diverted by Satan. The locally felt necessity for intricately combining verbal utterance and written reference points will prove important in analysing the services of a Pentecostal-charismatic church in Chapter 11.

However, as I demonstrate in Chapter 7, even recurrent and evidently apparent consultation of the Bible was not deemed to constitute ultimate confirmation that a given religious practice was of a genuinely Christian kind. In fact, the Bible was not only used in what were more or less undisputedly assumed to be Christian churches, but occasionally also in the religious practices of what Gwembe Tonga call *bang'anga* healers and *masabe* possession cults. This chapter thus discusses how the Scriptures were employed in these 'traditional' forms of religion and what criteria people used for identifying 'proper Christian' uses of the Bible. However, since many of my informants took part in different religious practices, either successively or concurrently, one and the same person occasionally recognized that different literacy practices might all have religious impacts – no single literacy practice constituted an absolute principle for them. The issues raised in the preceding chapter suggest that the label 'religion of the book' might not be as well defined as is commonly supposed. These issues thus serve as a starting point for Chapter 8 which outlines some general analytical questions and conceptual frameworks that will prove useful (later on in the present work) for examining Pentecostal-charismatic literacy practices. For example, here I discuss the canonization of religious texts, Biblical infallibility and the issue of scriptural intermediation.

Having recourse to the issues and findings of the earlier chapters, Part III of the book examines reading practices in Pentecostal-charismatic and, for comparative reasons, non-Pentecostal denominations with headquarters in Western countries. This is done by considering the status of religious publications, analysing indigenous conceptualisations of the relationship between readers and texts, and describing the settings and procedures of textual reception. With regard to the case study of a

Pentecostal-charismatic denomination in the area of my research, Chapter 9 demonstrates that, in the Spirit Apostolic Church, the Bible as a whole was deemed to be infallible. Yet Church members differed with regard to what particular version of the Bible they possessed; communal Bible readings thus often revealed the existence of conflicting versions of the same verse. The fact that, quite surprisingly, such conflicting versions of the Scriptures were treated with indifference had to do with the spiritual orientation of Church members. The reception of the Bible by a spiritually endowed person was said to require guidance by the Holy Spirit, which would function as a corrective spiritual power by redressing any faults in the Bible translation in the very act of reading it. To some extent the combination of spiritual orientation and indifference also related to other Christian publications. Far from being concerned about the origin of an unknown religious publication, people generally ignored indicators of denominational origin. Newly arrived publications were read with unlimited interest. If the publication then proved to contain assertions that could be recognized by a reader who was endowed with spirituality as having a divine origin the publication was accorded religious significance regardless of its denominational origin. Also dealing with the status ascribed to religious publications, Chapter 10 starts by demonstrating that – in contrast to non-Christian spirits – the Holy Spirit was presumed never to reside permanently in any particular material location. This idea in its turn informed the general opinion of Christians in my research area that it was not possible to achieve immediate contact with God or the Holy Spirit by reading the Bible. This detail makes the Bible seem rather insignificant in questions of spirituality. Yet, as shown in Chapter 6, making ostensible reference to the Bible was considered indispensable for an authoritative Christian discourse. Here, therefore, we are confronted with a use of the Scriptures that is based on two essential preconditions that must be combined: the Bible and the Spirit. The declared necessity for the mutual interaction of spirituality and scriptural usage also implies that, for those who are not regarded as having spirituality, the mediation of the Scriptures is of the utmost importance if they are to understand the Bible properly. Due to the felt need for scriptural mediation, scriptural readings were mostly undertaken during church services, that is, during those social events at which religious experts offered an authoritative and spiritually guided reading of the Bible.

Chapter 11 provides an analysis of the course of such events, showing that during sermons church elders cultivated a two-pronged performance in which the Scriptures and the congregation were connected. Only when the Scriptures had been orally infused with the power of the Holy Spirit by being uttered in a spiritualized state could they develop their empowering potential. And only when it was verbally and repeatedly exposed to such inspired preaching would the laity be able to receive the 'sediments of the spirits', that is, a spiritualizing deposit of the Bible's literal message. In this way, an interactional network that placed the mediation of the Church elders at its centre was continuously reproduced. The specificities of these findings become evident when they are compared to literacy practices among non-Pentecostal and non-charismatic denominations with headquarters in Western countries. In an examination of the Jehovah's Witnesses and the New Apostolic Church (*Neuapostolische Kirche*), Chapter 12 demonstrates how much the religious organisation of these two churches crucially depends on the distribution of denominational pamphlets and circulars. In the congregations that were functioning in the area of my research, these materials were reckoned to be merely subsidiary to the Holy Writ. Yet by situating denominational publications as 'obligatory passage points' (Callon 1986) for reaching a proper understanding of the Bible, the Bible became what these publications made it.[21] In both cases, to some extent the Bible became a promise that was perpetually being postponed, one in which supplementary publications represented small advances in the possibly unending passage to fulfilment. Chapter 13 compares these literacy practices with those of African-initiated Pentecostal-charismatic denominations and, by adding to the general discussion of 'religions of the book' in Chapter 8, develops the concept of 'literacy enablement'. This concept relates to those activities, qualities and devices which, in a particular socio-religious field, are seen as necessary for attempting to bridge between the divine-scriptural sphere and the worldly realm. These literacy procedures, qualities and devices are mostly understood as being secondary to the actual beholding or interpretation of the Bible. Yet, as I suggest, each 'enablement' is essential and highly influential for scriptural readings and processes of religious authorization. The concept of 'literacy enablement' is therefore useful in comparing the literacy practices of different religious communities. Taken together, for the members of the Pentecostal-charismatic Spirit Apostolic Church, reading the Bible in a divinely ordained way required 'enablement' through the Holy Spirit. For Jehovah's Witnesses and the members of the New Apostolic Church (*Neuapostolische Kirche*), by contrast, this 'enablement' was intricately linked to the publications of their own denominations. In general, the difference between these two types of church in my area of research was therefore not so much a difference between denominations in which supplementary writings were used and denominations in which they were absent: it was not, in other words, a contrast between 'literate' and 'oral' cultures. Instead, the divergence consisted in, first, how Christian publications were used and integrated with social interaction, and secondly, what was considered to be an essential precondition for a divinely ordained reading of religious writings.

The fourth and final part of the book (Part IV) analyses writing practices in Pentecostal-charismatic churches that took the form of what I call 'bureaucracy in the Pentecostal-charismatic mode'. Against the background of theoretical considerations about research on bureaucracies Chapter 14 discusses, among other things, the relationship between church offices and ascriptions of charismatic ability with regard to the case of a Pentecostal-charismatic church in the area of my research, the Spirit Apostolic Church. Here I show that the leaders of this church tried to resolve this (potentially) precarious configuration by having recourse to functional 'personal unions' in which bureaucratic and spiritual dimensions were balanced and at times conflated. The intricate relationship between bureaucracy and spirituality is particularly evident in the case of church secretaries who, among other things, are dealt with in Chapter 15. Some members of the Spirit Apostolic Church suggested that the office of church secretary was too low in rank to presuppose spirituality: thus anyone could be invested with the post. The very activity of documenting the religious practices of spiritually endowed church leaders, however, would itself bring the secretary closer to God. Observing and recording spiritually inspired activities would thus increase his personal association with the Holy Spirit. Others saw spirituality as a prerequisite for being appointed a church secretary, asserting that only a spiritually endowed secretary would be able to appreciate the main points of an ongoing religious practice. In both lines of argumentation, the work of church secretaries was linked to questions of spiritual power, with spirituality being seen as either a precondition or a result of secretarial work. Moreover, this chapter examines how bureaucratic inscriptions, in the form of religious certificates, identity cards, and registers, were used in the Spirit Apostolic Church in an attempt to establish durable relationships between the different levels of the church leadership, on the one hand, and between the leaders and members of the church, on the other. I show that although these written inscriptions were taken seriously by church elders and church members as a means of capturing and/or signalling socio-religious identities, they involved a complex bureaucratic-charismatic configuration that for the most part undermined efforts to exert disciplinary power through the construction of administrative 'networks of writings' (Foucault 1977).

Building on the foregoing discussion, Chapter 16 concentrates on the precarious relationship between church services and their planning and documentation in writing. As indicated above, many churchgoers understood spiritual potency to be an essential prerequisite for secretarial tasks. Since, however, church services were also assumed to be led by the Holy Spirit, a paradoxical constellation emerged: a divinely inspired agenda was prepared for a similarly divinely inspired religious practice, whose spirituality was seen to manifest itself in unpredictability and in the emerging quality of the performance. Lastly, religious practice was documented in the form of service reports by (spiritually endowed) secretaries. The paradoxical tensions between the three main elements in this constellation – schedules as revelations, unpredictable spiritual events during religious practices and the documentation of scheduled yet unpredictable practices – regularly caused conflicts within the church. The section analyses typical examples of spiritual/literal blendings and detachments, as well as the conflictual negotiations that accompanied this constellation. It is shown that criticism mostly concerned a lack of spirituality in bureaucratization. Thus, surprisingly, the criticism was ultimately aimed at achieving a re-spiritualization of bureaucratic practices. Why the bureaucratization of the Spirit Apostolic Church was pursued, despite the paradoxes mentioned above, is the topic of Chapter 17. Within the Church, the products of bureaucratization – reports, agendas, lists, etc. – attained the status of 'boundary objects', which permitted each of the parties involved to follow his/her own interests, while at the same time being engaged in shared literacy practices: local church leaders were administratively bound to the headquarters, while simultaneously pursuing spiritual activities in an unrestrained manner.[22] In this sense, bureaucratization represented a shared effort in generating a 'facade' that simultaneously concealed and made visible. A similar constellation can be found in the relationship between the Church as a whole and the Zambian state, which was locally assumed to be (potentially) coercive. Besides the internal rationalities discussed above, the bureaucratization of the Spirit Apostolic Church represented an attempt by the leaders of the Church to acquire a self-protective compatibility with state agencies by mimetically incorporating bureaucratic procedures. Bureaucratic products were thus created that were linked to dominant models of organizational formalization. At the same time, these bureaucratic products exhibited no trace of the practices that were deemed to be highly significant for the church: they appeared mundane, externalized and depersonalized. Spiritual practices were not documented in writing because they were deemed to be incompatible with the state.

As will have been demonstrated in the preceding chapters, however, the actual work of bureaucracy was associated with the very phenomenon that was kept out of the records, namely spirituality. In relation to state agencies, therefore, the bureaucratization of the Spirit Apostolic Church represented an intricate coming together of incorporation and transformation. The products created through bureaucratization were, among other things, directed at the Zambian state, whereas the production of this bureaucratization exhibited those very features that the bureaucratic product attempted to conceal. Taken together, therefore, it is argued that bureaucratization served here as both an internal and an external 'facade', being used to enable Pentecostal-charismatic practices rather than constraining them.

Notes

1. A remark is in order here regarding the terminology I am using. For the most part, the case studies examined in this book concern religious communities which resemble what the literature on 'African Initiated Churches' (Anderson 2001) calls, for example, 'Zionist churches' (Sundkler 1961a), 'prophet-healing churches' (Turner 1967a) or 'Spirit-type churches (Daneel 1971). In using the term '*Pentecostal*-charismatic' in relation to these communities in this book, I am taking account, first, of the historical fact that they 'emerged out of the global Pentecostal movement' (Maxwell 1999: 244; see also Maxwell 2006) which originated in Methodist and Baptist sanctification circles. Soon after the so-called 'Azuza Street revival' in the United States in 1906, this movement spread to South Africa, from where it diffused – or rather: was translated – to other regions in southern Africa. Though it cannot be determined with certainty, the historical origins of the main case study, the Spirit Apostolic Church, most probably lie with the Full Gospel Church of God in Southern Africa, a Pentecostal denomination established in South Africa in 1910 after one of its founders, Archibald Cooper, had received '"Apostolic Papers" published by the "Azuza" movement in Los Angeles' (Sundkler 1976: 52). Secondly, my use of the term 'Pentecostal' takes account of the fact that 'Pentecostalism is not a denomination or a creed, but a movement, a cluster of religious practices and attitudes that transcends ecclesiastical boundaries' (Cox 1994: 246). This 'cluster of religious practices and attitudes', which links my case studies to the wider Pentecostal movement, concerns especially the crucial importance ascribed to the working of the Holy Spirit in faith and religious practice. Thus, agreeing with B. Meyer that the 'focus on local communities does not of course imply any denial of the fact that these communities form part of a wider system' (1999: xix), this book is also an inquiry into a particular aspect of 'African agency in the appropriation of global culture' (van Binsbergen and van Dijk 2004).

Thirdly, my use of the term 'Pentecostal-*charismatic*' is not intended to establish a theological typology (cf. Anderson 2001: 110), nor is it a reference to what, since the 1960s, has been called the '(neo)charismatic movement' (cf. Robbins 2004: 121–22). Instead, I employ this term in order to highlight the fact that, in the churches concerned, inspiration by the Holy Spirit represents an essential basis for religious authority.

2. E. Keller similarly remarks that 'sober types of Christianities, like Seventh-day Adventism, fascinate less and seem to attract little attention' (2005: 42).
3. However, as M. Riesebrodt demonstrates, Weber's depiction of charisma as an innovating force cannot easily be reconciled with his actual examples of charismatic leaders, such as shamans, war heroes, 'berserks' (Weber 1968c: 19). Referring to one of these examples, Riesebrodt asks: 'What does the anti-traditionalism of a shaman consist of?', concluding that 'Magical charisma, by requiring no changes in "inner" attitudes, seems to be part of traditionalism rather than its antithesis' (1999: 8; see also Johnson and Anderson 1995: 11–12).
4. For reasons that can only be mentioned here but which will be elaborated further in Chapter 14, my treatment of 'bureaucracy' will, in contrast to Weber's, refrain from making questions of 'rationality' a pivotal topic. According to a common understanding, the striving for rational and instrumental efficiency represents a crucial characteristic of bureaucracies and organizational formalism. In these approaches, 'rationality' and 'efficiency' seem to reside somewhere beyond socio-cultural definitions. However, as neo-institutionalist perspectives have demonstrated, ideas of organizational rationality are highly dependent on their cultural, social and institutional contexts. According to J. Meyer and B. Rowan (1977), formalism and 'rationality' in organizations therefore represent 'myths' that are socially constituted and reduplicated for reasons of organizational self-legitimation.
5. See, for example, P. Wogan's (2001) article on B. Anderson's *Imagined Communities* (2006).
6. For studies that problematize this perspective, see, for example, Niezen (1991), Street (1984).
7. I. Hexham (1997: 367) and E. Parrinder (1953: 127–29) mention other examples where the Bible has been rejected by African Christians. Such rejections are commonly due to the association of the Bible with experiences of colonial oppression or, as M. Engelke (2005, 2007) suggests, to its very materiality, which contradicts the commitment of religious practitioners to immateriality.
8. See, for example, Behrend (1999: 148–71), Kirsch (2003, 2007), Prinsloo and Breier (1996), Probst (1992).
9. M. Sökefeld has observed, with regard to the anthropological debate on 'non-Western' selves: 'In this debate, the Western self is represented as an instance of the individual's providing it with boundedness, relative autonomy and independence, reflexivity, and the ability to pursue its own goals' (1999: 418). In conceptualizing 'non-Western' selves, in turn, 'the Western self was taken as the starting point and the non-Western self was accordingly characterized as its opposite: unbounded, not integrated, dependent, unable to set itself reflexively apart from others' (ibid.). My argument concerning the spiritual permeability of human bodies is certainly not intended to resonate with this problematic approach. Although 'individualism' has often been associated with Christianity (Dumont 1985), it is all too clear that in Western Christianity there also exist traditions in which human–spirit relations and the embodiment of spiritual entities are of the utmost importance. Therefore, the characterization above does not pertain specifically to African Christianity. In a similar vein, D. Maxwell has recently remarked, with regard to 'African Independent Churches', that 'it is precisely those phenomena in independency which [have often been] interpreted as most exotic or African – prophecy, divine healing, exorcism, glossolalia – which can be shown to be the most Christian part of the churches' (1997: 144). For the connection between conceptualizations of literacy and those concerning personhood in the Western history of ideas, see also Bloch (1998a).
10. This contrasts with the constantly growing body of scholarly literature dealing with the use of electronic mass media and film by religious practitioners in contemporary Africa. See, for

example, De Witte (2003, 2005), Hackett (1998), Meyer (2004b, 2006), Oha (2002), Schulz (2003), Ukah (2003).
11. Literacy productions by contemporary African Christians are dealt with by, for example, Behrend (1999: 148–71), Kirsch (2003, 2007), Maxwell (2001, 2006).
12. See, for example, Andersson (1958: 160), Dillon-Malone (1978: 34), Janzen and MacGaffey (1974: 22), Rasmussen (1996: 94).
13. See, for example, Dillon-Malone (1978: 35), Turner (1967c: 10).
14. See, for example, Daneel (1988: 129), Dillon-Malone (1978: 156), Janzen and MacGaffey (1974: 19, 23-24), Roberts (1970: 17), Sundkler (1976: 323–25), Turner (1967c: 39).
15. See, for example, Turner (1967b: 18, 210; 1967c: 22, 57).
16. See, for example, Rasmussen (1996: 41), Scarnecchia (1997: 93), Schoffeleers (2002: 243), Turner (1967c: 14).
17. See, for example, Daneel (1988: 280), Scarnecchia (1997: 98).
18. Similar 'blurrings' of religious functions have been noted by other anthropologists. M. West, for example, remarks of African-initiated churches in Soweto that some 'church leaders exercise both legal and charismatic authority over their congregation' (1975: 50). M. Daneel conceives the founder and leader of a church in Zimbabwe to be partly a 'case of integrating administrative and prophetic functions' (1987: 142). And M. Bloch states for early Madagascan scribes that they had the 'dual role of diviner-astrologers and secretaries' (1998b: 139). See also ter Haar (1992: 240–41).
19. This means that I do not subscribe here to the idea of a 'textuality' of culture and religion (cf. Buckland 1996), nor to the metaphorical extension of the term 'writing' as, for example, suggested by J. Derrida (1976). For an analysis of tropes in the discourse on 'orality' and 'literacy', see Tyler (1986).
20. See, for example, Kulick and Stroud (1993: 30–31), and the recent controversy between Postill (2003) and Bloch (2003).
21. M. Callon's notion of an 'obligatory passage point' is succinctly summarized by R. Rottenburg: 'Borrowing from military parlance, Callon (1986) speaks of an obligatory passage point if someone has convinced others that they cannot get what they want unless they pass through a narrow passage that can easily be controlled and utilized to generate power' (1996: 217).
22. The analytic concept of 'boundary objects' was first developed in an article by L. Star and J. Griesemer, who defined them as 'objects which are both plastic enough to adapt to local needs and the constraints of the several parties employing them, yet robust enough to maintain a common identity across sites. They are weakly structured in common use, and become strongly structured in individual-site use. These objects may be abstract or concrete. They have different meanings in different social worlds but their structure is common enough to more than one world to make them recognizable, a means of translation. The creation and management of boundary objects is a key process in developing and maintaining coherence across intersecting social worlds' (1989: 393).

PART I

HISTORIES AND ETHNOGRAPHIES

Chapter 1
Colonial Literacies

The role of literacy in Western colonial projects in Africa can hardly be overestimated. For the missionaries, the Bible simultaneously represented the divine assignment for evangelization, the essential script for proselytism, a means for its enactment and the pivotal symbol of self-representation. As metaphor and practice, religious literacy thus often represented the sine qua non for converting 'pagans' and transforming them into what the missionaries considered to be divinely ordained subjectivities. The colonial administration, on the other hand, was striving to regulate and control the colonized by entangling them in a network of passes, statistics and files. Theirs represented an attempt to identify and ultimately shape realities through acts of taxonomic classification, standardization and formalization that assumed the form of written records and translated colonial subjects into administered objects. Moreover, the cartographical inscription of colonial spaces on to maps (Worby 1994) and the linguistic standardization of vernacular languages in, for example, grammars and textbooks (Errington 2005; Fabian 1986; Posner 2003) also had an influence on cultural, ethnic and political configurations in the African colonies. Formal schooling, in its turn, conveyed to the colonized who had been subdued 'a sharp image of their place in the world' (Comaroff 1996: 28), while at the same time giving rise to new elites, thus introducing socio-economic differentiations based on the distinction between 'literates' and 'illiterates' (cf. Cook-Gumperz 1986).

Yet, as has been amply demonstrated by both anthropologists and historians, colonialism was neither 'monolithic nor omnipotent' (Cooper and Stoler 1989: 609), but a complex, contingent and contradictory process (see, for example, Dirks 1992; Elbourne 2002; Peel 2000; Pels 1997; Cooper and Stoler 1997) involving actors from different backgrounds, with disparate and changing agendas. Colonialism consequently represented a site of struggles and negotiations that altered not only the colonized, but also the colonizers themselves (Comaroff and Comaroff 1991, 1997).

This chapter sets out to trace some of the complexities of religious, educational and administrative literacies in colonial Northern Rhodesia (now Zambia). I shall not provide a comprehensive historical overview but will instead highlight certain features concerning the promotion and adaptation of colonial literacies that are important for the overall argument of this book. I shall indicate, for example, that the coalescence of 'religious literacy' and 'bureaucratic literacy' that is characteristic of contemporary Pentecostal-charismatic churches in my area of research is not a newly invented practice, but actually had its precursors under colonialism.

Mission, School and Printing Press

Right from the very start, the introduction of Christianity into southern Africa by European and American missionaries was intimately linked to school education as a principal method of evangelisation (Ragsdale 1986: 28–29).[1] Despite denominational differences in educational approach, for most missionary organizations: 'Schooling actually provided the model for conversion; conversion, the model for schooling. Each aimed at the systematic, moral reconstruction of the person in a world in which individuals were increasingly viewed as capable of being formed and reformed by social institutions' (Comaroff and Comaroff 1991: 233).

In a general address given to the General Missionary Conference of North-West Rhodesia in 1914, for example, Reverend J. R. Fell from the mission station of the Primitive Methodist Missionary Society (PMMS) in the Gwembe Valley outlined the educational ideals and methods of his mission society by laying emphasis on a triad of civilization, Christianity and school education:

> As a civilising force Education has no equal. It will make rational thinking men who perceive cause and effect instead of those believing the silly notions arising from generations of paganism. It is a valuable adjunct in Christianising. The spread of Christianity is largely dependent on education. … First and foremost, it must be Christian education. Instruction in the three R's [reading, writing, arithmetic] is an important factor in civilising the people, but we are not concerned with civilisation merely. The best in civilisation is the outcome of Christian influence and the civilisation best suited to the native is a Christian education. In all educational work we must have Bible and moral training (1914: 24).

In general, this assessment was unreservedly shared by most Protestant mission societies. Instruction in the 'three R's' and the emphasis on Bible training thus presupposed translation work and the publication and dissemination of various kinds of literature.

The missionaries of the PMMS, whose stations in the area of Northern Rhodesia were initially called the BaIla-BaTonga Mission, concentrated from the very beginning on linguistic work. In 1911, some parts of the Bible had already been translated into Chitonga and printed. It took up to 1949, however, for the whole of the New Testament to be published in the vernacular; the complete Chitonga Bible was only published in 1963. Various other literature had been translated and printed during the early decades of their activities. In 1906, for example, the first Tonga primer was published (cf. Doke 1945), while in 1914, Revd Fell is reported to have 'adapted our

Ila Hymnbook and (with additions) Catechism' (1914: 14). Fell had purchased a small hand-printing press – one of the first in Northern Rhodesia – which he henceforth used for printing works in the dialect of the Mweemba area in the Gwembe Valley (Baxter 1958: 489). In 1919, the BaIla-BaTonga Mission reported:

> The Mission Book Room acts as a distributing centre for our necessary literature both English and Vernacular as well as all school materials. Our vernacular books include School Primers, Folk tales, New Testament, Phrase books, Hymn Book, Catechism, Science Reader on Common Objects, Hygiene Reader, and Grammar of both Ila and Tonga. Other books are in preparation (1919: 18).

Translating, printing and distributing literature, and teaching with reference to writings, were among the preoccupations of the PMMS, as well as of most other mission societies.[2] Les Switzer thus remarks, in relation to South Africa:

> The mission's ultimate success ... stemmed from its monopoly over the written word. Mission station communities were centered on the church, school and either possession of or access to a printing press. Churches and schools were inseparable even on the more primitive stations, because the education of an African Christian community imbued with certain moral, emotional and intellectual qualities was deemed essential for the preservation and expansion of the Church. In turn, the preaching and teaching ministry was dependent on the mission's control and manipulation of literate culture (1984: 459).

Yet, it did not prove easy to introduce a 'literate culture', as J. P. Bruwer of the Dutch Reformed Church Mission remarked in a statement made to the General Missionary Conference of Northern Rhodesia in 1944. Under the heading 'The Problem of Reading', he states:

> The main fact is that the Bantu are not a reading people; they are a talking people. They know how to talk and find great delight in it. In addition to their conversational gifts, they possess a flexible and highly differentiated family of languages. Most of these have been reduced to writing, but the people on the whole still cling to the social gathering. The murmuring in the village square still has the power to lure the literate away from the new-found love of learning. Probably this problem of cultivating in a race of talkers a love for reading is one of the greatest that will have to be overcome. A welcome sign however in this respect is that the people are willing and even eager to listen for long periods if some one will read to them, whether because being read to approximates in some degree to talking, or because it requires less mental effort. We should make use of this possibility especially where a great number of people is still illiterate. This type of community reading should in

any case to my opinion come before any literacy campaign to cultivate in the people a thirst for more knowledge, and to persuade them to master the art of reading (1944: 27).

In these quotations, mission activities, which are claimed to depend on a 'love for reading', must still be stimulated by public readings that ultimately promise to raise interest in the 'art of reading'. Bruwer also observes that certain environmental aspects are hampering the development of an indigenous reading public: 'The African hut was evolved by and for a non-reading community ... The absence of lamps or other artificial light in the African home may be overcome if there is a reading room for the community. This room may well replace the talking hut or yard of the old African village' (1944: 27–28).

He thus suggests that libraries should form the centre of social and political life. Houses with chairs, desks, books and windows will ensure the Africans' enlightenment, in a metaphorical but also a very literal sense. Under the heading 'The Problem of Printing', Bruwer also advocates setting up local presses to produce texts in the vernacular: 'There are also great possibilities for small handpresses, and even for duplicating machines. Every Mission Station should have one of these. Summaries of lessons and talks given at refresher courses, synopses of lectures, tracts and pamphlets may with success be produced on these' (1944: 29).

Nevertheless, paper shortages and distribution difficulties would pose problems for such enterprises. An indigenous reluctance to purchase literature would also be detrimental to the 'art of reading':

> The Africans are utilitarians, and they are not easily induced to buy books unless they are convinced of their usefulness and necessity. On the other hand they will read anything that is given free, probably as much because it is free as because it is reading matter. ... Perhaps the outstanding difficulty is that the African has not yet developed a book-sense (1944: 30).

On the whole, Bruwer's statement concerning Christian literature provides us with some impressions of the Protestant missionaries' ideas and aims in developing an African reading community. Their ideas on literacy were frequently informed by notions of 'fine art' and enlightenment, and literacy itself was also seen as promising 'the ascendance of the reflective, inner-directed self: a self, long enshrined in Protestant personhood' (Comaroff and Comaroff 1991: 63). The famous Swiss missionary and anthropologist Henri-Alexandre Junod, for example, who at the turn of the twentieth century worked in South Africa, 'felt that deciphering the characters printed on a page ... concentrated the mind and encouraged reflection' (Harries 2001: 409) and that 'reading, as a silent, private practice, would cause Africans to think about personal choice and individual responsibility' (ibid.: 411). Literacy as cognitive and social practice was consequently envisaged as being a medium for the construction of new subjectivities.

That such efforts were ultimately only partially successful will become clear over the course of this book, as we examine the literacy practices of Pentecostal-charismatic churches in rural Zambia. More than fifty years after Bruwer wrote many Christians in the area of my research had become 'a reading people', though they had actually developed a 'book-sense' of a different kind. This difference still had to do with what Bruwer had already indicated in 1944: the problem of illumination, the crucial role of public readings and a certain disinclination to purchase books. But most importantly, it also had to do with notions concerning the spiritual permeability of the human body, discussed in Chapter 10. The idea that 'personhood' might not (only) enshrine a human self but also (temporarily) spiritual entities imbued literacy practices with epistemological premises that differed significantly from those projected by the early Protestant missionaries.

Steps towards Secularization

The early mission societies' training of converts was also aimed at the diffusion of school education. Describing common practices among his colleagues in 1908, Revd A. Baldwin of the PMMS states:

> The new policy is really the employment of converts as active Christian workers. The principle is that, as soon as a young man has given adequate proof of conversion, and has made some advancement in school knowledge, he is encouraged to go out and take charge for a term of a village school. He may know little, but that little he can go and teach others. He then comes back for a further spell to the head station to carry his own studies on a further step. He not only teaches, but holds religious services, and preaches what he knows of the rudiments of the gospel (cited in Ulrich Luig 1997: 111).

The establishment of out-schools in the villages using indigenous teachers was a common practice among the early mission societies in the territory of Northern Rhodesia (Ragsdale 1986: 33; cf. Gray 1990). Providing a means of 'evangelization-on-the-cheap' (Fields 1985: 45), out-schools not only compensated for the shortage of Western staff, but also enabled the missions to expand and demarcate their respective spheres of influence: wherever a mission society had established schools, other missions were less inclined to embark on evangelisation activities.

The colonial administration, however, was often rather critical with respect to such out-schools. A Native Commissioner's report for the year 1917, for example, states with regard to PMMS educational activities in the Gwembe Valley:

> There are four outside schools each in the charge of a native teacher, one of whom is a Masuto and the others Batonga. These teachers have little influence being stationed alone and at some distance from the European Missionary. The headmen of the villages do not send their children to these out-schools and the result is that the teachers have nothing to do. Under white supremacy these native teachers might be put to some good use which

at present they are not. ... When one realizes that this Primitive Methodist Mission has been established on the Zambezi since 1908 *[sic]* one cannot help feeling that little progress has been made and that the mission has little to show for all these years. There is no doubt however that the material on which they have to work is of a very inferior kind, for the Banamwemba [the people from the Mweemba area of the Gwembe Valley where the Kanchindu mission was located] belong to one of the lowest classes of Central African tribes. The fault however does not only lie with the native but in the policy pursued by the Mission authorities. One European by himself cannot hope to make a success of any Missionary enterprise, much less can he do so if he has to control four out-schools situated at a distance of some thirty miles from the central mission station.[3]

This report highlights a theme that was to become a constant object of contention between administrative agencies and mission societies in the territory of Northern Rhodesia: the question of control over the indigenous teachers at out-schools. The British South Africa Company (BSAC) and later the British colonial government generally approved of the expansion of school education through mission societies, yet refused to provide financial assistance for 'native education'. What thus evolved was a collision between 'evangelisation-on-the-cheap' and 'colonialism-on-the-cheap' (Kilson 1966: 24).

Already during the first General Missionary Conference in 1914, the mission societies had issued a resolution urging the BSAC 'to consider the advisability of subsidizing all the approved schools in the country' (1914: 23). Yet, though the expansion of the out-school system aggravated the missions' financial and logistical difficulties, the administration persisted in denying public funds to 'native education', while nonetheless in 1918 releasing a Native Schools Proclamation that assigned the administration the power to control schools and teachers. This proclamation, which was revised in 1919 and 1921, also declared that missionaries should tour their respective out-schools at least four times a year and that all teachers should have certificates issued by an officially recognized denomination (Ragsdale 1986: 59–68). The missions opposed some points in the Native School Proclamations since they placed certain obligations on missionaries while simultaneously empowering the administrators with what to the missions seemed a disproportional degree of control over their work. All the same, the proclamations reflected the increased involvement of administrative agencies in questions of 'native education', which became even more pronounced when the British colonial government took over the territory from the BSAC in 1924. After the Phleps–Strokes Commission had made an assessment of the educational situation in Northern Rhodesia that same year, missions and government agencies started to cooperate more closely. This meant that the administration provided 'grants-in-aid' to schools while the missions had to conform to political regulations if they wanted to obtain such public funding. In the mid-1920s, a Department of Native Affairs was established that included the sub-department of 'Native Education'. It pursued a policy:

to allow sub-schools, provided that they are conducted without prejudice to good government, to encourage missions to concentrate on the improvement of 'schools' which are defined in the Schools Ordinance as a class for the teaching or instruction of natives, whether held in a building or not, conducted for not less than one hundred and twenty days a year, and in which instruction is based on a code approved by the Director of Native Education and the Advisory Board of Native Education.[4]

The Phleps–Strokes Commission also recommended that the colonial administration should provide secular education. But it was only much later that the colonial government actually started to set up non-denominational primary and secondary schools. In 1935, only 2 per cent of the school population were enrolled in government schools; ten years later, it was 6.5 per cent (Henkel 1989: 131). Up to the mid-1950s, by which time the percentage of the school population in government schools had risen to 22 per cent, almost all schools were run by missions. They thus represented institutions where Christianity and formal school education were intimately linked. It was only after Zambian independence in 1964 that most primary schools were handed over to the government (Henkel 1989: 41).[5]

Counterforce in Writing

The attempt to control schools reflected a certain ambivalence towards 'native education'. Some government representatives and especially the white settler communities regarded the missions' educational work with great scepticism. Conflicts with the indigenous Watchtower movement during the early decades of the twentieth century nourished their fear that schooling might upset the colonial hierarchy. There was actually something in this: upon returning to Northern Rhodesia from the mines in Southern Rhodesia and South Africa, some migrant workers in 1908 had started African Christian movements whose millenarian and anti-colonial rhetoric appeared to threaten the colonial order and the Western missions' standing.[6] One of the leading exponents of these early movements was Elliott Kenan Kamwana, who has been described as 'a product of the church's schools, [who] was among the most promising pupils of the 1899 middle-school class, and [whose] name appeared on the Livingstonia honor roll in 1901' (Fields 1985: 105). Kamwana had received some instruction in Watchtower doctrines from Joseph Booth, a British businessman with an enigmatic missionary career in sub-Saharan Africa (Langworthy 1996). And since Booth's religious teachings were suspected to have been responsible for the so-called Chilembe Rising of 1915 in Nyasaland (now Malawi), indigenous Watchtower activities in Northern Rhodesia were increasingly viewed with alarm and anxiety by the colonial administration (Shepperson and Price 1958; Yorke 1990).

In subsequent decades, conflicts repeatedly flared up between the colonial authorities and the organizationally fragmented, fluid and mostly surreptitious working movements. The strong rhetoric of the Watchtower literature and the association of the African churches with incidents of occasionally lethal witchcraft eradication movements led to the conviction on the part of both the colonial administration and the established Western missions that Watchtower was potentially seditious and dangerous to public welfare.[7] Attempts were thus made to suppress or at least to channel the religious movements. In the period up to the 1960s, Watchtower publications were continually being censored and were even at times banned from the country. Yet, since the African Watchtower movements were organizationally autonomous, tracing the passage of such publications into the colony from South Africa, Nyasaland or Southern Rhodesia was almost impossible. The administration thus sought to persuade the Watchtower Bible and Tract Society's regional headquarters in South Africa to refrain from sending publications to Northern Rhodesia. Previously, after witchcraft eradication activities had led to the death of alleged witches, the Watchtower Bible and Tract Society had declared that it had nothing to do with the Northern Rhodesian indigenous movements. Nonetheless the Society was not willing to follow the colonial administration's request. For this denomination, evangelisation crucially depended on the dissemination of its literature.

The conflict between the Northern Rhodesian administration and the Watchtower Bible and Tract Society was further aggravated by the so-called Copperbelt disturbances of 1935, which the commission of enquiry saw as resulting from indigenous Watchtower activities. Around that time, the colonial authorities eventually changed their strategy and endeavoured to accommodate the movements by cautiously cooperating with the denomination's headquarters. Admitting white representatives from South Africa to enter Northern Rhodesia was thus linked to the expectation that supervision by a larger denominational organization might domesticate its rather unruly African element. This supervision resulted in organisational reform, as well as in attempts to control how the publications of the Watchtower Bible and Tract Society were used by the indigenous population.[8] I shall return to this latter point in Chapter 12, when I analyse the literacy practices of contemporary Jehovah's Witnesses in my area of research.

During these conflicts and efforts to restrict the use of Watchtower publications, the high availability and affordability of these publications in Northern Rhodesia had spurred other mission societies to erect a 'counterforce in writing'. For the majority of the indigenous population, the Watchtower publications 'formed the bulk of available literature, as the distribution of African news papers was scanty or non-existent' (Cross 1977a: 93). Following the Copperbelt Disturbances of 1935, the commission of enquiry suggested that 'attention should be drawn to the fact that the circulation of Watch Tower literature has been rendered easy by there apparently being no other literature available in convenient and cheap form for natives who wish to read English. There would seem to be little difficulty in supplying that want by the provision of cheap and suitable literature' (1935: 49).

The publication and dissemination of cheap writings now became one of the pillars stabilizing the colonial order. In the territory of Northern Rhodesia, this induced the sharing of reading rooms and later on logistical arrangements for the distribution of books among the Western mission societies (Msiska 1986; Shaw 1958). These arrangements, as well as the launching of the first newspaper in vernacular languages, *Mutende*, in 1937, can thus be seen as an effort to compete with the magazines and pamphlets of the Jehovah's Witnesses.

In this way, the freewheeling use of denominational literature by scattered religious groupings had an influence on the development of literacy networks on a wider scale. African Christian initiatives in religious literacy, which represented modified adaptations of what was being promoted in the mission schools, thus led to adaptations to the colonized on the part of Western mission societies and the colonial administration. This influenced how these agencies interacted with one another, gave rise to an expansion of what might be called 'literacy infrastructure' and had an impact on the types of written materials that were subsequently published and distributed.

What is a School?

The colonial administration's insistence that indigenous teachers should be supervised also had to do with what were perceived to be drawbacks in the convergence of church and school. Karen Fields has argued that 'the colonial structure had a ready-made space for the God of the Watchtower millennium, because quieter but kindred gods were cemented into its very foundation, because the propagation of belief helped to maintain it erect' (1985: 21–22). She powerfully demonstrates how baptism and glossolalia in such colonial settings, with their merging of religious and political dimensions, can be comprehended and used as tools for anti-colonial struggle. A similar coalescence was to be found with regard to the dimensions of 'school' and 'church': since teachers usually acted as preachers, and since school buildings were often used for Sunday services (Shewmaker 1970: 82), an 'understanding of the church as school and the school as church' (Ulrich Luig 1997: 110) evolved. This implied that the roles of 'teachers' and 'preachers' were not always distinguishable.

The same held true for indigenous Christian movements. As in the mission societies, their 'preachers' were occasionally also 'teachers' who opened 'schools' (cf. Turner 1975). It is in view of such developments that the Native School Proclamation of 1918, already mentioned, cited religious instruction and educational work in one breath. The equation of school and church was now deemed to represent a potentially dangerous blurring of genres, which had to be redressed through institutional controls.

During a special conference in Livingstone in 1919, mission societies discussed amendments to the first draft of the Native School Proclamation. This included attempts to outline basic definitions: 'Schools means a school or class for the teaching of natives whether held in a building or not but shall not be interpreted to mean the holding of a religious service in accordance with the practice of any recognized Christian Denomination'.[9] The aim of this definition was to 'distinguish school teachers from "natives engaged in preaching and religious teaching". The latter were to hold certificates of authorization from a missionary in charge of the mission to which they belonged' (Ragsdale 1986: 65). But since 'No person shall be a teacher in any school unless only qualified under the conditions prescribed by the regulations of this Proclamation,' the teachers were also to obtain specific certificates:

> A Native teacher or inspector in charge of a school or schools must hold a certificate signed by the head of the mission. Such certificate is only to be granted to such as have satisfied the conditions laid down by the Mission in regard to educational attainment and length of training and hold a two years certificate of good character signed by a European who has known him during the whole of that period.

Although the missions generally accepted the demand for administrative and legal regulations for 'native education' in Northern Rhodesia, they strived to retain the authority to determine the criteria for selecting their respective teaching staff. In a similar vein, they suggested that the annual form that the Native School Proclamation required to be submitted to the magistrate by the missionary in charge should not include the item 'qualification of the teacher'. The conference report concluded with an appeal to the administration to draw up an educational 'code', to appoint an 'expert to supervise school-work and advise in regard to it' as well as to render 'financial aid or otherwise'. The last sentence reads as follows:

> whilst the Conference is in accord with the publication of the Proclamation and Regulations as amended by their suggestions it feels it right to put on record that most of the difficulties which have presented themselves have arisen from the fact that two distinct subjects are dealt with and would suggest that many of these difficulties would be removed by the promulgation of two different proclamations, one dealing with matters purely educational and the other in reference to matters purely religious.

In this interesting shift in their argument, the mission societies – which had themselves starting merging church and school – call for a laicizing separation of 'purely educational' and 'purely religious' matters. Apparently only this regulatory separation could secure the sought-after financial assistance from administrative agencies.

The efforts to redefine the boundaries of school and church – and eventually to control 'native teachers' – caused an increase in the standardization of the curriculum. And whereas becoming an indigenous teacher in the early years of the missions often merely required some basic abilities in reading and writing (Snelson 1974: 129), the introduction of compulsory certificates for teaching and preaching in 1924 was aimed at the professionalization of the missions' indigenous staff (Henkel 1989: 130), while simultaneously controlling access to teaching occupations by outlawing 'teaching' outside the officially accredited institutional networks.

Yet, the separation of school and church remained a highly politicised issue in the following decades. In a case brought before the Court at Litembwe in Luangwa Province in March 1934, for example, one William Nsofu was accused of preaching in Chief Chikupiri's area without authorization by a 'recognized religious denomination'. During the hearing of witnesses, Chief Chikupiri declared that:

> William Nsofu has built a school in my country. I have not seen it myself. It is a grass house. They have not begun to *teach* in it, but they *preach* in my country at Nkotami and Libengwa. I have not the least desire to have them in my country, if I had my way I could drive the whole lot of them away. ... These people have come round my back and built this school at Libengwa village.[10]

Another witness maintained: 'I know it was a school because William himself told me so; he said "Yes of course it is a school, you can take me to the Boma about it if you like"'.[11] And on being interrogated, William Nsofu himself stated:

> I admit that I built a school to *teach Chitawala* [i.e., 'Watchtower']; but it was because the rains were wetting our disciples very much and we wanted shelter. ... I do not deny that I *preach Chitawala*. I preach it everywhere in Nkole's country and in Chikupiri's and at Nkotami's as well as Libengwa's villages. Jeremiah Gondwe [one of the most famous Watchtower 'activists'] sent me and I am Jehovah's (Lesa's) witness. This is my certificate.[12]

The expression 'to teach Chitawala' – that is, 'to teach Watchtower' – as well as the fact that the words 'to teach' and 'to preach' in these statements appear to be interchangeable, indicate that indigenous Christian movements did not see much difference between 'school' and 'church'. For the colonial administration, however, the distinction was of crucial importance with respect to the legal judgement of the case. In reporting the case to the Provincial Commissioner of Luangwa Province, District Commissioner J. P. Murray accordingly wrote:

> William's action in commencing to build what he calls a 'school' at Libengwa's Village, seems to be carrying things a bit far, but it is assumed that what they call a 'school' (Lishikulu) should perhaps more properly be translated 'church' or 'chapel' and does not come within the law.

The final judgement referred to the Native Education Ordinance of the 1920s, which distinguished between 'schools' and 'sub-schools' (Ragsdale 1986: 83):

> This is not a 'school' within the definition of s.2 [i.e., section 2] of the Ordinance, because it is not conducted for 120 days a year, nor is it based on a code approved by the Director of Native Education. Nor is it a 'sub-school' because it does not give instruction in what may properly be described as secular subjects. However the accused seem to make no

concealment of their religious views and the Ordinance seems definitely to prohibit unauthorized preaching.[13]

On the basis of the Native Education Ordinance, William Nsofu's grass-thatched shelter was denied the status of a 'school', and his certificate issued by Jeremiah Gondwe was not recognized as appropriate authorization for preaching. Being neither a proper 'teacher' nor a lawful 'preacher', William Nsofu was found guilty.

Taken together, these findings suggest that colonial agencies in Northern Rhodesia embarked on the separation of 'church' and 'school' only *after* African Christian movements had actively appropriated the early colonial practice of coalescing the two. The ensuing process of 'modernization', in the form of a functional differentiation between 'religion' and 'formal education', represented an attempt to control the indigenous population, just like the earlier coalescence of 'church' and 'school'.

Resistance and Non-religious Literacies

Many of the indigenous population readily accepted and embraced 'formal learning as the *fons et origo* of European potency' (Comaroff 1996: 20; cf. Hastings 1996: 457). Yet for some, schools and literacy were not only equated with missions but, problematically, also with the colonial government. Criticizing the educational monopoly of the mission societies and seeing in the mission schools an instrument of colonial oppression, indigenous Christian movements thus demanded – and, as we have seen, actually opened – their own schools and made schooling a 'political battlefield' (Fields 1985: 238; cf. Berman 1974; Ranger 1965a; Summers 2002). Parents belonging to the early Watchtower movement often refused their children access to mission schools, and even much later the mission societies' schools were objects of contention. Violent conflicts with the Lumpa Church of the prophetess Alice Lenshina started in 1964 when she forbade her followers to attend mission schools (Roberts 1970: 44). In a letter from a catechist of the Lumpa Church to Chief Makasa, the writer stated that 'we want a Lenshina school not a European one' (cited in Oger 1960: 50).

Alongside the equation of missions with colonial hegemony, another dispute pertained to the question of how much 'religion' should be taught in the mission schools. When the Paris Evangelical Mission opened the first school in the territory of what was later to become Northern Rhodesia in 1867, the 'mission regarded education as primarily a preparation for the Christian life', whereas the BaLozi aristocracy and King Lewanika saw it 'as the means of providing the Lozi state with qualified clerks, interpreters, artisans and so on' (Ranger 1965b: 30). The Secretary for Native Affairs observed in 1907 that the BaLozi 'recognize the value of technical education and have long been dissatisfied with the teaching of the missionaries which is confined to the Bible, singing and a smattering of imperfect English' (cited in Ranger 1965b: 31).[14] Against this background of discontent, in 1903 Lewanika contacted the African Methodist Episcopal Church (AMEC) in South Africa, which to him seemed to offer the BaLozi a truly modernizing education. Yet, when the provision of school education through the AMEC eventually failed, the BSAC, fearing another 'Ethiopian activity' (Ranger 1965b: 37), set up the aforementioned secular Barotse National School in 1906, which was the only school ever founded by the British South Africa Company in the territory.

Thus, although the church–school relationship in the early history of Northern Rhodesia was generally characterized by a marked degree of overlap, the local population did perceive a potential in formal schooling that lay beyond the religious domain. For Lewanika, trainings in secretarial and administrative tasks, including typing, were among the principal educational objectives. And success in a mission school generally promised employment in the colonial administration: the first generations to receive schooling not only had considerable opportunities for promotion within their mission society as teacher-evangelists, but also in obtaining salaried jobs in government service. With Zambian independence in 1964, the demand for administrative staff increased even further. As Colson and Scudder (1980: 21) have pointed out, 85 per cent of the first generation of secondary school leavers in the Gwembe Valley became employees in the administration. Schools and literacy were accordingly not only associated with Christianity – and for some with colonial hegemony – but also with administration and bureaucracy.

Colonial Bureaucracy

When registering the indigenous population for, among other things, purposes of taxation, forced labour or occasional famine relief, the colonial administration made extensive use of various kinds of forms, documents, law books, files and registers. These administrative procedures, which involved indigenous staff, strove to follow Western models of a rather centralised bureaucratization. Evaluating the local administrative staff after a tour of the Gwembe Valley in 1938, for example, the District Officer noted:

> The Court Clerk has many good points and he is especially good at intercepting men on leave and entering their taxes in his copy of the register, which was very up-to-date in this respect. Against that he had not compared his register with the 'master copy' at the Boma for a long time and since he had been entering youths in his register in anticipation of them being written in the same spaces when they got their Identification Certificates at the Boma some confusion resulted.[15]

One of the main difficulties faced by the colonial administration accordingly consisted in making the different types of written registration and identification compatible with each other. Even among different administrative territories of the British colonial empire, such compatibility frequently could not be taken for granted. Stating that many taxpayers in his area had already paid their taxes in Southern Rhodesia, where they had been working as labour migrants, the District Officer complains: 'I regret that it is rare to be able to identify a man from the copies of Southern Rhodesian tax receipts which reach the Boma'.

Besides such lack of practical standardisation in the British administration itself, certain subversive strategies on the part of the indigenous population also undermined bureaucratic registrations:

> The habit of changing name on every possible occasion is becoming an absolute pest and it is against the best interests of the Africans themselves. It is sometimes done because the owner thinks he may wish sometime or other to cover up his tracks. But more often it is a matter of caprice without any particular motive. I am particularly keen on devising some system of establishing identity apart from the Pass Laws, but I should like it to be uniform for the territory.[16]

The Provincial Commissioner of Central Province gave an example of this 'habit of changing names'. Referring to a minute of a District Commissioner, he wrote in April 1943:

> There is a growing tendency on the part of modern youths to drop the childhood name, which tendency I consider should not be encouraged. For instance, a man named John Chisenga has a son who is given the name of Kalunga at birth. As a youth Kalunga adopts the name Isaac. His full name should be Isaac Kalunga Chisenga, but he thinks it grand to call himself Isaac John, and he probably becomes registered as such. Inevitably, if this trend is allowed to become general, Africa will be peopled by 'bicycle', 'ticket' and 'football', and native names will be forgotten. It would be a tragedy if such actually happened, and this order mentioned is an excellent method of preventing this. I consider it would be an excellent thing if all clerks engaged in the work of registering – particularly in industrial areas, would be instructed not to accept such names as 'Isaac John' when forwarding applications for identity certificates to rural areas.[17]

Ironically, administrative necessities here suggest restricting the cultural hybridity that prevailed in the newly established industrial areas in the colony in order to retrieve an 'African identity' (cf. Ranger 1986a). Unequivocal and 'authentic' African names appear to guarantee a similarly unequivocal bureaucratic colonial type of registration.

The colonial administration in Northern Rhodesia thus faced severe difficulties in creating a constellation such as the one Michel Foucault has described for European history, where surveillance, normalising judgements and examinations brought about the subjugation and inscription of 'subjects' into existing power relations. This mostly had to do with the fact that they did not manage to inscribe clearly identifiable 'subjects' into an authoritative 'network of writing' (Foucault

1977: 201). The Report of Native Affairs of 1932 for Batoka Province, which at that time also included a portion of the Gwembe Valley, notes:

> Up to date 19,200 identity certificates have been issued here. The impunity with which natives can discard their certificates and obtain new ones makes the success of the scheme appear very doubtful. At this office nearly three hundred duplicates have been issued during the past three months. Enquiry is made into every case before the issue of a duplicate, incidentally a good deal of valuable time is wasted in so doing, but if a native puts up a plausible story to account for the loss of a chitupa [a pass], one has seldom or never means of proving its falseness, though as undoubtedly frequently happens, he may have simply walked out of his employment and thrown away his identity certificate.[18]

Besides identity certificates and tax registers, the administrative staff of colonial Northern Rhodesia were also preoccupied with, for example, annual reports, station cash accounts, diaries, travel reports, statistical documentation and various types of notebook. Writing was thus also aimed at the temporal stabilization of social relationships: 'When a District Officer goes to a village and reads out the names of all natives written in that village it serves to *cement* the village and prevent the disintegration of villages that is considered to be unfortunate'.[19]

Such administrative writing, however, was not confined to the British staff. 'Native clerks' were also employed (cf. Derrick 1983), while indigenous messengers were provided with passes and had to write reports after investigating particular cases in the areas under their responsibility. The village headmen, on the other hand, had to have a 'Village Note Book'. The common vernacular designation in Chitonga, which is still used today for village headmen (*sibbuku*, 'the man with the book'), is a reference to this book.

The administrative obsession with the written form is most clearly expressed in a letter by the Provincial Commissioner (Abercorn) of 22 June 1932, who states that 'numbers of District Officers regard their registers rather as *fetish*, to be treated with great reverence'.[20] Despite the limited efficacy mentioned above, the work of the colonial bureaucracy was thus pursued with great solemnity involving 'bureaucratic ritualism':

> One of the prominent features of colonial administration was an overemphasis on bureaucratic rituals, especially when it came to European superiors dealing with African junior officers and clerks. This revolved on an administrative orthodoxy which required strict adherence to routinised procedures and the drilling of African officials into imitative behaviours (Lungu 1985b: 46).

This conjunction of dubious effectiveness and solemn ritualism, in which documents became 'ritualized instruments of ruling and … a way of drawing boundaries' (Hofmeyr 2002: 450), must have been one of the most striking impressions made by 'bureaucracy' on the indigenous population.

At the same time, this population was provided with the products of bureaucratization: taxpayers, for example, 'were given a receipt (*citipa*), stamped with emblems (usually birds or animals which changed yearly' (Vickery 1986: 72). And 'certificates' were made obligatory for 'teachers' and 'preachers'. As in the case of William Nsofu, mentioned above, however, the question of who was allowed to issue such 'certificates' was a constant subject of contention. During the hearing of his case, Nsofu had presented a certificate issued by Jeremiah Gondwe, who for Nsofu represented the relevant authority, though he did not belong to any of the officially recognized denominations. In another instance from 1935, a Kaonde of Mumbwa District was accused of pursuing 'the business of a hawker by travelling from place to place selling or offering for sale certain tracts of the Watch Tower Society at 3d each, not being the growth, produce or manufacture of N. Rhodesia, without holding a licence authorizing him to do so'. The accused pleaded 'Not guilty. "My licence is in the booklet *The Crisis* pages 31 and top of page 32"'.[21] These references to one of the Watchtower Bible and Tract Society's publications ultimately implied a reference to God and thus opposed divine to worldly authorities. The accused agreed with the court that written licences are an appropriate means of self-authorization in the religious realm, but he disagreed with it in respect of who should be the authority behind such licences.

Evangelists as Administrators

But not only secular colonial authorities engaged in bureaucratic procedures: certifying, documenting and registering in writing had also been common practice among Western mission societies. The Universities Mission to Central Africa, for example, outlined its mission procedures as follows: 'After preaching in the town names would be written down of those who wish to put themselves under instruction as hearers; hearers are taught for at least one year before they are admitted as catechumens, and catechumens are under instruction for at least two years before baptism' (1914: 18).

An interest in religious matters was expressed by having one's name registered. And the subsequent religious advancement followed a sequence that was structured less by individual achievements than by a strict timetable. Miss O.C. Doke of the South African Baptist Mission also emphasised the use of registers when conducting 'Hearers' Classes', that is, when giving religious lessons to those 'who had their desire aroused to know more of "The Way of Life"':

> A register of these classes is very necessary and should be kept always up-to-date. In fact it is advisable to have two registers, one to be kept at the village, in which a careful note is made about the whereabouts of each member (as they are often at work, etc.) and also a record of any 'cases' that he or she may bring to be settled and the progress of the same; and then one carried by the visiting Evangelist or Missionary which is always brought back to Headquarters filled in to date (1931: 43).

Comparing this to the procedures of the colonial administration, one hardly finds great differences between them: most missions also aimed to construct a 'network of writing' that recorded the identity and 'whereabouts' of 'hearers' and members, and to bring local registries into line with superordinate registries at the respective mission's headquarters. That such procedures of registration were common among the mission societies of Northern Rhodesia is also described in Brian Garvey's analysis of the Catholic White Fathers:

> The proposal for a special school for the training of evangelists became one of the main points of dispute between Bishop Dupont and his priests after 1908. Missionaries complained that the handwriting of the catechists was so bad that they could not keep the simple lists of names required of them. By 1909 a Council of the whole vicariate had agreed on the establishment of what they termed a 'Central School' for the southern half of the vicariate, that is to say the missions in Malawi. In the north, the missions of Bembaland, each station would continue to take responsibility for the training of its own catechists (1994a: 101–2).

The catechist instruction of the White Fathers accordingly aligned training in religious matters with instructions in denominational administration. Their evangelists were simultaneously responsible for proselytizing, for general ministerial tasks and for the bureaucratic administration of the smaller religious communities.

Besides the personal union of 'preacher' and 'teacher', described above, much missionary work in Northern Rhodesia accordingly involved a personal union of 'preacher' and 'administrator'. Given the frequent shortage of mission staff, practising Christianity not only involved the metaphysical, it also meant engaging in the physicality of administrative bureaucracy – a bureaucracy in the religious mode.

Frederick Cooper once remarked: 'It is far from clear what Africans thought about the symbolic structure of the colonial power or the identities being inscribed on them. The cultural edifice could be taken apart brick for brick and parts used to shape quite different cultural visions' (1994: 1,527). As has been shown in this chapter, Western mission societies in Northern Rhodesia projected 'literate culture' as a means of 'inscribing' new identities on to the colonized. In this endeavour, 'church' coalesced with 'school', while 'preachers' also acted as 'administrators'. The colonial administration, on the other hand, struggled to position colonial subjects within an authoritative network of bureaucratic inscription while also demonstrating bureaucratic ritualism and an attitude that occasionally came close to a veneration of administrative writing.

Cooper is certainly right in noting that one cannot be sure what in particular the African population thought about all this. But what is clear is that while some features of these literacies were evaded or subverted, others were adopted and made to suit indigenous aspirations. I have tried to demonstrate in this chapter that this adaptation not only concerned literacy as a means of self-empowerment, but also particular ways of coalescing 'religious literacy' with 'schooled literacy'. It was, paradoxically, this very appropriation that made colonial agencies adapt to the colonized by, for example, increasingly stressing functional differentiation and promoting 'secular literacy'.

As we shall see later in the course of this book, things have changed a great deal in contemporary Zambia. Yet certain features of these early constellations in Northern Rhodesia are also characteristic of the literacy practices I observed: the association of literacy with Christianity, the association of Christianity with bureaucratic forms of administration, the existence of religious-bureaucratic personal unions, and the association of bureaucracy, not with obvious effectiveness, but with a certain ritualism.

Notes

1. Protestant and Catholic missionaries to southern Africa had different educational ideals (cf. Henkel 1989: 127; see also Garvey 1994a: 101). In the following, I shall concentrate on the Protestant missions' school activities, since they were the prominent representatives of early Christianity in the area of my research. For Catholic educational initiatives, see Carmody (1991, 1992, 1999), Garvey (1994a, 1994b), Hinfelaar (2004), Simpson (2003). For a general history of missionary activities in Northern Rhodesia up to 1924, see Rotberg (1965).
2. R. Moffat of the London Missionary Society, for example, describes returning to his mission station from a journey to Cape Town in 1831 as follows: 'Never since missionaries entered the country was such a treasure conveyed to the mission as on the present occasion, for we brought with us an edition of the Gospel of Luke, and a hymn-book in the native language, a printing press, type, paper, and ink ...' (1842: 563).
3. Annual Report for the Year Ending 31 March 1917. NAZ: KDB 6/2/1.
4. Annual Report on Native Education for 1931. Lusaka: Government Printer.
5. For detailed discussions of the history of school education in Zambia, see Snelson (1974), Ragsdale (1986), Lungwangwa (1987), Carmody (1999).
6. The history of the early Watchtower movement in Northern Rhodesia has been extensively treated by Quick (1940), Cunnison (1951), Lehmann and Taylor (1961), Hooker (1965), Long (1968), Assimeng (1970), Cross (1970, 1977a, 1977b), Fields (1985), Epstein (1986), Henkel (1989), Gifford (1998).
7. The most famous of these witchcraft eradication movements was launched by Tomo Nyrienda, already mentioned, who is said to have killed about two hundred alleged witches (cf. Ranger 1975).
8. In subsequent decades, the Watchtower Bible and Tract Society managed to include many of the indigenous movements' congregations into its own organizational structure. Others, however, never joined but continued their rather autonomous religious practice, although in a more law-abiding manner.
9. This and the five subsequent quotations, apart from J. Ragsdale's (1986), are taken from the Report on the Conference of Representatives of Missionary Societies, 1919. NAZ: B1/62/2.
10. Case Record of Mukusi Division in Luangwa Province, 22 March 1934. NAZ: Sec2/1175; my italics.
11. A *boma* was a regional administrative centre of the colonial government.

12. Case Record of Mukusi Division in Luangwa Province, 22 March 1934. NAZ: Sec2/1175; my italics. For an analysis of Jeremiah Gondwe's role in the Watchtower movement, see Cross (1970).
13. Case Record of Mukusi Division in Luangwa Province, 22 March 1934. NAZ: Sec2/1175.
14. In a letter to the missionary F. Coillard of the Paris Evangelical Mission, for example, Lewanika wrote: 'What do we want with all that rubbish heap of fables that you call the Bible? ... What does your school do for us? ...it is a purposeless and unprofitable folly. What I want is missionaries ... who build big workshops and teach us all the trades of the white man. ... What I want is carpenters, blacksmiths, armourers, masons. ... That's what I want, industrial missionaries; that is what all the chiefs want. We laugh at the rest' (cited in Campbell 1995: 192–93; see also Prins 1980). With the growing urbanization and industrialization of Northern Rhodesia, however, the indigenous assessment of mission schooling changed. Colson and Scudder remark, on the Gwembe Tonga: 'The early educational stress on agriculture and on manual labor was less relevant to villagers than a curriculum that would enable them to acquire skills in demand in towns and industrial areas to which Gwembe men were increasingly drawn in the search for a cash income' (1980: 51).
15. Gwembe Tour Report No. 8, 1954. NAZ: Sec 2/1018.
16. Letter of Provincial Commissioner (Ndola) to Chief Secretary of the Northern Rhodesian Government, 12 February 1943. NAZ: Sec 2/430.
17. Letter of Provincial Commissioner (Broken Hill) to Chief Secretary of the Northern Rhodesian Government, 6 April 1943. NAZ: Sec 2/430.
18. Report on Native Affairs for the Quarter Ending 31 March 1932, Batoka Province. NAZ: Sec 2/68, Vol. 4.
19. Letter of District Commissioner (Ndola) to Provincial Commissioner (Ndola), 2 September 1932. NAZ: Sec 2/337, Vol. 1; my italics.
20. Letter of Provincial Commissioner (Abercorn) to Chief Secretary of the Northern Rhodesian Government, 22 June 1932. NAZ: Sec 2/337, Vol. 1; my italics.
21. Case Record of Kapotwe Village in Mumbwa District, 30 March 1935. NAZ: ZA 1/9/62/1.

Chapter 2
Passages, Configurations, Traces

The area in which I conducted my ethnographic fieldwork, namely the Gwembe Valley and the adjacent Central African Plateau in the Southern Province of Zambia, has been extraordinarily well covered by the longitudinal studies of the Gwembe Valley Research Project (in particular by Elizabeth Colson and Thayer Scudder), the main exception being African Christianity. In now laying the groundwork for the subsequent analysis of literacy practices among African Christians by sketching out the general ethnographic setting of my research, I shall draw on their findings. But I shall also adopt an approach that takes the biographical narrative of one of my local interlocutors as a starting point in order to indicate in an exemplary manner how the wider developments in this area were related to lived experience. In a similar vein, my remarks concerning the 'religious field' in my research area will partly adopt the perspective of members of a particular religious community, the Spirit Apostolic Church. This allows me, first, to elaborate by way of an example the contextual embeddedness, flexibility and contingency of religious practices and, secondly, to introduce important features of an African Christian community that, in the course of this book, will serve as one of the major ethnographic case studies.

At the Edge of the Road

When narrating his life history one day in 1999, the Bishop of the Spirit Apostolic Church, Rabson, started by describing what he said was the most impressive experience of his childhood in the 1950s. His parents' homestead was situated in the rugged hills of the escarpment between the Central African Plateau and the Gwembe Valley.[1] At that time, access to the Valley and the thinly populated hills was difficult (Colson 1962a: 611). Some minor paths led through the escarpment, paths which were used by the Gwembe Tonga for bartering with the Tonga on the Plateau,[2] purchasing commodities, small-scale trading, and seeking labour in the towns and commercial farms adjacent to the railway line connecting Lusaka with Livingstone and with the mines in the South and on the Copperbelt.[3] Most of the scattered villages on the escarpment were only accessible using such paths. The homestead of Rabson's parents, however, was located close to the Old Road, the only road in this area allowing one to travel from the plateau to the Gwembe Valley using a motor vehicle:

> I cannot remember how often I was standing there, close to the edge of the road. I was still a young boy. But I really enjoyed watching the cars and lorries passing by. There were not many cars in these years, but whenever I heard the noise of engines, my friends and I made sure to stand close to the road. I guess it was at that time that I started having the wish of becoming a driver.

The Old Road was a gravel road that had been built by the British colonial administration in the 1930s, when another drought-induced famine had struck the Gwembe Valley (Colson 1979; Scudder 1962: 215–47; see also Cliggett 2005). It stretched from the railway line to a settlement close to the Sinazeze creek, where a depot for famine relief had been constructed, and then to the mission station of the Primitive Methodist Missionary Society at Kanchindu (Read 1932: 18). The colonial government had not always cared much for the Gwembe Tonga, who administrators and missionaries, neighbouring groups like the BaLozi, and even the socio-culturally related Plateau Tonga all tended to consider a 'primitive' and 'backward' people. Despite the fact that it was just about impossible to find work within the Gwembe Valley, the colonial administration had imposed a hut tax on male inhabitants in 1904 (Read 1932: 8), registering taxpayers and prosecuting those who tried to avoid payment. The high temperature – especially during the hot season (*cilimo* and *kumwaka*), which starts in mid-August – the poor soils in most areas, the unreliability of the rainfall and the distance of the Gwembe Valley from the railway line all prevented commercial farming on a large scale.

Up to the mid-1950s, only a small number of European traders were active in the Gwembe Valley, and even the British missionaries periodically shifted their mission station from the Valley to the better climate of the Plateau.[4] Apart from some limited initiatives in growing cash crops like tobacco and cotton, it was mostly labour migration that provided the Gwembe Tonga with the money they needed to pay taxes and purchase at least some of the highly valued commodities of the whites (*bakuwa*).[5] In 1956, more than 40 per cent of the male taxable population had left the villages as labour migrants (Colson 1960: 32). Since the 1930s, opportunities for wage labour within the Valley had slightly improved, for example, in road construction and maintenance. Generally, however, prior to the mid-1950s there were fewer than five hundred paid jobs in the Gwembe Valley (Colson and Scudder 1980: 8), which, according to a census conducted by the colonial administration, had a total population of almost fifty thousand in 1956 (Colson 1960: 41).[6]

Like most other Tonga, Rabson's parents thus relied on subsistence farming, that is, maize, sorghum and different types of millet, as well as goats, chickens and some cattle (Scudder 1962). Since their village was close to a small tributary, which flowed into the Zambezi River further down in the Gwembe Valley and carried water for most of the year, they were not totally dependent on the rainy season (*mayinza*), which in good years started in November and lasted until March or April. On the banks of this tributary, they maintained small semi-permanent gardens with, for example, banana, tomato, pumpkins, rape and beans. A similar agricultural system was followed on the banks of the Zambezi River, which were flooded annually. Villages (*miinzi*) consisted of scattered homesteads clustered around the riverside; two to seven villages made up a neighbourhood (*masi*), the largest indigenous political unit in the Valley (Colson 1960: 57–65, 162–95). Some fertile alluvial soils on the banks of the river allowed cultivation twice a year, although irrigation was not common among Gwembe farmers. Individuals of both sexes could own gardens, which were generally inherited through the matrilineage, but whose right of use could also be transferred to spouses, distant kin, or even strangers who wished to settle in the area. A pioneer farmer could claim land he had cleared for the first time (Scudder 1962: 63–71; see also Colson 1963, 1966a, 1971a).

Rabson's father had been one such pioneer. When he moved from the southern banks of the Zambezi to the escarpment on the northern side of the river in the 1940s, he had to apply for permission from the headman of his new village to clear land and to settle.[7] This shift in residence also meant that he was now living in another chieftaincy, although he personally never had any contact with his new Paramount Chief.[8] In subsequent years, Rabson's father frequently visited his relatives on the other side of the Zambezi.[9] When the Kariba Dam was built in the Gwembe Valley in the mid-1950s, however, this contact was cut off completely. The construction of the dam, which created what at that time was the largest man-made lake in the world and which was intended for the production of electricity, necessitated the resettlement of about 57,000 people and induced rapid infrastructural developments. An accelerated influx from the outside world, the increased incorporation of the area into the market economy system and the initial stages of urbanization were all facets of this rapid change, which also caused the disintegration of many customary ways of living (Colson 1971b; Scudder 1969, 1993).

Rabson grew up during this time of marked socio-cultural and economic transformation. When in 1999 he began his biographical narrative with the Old Road, he therefore not only presented it as a symbol of the development of the Gwembe Valley as a whole, but also as a symbol of what seemed to be his personal future.

On the Road

When Rabson's father died, his mother was married to the elder brother of her deceased husband. The relationship with his 'new' father was strained, since there were now three wives struggling for their joint husband's attention.[10] Being the third child of the last wife, Rabson felt neglected, since he was only allowed to attend the village school for four years and was afterwards pressured into tending the cattle. One day, he decided to run away:

> I had heard that there was a camp at Batoka where all the construction workers for the new road were living. It was a long distance from my village,

but I went there and then I just knocked at the door of the first house I saw and asked to be given some piecework. I wanted to be a driver or at least to be close to the vehicles. After all, I thought, I might get somebody to teach me how to drive.

The township of Batoka on the Plateau near the escarpment had a small train station and was surrounded by commercial farms, which mostly raised cattle for sale in the larger towns and the mining areas. Compared to the inhabitants of the Gwembe Valley, the Tonga on the Plateau had experienced colonialism over a longer period of time. Wage labour and the money economy, urbanization, formal schooling and Christianization had all exerted an early and far-reaching economic and socio-cultural impact on the areas near the railway line.[11] The introduction of extended farming areas in the colonial period had forced the local population to settle in unattractive 'Native Reserves', whose sandy soils only produced bad harvests for the most part. Siamujulu village, where the headquarters of the Spirit Apostolic Church was established later on, was situated in one of these residential areas, near Batoka.

After residing in Batoka for some months, Rabson joined the crew of a British construction company that was building the new road from Batoka to Maamba in the Gwembe Valley, where open-cast coal mining had recently begun. This new road in some sections followed the Old Road, yet for the most part deviated from the latter's meandering course instead taking a straighter route. When Rabson joined the crew, the hilly escarpment and part of the Gwembe Valley had already been finished. The tarmac road passed the area of Nanyenda, where in the 1970s a development aid organization set up its camp, and where in the early 1980s a congregation of the Spirit Apostolic Church was established. Then the road proceeded to Sinazeze, which by this time had become a small township with some shops and a rural health centre.

While being employed as a construction worker and moving ahead with the gradually extending tarmac road, Rabson managed to learn how to drive. Soon afterwards, he stopped working for the construction company, subsequently finding employment with a number of different companies. He worked as a lorry driver for a garage in Choma on the Plateau, as a driver for the development aid organization in the Gwembe Valley, and periodically as a taxi driver shuttling back and forth every day between the Plateau and the Valley. Thanks to his highly mobile occupation, he travelled to different destinations, mostly in Zambia's Southern Province. Wherever he went, Rabson tried to set up new branches of the Full Gospel Church of Central Africa, which he had joined in the early 1960s, and from which the Spirit Apostolic Church separated in the early 1990s. Several other elders of this same Church also worked as drivers, others were supported by Rabson while they tried to obtain a driving licence, and yet others worked as his assistants. Among the founders of the Spirit Apostolic Church there were then a comparatively high number of people whose occupation had something or other to do with vehicles and motor transport. Their employment provided opportunities to spread the Church more widely than other African-initiated denominations could dream of doing.

1. Thatching the roof of a new church building, Nanyenda village, 1993.

However, in contrast to those church elders who were employed as drivers and thus had a regular income, most members of the Full Gospel Church and later of the Spirit Apostolic Church lived on the edge of poverty. Since the mid-1970s, the local impact of the Zambian economic recession, declining opportunities for wage labour and labour migration, and repeated droughts have had a deteriorating effect on the Valley's economy (Scudder 1985). For the majority of people in my research area it was, therefore, difficult to even get enough for their daily food.

Early Evangelisations

My interlocutors from different denominations were generally among the first Christians within their respective families. This is surprising when seen in the light of the comparatively long history of Christianity among the Tonga.

During his journeys through southern Africa in the mid-1850s, David Livingstone of the London Missionary Society passed through the Gwembe Valley and the lands of Chief Monze on the Tonga Plateau (Livingstone 1857). The Primitive Methodist Missionary Society, which had separated from the Wesleyan Methodist Church in Britain and had been active in South Africa since 1870 (Henkel 1989: 31), opened the first mission stations among the Balla on the plateau in the late nineteenth century, and then gradually extended its activities into the territories of the Tonga. In subsequent decades, representatives of various other churches, such as the Seventh-day Adventists, the Jesuits, the Brethren in Christ, the Universities Mission, the Church of Christ, the Pilgrim Holiness Church and the

Salvation Army, came to settle on the Tonga Plateau. The Gwembe Valley, on the other hand, had experienced an abortive attempt by Jesuit priests to establish a mission station in 1880 (Kubera 1998: 195–96). In 1901, representatives of the Primitive Methodist Missionary Society came to settle in Sijoba village and subsequently at Kanchindu (Ulrich Luig 1997: 86–89). From there, outstations were built so as to extend the scope of its mission activities in the Gwembe Valley, which from the early 1920s also became a site of missionary work by the Salvation Army, the Jesuits, the Seventh-day Adventists, and from the mid-1930s the Pilgrim Holiness Church (Colson and Scudder 1980: 49–60).

It had been the policy of the colonial government and of early Western mission societies to divide the territory of Northern Rhodesia (now Zambia) into various exclusive 'mission spheres of influence' (Henkel 1989: 103–11), in an attempt to prevent rivalry between the different churches. Most Tonga in the early twentieth century thus had no real choice between the various Western denominations. Up to the 1950s, the Primitive Methodist Missionary Society had something of a monopoly of Christianity in the chieftaincies of Mweemba and Sinazongwe in the Gwembe Valley, while the Pilgrim Holiness Church concentrated on the regions further down the Zambezi River. Siamujulu village, near Batoka on the Plateau, on the other hand, was mainly located in the 'sphere of influence' of the Brethren in Christ, who had a mission station at Sikalongo from 1921.

On the Plateau, this spatial separation of Western denominations had to some extent been undermined by African Christian movements. In the first decades of the twentieth century, labour migrants returning from Nyasaland (now Malawi), Southern Rhodesia (now Zimbabwe) and South Africa set up independent churches in Northern Rhodesia. The first documented church with a purely non-white leadership in the territory of Northern Rhodesia was the African Methodist Episcopal Church, which was established in Barotseland around 1900 (Ranger 1965b). In the northern parts of the territory, preachers belonging to the indigenous Watchtower movement, mentioned in the preceding chapter, succeeded in winning adherents in the period after the First World War (Cross 1977b). This movement, which henceforth spread rapidly throughout Northern Rhodesia and repeatedly came into conflict with the colonial authorities, was influenced by the literature of the Watchtower Bible and Tract Society without, however, being organisationally linked to the official headquarters of this denomination. From the 1920s and 1930s, Watchtower preachers also toured Southern Province. In the so-called *Mwana Lesa* movement of 1925, which had parallels with the *muchape* movement (Richards 1935), baptism was employed for witch-finding. When it emerged that several hundred alleged witches had been drowned, the colonial administration sentenced the movement's leader to death. However, most early Watchtower activities on the Tonga Plateau seem to have grown up in the Mazabuka area (Fields 1985: 7, 139, 203–4, 230). These movements were observed with unease by the British administration. Their perennial conflicts with 'traditional' political authorities, their anti-colonial rhetoric, and their uncontrollable growth seemed to foreshadow sedition. Striving to maintain colonial rule, yet shrinking from curtailing religious freedom altogether, the administration alternated between taking a liberal stance towards African-initiated churches and attempting to suppress them.

In contrast to the Tonga Plateau, for which ample evidence of early Watchtower activities exists, it is now hard to judge the impact of African indigenous movements on the Gwembe Tonga in the first half of the twentieth century. One of the rare pieces of evidence for the presence of these movements in the Gwembe Valley is contained in the Annual Report upon Native Affairs of 1935, where it is reported: 'Watch Tower preachers have made some headway especially in the Kafue and Zambesi Valleys. The people there, always independent, and without other religious teaching, have been only too ready to adopt a creed which appears to advocate complete independence and contempt of authority'.[12]

In most other administrative reports of the same period and for the same area, however, there is no reference to indigenous religious movements. It is highly probable that the Gwembe Tonga were acquainted with Watchtower doctrines even before the 1950s, because the Valley lay on the labour migration route from the North prior to the building of the railway bridge over the Zambezi at Livingstone in 1905 (Vickery 1986: 56), and because the labour migrants from the Gwembe Valley also travelled to the mines in the South (like Bulawayo and Wankie), where the various movements were strong. All the same, these African indigenous Christian teachings and practices initially do not seem to have had a strong impact on the Gwembe Tonga. And although the Western missions gradually enlarged their range of activities in the Valley by setting up outstations and holding religious services in various villages each Sunday, even their efforts could hardly be termed successful:

> On the whole, the missionary evangelism proved to be a largely ineffective means to convert the Valley Tonga to Christianity. Apart from the unprofessional and superficial way in which it was performed, the underlying clash of the distinct and mutually exclusive world views and religious practices must be seen as lying at the heart of the matter. Although the people in the villages apparently welcomed the entertaining performances of such services and were prepared to adopt new cultural elements like songs or stories, they remained, on the whole, thoroughly reluctant to give up their own beliefs and religious praxis (Ulrich Luig 1997: 105).

It was only after the mid-1950s that Christianity increased its impact in the Valley. Mining and the construction of the Kariba Dam created new infrastructure, which opened up the Gwembe Valley to the Plateau and thus cleared the way for both Western and African-initiated churches to enter the area. Around Sinazeze, where the Primitive Methodist Missionary Society had formerly been dominant, a 'free market of Christianity' (Ulrich Luig 1997: 231) emerged.

Christianity in the 1990s

In the 1990s, most of the younger generation in the area of my research were associated with a Christian congregation (cf. Cliggett 2005: 117–18).[13] A considerable number of Western and African-initiated churches co-existed in mutual competition for members. In 1999, for instance, eighteen different denominations could be found within the range of an hour's walk starting from the township of Sinazeze. Some of these even had two or three congregations within this, for the most part, sparsely populated region. In the area of Siamujulu village on the Plateau, five denominations existed within a similar range. And since these churches worked alongside different 'traditional' religious forms, my research area was marked by a high degree of religious pluralism (Fabian 1985).

The Christian practices of the Tonga were characterized by a marked selectivity, in that changing one's church affiliation repeatedly (although sometimes only temporarily) represented the rule rather than the exception. To a large extent, people were free to attend the church of their choice, and even after making a selection (*kusalaula chikombelo*), they often tended to be sceptical of absolute claims to religious authority. Although young children generally attended the same church as their parents, at the age of ten to twelve they often decided to change to another denomination. And although women were mostly expected to join the church of their husbands after marriage, I observed many instances where husbands and wives belonged to different denominations.

This marked degree of 'affiliational mobility' (Murphree 1969: 165) and selectivity, which has certain parallels in Tonga social organisation in general, will be important for the analysis undertaken in this book. Particular families certainly had preferences for particular denominations. On the whole, however, the choice of church affiliation was a decidedly individual affair. Nobody could be forced to attend a certain denomination by either their relatives or the church authorities. Given this background, it is clear that the various denominations had to struggle to maintain a following. Their authority was not fixed, but had to be continuously confirmed or even, sometimes, constituted anew. Being embedded in a highly competitive religious context, church leaders were thus at pains to demonstrate that their own denomination had been divinely ordained. If they failed to make their claims plausible, their congregations slowly drifted away.

The selectivity of the Tonga with respect to church affiliation crucially had to do with the local view that Christian authority cannot be permanently fixed (see also Chapter 10). That church elders might easily fail to contact and interact with God (*leza*) due to their inevitable human fallibility and to the workings of evil spirits was considered a truism. Scepticism of claims to absolute religious authority thus provoked constant judgement (*kumuyeyela mumizezo*) on the part of the churchgoers as to whether a specific religious practice had been divinely ordained or not (cf. Turner 1967c: 133). The criteria for such evaluations, however, differed from person to person, and even from time to time (Kirsch 1998: 40–46). Whereas a given church might be seen as being divinely guided by some, others regarded the same church as representing the abode of Satan. And when people changed from denomination to denomination, they frequently claimed that the previous church had lost its association with the Holy Spirit (*muya usalala*) and had instead started to employ evil powers (*madaimona* or *muya mubi*) that only resembled this divine being. Like other spiritual entities, the Holy Spirit was identified by its phenomenological appearance, but, as Judith Irvine points out with respect to the interpretation of spirit possession:

> the emergence of an interpretation will also depend on contexts of situation; it will depend on the observers' knowledge of participants' past histories; and it will depend on the motives and interests of the various observers who interpret what is going on. In other words, interpretation is a creative process, incorporating a historical trajectory, and involving active collusion among participants (1982: 257).

Among the churchgoers in my area of research, the Holy Spirit was thus not part of a unanimously shared and timeless system of classification. Besides the common view that the Holy Spirit was a basically benevolent being, its concrete characteristics and powers, and the *loci* of its manifestations, were constantly being negotiated and renegotiated in different social constellations.

The Holy Spirit was of particular relevance in what Harold W. Turner has called 'prophet-healing churches' (Turner 1967a), that is, in those African-initiated Pentecostal-charismatic churches where the divination and healing of afflictions played a 'pivotal role with regard to doctrine, pastoral praxis and the recruitment of members' (Schoffeleers 1991: 2). Such churches in my area of research were of African origin, their historical roots being in Nyasaland and Southern Rhodesia. In the Gwembe Valley, the congregations of the Spirit Apostolic Church (SAC), which can be counted among the prophet-healing churches, were located next to branches of the following African-initiated Pentecostal-charismatic churches: African Apostolic Faith Mission, Apostles of Jesus, African Church, Church Service of Christ, Full Gospel Church of Central Africa, Foundation Church of Jerusalem in Zambia, African Apostles of John Maranke, Zion Church, St Moses God's Holy Spirit Church of Zambia, Spiritual Church of Kabwe, and Pentecostal Word of God Ministry. Branches of the Apostles of Jesus and of the Zion Church were also located close to the headquarters of the SAC in Siamujulu village on the Plateau.

It is important to note, however, that – at least until my last visit to Zambia in 2001 – not one of these churches in my area of research was actively taking part in the neo-Pentecostal and neo-charismatic movements which had begun proliferating in many parts of Africa over recent decades and which have attracted much attention from anthropologists.[14] In broad outline, these movements can be described as being predominantly urban and mass-based; they display a global orientation and have active transnational connections; and they use (electronic) mass media to disseminate their ideas. Born-again adherents to these movements are expected to 'make a complete break with the past' (Meyer 1998), undergoing rituals of 'deliverance' that aim at liberating them from the influence of satanic forces (Anderson 2006; Hackett 2003) and often being taught a 'prosperity gospel' in which material success is interpreted as a sign of God's blessings (Coleman 2002; Gifford 1990; Hackett 1995; Maxwell 1998). Therefore, with regard to the latter point, according to David Maxwell the 'stereotype of the African Pentecostal who drives to church in a Mercedes, wearing the finest clothes and jewellery is not far from the truth in the new urban mega-churches found in large African cities' (2006: 9). Yet, as becomes clear in this and subsequent chapters of the present book, in many respects this stereotype is a far cry from Pentecostal-charismatic realities in my own area of research.

2. Baptism ritual at a river, Simanzi village, 1999.

In these Pentecostal-charismatic churches, an attempt was made to employ the 'life-transforming power of the Holy Spirit' (Hammond-Tooke 1986: 157). Against the background of a 'polyvalent metaphor of healing' (Comaroff 1985: 197), the African-initiated Pentecostal-charismatic churches engaged in the treatment of bodily afflictions, mentally or socially odd behaviour, and cases of sterility. As in most indigenous Christian churches in Southern Africa, witchcraft was considered the main cause of human afflictions (cf. Colson 2000). Some African-initiated Pentecostal-charismatic churches in my area of research – like those belonging to the *mutumwa* movement – accordingly offered protective measures against the activities of witches (*balozi*).[15] The search for the cause of misfortune (Whyte 1997) or an affliction (*kunsinsima*) was usually pursued by means of 'mediumistic' (Devisch 1985: 51) divinations, which required the prophet concerned to be possessed by the Holy Spirit. The treatment, on the other hand, generally involved spiritualized praying with the laying on of hands (*kupailila*) and the singing of spiritual hymns (Kirsch 1998: 64–73, 97–105). Some churches even provided herbalist treatment that resembled the practices of 'traditional' healers (*bang'anga*).[16] In both cases, however, success in healing presupposed that the respective healer was associated with the Holy Spirit, which was conceptualized as the main antagonistic force against witchcraft and demons. Against this background, religious authority in these African-initiated Pentecostal-charismatic churches was intricately linked to the idea that certain human beings have a privileged association with the Holy Spirit, who assists them in acquiring divine knowledge and curing afflictions.

Other denominations at work in the same area had organizational connections with headquarters in Europe or the United States of America: Apostolic Faith Church, Jehovah's Witnesses, New Apostolic Church, Pilgrim Wesleyan Church, Roman Catholic Church, Seventh-day Adventist Church, and United Church of Zambia. The Bahá'í Faith had also won adherents in the Sinazeze area since the mid-1990s. The organizational links with their respective headquarters were mostly evident in administrative forms and transactions, as well as in the fact that the branches more or less regularly received instruction and religious teaching in writing from them. This latter feature will be analysed in a subsequent chapter with respect to the Jehovah's Witnesses and the New Apostolic Church (*Neuapostolische Kirche*).

When compared with the African-initiated Pentecostal-charismatic churches in my area of research, the religious communities that had associations with Western church bodies placed less emphasis on the workings of the Holy Spirit. All the same, when seen from the members' perspective, this difference was not as clear-cut as might be expected at first glance: it was common for members of the denominations mentioned above to change their church affiliation temporarily if they were affected by witchcraft or health problems. In cases of affliction, the 'therapy management group' (Janzen 1978: 4), which was made up of the patient's relatives, some of whom were frequently non-Christians, decided which type of therapy would be appropriate for the particular problem: the hospital, the *masabe* possession cult, the 'traditional' herbalist (*mung'anga*) or an African-initiated Pentecostal-charismatic church. In classifying afflictions according to phenomenological appearance or the social context of occurrence, some diseases were thus considered to require Christian spiritual treatment. This, in its turn, made temporal visits in African-initiated Pentecostal-charismatic churches inevitable, since the leaders of Western-oriented denominations were generally disinclined to provide such therapies.

The prevalent 'floating fringe' (Aquina 1967: 208) of membership in the African-initiated Pentecostal-charismatic churches was thus also due to temporary affiliations of people who otherwise belonged to a different denomination. On the whole, such practices helped diffuse religious discourses and practices. It was not only that churchgoers were continuously being confronted with other religious practices within their immediate social context; they also usually had first-hand experience of a variety of Christian churches themselves (cf. Sundkler 1961b: 203). By 1999, for example, the bishop of the SAC in 1999 had actually attended ten different denominations during his lifetime; the general secretary had been a member of six different churches prior to the Spirit Apostolic Church; and the pastor of the Nanyenda congregation of this Church had experience of as many as thirteen denominations.

When attending a new denomination during a 'quest for therapy' (Janzen 1978), people generally tried to adjust themselves to whatever religious practice was being pursued there. Since the African-initiated Pentecostal-charismatic churches were ultimately judged according to their effectiveness when dealing with afflictions, such judgments represented *post hoc* assessments. Unanimity within a religious community was considered a prerequisite in successfully making contact with God. The temporary visitors in an African-initiated Pentecostal-charismatic church thus made its discourses and practices their own, so as to learn later on whether they were working effectively or not. Although such discursive adjustments frequently entailed suggestions of exclusivity – in the sense that 'our Church is the only divinely ordained community' – the intersection of different Christian practices during the lifetime of any one person in the long run built up to a certain variable stock of Christian knowledge that could be recalled according to the situation and matter at issue. Churchgoers would clearly advocate a particular Christian practice and reject others at one point in time, while confidently adopting just the opposite on other occasions. A similar observation is made by Benetta Jules-Rosette in her book on the African Apostles of Johane Maranke: 'I learned to expect that the rhetorical strength of a single interpretation was more important than consistency operating across explanations' (1975a: 207).

When seen in a wider perspective, therefore, the religious discourses and practices of different denominations in my area of research did not represent mutually exclusive stocks of knowledge but rather parallel worlds, which were intersected by churchgoers' affiliation practices. Since each of these experienced 'worlds' might be deemed plausible and religiously adequate, they could be invoked at specific times and for specific purposes.

Against this background, even within a given church there was often much less unanimity in basic doctrines than one might expect. The Bishop and the Vice-Bishop of the SAC, for example, did not always agree over the question of whether Jesus Christ had been the son of God or a manifestation of God himself. Likewise, the monogamists among the church elders occasionally deplored the polygamy of Bishop Rabson, while at other times advocating it as an acceptable Christian way of life. The discursive malleability brought about a marked flexibility in religious dogmas. Churches like the SAC thus represented 'discursive fields', which Werner Schiffauer defines as follows: 'A discursive field is an arena in which different social actors are engaged in symbolic struggles. This means conceptualising religious community less as a group that shares a system of symbols than as an open network of believers in ever new constellations in which interpretations and meanings are argued over' (2000: 320; my translation).

As the following shows by way of an example, these struggles concerned not only Christian beliefs, but also other ('traditional') religious forms that in general played an important role in the lives of my interlocutors.

Religious Intersections

In September 1999, the church elders of the Spirit Apostolic Church (SAC) assembled at the homestead of Cephas, the pastor of Nanyenda in the Gwembe Valley. This homestead consisted of seven small grass-thatched houses surrounding a yard at the centre of which were situated three cooking shelters. One of the houses belonged to Cephas and his wife and children. Another house was inhabited by his nephew, who had recently married after returning from Livingstone, where he had been attending secondary school. While he had previously been a member of the Church of Christ, he now usually attended the United Church of Zambia, since it was the nearest to his home and to him resembled his former denomination.

Two other houses were occupied by Cephas' elder brother, Miliot, and his two wives. Miliot had been one of the first members of the SAC in Nanyenda and had acted as a healer and evangelist up to 1996. The bishop in 1999, Rabson, had helped him obtain a driving licence, so that he eventually succeeded in finding work as a taxi driver in Lusaka, Zambia's capital city. Some months later, however, two clients threw him out of his car and drove away in it. Fearing that the police might suspect him of being involved in the theft of the car, yet being financially stranded, he had gone into hiding and sent a letter to his relatives to help him. And now, after a rather demoralizing and furtive return to his homestead, he felt he was in a kind of limbo. He hesitated to join the SAC because he knew that, following his years away, he would have to subordinate himself to Cephas, his younger brother. And even more generally, he felt uncomfortably dependent on Cephas: he had not cultivated his own fields that year and therefore had to rely on the crops of his wives and on those of Cephas. His younger brother consequently had some control over him, despite the fact that it was actually Miliot who had inherited the spirit (*muzimu*) of a deceased uncle of their mother's lineage, which otherwise ought to give him authority over the family.[17] Miliot had admittedly never enacted the rituals associated with ancestral spirits because he had never been required to do so by his relatives. All the same, his current situation, which seemed to undermine his authority, disquieted him. He felt that he was a guest in his younger brother's homestead, although it should ideally have been the other way round.

One of the other houses of the homestead belonged to Cephas' mother, Selina. She had refused to be remarried when her husband died in 1995. During his lifetime Cephas' father had worked as a blacksmith specialising in hoes, axes and spears. When he was forcibly recruited to work on building the Old Road in the 1930s, he also learned how to produce ploughs. Many decades later, he instructed his youngest son, Cephas, in the craft of blacksmithing. However, although Cephas received even more training in Zambia's Eastern Province he soon stopped working as a blacksmith, since the informal gasoline business proved more profitable. After her husband's death, Cephas' mother made a living by brewing and selling alcohol. About once or twice a week she would beat drums in order to attract customers, who would then sit around the homestead gradually getting drunk. Although Selina did not disapprove of her children's involvement in churches, she had never actually been a Christian herself. Instead she made sure that certain non-Christian religious practices were observed by the churchgoers among her descendants. When Cephas' wife, who acted as the chairlady of the SAC congregation in Nanyenda, gave birth to a son in 2001, Selina placed small pieces of paper and cloth at the entrance to the homestead so that pregnant women would not step into the yard. Otherwise, she claimed, there might be a miscarriage. In addition, Cephas occasionally approached his mother to narrate his dreams. One morning in 1999 he reported a vision of a particular type of tree. Selina interpreted this as indicating that he might become a 'traditional' herbalist (*mung'anga*), since this particular tree might eventually turn out to have healing powers. Cephas initially laughed at this suggestion, but then recalled that even his own father had been endowed with powers of curing. Finally he decided to wait until another dream revealed the kind of affliction that could be healed using the leaves of the tree he had seen in his vision.

Cephas' elder sister, who lived in the house next to her mother's, was a member of the New Apostolic Church (*Neuapostolische Kirche*). She had got divorced some years before and now helped her mother with brewing beer. When Cephas was a young boy, he accompanied her to church. Some years later, however, he became involved in the SAC, where he soon attained the position of pastor. Since then, he occasionally organized night-time gatherings of the SAC at his homestead, at which his sister used to join the choir.

The very day on which the elders of the SAC gathered at the homestead in Nanyenda in September 1999, another of Cephas' older sisters entered the yard. Since she had been sick for some months, her mother had recommended that she consult the healer of a neighbouring *masabe* possession cult.[18] While the church elders were waiting on one side of the yard for their Christian conference to start, preparations for a *masabe* divination were made at the other end. After some time, the *masabe* healer called on the residents of the homestead to assist her in singing a particular song. If the patient's hands shook during the song, then the afflicting *masabe* spirit might be identified. The singers eventually included most of the inhabitants of the homestead, regardless of what Christian church they belonged to. Cephas, who, as the pastor of the SAC branch of Nanyenda, was hosting the elders' conference, found himself in a precarious situation. According to the main teachings of his Church, the *masabe* were demons. Yet he also realised that he was expected to show solidarity with respect to his sister's affliction. Ultimately, he chose a compromise position by endlessly walking around to urge others to join in the singing, while avoiding joining the group himself.

Most church elders of the SAC watched the proceedings from the other side of the homestead with disgust. Being Cephas' guests, however, they refrained from explicitly voicing their disagreement and instead acted as if nothing unusual was happening. A number of them, indeed, watched the *masabe* divination with barely concealed curiosity. To the church leaders of Siamujulu village on the Plateau, *masabe* possession cults were not as familiar as they were to those in the Gwembe Valley.

This episode and the specific social configuration involved both highlight several important aspects that informed Christian practices in my area of research: First, besides going to church, most Christians were also associated with various non-Christian religious forms: Miliot had inherited an ancestral spirit (*muzimu*); Cephas would not deny completely that his dreams might be a sign of his becoming a 'traditional' herbalist (*mung'anga*); and Cephas' wife had joined the singing of *masabe* songs, although she was a regular member of the SAC.[19] Second, it was usually impossible for churchgoers to refrain completely from participating in such religious practices. Especially where cases of affliction among relatives were concerned, they were expected to give their support, even when the treatment chosen by the familial therapy management group fundamentally contradicted the teachings of the denomination otherwise attended by the churchgoer concerned. Third, some religious practices which could still be found in 1999 in the Gwembe Valley had ceased to be significant on the Plateau decades earlier. Seen in a wider perspective, the SAC thus displayed a marked asymmetry in relation to alternative non-Christian religious practices. *Masabe* possession cults, for instance, were a common childhood experience for most church members in the Gwembe Valley. Many had attended *masabe* rituals as spectators because of their sheer entertainment value, and others had even taken part as drummers in the course of the rituals. In the area of the church headquarters in Siamujulu village on the Plateau, by contrast, dancing *masabe* never occurred.

Practices like those of the *masabe* cults were usually despised by the church elders of Siamujulu village, who considered them 'heathenish' and 'satanic'. However, simultaneously being aware of the fact that most branches of their Church – indeed all of them apart from headquarters – were unavoidably embedded in the contexts of such practices, they did not explicitly argue against them in the presence of people from congregations in the Gwembe Valley. They feared that outspoken opposition, let alone prohibition, would lead to a loss of members or even secession. Certain points of view concerning the religious and socio-cultural flexibility of churchgoers consequently remained unspoken. This situation will prove significant in one of the later chapters of this book, where the double gesture of presentation and concealment in the bureaucratic practices of the SAC will be discussed.

Yet even among the senior church elders of Siamujulu, there was no unanimity concerning whether or not the 'traditional' religious practices of the ancestors represented something completely different from Christianity. For some, Christianity was a novel religion that had been introduced by the Europeans to their previously altogether 'ignorant' and 'pagan' ancestors. Many others, however, emphasized that the Tonga had practised some form of Christianity even before the arrival of the Europeans, stating that their ancestors had also prayed to God (*leza*) – although only via the spirits of the deceased.[20] They also maintained that the local rain shrines (*malende*) had been the 'churches' of the ancestors. Elderly people thus recalled that the European mission churches had initially been called *malende amukuwa* ('the shrines of the whites'). In this interpretation, which stressed the continuity of religious practices, there were only two genuine innovations that had been brought by the Europeans: the Bible, and the idea that God could be addressed directly. Both versions – Christianity as an innovation and as a certain continuation

– agreed that previous religious practices had lost effectiveness after the coming of the Europeans since, for example, God had replaced worshipping at the *malende* with praying in 'churches'.

On the whole, however, most younger churchgoers in my area of research had difficulties in classifying the different kinds of 'traditional' (non-Christian) spirits (cf. Cliggett 2005: 132). The term *basangu*, for instance, had formerly been used to denote the spirit of the guardian of the local rain shrines (*malende*) (cf. Schoffeleers 1978), who in turn was called *sikatongo* or also *basangu* (e.g., Colson 1948, 1960: 61–66, 163–66; Scudder 1962: 111–23).[21] In 1999, many of my informants could not say what a *sikatongo* was supposed to do, and their interpretations of *basangu* spirits differed crucially. Whereas some people classified this type of spiritual being among the largely benevolent ancestral spirits (*mizimu*), or even among those ancestral spirits who had turned malevolent because of the neglect of their own descendants (*zyeelo*),[22] others classed them as a particular type of *masabe* spirit.

Several characteristics of this religious field must be kept in mind when examining literacy practices in the Pentecostal-charismatic churches that are the focus of this book. In my research area, people's flexibility and selectivity in choosing the religious practice of their liking made religious authority a fragile affair that had to be continuously confirmed or even constituted anew. This flexibility and selectivity was, first, related to local notions concerning the evanescent nature of the Holy Spirit, and secondly, due to the fact that the classification of spiritual entities and the loci of their manifestations were constantly being negotiated and renegotiated. Against this background, the use of objectifications in the form of writings promised a stabilization of religious authority. Before coming to this issue in the following chapters, however, I shall first outline how 'schooled literacy' and 'schooled religion' were experienced by my interlocutors.

Notes

1. The Gwembe Valley lies about six to seven hundred metres below the Central African Plateau and extends from the Devil's Gorge on the Zambezi to the confluence of the Zambezi with the Kafue some 300 kilometres further downriver. The north-west part of the valley belongs to Zambia, the south-east to Zimbabwe. Here I am dealing solely with the Zambian part.
2. E. Colson points out that for the precolonial Bantu-speaking Tonga: 'No clear-cut linguistic, cultural or political boundary separates the Valley from the Plateau Tonga' (1960: 14). Considerable socio-cultural variations occur in the Gwembe Valley (cf. Colson 1960: 18–25).
3. For early inter-regional trading activities of the Plateau Tonga, see Miracle (1959); for later developments in the relationship between the Valley and the Plateau, see Colson and Scudder (1975).
4. As for trading activities, a Gwembe Tour Report from 1952 states: 'There are no village stores in the area [of chief Sinazongwe] and if they have to do any shopping, the people generally go to Siazwela or Batoka. At the present time cash is not plentiful and all income is derived from those away at work' (Gwembe Tour Report No. 3, 1952. NAZ: Sec 2/1016).

5. For trans-Zambezi labour migration at the end of the nineteenth century, see Makambe 1992; for a historical perspective on labour migration among the Gwembe Tonga, see Ute Luig (1997); for contemporary Gwembe Tonga migration, see Cliggett (2000, 2003).
6. According to an estimate of the Zambian Central Statistical Office the Sinazongwe District, where my research area is situated and which constitutes one of the seven chiefdoms in the Gwembe Valley, had a total population of about 100,000 in mid-1999.
7. The role of the village headman (*sibbuku*) among the Tonga can best be described as that of 'arbitrator'. In everyday life, they are *primus inter pares* (cf. Colson 1960: 58).
8. The village as an administrative unit and the chieftaincies had been introduced by the British colonial authorities (Colson 1960: 31). E. Colson and T. Scudder, who describe the precolonial Tonga as an acephalous society, remark that most of the population regarded these governmental structures as having been 'superimposed upon them' (1980: 9). For a different perspective, one which describes the precolonial Tonga as having a degree of politico-religious centralization, see O'Brian (1983).
9. For an analysis of the Tonga on the southern shore of the Zambezi river (and later Lake Kariba), see Weinrich (1977).
10. The largest corporate kin groups among the Gwembe and Plateau Tonga are dispersed exogamous matrilineages (*mukowa*; cf. Colson 1960, 1980). Although clans exist, they do not play an important role in social life. The social organization of the Tonga was, and still generally is, markedly segmentary in type. Residence after marriage is virilocal, that is, the bride moves to the household of her husband; adolescent males enjoy great freedom in selecting their place of residence at the homesteads of either matrilineal or patrilineal kin (Colson 1960: 98–101). According to S. Clark et al. (1995: 99), the proportion of polygamous marriages has declined in recent decades and in 1991 made up 20 per cent; N. Price (1995: 11), by contrast, calculates the proportion of polygamous marriages in the area of Chief Sinazongwe, where my research area was situated, to be 50 per cent. After a married man dies his widow is usually inherited by a man from his lineage. Nowadays, however, awareness of AIDS is causing some reluctance among some men to inherit a widow (Malungo 2001).
11. For a detailed discussion of this impact, see Vickery (1986); for general ethnographic analyses of the Plateau Tonga, see Colson (1949, 1951, 1955, 1962b, 1965).
12. Annual Report upon Native Affairs for 1935, Southern Province. NAZ: Sec 2/1286.
13. This contrasts with E. Colson's findings in the 1970s: 'as far as I have been able to discover, people remained indifferent to the appeal of the evangelists and missionaries' (1970: 146). According to an estimate of P. Gifford's, three-quarters of the total Zambian population are Christians today (1998: 183).
14. For (neo-)Pentecostal and (neo-)charismatic movements in Africa, see Anderson (2005), Englund (2003), Gifford (2004), Maxwell (2006), Meyer (1995, 1998, 2004), van Dijk (1999, 2002, 2005). For the global character of Pentecostalism and charismatic movements, see Anderson (2004), Coleman (2000), Robbins (2004).
15. Witch-finding was occasionally also undertaken by itinerant *muchape* witch-finders; see Luig (1993a).
16. These churches used herbs and roots in the healing of patients. Water that had been blessed or salted was used for washing the body or for drinking, and burning roots or vapours from a pot of boiling water in which medicine had been dissolved was inhaled. Occasionally, the wooden rod of the diviner/healer or the Bible was placed on the afflicted part of the patient's body.
17. At death, the spirit (*muzimu*) of a person is usually inherited by an appropriate member of the matrilineal kin group, who henceforth acquires some of the rights and duties of the deceased. This includes the ritual responsibilities of 'appeasing' the ancestors, which are said to induce afflictions if they are not remembered by their descendants or if their demands are not fulfilled (Colson 1955, 1960: 122–61). During the 'inheriting' ceremony, the spirit is attached (*kwanga muzimu*) to the heir without entering (*kunjila*) his/her body; it henceforth stays close to the person concerned. The practice of inheriting *mizimu* (pl.) has considerably

decreased in recent decades, among other things because of the teachings of Christian churches. And as N. Price and N. Thomas (1999: 521) note, even the sequence of inheritance has diminished: 'In the past, when the inheritor died the shade [i.e., the *muzimu*] was passed to another member of their lineage, and after two generations the shade would be forgotten. Nowadays, transfer rarely extends beyond the first inheritor, meaning that the cult of the shades now concerns the dead who are usually only one generation, and at most two generations, from the oldest living members of society'.

18. *Masabe* possession cults deal with the incorporation of spirits that represent 'alien humanity' (Colson 1969: 71), foreign cultural practices and technologies, as well as the wild (Colson 1969; Luig 1992, 1993a, 1993b, 1993c, 1994). The incorporation of these spirits manifests itself while dancing *masabe*, which is accompanied by drumming and particular songs. Such temporary incorporations are, among other things, thought to provide some protection against affliction.

19. As we shall see in Chapter 7, some members of the SAC were even regular participants in possession cults and were said to have incorporated *masabe* spirits. This fluidity and simultaneity of different religious practices has repeatedly been pointed out for Southern Africa. T. Ranger, for instance, remarks: 'A hypothetical man in precolonial Southern Africa could belong successively, or even simultaneously, to all these overlapping networks of religious relationships: for example, he could express his control of his household through a localised ancestral cult, carry tribute to a distant territorial shrine, belong to a gun-hunter's guild, and be an initiate of a possession cult that linked him to the men and women who lived along a trading route' (1993: 74). G. Bond (1987) analyses the co-existence of Protestant churches and ancestral cults, while A Anderson states for the members of the Zion Christian Church in South Africa: 'For some ZCC members the offices of prophet and diviner coalesce; and sometimes the prophet is not only the agent of the Holy Spirit but also of the ancestors. … A person with these powers could use them to function as a diviner at home, and could use the same powers to prophesy in the church. In both cases the person was a channel of God or of the ancestors, telling people what God or the ancestors wanted them to do. The implication was that the ancestors in fact spoke the word of God to people; and there was no perceived contradiction between the two' (1993: 5). For the Tonga, see Luig (2000: 16).

20. Even before the coming of the European missionaries, the Tonga had a concept of a *deus remotus* (*leza*), who was considered to represent the 'ultimate reality of power' (Colson 1971b: 233) and to have created the world (cf. Hopgood 1950). In precolonial times, however, there was no cult addressed directly to *leza*, contact with whom was thought only to be possible through mediating spirits like *mizimu* or the *basangu* spirits discussed below. The term *leza* was adopted by early Western missionaries when translating the Bible. Nowadays, this term is generally associated with Christianity. For the precolonial High God (*leza*) of the BaIla, who are culturally related to the Tonga, see Smith and Dale (1920: 197–212).

21. The *basangu* spirits are the spirits of the first settlers in a particular area and are considered to have protective power and to be responsible for the local community's welfare with regard to the agricultural cycle. These spirits are inherited within the matrilineage, the heir (*sikatongo*) being responsible for the local rain-shrine (*malende*). Due to their highly localized nature, the socio-religious importance of the rain-shrines and the *sikatongo* connected with them decreased considerably after resettlement in the mid-1950s (Colson 1971: 225–33, 1977: 130–34). Many *malende* were simply flooded by the Kariba dam. And even the territorial rain-prophets (*baami ba imvula*), who, in contrast to the *sikatongo*, fell into trance with *basangu* spirits and were irregularly appealed to in order to redress crises in the relationship between humanity and 'nature' (Scudder 1962: 111–23), lost significance after the construction of Lake Kariba (Colson 1977).

22. The *zyeelo* have no message for the living (Colson 1969: 72), but instead represent the 'perverted human order' (Luig 1993c: 112), and can also be deployed by witches.

Chapter 3
Schooled Literacy, Schooled Religion

In her article 'Literacy and Schooling: An Unchanging Equation?' Jenny Cook-Gumperz (1986) retraces the relationship between literacy and formal school education in Western societies. She demonstrates that although 'school' and 'literacy' nowadays appear as inseparably interlinked, this association is actually a relatively recent phenomenon with an astonishing temporal sequence:

> the shift from the eighteenth century onwards has not been from total illiteracy to literacy, but from a hard-to-estimate multiplicity of literacies, a *pluralistic* idea about literacy as a composite of different skills related to reading and writing for many different purposes and sections of a society's population, to a twentieth-century notion of a single, standardised schooled literacy (1986: 22).

According to Cook-Gumperz, standardizing literacy through public schools represented an attempt to control previously unrestrained 'popular literacies' (Soltow and Stevens 1981) and simultaneously instituted a new social division between the 'educated' ('schooled') and the 'uneducated' ('non-schooled') (cf. Goody 1982: 212–14).

In anthropology, this perspective on literacy and power in modern nation states has recently been taken up by James Collins and Richard K. Blot who, among other things, examine 'links between political, economic and religious power and the desire to regulate literacy as a means of regulating conduct more generally' (2003: 67). In Northern Rhodesia, the colonial attempts to constitute new subjectivities through literacy, outlined in Chapter 2, certainly represent an example of such visions of a literate empire. Yet, as has been shown already, these endeavours were only partially successful. And, as we shall see in what follows, even in contemporary Zambia, many people 'remain effectively outside the scope of this textual-institutional subject forming' (Collins 1995: 83).

At present, local primary schools represent the main institution for literacy acquisition. They can therefore be expected to have a crucial influence on literacy practices and perceptions of literacy in general. But how did people in my area of research actually experience 'schooled literacy'? Since most members of Pentecostal-charismatic churches had attended formal school education for at least a number of years, this chapter examines the role of primary schools in my area of research and the literacy practices they promoted. This will help us assess the extent to which these schools achieved a (hegemonic) standardization of literacy, how formal schooling was related to everyday life (cf. Bloch 1993), and whether – at least as far as the major case study of this book, the Spirit Apostolic Church, is concerned – the social differentiation between the 'schooled' and the 'unschooled' had any correlation with religious hierarchies between laity and religious specialists. Besides raising questions about churchgoers' literacy skills, this latter point evokes considerations of how the relationship between 'school' and 'church', discussed for the colonial period in Chapter 2, was perceived by my interlocutors in the present day.

Enrolment in School

When Elina of the Spirit Apostolic Church (SAC) enrolled in Nkandabwe Primary School in 1991, she was eight years old. During her first year, only the teacher had a textbook: the pupils were taught the alphabet by writing it with their fingers in the sand. Starting from the second grade, books were occasionally handed out to pupils so that they could decipher and repeat aloud those syllables that the teacher was reading. At the end of the school day, however, these books were stacked away again. It was only in the ninth grade, that is, in 1999, that Elina acquired her own schoolbooks to take home and study whenever she wanted to. In previous years, she had had to share books with two other pupils, which meant that she rarely had a chance to prepare or re-read school lessons at home. And since her parents were rather disinclined to spend money on writing implements and exercise books Elina was frequently not even in a position to do homework. If she wanted to pass her examinations at the end of the term, she had to memorize as much as possible during the school lessons. But it was still doubtful whether she would be allowed to sit the exams, since she had not been able to pay the examination fees. Her relatives again proved hesitant: after all, Elina was already seventeen years old and could be expected to marry soon – other girls of her age had stopped schooling much earlier. So why bother to pay for more school education? And if Elina passed the final examination, she might ask to be promoted to secondary school. This would mean that she would leave the village for one of the boarding schools in Choma, Maamba or Pemba, that she would be exposed to the noxious influences of town life, and that her parents would have to continue paying school fees. In fact, Elina did not expect to be supported any longer.

Elina's formal school education covered an unusually long period of time when compared to other girls in her age group, or even to the average female and male population of Zambia's Southern Province in general.[1] In SAC congregations in 1999, for example, the mean duration of schooling ranged from one to five years. These figures already indicate that the congregations of the SAC differed crucially in how long their members had attended school on average. However, even within a given congregation the duration of schooling diverged to a high degree. In the congregation of Siamujulu village, for example, people who had not attended school undertook religious practice alongside members who had attended secondary school.

These discrepancies did not generally reflect differences in physical access to school (*ichikolo*): there was no church member who had permanently been denied access to school because of over-enrolment in classes. And even the spatial distribution of schools cannot be seen as the sole explanation for the differences in schooling: in the Siamujulu, Sinazeze and Mazwange areas, schools were accessible, although certainly not always easily. Only in Intema village was distance an almost insurmountable obstacle, since schools were almost four hours away from there. This partly explains the remarkably short average duration of formal schooling among the members of this congregation which posed severe problems for the branch, since almost none of the junior members were able to read the Bible. For the churchgoers of the other congregations, unwillingness on the part of relatives or other potential sponsors to finance prolonged schooling was the main reason for ending school attendance (cf. Colson and Scudder 1980: 83). Pupils also faced social expectations concerning social reproduction or cooperation in work. These two aspects, combined with the lack of foreseeable opportunities for the future practical application of knowledge obtained at school, made prolonged schooling a 'luxury' that could only be enjoyed by a privileged few.

There were also apparent differences between the genders, as well as between the laity and the church elders: in some congregations men had almost twice as much school education as women. In Mazwange village, for example, male members had an average of 2.7 years, while female members had only 1.4 years. In other congregations, the ratio was more balanced, as in Siamujulu village (5.5 years compared to 4.4 years). Nonetheless, in all congregations of the SAC women had on average less school education than men, and there were also a higher number of women than men without any schooling at all. The leaders of the church had usually attended school for a longer period than the male members of the laity (5.6 years compared to 3.0 years).

The hierarchical structure of the SAC thus mirrored social differences associated with formal school education. Yet when examining the levels of church hierarchy, it becomes clear that the leaders at 'local branch level' generally had almost the same amount of schooling as those of the superior 'mainboard' (5.4 years compared to 5.7 years). This finding suggests that positions within the church hierarchy did not necessarily correlate with the length of school education. In some cases church elders even had much less formal school education than members of the laity: one church elder had never attended a school, others had done so only for one or two years. Reading and writing skills were thus not considered a prerequisite for church leadership.[2] And the three members of the SAC who had secondary school education were two ordinary male church members and the branch secretary of Siamujulu village – none of them belonged to the group of senior church leaders.

Taken together, there were great differences between congregations, as well as within one and the same congregation, when it came to the question of length of schooling among the members of the SAC. Men were more likely to have attended school than women, and their schooling in general tended to be longer. Furthermore, the church elders usually had more school education than the laity, although positions in the church hierarchy cannot be said to reflect levels of formal school education.

After the Ringing of the Bell

Despite these differences, Elina's educational career reveals recurrent patterns of contemporary school education in the rural areas of Zambia's Southern Province. In contrast to what Elina experienced, pupils in preceding age groups had mostly been provided with schoolbooks, exercise books and writing implements. During much of the colonial period and the early years of government by the United National Independence Party (UNIP), which after Zambian independence in 1964 planned to introduce Universal Primary Education, school materials had been supplied by government agencies. Since the 1980s, however, shrinking resources on the part of the Ministry of Education have led to a shortage of instructional materials and equipment (Kelly 1999: 196). In 1991, shortly before the Movement for Multiparty Democracy (MMD) came to power, a report entitled 'Zambian Declaration on Education for All' outlined educational reforms which, among other things, called for increased involvement by the parents and the community in which the family lived.

The policy of assigning educational responsibility to local level structures was adopted by President Frederik Chiluba, who from 1995 took steps to decentralise the educational system. In the course of this decentralisation, Education Boards, local School Committees and Parent–Teacher Associations (PTA) were entrusted with responsibilities for allocating and monitoring government funds as well as for raising additional resources if needed. Since the mid-1990s, private households accordingly had to bear an increasing share of the expenditure for school education. Besides compulsory contributions to the General Purpose Fund – levied, among other things, for cultural activities – additional fees determined by the local School Committees and Parent–Teacher Associations had to be paid by the students' parents each term. Families also had to provide the pupil's exercise books, writing implements and textbooks. Although the regulation concerning school uniforms, which had formerly been compulsory and had thus posed another financial burden on parents, was liberalized in 1997, the overall cost of school education was hard to bear for most families in my area of research. Once the required school fees had been settled, they were frequently reluctant to spend additional money on items like exercise books or ballpoint pens.

Many schoolchildren therefore never did any homework. They had nothing to take home from school – no scribbled notes, copied lectures, or textbooks. For them, formal school education inevitably ended with the ringing of the bell. On a very basic level, formal schooling and everyday life thus ran almost parallel to one other.[3] Schooling represented a clearly demarcated section of life that to me often appeared practically detached from what the children did otherwise. Whatever influence the school exerted on the pupils' thinking and world view, it was largely confined to what had been memorized, experienced or rather unintentionally retained by the students while they were at school.[4]

The literacy practices that were usually encountered by churchgoers in school, as well as teacher–student interactions, which revolved around the use of school books and will be dealt with in the next section, are significant aspects in this regard.

Recitations of Syllabi

The allocation of educational responsibilities at local level just described implied that the quantity and quality of school facilities and instructional equipment in any given school crucially depended on the efforts of local agencies. There were therefore significant variations in equipment from school to school. In 1999 Mazwange village, for instance, had managed to obtain doorframes and iron sheets for new school buildings through the help of a minister and donations from a non-governmental organization; some classrooms in Sinazeze Basic School, by contrast, had been left unfinished for years. And whereas, moreover, the people of Mazwange had basically constructed these buildings on their own, other schools had failed to summon the Parent–Teacher Association to discuss future school activities.

Such differences between schools could also be found in respect to textbooks and instructional materials. Due to the varying degrees of commitment on the part of different headmasters, not all schools had the same schoolbooks nor, therefore, the same type of curriculum. Up to 1997, some of the schools in my area of research had used the textbooks of the *Zambia Primary Course*, a curriculum that had first been developed in the 1970s. Others had at that time already started to employ the textbooks for the new curriculum, the *Zambia Basic Education Course*, which had been introduced in the mid-1990s.

These two curricula differ in a number of ways. The more recent *Zambia Basic Education Course* gives schoolteachers a comparatively high degree of freedom in how actually to teach lessons; methods of practical learning and the use of illustrative materials are recommended. As such, this syllabus requires teachers to prepare the lessons in advance and allows them to depart from the instructions in the respective textbook. The *Teacher's Handbook for the Zambia Primary Course* (ZPC), on the other hand, contains elaborate instructions on how each lesson should be conducted. Two examples taken from the handbook for *English Language and Reading* (Grade V, Term 1) illustrate this. The Oral Language exercises are 'designed to teach the pupils one or two important language patterns, or important single words, which will enable them to express more and more complicated ideas in English' (ZPC 1971: ii). The first oral exercise in this handbook gives the following instructions to the teacher:

Say to the class:
Teacher: We've got a garden at school, haven't we?
Class: Yes, we have.

Teacher:	Our garden's watered every day except Saturday and Sunday. It's watered every day. Say together 'The garden's watered every day'.
Class:	The garden's watered every day.
Teacher:	Yes, the garden's watered every day. Say together 'The garden's watered every day'
Class:	The garden's watered every day (ZPC 1971: 1).

And in the section 'New Reading Items' relating to words 'which the children have learned orally in the Lower Primary course, but which they have not yet learned to read' (ZPC 1971: vi), the *Teacher's Handbook* gives these instructions:

Step 1	Revise 'fisherman' briefly by using it in two or three sentences.
Step 2	Write 'fisherman' on the board, point to it, and read it out two or three times.
Step 3	Point to 'fisherman' on the board and get the whole class to read it aloud two or three times.
Step 4	Get individual pupils to read the word as you point to it (ZPC 1971: 12).

Such detailed directions in the *Zambia Primary Course* prefigure, anticipate and thus standardize student–teacher interactions and almost all the activities of the teacher in the classroom.[5] The teacher's handbook points out in the introduction that the Oral Language exercises should be conducted in a 'natural situation' whenever possible, and that language drilling 'must be brisk and lively; nothing is more boring (or more ineffective) for teacher and pupils than slow, monotonous language drilling' (ZPC 1971: ii). Nevertheless, my interlocutors asserted that most of their teachers had actually stood in front of the class, reading the *Teacher's Handbook* and accurately following its instructions step by step. And even the teachers I talked to conceded that the *Zambia Primary Course* had encouraged them to stick close to the pages of the handbook. They maintained that there was a great difference between their own school education, which had partly been in mission schools, and the contemporary conditions of schooling. Ackim, who had been the primary schoolteacher of many of my interlocutors in Sinazeze area, recalled that during colonial times his own teachers used to supervise the individual reading skills of their pupils:

> All the children had books and were reading silently; and the teacher was going from desk to desk, checking closely. Sometimes he made them read aloud individually. Nowadays, education is spoon-feeding. The teacher is writing a word on the blackboard and then makes the whole class read it aloud. School, nowadays, is rather talking than reading. And even if the pupils repeat the word, you cannot be sure if they were really reading it from the blackboard. Maybe they just look around somewhere and just repeat what the teacher has said. This is not how to learn reading. But what can you do? No books, no proper reading.

Almost all adolescent church members of the SAC had been taught to read and write on the basis of the *Zambia Primary Course* discussed above. They thus shared the experience that literacy practices in school were largely based on an asymmetry between the teacher and the pupils when it came to the possession of textbooks: it was often only the teacher who possessed a book, which he continually consulted during the course of the lesson. The pupils, on the other hand, were trained in literacy less through silent reading than by reading aloud those words and sentences that the teacher had written on the blackboard. And since for them school literacy mostly meant collective verbalization, pupils' individual reading and writing skills were only rarely controlled. The *Zambia Primary Course* thus implied a high standardization and distanced formalization in teacher–student interactions, while little attempt was made to determine whether this interaction also brought about a standardization of pupils' literacy skills.

Against this background, the literacy skills of a school-educated person in my area of research could not be inferred simply by considering the length of schooling (see also Nielsen and Westergard-Nielsen 2001: 374). I met pupils in the third grade who were quite proficient in reading and writing, as well as others in the fifth grade who were having obvious difficulties. Some were good readers but could not write, while others were literate in Chitonga but not in English. And since many of them skilfully compensated for personal handicaps by, for example, engaging in collaborative writing (cf. Shuman 1993), it was frequently hard to judge who in a particular group had what level of proficiency in reading and writing.[6]

There was one particular aspect of the schools' literacy practices that had been adopted by almost all my interlocutors, namely a certain inclination to plan writings using a formalized layout. Documents were often structured by subdividing pages into sections and numbering lines. In addition, reading practices during the SAC services, which will be described and analysed in Chapter 11, had certain parallels with the school practices described above, since recitation and repetition played a significant part in both cases. Overall, however, religious reading for purposes of spiritual advancement was considered to be completely different from what most members had experienced during their schooling. This is certainly not surprising in the case of language lessons like those outlined above. But even school lessons dedicated to 'religious education' were deemed to represent a rather mundane affair. This assessment is especially striking with regard to mission schools that laid great emphasis on Christian instruction and Bible reading.

Experiences with Mission Schools

Some of the elder members of the SAC had attended mission-run schools. Two had been enrolled in the Pilgrim Holiness Mission's school at Sinanjola, while three had attended schools run by the Primitive Methodist Missionary Society. Another three members, who lived on the Plateau and the adjacent escarpment, had been enrolled in schools run by the Brethren in Christ.

The retrospective accounts of these members that I collected in 1999 displayed a marked ambivalence. Although the mission schools were said to have been charitable towards their students – among other things because they had provided writing implements for free – at the same time it was emphasized that the schools were coercive in character: my interlocutors recalled that it was compulsory for pupils to attend the church services of the particular mission. The teachers were partly Tonga from the Plateau and had also acted as evangelists. The school day generally started with a prayer, and religious education made up a considerable proportion of the instruction. Schooling implied becoming a member of the associated denomination. This membership, however, appeared rather pragmatic in retrospect. Those who wanted formal school education had to conform to the demands of the institution providing the schooling, which meant that they formally had to become Christians. They maintained that this school Christianity had not exerted any prolonged influence over them and had even represented something of nuisance for most pupils. Since their teacher-evangelists received salaries, they doubted whether the missions' religious work was of a genuinely Christian kind. In the 1990s, none of them could recall any of the basic religious teachings of the Pilgrim Holiness Mission, the Primitive Methodist Missionary Society or the Brethren in Christ, except, perhaps, that polygamy was prohibited and how baptisms were conducted.

All agreed, however, that these Western churches had not had any spiritual power and that religious education in school had been just like any other subject – it was 'knowledge' to be memorized for subsequent examinations. School appeared to be a tactic for swelling attendance at the missions' church services. Their own feigned conversion to Christianity was thus considered an equitable counterpart to the (alleged) hidden agenda of the missions. Nonetheless, my interlocutors complained strongly about the collaboration between the Western missions and the local political authorities: if a student repeatedly failed to attend school, he or she was disciplined by the latter. One of the senior church elders of the Spirit Apostolic Church recalled how he had been chased to school in front of a *boma* messenger on his bicycle; another said that his punishment for non-attendance at school was to carry stones from one village to another. It was such instances that encouraged some of my interlocutors to associate mission schools with forced labour of a colonial type.

The accounts of those who had been most strongly exposed to mission schooling in the 1950s and early 1960s accordingly criticized the convergence of church and school as reprehensible. In contrast to such convergences among the early indigenous Christian movements that were discussed in Chapter 2, my interlocutors distinguished clearly between the domains of school education and of religion. It was the former that was initially sought after; Christianity appeared as an almost tiresome by-product that had to be swallowed if one wanted to receive some formal schooling. Thus there was deemed to be no inherent association between Christianity and formal school education. Furthermore, in criticizing instances of collaboration between missions and government agencies, my interlocutors advocated a strict secularism: religious affiliation should not be made a precondition for schooling, and no denomination should receive special support from the government.

These retrospective assessments from 1999 were certainly shaped by my interlocutors' experiences with and knowledge of the secular system of formal school education that had evolved after Zambian independence in 1964. Yet already in the years antedating this change in educational policy, it seems to have become more difficult to distinguish mission and government schools. The out-schools of the Primitive Methodist Missionary Society in Sinazeze and Nkandabwe, for example, had not always provided religious education or Bible courses. The teacher Ackim, mentioned earlier, whose schooling started in the mid-1950s, recalled that he had received no Bible training during his four years in Sinazeze Primary School until he was allowed to pursue further education at the Kanchindu Mission. Others could not say whether the school they had attended as children, that is, the primary school in Nkandabwe, had actually been run by the government or by a mission. One churchgoer categorized all schools as 'government schools', which he felt were connected with the political realm: he had attended the Nkandabwe Primary School in 1960, which he knew had been built using government resettlement funds. In an interview in 1999 he nonetheless maintained that this school had been founded by Henry Nkumbula, at that time a leader of the African National Congress of Northern Rhodesia, which was engaged in anti-colonial opposition.[7] This latter interpretation to a certain extent agrees with how mission schools were understood, because neither they nor government schools were considered 'neutral' institutions. For the Tonga, they represented institutions with close connections to particular (political or religious) interest groups.

Contemporary Religious Education

The separation of church and school, which had progressively evolved during colonial times, increased further after Zambian independence, when the mission societies turned most of their primary schools and some of their secondary schools over to the government. In the 1970s, President Kenneth Kaunda proposed to make 'scientific socialism' part of the school curriculum, though this was dropped after strong opposition from Western church representatives. Under the subsequent presidency of Frederik Chiluba, a discussion was started about the restoration of mission primary schools (Carmody 1999: 132–38). This was paralleled by a political culture that increasingly relied on Christian rhetoric and symbolism (Gifford 1998). Nonetheless, the primary school children of the 1990s whom I encountered generally perceived formal school education as something detached from religious matters.

When attending primary school, most adolescent members of the SAC had been instructed in 'Religious Education', a course which has been called 'Spiritual and Moral Education' since 1997. Given the differences (just mentioned) among the schools in my area of research, however, not all pupils were actually trained in this subject. Some students in the Sinazeze area had completed five years of schooling without having had any lessons in religion. Those who had attended Religious Education lessons recalled that such courses were mainly devoted to discussions of spiritual and ethical issues, in which Christianity was treated alongside other religions like Hinduism, Islam and African 'traditional' religions (cf. Simuchimba 2001; Katulushi 1999). Concerning the latter, the teachers usually pointed out similarities between the Christian faith and 'traditional' forms of religious practice, for example, when outlining analogies between Christian rites of passage and initiation rituals among the BaLuvale of north-west Zambia. And even with regard to differences in pupils' church affiliation, primary schools tended to take an ecumenical stance: my interlocutors asserted that they had never experienced discrimination because of their membership of a particular church and that their teachers had, rather, accentuated shared Christian values.

The curriculum for religious education was identical in the government and the mission-run primary schools.[8] Yet differences between these two types of school emerged when it came to the overall religious framework of the respective school education. Enos, from the SAC congregation in Siamujulu, for example, spent his first year of schooling in Siamujulu Primary School. In this school, which was run by the government, many teachers were not active Christians and there were no prayers at the beginning of the school day. Yet at the Bbombo Primary School that he subsequently attended, whose facilities were largely provided by the Brethren in Christ, each morning started with an obligatory prayer by one of the students. Every second school day, the schoolchildren also held a parade, which involved short sermons being given by the pupils. There were, however, no official guidelines for such sermons or for morning prayers: the schoolchildren, who on Sundays attended a variety of different churches, were more or less free to develop their own ideas.

This brief example of a contemporary primary school highlights the fact that religious education nowadays generally follows pluralistic ideals: even in mission-run primary schools, there is no compulsion to become a member of that particular denomination. Different religions are covered during the courses, the pupils usually belong to different churches, and teachers attempt to prevent potential interdenominational conflicts. This pluralism contrasts markedly with the experiences of those among my interlocutors who had attended mission schools in the 1950s and early 1960s and who, as already mentioned, had mostly been obliged to become members of the associated church. In the 1990s, the pupils were not only free to choose a church of their liking, they also encountered the teachings of other denominations during their schooling: pupils from different churches alternated in saying the morning prayers and in holding public sermons. School attendance thus provided students with a certain degree of knowledge about a variety of denominational practices.

Like those who had attended mission schools, however, the primary school children of the 1990s stressed that the religious education of their schooling had actually not affected them to a significant degree. Several explained that even the issue of polygamy had never been treated in school, which surprised them, since they knew that the Brethren in Christ advocated monogamy. They also pointed out that 'school Christianity' differed crucially from 'church Christianity'. While they characterized the former as 'useless theorizing' and as being 'somehow of a worldly type', their personal church affiliation was depicted as involving a promising search for religious and especially spiritual growth. And as we shall see in subsequent chapters, this spiritual search was associated with particular 'non-school literacies'.

In summarizing these findings, we find several aspects that are noteworthy. First, with regard to the contemporary role of primary schools in my area of research, we have identified certain discontinuities between school and home and a lack of occasions for the practical application of school knowledge. Secondly, the actual experiences of literacy acquisition in school were characterized by a lack of reading and writing materials, differences in the curricula used in the schools, a high degree of distanced formalization in teacher–student interactions, and a strong focus on rote learning that was not conducive to overcoming the students' general feelings of alienation.

In view of these findings, I suggest that the primary schools in my area of research did not lead to the formation of 'schooled' subjectivities that had an impact beyond situated school contexts. And although the schools were certainly the primary site for literacy acquisition, the described specificities of 'schooled literacy' left ample space for alternative literacies outside school. Moreover, in contrast to what was described above for the colonial missions' educational initiatives, I have shown that my interlocutors perceived a clear disjunction between (religious) education in the schools and their own quest for spiritual empowerment. It may have been for this reason that there was no direct correlation between duration of schooling and promotion to church leadership. Pentecostal-charismatic churches, like the Spirit Apostolic Church, were composed of people who differed crucially in how long they had attended school and in what particular type of formal education they had experienced. Thus, instead of following a standardized literacy developed in the educational system, members of these churches constituted textual communities that determined their own criteria for deciding what was a religiously adequate literacy practice. Before examining such African Christian literacies, I shall first address another important aspect of literacy practices: the physicality of texts.

Notes

1. The Zambian Statistical Office indicates a 'Grade 7 Dropout Rate' of 67.6% for 1995 (Zambian Situation Analysis 1997: 4). According to an estimate of the WHO, almost 78% of the Zambian population are literate (World Health Report 1999: 87).
2. This contrasts with some other African-initiated churches, like the Nigerian Christ Apostolic Church, where trustees 'must be able "to read and write in English"' (Crumbley 2000: 175).
3. W. Hoppers remarks for the comparable case of school-leavers in the North-Western Province of Zambia: 'School practise allows learning to remain rather separated from actual rural reality and it contains little – in terms of skills or attitudes – that would enable school-leavers to act innovatively in that environment' (1980: 732). He continues: 'There was also little indication that boys were regularly asked to share their knowledge. Apart from letting them read or write

4. their letters or do some counting, people hardly ever seemed to ask the boys to explain anything' (ibid.: 735; see also Serpell 1993: 18).
4. For the early schools' impact on Tonga socio-cultural practices, such as puberty seclusion, see Colson and Scudder (1980: 67, 144–52).
5. The introduction of this kind of curriculum was due to the severe lack of trained teachers at the time of Zambian independence. In 1964, 97.85% of the teaching staff in African primary schools had never attended a secondary school (Lungwangwa 1987: 150). The *Zambia Primary Course* thus represents a legacy of the shortcomings of the British colonial educational system. It was devised for newly recruited and cursorily trained teachers who were employed to attain the national aim of Universal Primary Education.
6. There is a long and heated scholarly debate about what 'literacy' actually means and how 'literacy skills' can or should be measured. Some definitions take a technological stance, as for example the notion of 'basic literacy', which is specified as 'the ability to pronounce and write the alphabet, read and write words and simple paragraphs, and comprehend simple reading materials' (Education Forum Basic Literacy-Numeracy Manual 1993). Since World War II, however, scholars have also attempted to develop the 'notion of a level of literacy more sophisticated than mere capacity to write one's name and to read a simple message, but less than "full fluency"' (Levine 1982: 250). This has led among other things to definitions of 'functional literacy' like the following: 'The possession of skills perceived as necessary by particular persons and groups to fulfil their own self-determined objectives as family and community members, citizens, consumers, job-holders, and members of social, religious, or other associations of their own choosing' (Hunter and Harman 1979: 7). In a similar vein, some scholars have criticized attempts to formulate a 'single literacy measure' (Canieso-Dornonila 1996: 1) and instead emphasize the necessity of contextualizing the definition of 'literacy' with a view to the specific social practices of reading and writing in a given socio-cultural setting. This ultimately implies a reorientation of 'the focus of discussion from differences in individual performance ... to a concern for the social/cultural/historical context of literacy' (Mitchell 1991: xviii). In my own research I never aimed at the quantitative testing of literacy skills among my interlocutors, not only because I lacked the training for such an enterprise, but also because I doubted its usefulness. When observing that one of the church elders of the Foundation Church of Jerusalem, who had never attended school, could not decipher words that were new to him but could recognize the iconographic appearance of phrases that he had previously encountered and memorized from the Bible, should I say that he was illiterate?
7. This idea of an opposition leader establishing schools was not as implausible as might appear at first glance. A Gwembe Tour Report of 1954 remarks: 'Nkumbula, in his visits last year, urged the villagers not to co-operate with the school authorities and in the case of a Monga School collected money from the villagers with the intention, it is said, of building a Congress School in the area' (Gwembe Tour Report No. 3, 1954. NAZ: Sec 2/1018).
8. In both types of schools, the teachers are paid by the government, which also provides a curriculum. One of the main differences between them is that the equipment for mission-run schools is provided and maintained by a Christian denomination.

PART II

LITERATE RELIGION

Chapter 4
Literate Cultures in a Material World

Whenever Sepiso opened his Bible during a service at his church, a slight smell of gasoline spread throughout the building. Almost two years before he had been travelling to a church meeting on the crowded back of a lorry, where he was forced to crouch near a leaking barrel of diesel. Since then, his Bible resembled a palimpsest: it was so thoroughly soaked with gasoline that its pages were almost transparent; the letters of any particular page intermingling intimately with those of the succeeding pages. The Bible of Patias, on the other hand, had lost its rectangular trim size. He had been confined to bed during a prolonged sickness and had failed to notice that termites were gradually consuming the edges of the text area. Since then, the lines on the page ended abruptly, sometimes in the middle of a sentence. And in the Bible of Aspin, the Book of Genesis was missing completely. One day, he recalled, he had thoughtlessly left his Bible on a small table in the yard. The next morning, he found that goats had devoured the cover and the first book of the Pentateuch. Since then, he concluded with a smile, there is no Genesis in Intema village, no more sermons about the creation of the world. His copy of the Bible was the only one in the whole congregation.

As these anecdotal cases indicate, this chapter is an attempt to locate the study of literacy practices within the physical world and the realm of material culture. Criticizing approaches in medieval studies that equate 'texts' with 'symbolic representations', John Dagenais points out, in his article 'That Bothersome Residue: Toward a Theory of the Physical Text':

> the first thing we have to do in order to get at this physical text is to free it from relations of representation, that is, from the idea that it represents, badly, an originary, authentic text. What I would propose as the first level is a simple shift in the unit we study from 'text' to (for medievalists, at least) the individual, unique concrete manuscript codex. This would mean, for example, that instead of studying the Poema de mio Cid we would study Madrid, Biblioteca Nacional, MS Vitrina 7–17 (1991: 252).

Similarly, as 'physical texts', the ragged, dog-eared, eaten-away Bibles described in the examples above may not be the general rule, but they illustrate nicely that

Christianity as a book religion can be quite a mundane affair. Reading the Bible first of all means making use of a material object. Beyond questions of biblical canonicity, the integrity of the biblical text can be affected by termites, gasoline and goats. It would thus be meaningless to pursue an analysis of African Christian hermeneutics, for example, without taking into account the sensitivity and frailty of paper. To a considerable degree, Sepiso's biblical hermeneutics were linked to his attempts to make out words and sentences against the murky background of multi-layered letters. Patias's Bible reading was informed by continuous guesswork, in an attempt to transmute the fallibility of the dilapidated text into the infallibility of a proper interpretation. And the missing Book of Genesis in Aspin's Bible places certain doubts on Jack Goody's assertion – admittedly expressed in connection with a completely different argument – that: 'A written work necessarily has a beginning, a middle, and an end' (2000: 13). Thus, instead of describing Christianity as a 'religion of the word rather than the object' (S. Coleman 1996: 108), and instead of embarking on the study of literacy practices by imagining an 'ideal reader' or an 'ideal writer' in a likewise 'ideal setting', the following discusses issues concerning the materiality, availability and ownership of (religious) writings.

The Bible as an Everyday Object

Many accounts of the Bible in Africa describe an almost 'fetishist' attitude to the treatment of the Scriptures. The Nigerian theologian Ernest M. Ezeogu, for instance, recounts his first encounters with the Bible during his childhood in an Igbo village as follows: 'My father could not read or write, yet he owned a Bible. Nobody ever read this Bible. It was not acquired to be read like ordinary books. My father's Bible was carefully wrapped in white cloth and kept under lock and key in a wooden cabinet in which my father kept things he particularly treasured' (1998: 25). Some accounts of early Western missionaries in Africa highlight a similar veneration of the Scriptures. Robert Moffat of the London Missionary Society ends his famous book *Missionary Labours and Scenes in Southern Africa* (1842) by describing how he and his travelling company were refused assistance by the inhabitants of a village on the banks of the Orange River until one woman offered them water and food. Emotionally moved by this unexpected gesture, Moffat interrogated her:

> On learning a little of her history, and that she was a solitary light burning in a dark place, I asked her how she kept up the life of God in her soul in the entire absence of the communion of saints. She drew from her bosom a copy of the Dutch New Testament. ... 'This,' she said, 'is the fountain whence I drink; this is the oil which makes my lamp burn.' I looked on the precious relic, printed by the British and Foreign Bible Society, and the reader may conceive how I felt and my believing companions with me, when we met with this disciple, and mingled our sympathies and prayers at the throne of our heavenly Father (1842: 619–20).

It is not clear why this woman stored her Bible where she did and what this particular depository meant for her. But for the Western reader of Moffat's description storing the 'precious relic' in the 'bosom' must have had connotations of sweet privacy coupled with the greatest esteem. The rhetoric and imaginaries of this account thus make it hard to discern who was actually the greater 'fetishist' in questions of where the Bible should be kept: the woman or the missionary.[1]

In the area of my research, churchgoers also accorded great importance to the possession of a Bible (*bbaibele* or *ibbuku lisalala* ['the holy book']). In contrast to the foregoing accounts, however, this attribution of high value did not mean that the Bible as a physical object was treated in everyday live with exceptional respect, obedience or cautiousness. The owner of a Bible admittedly faced problems in storing it: in the thatched roofed and mud-brick buildings commonly encountered in Zambia's Southern Province, paper easily falls prey to natural enemies like ants and rats or the disrespectful hands of children. And for polygamists, who alternate between the dwellings of their spouses and usually take care that their belongings are distributed fairly among those dwellings, the safe storage of a Bible is even more challenging, since its location is often changed several times during the course of a week. Yet all the same, I never came across serious efforts to anticipate or prevent damage to the Bible as an object. For my interlocutors of different denominations, the Bible (as a book) constituted a mere thing (*cintu*) whose pages were heedlessly turned, creased and folded, and which was occasionally carried around in plastic bags. Most of them stored their Bibles unceremoniously on shelves which also contained a variety of other paper materials, like school exercise books, pamphlets of different denominations, or booklets from AIDS campaigns (see also Keller 2005: 92). There was just one exception to this generally laissez-faire attitude: people usually took care to ensure that the Bible kept its integrity as a bounded whole. Patias and Aspin complained about their incomplete copies of the Scriptures, and when a child tore the cover off his uncle's Bible, it was sewn with a few stitches to ensure that no pages would get lost. For many, the integrity of the Bible also meant that one should refrain from scribbling notes or references on to its pages. This marks an important contrast to the use of all other written materials, which – given the general lack of paper in my area of research – were constantly being used for new purposes.

Literacy in Times of Paper Shortage

None of the regular shops in my area of research provided reading materials; they sold neither books nor magazines nor newspapers. That a small store in Sinazeze had the publications of the Jehovah's Witnesses in stock and that it was possible even for non-members to buy the publications of the New Apostolic Church (*Neuapostolische Kirche*) in a nearby private home was unknown to most. Whoever wanted to purchase a current newspaper in the Sinazeze area had to make an arrangement with the driver of a minibus going to the small town of Choma. About eighty kilometres from Sinazeze in the Gwembe Valley and thirty kilometres from Siamujulu village on the Plateau, vendors could be found here and there in the streets of Choma, who sold, for example, the *Times of Zambia, The Post* or *The Daily Mail*. Yet even in Choma, the price of a newly issued newspaper remained the same for one week; its news value expired over a comparatively *longue durée*. Such arrangements with a driver, however, were only rarely made by people from Sinazeze, since they presupposed a good relationship with a trustworthy driver. They were impossible to make for the residents in Siamujulu village on the Plateau or for those in many other areas of the Gwembe Valley, since the minibuses to Choma did not stop regularly in their villages.

On the whole, books, newspapers and magazines were most likely to be brought to the Gwembe Valley and to Siamujulu by residents who were returning from a visit to more or less distant locations. These reading materials then circulated among relatives and friends until they were eventually used as packing paper, cigarette paper, notebooks or toilet paper (cf. Engelke 2004: 87). Many of the religious tracts and free booklets that arrived in my area of research were subject to the same fate. Only in those rare instances where someone got hold of a 'proper' book did its potential monetary value tend to curb such creative changes of use. It was perfectly possible to purchase school exercise books and toilet paper in the stores, yet most people could not afford to do this on a regular basis or were hesitant to spend their money on such items when alternatives were available. Thus, the margins of publications were used for memoranda, notes and lists of any kind. Smokers and rural street vendors selling buns or vegetables relied heavily on small strips of out of date newspapers. And as far as toilet cleansing habits were concerned, the period from October to February usually posed the biggest threat to printed materials, since the stock of corncobs – which are normally used instead of toilet paper by ordinary villagers – had mostly been used up for that year, so that other materials like pamphlets had to take their place.

The creative re-use of paper materials affected most publications, whether of a worldly or a religious kind. In the homestead of a Christian family in Siamujulu village, for example, the monthly magazine of the New Apostolic Church (*Neuapostolische Kirche*), *Our Family*, was occasionally used as toilet paper, even though it contains sermons and biblical references. Christianity as a textual topic thus did not preclude use changes in respect of a particular publication. The preservation of Christian printed materials (*mabbuku aleza*) depended rather on personal attributions of religious relevance and on their social embeddedness, which exercised a certain compulsion not to behave as usual thereby misappropriating a particular piece of writing. In the case of *Our Family* such social embeddedness was absent, since none of the family members belonged to the New Apostolic Church.

On a more general level, it is therefore important to note that the paper shortage created competition between different uses for paper, competition in which *reading* printed materials constituted just one of the potential alternatives. Because of their rarity publications were read and circulated, but they generally had quite a short lifespan. Thus, whereas scholarly studies on literacy generally take it for granted that written matters pertain to writers and readers, in my area of research it is clear that literacy practices must be seen in relation to alternative uses for paper. It is especially this latter point that has to be kept in mind when analysing African Christian literacy practices: the production of written materials in my area of research was crucially informed by the fact that the writers were well aware that the recipients of their writings might easily convert their scripted products to a type of use that they themselves had not intended. Against this background, they struggled to endow their documents with an aura of significance. Among other things, this was done by avoiding distributing one's own writings: even if a series of copies had been made, the documents were shown around rather than handed out. The withholding of written materials, which will be explored in more detail in Chapter 16, thus represented not only a powerful gesture that constructed authority through scarcity and control, but also a desperate gesture in the writers' struggle for control over paper-use.

Getting Hold of Christian Publications

Although some Christian publications circulated freely in my area of research and were obtained rather circumstantially, efforts actively to procure Christian literature proved to be rather difficult, especially when anyone wanted to get hold of a Bible. In some cases, second-hand Bibles were passed on to relatives if anyone did manage to buy a new copy. At the death of a Christian, the inheritance of his Bible followed no particular convention: it was simply added to all his other possessions to be distributed amongst the heirs. Most of my middle-aged and elderly male interlocutors had actually bought their Bibles when they were involved in labour migration or in small-scale trading to rather distant locations, or while working as drivers. Possessing a Bible was thus closely linked to travelling. To some extent this was also true of those who intended to purchase a Bible but who were residing permanently in the Gwembe Valley or the Siamujulu area on the Plateau. In 1999 there were four bookstores in Choma that provided Christian literature, and some of my interlocutors repeatedly tried to get hold of a Bible there. Yet, during the period of my fieldwork, none of these shops had vernacular Chitonga Bibles in stock, only a supply of well-produced Bibles in English, which customers in rural areas could not afford. My interlocutors thus returned from Choma empty-handed.

But there was still another method of getting hold of Christian literature, a method which was mostly resorted to by adolescent male Christians in the Siamujulu area. During the evenings they would gather around a radio to listen to Christian broadcasts, which occasionally gave out contact addresses for evangelists in Europe or the United States. In April 1999, for example, Enos received post from an Irish clergyman. A neighbour of Enos had previously written a letter to one of the preachers who had been mentioned on the radio and had then received a questionnaire, on which he had to fill in his age, gender, church affiliation and the addresses of six close friends. One of the friends he named was Enos, who shortly afterwards received post which contained a sermon in the form of a letter, a list of almost fifty different evangelists from Australia, Canada, Ireland, Norway and the USA, and confirmation that he could receive Christian literature from any one of these preachers. Enos wrote letters to most of the evangelists on the list, tied them up, and arranged for someone to take them to an agent of that particular interdenominational organization in Livingstone, who then took charge of them for onward postal transmission. Later he received more post, consisting this time of another questionnaire, a small booklet with psalms in English, a recording of a sermon on an audiocassette, and another list with the contact addresses of international evangelists. Enos had no idea which church the preacher on the audiocassette belonged to.[2] Having read the pamphlet, he thought that he might be a member of the Seventh-day Adventists. But he eventually assigned no real importance to the denominational origin of the publications.

I shall return to this indifference concerning the denominational background of Christian publications in Chapter 9. Like other adolescent males in the Siamujulu area, Enos made efforts to acquire such publications, regardless of their exact provenance among different Christian denominations. Procuring Christian literature by means of radio and correspondence – alongside those publications that had been obtained circumstantially – thus led to a collection of publications offering different theologies (cf. Turner 1960). They were all consulted, although some of them obviously contradicted the religious outlook of the church they normally attended.

This transaction by letter contrasts with the mode of obtaining religious literature pursued by middle-aged and elderly Christians in the same area who, as we have seen, generally acquired their Bibles or other Christian publications during periods of labour migration, when working as a driver, or when engaged in small-scale trading in rather distant towns. Many adolescent men in the Siamujulu area felt discouraged from seeking employment in distant locations, since they knew of other young men who had looked for a job in Lusaka in vain and eventually had to be assisted financially in order to find their way back to their home villages. None of them had the driving licence that was necessary to be employed as a driver, and they all lacked the economic means to start a business that involved the use of public transport. Instead of migrating or travelling themselves, adolescent Christians thus relied on the media to contact the world beyond their rural areas. Residing in a homestead in Siamujulu village and pondering their future lives, they tuned in to the BBC, heard about the Kosovo war and the solar eclipse in Germany in 1999, and eagerly listened to Zambian national news. Theirs was a highly localized globalization, a virtual mobility achieved by listening to broadcasts and writing letters to addresses given out over the radio.

Receiving Christian literature by such means brought the world to their locality. But it was the world in an envelope. There was a stamp, a sender and a destination. This ultimately implied that such publications were not assigned the same prestige as those that had been brought personally from a distant location. The pamphlets and booklets presented by returning labour migrants originated in a rather undefined space and were frequently accompanied by accounts of how the migrants had (miraculously) encountered spiritualized Christians who had given the particular publications to them. For the residents in the home village, the source of these publications was thus quite opaque or was associated with a centre of spiritual origin somewhere beyond their own world. In this sense, migrants' Christian publications at times attained the status of a source of outstanding religious knowledge that to a certain extent paralleled knowledge acquired through a prolonged period of meditative seclusion. Like those elders of Pentecostal-charismatic churches who, after going into the mountains to pray, announced divine messages, a returning migrant was occasionally seen as a messenger bringing religious news from another sphere. His message had the form of Christian literature, and it was the very fact of having travelled from afar that made him a messenger.

The envelopes of the adolescent Christians, on the contrary, were delivered to non-migratory residents and with a clear return address. The enclosed pamphlets and booklets admittedly provided them with a message, but this did not make them messengers. It was all too clear to everybody how this religious knowledge had been acquired. In this context, one of my elderly interlocutors referred to the proverb '*muzoka ulya kwendenda*' ('a snake eats while moving'), which he understood as expressing the idea that Christians have to be mobile if they want to obtain outstanding religious knowledge or to enter a close relationship with the Holy Spirit – in other words they have to move into a distant social realm or into the non-social sphere of the mountains.

In general, how Christian publications were obtained accordingly had an influence on perceptions of their religious significance. Given the emphasis on procurement by travelling and the adolescents' relative immobility, this implied that it was difficult for adolescent men to achieve prestige or augmented religious status through the pamphlets and booklets they had received via post. Moreover, as we shall see in Chapter 9, the view that this mode of procurement was a rather mundane affair crucially informed how the publications were used.

Publications as Property

The findings above provide us with an indication of which social circles actually possessed which kinds of publication. In 1999 copies of the Bible were mostly owned by middle-aged and elderly male Christians. Tracts, booklets and other Christian publications in smaller formats, on the other hand, could be found especially among male Christians of a younger age. The latter group thus owned Bible commentaries rather than the Bible itself. This constellation reveals an asymmetry, which was mostly due to differences in occupational biography and age-specific uses of the media. Periods of labour migration and mobile economic occupations had provided middle-aged and elderly men with the financial means and opportunities required to purchase a copy of the Bible. For unemployed young men who did not travel much, if at all, however, the acquisition of a Bible proved to be a highly challenging matter.

This asymmetry produced implicit tensions between the generations, since the young men were to some extent dependent on the Bibles of the elders. The free publications that the former collected avowedly referred to the Bible and even quoted some of its chapters and verses. The adolescents' knowledge of the Bible thus to a certain extent derived from commentaries and supplements to it. But it was frequently felt that this was only second-hand knowledge, which was no compensation for owning a proper Bible. Middle-aged and elderly Christians who owned a Bible therefore tended to talk about such publications condescendingly. Against this background, the adolescent men developed skills in displaying biblical expertise through the use of such publications, while simultaneously trying to conceal the fact that their knowledge actually came from Bible commentaries.

Another asymmetry related to gender (cf. Rockhill 1993). Literacy and everything associated with it was widely assumed to be a male domain. There were cases of a woman owning a Bible while her Christian husband did not, but these were rare. This asymmetry undoubtedly had to do with the fact that the rate of literacy was lower among females than among males, and that more men than women were pursuing profitable mobile occupations. Yet it would be reductionist to explain the relative absence of Bibles and Christian publications among women solely on the basis of these two factors. We should also take into account the fact that women's Bibles were received as gifts from relatives rather than bought by the women themselves. Those women who pursued trading activities and who had the financial means and opportunities to acquire a Bible tended to spend their earnings on subsistence food or items that were immediately useful to their business or household. I rarely encountered women who had purchased extras like a radio, a torch, or other 'luxury' items like Bibles. Buying a copy of the Scriptures, as well as gathering around a radio to obtain contact addresses, was part of the male sphere of life. The distribution of the Bible in my area of research was therefore also a matter of gender-related preferences in consumer behaviour.

According to John Dagenais, the physical text is caught in a paradox because 'it is superfluous, a by-product of writing and reading ... and yet its presence is essential if these twin acts, writing and reading, are to take place' (1991: 246). The present chapter has addressed some aspects of this paradox as they concerned literacy practices in my area of research. Given the scarcity of reading materials and the generally high appreciation of religiously stimulating input, churchgoers sometimes went to great efforts to procure Christian texts, such as pamphlets and booklets. Yet, because of the paper shortage, *reading* these materials represented just one way of using them. In addition, denominational publications and the Bible as physical objects were for the most part treated rather heedlessly and unceremoniously. For reasons that will be described in Chapter 10, none of them was treated like a 'fetish' in the commonsensical anthropological meaning of the word (see Ellen 1987: 218).

At the same time, the pattern of ownership of religious publications is clearly age and gender specific. In comparing middle-aged and elderly men with younger male churchgoers, it became clear that these two social circles had different degrees of access to Christian publications which, in turn, resulted in differences in how published materials were employed for religious self-authorization. Publications that had been procured while travelling to distant locations were commonly ascribed greater prestige than those received by post. The perception of the religious significance of a publication consequently depended not only on its contents and its social embeddedness, but also on how it had been obtained.

Notes

1. It should here be noted, however, that Moffat's book aimed at fund-raising for mission societies (Chennells 1977: 48). His rhetoric thus clearly reflected what he expected to be the book's Western readership.
2. The organisation Truth for the World, which had initiated this correspondence, actually presents itself as a non-denominational association of the American Churches of Christ.

Chapter 5
Indices to the Scriptural

Churchgoers are widely described as 'book people' in sub-Saharan Africa, an allusion to the central role of the Bible for Christian identity and self-representation. The present chapter deals with two dimensions of such identificatory and emblematic uses of the Scripture. First, in dealing with the question of how the Bible formed part of oral discourses in my area of research, I shall demonstrate that quotations of biblical phrases served the formation of religious group identities by providing not only a mutually shared language, but also a means for covering up disagreements and avoiding (possibly dangerous) frank talk where, for example, witchcraft accusations were concerned. Secondly, I shall address locally prevalent conceptions concerning the material visibility of the Bible, which stood in contrast to the rather clandestine paraphernalia of 'traditional' religious practitioners. Generally speaking, the following thus describes how Christian identities, discourses and practices in the area of my research were linked to overt scriptural referentiality.

Bible Talks

Brian Stock's book *The Implications of Literacy* (1983) demonstrates that the new patterns of communication which emerged in the European high Middle Ages were 'not so much from oral to written as from an earlier state, predominantly oral, to various combinations of oral and written' (1983: 9). Similarly, the introduction of reading and writing in sub-Saharan Africa gave rise to a heterogeneous variety of oral–written interactions. In her work on oral poetry, for instance, Ruth Finnegan points out: 'A poem first composed and written down … may pass into the oral tradition and be transmitted by word of mouth, parallel to the written form; oral compositions, on the other hand, are sometimes preserved by being written down. In short, the borderline between oral and written in these areas is often by no means clear-cut' (1970: 52).

Following Finnegan's lead, recent decades have seen a series of studies dealing with the question of how literacy was taken up in sub-Saharan Africa and what kinds of interactions evolved between oral and literate modes of communication (e.g., Gunner 1988, 2000; Guy 1994; Hofmeyr 1991, 1993, 1995b; Opland 1986).

Yet, there is a noteworthy and problematic inclination in many studies to associate 'African orality' with authenticity, creativity, dialogue and resistance, while 'literacy' is associated with spuriousness, standardization, monologue and domination. To put it metaphorically, the opposition between 'orality' and 'literacy' is here cast in images of 'sound versus silence' or 'life versus death' – which, as has been demonstrated in the introduction to this book, resonate with the Pauline dictum that 'the letter kills, but the spirit gives life' (2 Corinthians 3: 6). Elizabeth Gunner, for example, writing about the use of literacy by Zulu *izibongo* praise poets, cautions that 'an over-reliance on the resources of print could reduce ... dialogue to silence' (1989: 55). In a similar vein, Kevin Maxwell eloquently offers this description of what he calls 'the Bemba oral way of life': 'As soon as this living religious world is written down, it is rendered soundless and its living words become muted and immutable. The hegemony of sight dulls the polysemous world of sound carried in a chorus of omnifarious authorities. The missionary writers anaesthetized the flow of oral plurality into a single textcentric purpose' (1983: xix).

Such arguments are surprising when they are voiced by authors who themselves vividly participate in a thriving dialogic, pluralist, literate culture, namely science. It is probably with similar statements in mind that Stephen Tyler has criticized anthropologists for invoking 'native speech out of nostalgia, a guilty longing for a past before writing and the corruption of civilization that writing creates and symbolizes' (1986: 135).

Related to this romanticizing attitude towards 'African orality' is the fact that, according to Gesine Krüger (2006), analyses of African literacy practices and African literature have tended to focus on 'orality in literacy', that is, on showing how African appropriations of literacy are informed by features of oral communication. This is certainly an important topic when dealing with oral–written interactions. Yet, rather surprisingly, the reverse question, namely to what extent and in what way 'literacy' and written discourses inform oral discourses, has rarely been made an issue in research on sub-Saharan Africa.[1] The present section engages in such an inquiry by examining how actors in my area of research explicitly linked their oral utterances to the written scriptures as a source of propositions.

Quoting scriptural verses in an almost proverbial manner, alluding en passant to stories in the Bible and casually referring to one of the Apostles were common in my area of research. Conversations, prayers and songs reiterated passages from the Bible, and when churchgoers told one another about their dreams, the narratives frequently linked spiritual experiences to Biblical references. Recounted, quoted, recited or sung portions of the Scriptures therefore represented an integral part of everyday Christian oral discourses. In conversations among Christians, references to scriptural verses were exchanged like emblematic tokens, allowing a whole line of argument to be condensed by simply mentioning the name of a book in the Bible together with chapter and verse. Those who had to ask for an explanation or who failed to respond with biblical quotations during such conversations fell outside the 'community of quotation'. Memorizing Bible verses and references thus helped distinguish outsiders from insiders, that is, devout churchgoers from less active Christians (*bana baleza*) and from 'heathens' (*bana basatani*). Fundamentally this played a role in the formation of a Christian group identity in general and in the construction of denominational unity in particular.

All the same, the common practice of quoting Biblical verses also contributed to obscuring differences in theological outlook: symbolic quotations were sometimes used to avoid discussions about controversial issues. In such cases, allusions to the Bible bridged disagreement by providing an atmosphere of religious solidarity and compatibility. Consensus was created not with respect to particular theological questions but through agreement that the Bible represented a shared source of citations and the common reference point for all Christian discourse and practice. In this respect, the way the Bible was used corresponded with what Anthony Cohen has described as the role of symbols in the construction of social communities. They are:

> ideal media through which people can speak a 'common' language, behave in apparently similar ways, participate in the 'same' rituals, pray to the 'same' gods, wear similar clothes, and so forth, without subordinating themselves to a tyranny of orthodoxy. Individuality and commonality are thus reconcilable. Just as the 'common form' of the symbol aggregates the various meanings assigned to it, so the symbolic repertoire of a community aggregates the individualities and other differences found within the community and provides the means for their expression, interpretation and containment (1985: 21).

But quotations from and references to the Bible were also employed as shorthand symbols when frank talk was deemed inappropriate. During a church meeting of the Spirit Apostolic Church in July 1999, for example, the provincial chairlady consulted the vice-bishop on how the church's women's association (*ruwadzano*) should prepare young girls for their future role as married women. Since this conversation touched on issues of sexuality that could not be addressed directly by the two church elders, the discussion revolved around Biblical references without ever mentioning the actual topic being considered.

Similar constellations emerged when the elders of African-initiated churches had to deal with moral failures (*zibi*) among the laity. Those suspected of, for example, adultery and drinking were rarely directly confronted with their faults. In the presence of the person concerned, the church elders preferred to take recourse in citations from the Bible that dealt indirectly with the particular moral failing. Fearing that straight accusations might be taken as rude affronts and that the accused person might withdraw from church attendance, they made use of the Bible's metaphorical language instead. Quotations from the Bible therefore served as a way of avoiding overt conflicts. Responsibility for moralizing was left to the Bible, one's own voice being disavowed or at least partly concealed.

Such indirect and figurative speech (*mambila mbali*) was also used in the presence of someone suspected of being engaged in witchcraft. Forthright accusations of witchcraft (*kutama bulozi*), it was feared, might stimulate attacks by the accused if he or she was really a witch. Resorting to quotations from the Bible in matters of witchcraft thus provided protection. Yet the avoidance of direct statements in the presence of (alleged) witches had an almost paradoxical outcome. If a suspected witch was present, witchcraft was discussed metaphorically, using Biblical quotations. Frank talk about witchcraft, in contrast, was an indication that nobody present was locally suspected of being a witch.[2]

In the case of suspicions of witchcraft, delegation of responsibility was also connected with Zambian national law. Like the Witchcraft Ordinance of 1914, which had been implemented by the British colonial administration, the present day Witchcraft Act makes accusing others of witchcraft an offence. Most churches were thus unwilling to condemn witches explicitly. The leaders of all denominations in my area of research admittedly understood witchcraft to be one of the greatest problems of humanity, they were occasionally asked for help in cases of affliction where witchcraft was assumed to be involved, and they even feared being attacked themselves by witches among their neighbours, members of the same church or even their colleagues. Many of these leaders had at some point in their lives gone to see a 'traditional' diviner who offered clues as to who was responsible for their respective afflictions. On the whole, however, naming a witch was a delicate matter for all religious experts. Apart from the witch-finders of the *mutumwa* congregations, mentioned in Chapter 3, it was only certain *bang'anga* (some of them called *musondi*) and *muchape* witch-finders who occasionally dared to come into conflict with Zambian national law by openly making witchcraft accusations.[3] Most other religious experts of Christian provenance simply declared that praying at the homestead of the afflicted would suffice to defeat attacks by witches and to destroy their magical paraphernalia, and they resisted all attempts to name witches. Others resorted to identifications of a rather symbolic kind. In April 1999, the inhabitants of Kabanda village near Sinazeze called in the witch-finder of a neighbouring *mutumwa* congregation because it was suspected that one of them was engaging in witchcraft. After going into trance and running around the village, this witch-finder eventually came to a halt at the cooking shelter of an elderly couple, where he revealed that he had seen a bird coming out from under the fireplace and then flying to a young man's maize granary in the neighbouring homestead. Although the witch-finder did not name the witch, this symbolic statement was interpreted by the villagers as clear proof that the old man had actually damaged his neighbour's harvest.

Others avoided conflict with the Witchcraft Act by combining Bible verses in such a manner that witches could be identified indirectly. While praying for a patient during a divinatory session at the end of a service of the Spirit Apostolic Church in Siamujulu, for instance, the prophet (*musinsimi*) who was in attendance started speaking in tongues. He disclosed that a dog had appeared in his visions (*kubona chilengaano mumuya usalala* [to see a vision through the Holy Spirit]), which he explained as signifying that the affliction had been induced by witchcraft. Instead of giving details of the culprit, however, he quoted a passage from the Bible: 'But the beast was captured, and with him the false prophet who had performed the miraculous signs on his behalf. With these signs he had deluded those who had received the mark of the beast and worshipped his image. The two of them were thrown alive into the fiery lake of burning sulphur' (Revelation 19:20).

When the patient and her relatives who were witnessing this asked for further explanations, he refused and ended the session by mentioning that he had also seen 1 Samuel 17:35 during his trance; no further explanations were given. If the patient and her relatives subsequently consulted this verse they would have read: 'I went after him, struck it and rescued the sheep from its mouth. When it turned on me, I seized it by its hair, struck it and killed it' (1 Samuel 17:35). Whatever actually occurred after the divinatory session, I was informed some days later that the patient's relatives had demanded compensation from an old man on the other side of Siamujulu village. This old man undertook herbalist treatments (cf. the 'false prophet' of Revelation 19:20), lived close to the only permanent pond in this village (cf. the 'lake' of Revelation 19:20), and had comparatively long hair and a beard (cf. the 'hair' of 1 Samuel 17:35), characteristics that aptly suited a combined reading of 1 Samuel 17:5 and Revelation 19:20. Although there is admittedly an element of my own guesswork here, this was undoubtedly the very kind of guesswork that had been intended by the prophet. He had revealed that the affliction had been caused by a witch and had given some clues to how this witch could be identified. The rest was up to his audience.

For the elders of African-initiated Pentecostal-charismatic churches, therefore, referring to and quoting Biblical verses allowed the shifting of responsibility for the identification of witches from themselves to the authority of the Bible and to the listeners, who were burdened with the hermeneutic task of making sense out of seemingly disparate verses. In contrast to most 'traditional' divinatory procedures known in southern Africa, here divination was divided into two temporally and spatially distinct parts: the public session in the presence of the patient and the prophet together; and the private consultation and interpretation of the Bible in the homestead of the patient's relatives.

In comparison to the *mutumwa* witch-finder, mentioned above, who also identified the witch symbolically but clearly bore responsibility for the particular symbolism, quoting verses from the Bible seems rather innocent: it obliterates the intentionality of the speaker, who does not create the symbols for himself/herself but instead resorts to an already available and widely accepted symbolism. All the same, the speaker clearly retains a certain agency because it is he or she who actually combines Biblical quotations in a particular way. In this sense, indirectly making witchcraft accusations by quoting from the Bible discharged the church elders from any responsibility concerning the actual results of their suggestions, while they simultaneously acquired a reputation among the laity for their part in the act of witch-finding.

Programmatic Visibility

It has been demonstrated in the foregoing section that allusions to and citations from the Bible made up a substantial part of everyday Christian discourses in my research area. But merely quoting the Bible was not considered sufficient: Christians were also expected to use the material object that was a 'Bible' as a visible emblem of identity (cf. Etherington 2002).

During services and church meetings, the male elders of African-initiated Pentecostal-charismatic churches would often be dressed in white gowns and carry wooden staves; those of denominations with headquarters in Europe or the United States of America usually wore black suits or at least dark coloured jackets. Female members of the Pentecostal-charismatic churches generally covered their heads with a scarf; those of other denominations wore skirts in Western style instead of the usual wrap-around *chitenge* (long loincloth) material. Churchgoers of both types of denomination, however, agreed that openly displaying the Scriptures was an essential marker of self-identity. And when posing for a photograph, both church elders and members made sure that they were holding copies of the Bible in their hands or at least had one on a small table in front of them.[4]

Like the quoting of Bible verses, this visible displaying of the Bible signalled church membership and devotion to Christianity. But it simultaneously entailed connotations that went beyond this identificatory dimension: openly displaying the central basis of Christian worship and practice constituted a contrast with the rather secret paraphernalia of 'traditional' herbalists and witches.

It has repeatedly been pointed out that 'traditional' herbalists (*bang'anga*) are generally regarded in southern Africa as having magical powers that can be used in either a beneficent or malevolent manner (e.g., Luig 2000: 17). In Zambia's Southern Province there was widespread agreement that becoming a *mung'anga* often required killing someone in order to use the spirit of the deceased for divinations and in the procurement of herbalist medicines henceforth. Other *bang'anga* were said to have inherited empowering ancestral spirits (*kukona mizimu*) from a relative. Nonetheless, since witches (*balozi*) were assumed to follow similar procedures of self-empowerment, *bang'anga* were not always distinguishable from *balozi*. The term for medicine, *musamu*, denotes the herbs and roots used by a *mung'anga* as well as some of the magical items used by witches (cf. Luig 1993a: 3). Those who attended a 'traditional' herbalist because of an affliction were thus occasionally suspected of having become witches during their treatment. This assessment was based on the idea that healing by a *mung'anga* actually involved initiation into witchcraft.

Balozi and most *bang'anga* also had in common the fact that their practices entailed the handling of more or less secret paraphernalia. Herbalists stored medicines and objects for divination and treatment in their houses, that is, in a private space that usually only close relatives were allowed to enter. Even those churches in my area of research that provided herbalist cures, such as the congregations of the *mutumwa* movement, hid (*kusisa*) their herbs and roots away at the back of a house. Moreover, although the *mutumwa* congregations conducted divinatory sessions in public, that is, in front of the congregation, the medicine was given to the afflicted person in private. Similarly, a considerable proportion of a *mung'anga's* divination and treatment was carried out within the house and in the presence of just the patient and one or two witnesses. The divinatory procedures, the negotiations between the healer and the patient, and the actual objects used for the treatment were thus subject to a degree of secrecy.

Such secrecy was even more pronounced in the case of witchcraft. For example, witches were said secretly to raise *ilomba* (i.e., spirit familiars; often a snake with a human head) within their houses; it was assumed that they privately possessed *katobolo* (i.e., magic guns made, for example, out of a dead child's bones); and they were believed to hide *insengo* or *chifunda* (i.e., horns or small containers filled with destructive medicine [*musamu*]) in the thatched roof of their victim's home, as well as *chinaile* (i.e., needles with magical powers) in dust roads, so that the victim would die when stepping on it. The magical items used by witches were thus all associated with surreptitious concealment. Furthermore the dark night was assumed to be the preferred time for witchcraft activities.

Some of my observations suggest that secrecy is even essential to the magical power of witchcraft items. One morning in June 1999, a building belonging to Sinazongwe District Council in Sinazeze was found to have been sprinkled with a brown liquid the night before. A small capsule wrapped in a cloth and smeared with an unknown substance had been placed in front of the door. It was widely agreed that the liquid was witchcraft medicine (*musamu*) and that the capsule was a *chifunda*. The clerk, who was a member of the New Apostolic Church (*Neuapostolische Kirche*), consequently refused to enter the building unless a witch-finder provided some counter-magic. However, since nobody was in a position to pay money for a witch-finder – the District's bookkeeping had no provision for such expenses, and the clerk did not want to pay them himself – the *chifunda* remained in front of the Council building. Nobody dared to touch it. After some weeks, however, several people told me that this magical object could soon be removed by any ordinary person at any time: the *chifunda* would gradually lose its destructive power because it was visible to everybody. Prolonged visibility was thus assumed to make witchcraft powerless. Similarly, when Sinazeze was electrified in July 1999 many residents expected a decrease in witchcraft activities in their neighbourhood. To them, electric light promised a degree of protection against witches, who were presumed to dance at night in the yards of their victims and also to hide magical objects under the shelter of darkness.

In view of the suspicious nature of this secrecy, the commonly practised public display of the Bible by Christians was a clear indication that they had nothing to hide and that they were in some way accountable to the public. Divinatory sessions in African-initiated Pentecostal-charismatic churches were in accordance with those of other religious experts in that all of them aimed at the disclosure of hidden or secret phenomena. In contrast to the others, however, Christian divinations made no secret about how these revelations were actually accomplished. The divinations were pursued in a more or less public social space, and if an object was used for them, it was one that was visible and potentially available to everybody, namely the Bible. Except for the *mutumwa* congregations, none of the churches in my area of research had religious items hidden behind the house, and the treatment of patients was never carried out in complete privacy. In most denominations there were not even confessions, a practice which for most Western churchgoers would represent the epitome of confidentiality in Christianity. And in those rare cases of African-initiated

Pentecostal-charismatic churches in which lay members were expected to confess regularly, the confessions were public in nature. Among the African Apostles of John Maranke, the churchgoers had to pass a 'gate' formed by two prophets before entering the place of worship (cf. Jules-Rosette 1975a); whoever was picked out by the prophets had to confess his or her sins publicly in front of the congregation. In contrast to other religious practices, the power of Christianity thus largely lay in its programmatic visibility. And the Bible was the symbol of this transparency.

References to the Book

Besides quoting from the Scriptures and taking the Bible as a symbol of transparency, it was unthinkable for the Christians in my area of research to dispense with the Bible as a material reference point (cf. S. Coleman 1996). At first sight this might not seem surprising, since the Scriptures plainly represent the essential cornerstone of Christianity as a religion of the book. Yet looking more closely, the particularity of this finding can be highlighted: even when churchgoers had memorized large portions of the Bible, it was deemed inappropriate for them not to resort to the 'Bible' as an object in an obvious manner while preaching. Knowing the Bible by heart, having internalized it and being in a position to quote it freely and recite passages from it therefore did not imply that the Bible *as a book* could be forsaken. A proper Christian was not only expected to quote from the Bible and to refer to it by means of allusions, but also to refer to it in a very physical manner: to skip its pages, to read verses aloud, to hold it while preaching.[5]

There was accordingly a widespread view in my area of research that treating Christianity as 'mere talking' entails certain risks. If it was not backed up by recurrent consultations of the Bible it was assumed that Christian talk might easily be diverted by Satan. My interlocutors insisted that preachers without Bibles in their hands should be carefully scrutinized, because they might say something that was not consonant with the Scriptures. The articulated need for the Bible as a material reference point was thus also a demand for self-discipline: everyone ought to check continually whether the Bible verses and Christian utterances he or she had memorized were in conformity with the Bible. This demand, which assigned to Christians responsibility for controlling their own personal religious discourses, has to be seen – among other things – in the context of the restricted availability of the Bible in my area of research that has already been mentioned. Since not everybody had the opportunity to check a sermon, the preacher was expected to demonstrate his accountability to the audience by constantly monitoring his own actions by means of Bible consultations (see also Presler 1999: 198).

In line with William Graham's suggestion that 'a scripture can be an oral as well as ... a written reality' (1989: 130), this chapter has shown, first, how religious practitioners employ oral quotations from biblical writings for the constitution of

Christian identities as well as, at times, as a way of bridging disagreements, avoiding frank talk and deflecting responsibility from themselves on to the Scriptures. Secondly, I demonstrated that in my area of research, Christians were expected to use the material reality that was a 'Bible' as an emblem of identity and to refer to it constantly and visibly in their religious practices. Serving as a symbol for Christian transparency and accountability, the Bible here on the one hand stood for the rejection of the secrecies associated with 'traditional' religious paraphernalia, while on the other hand it was also regarded as a material guarantor that 'Bible talk' was not corrupted by evil forces. The latter point will again prove significant when later examining how sermons were conducted in a Pentecostal-charismatic church.

At first sight these findings seem to suggest that use of the Bible was unanimously identified with Christianity. Yet, even recurrent and visible consultations of the Bible were *not* deemed to constitute ultimate confirmation that a given religious practice was of a genuinely Christian kind. As we shall see in the following excursion into the fringes of Christianity, even some 'traditional' religious experts at times resorted to the Scriptures.

Notes

1. But see, for example, Engelke (2004), Opland (1995), Muller (1997, 2003).
2. However, in contrast to what has been described for the *zar* cult of North Africa (e.g., Böhringer-Thärigen 1996: 39), where reciting the Quran provided protection against demons, the everyday quotation of Bible verses was not assumed to protect against demons or witchcraft in my area of research.
3. For *muchape* witchfinders, see, for example, Richards (1935) and Probst (1999) for recent developments.
4. According to H. Behrend, a Christian fundamentalist movement in East Africa even used photographs as 'counter-sorcery: if one had oneself photographed with a Bible, the sorcery would not work' (2003: 135).
5. Even in the wider history of Christianity, it is rare to find the idea that one can discard the Bible as an object, for example, after memorizing the whole Scriptures. In a famous narrative about an ascetic monk of the fourth and fifth century that first appeared in the *Practicus* of Evagrius, it is stated, with amazement: 'A brother owned only an evangelarium. He sold it and used the profits to feed the hungry, thereby uttering the following memorable words: "I have sold the logos ... that told me: 'Sell whatever you have and give the yields to the poor (Matt. 19.21)'"' (cited in Bartelink 1999: 27; my translation). And the contemporary prophet Olumba Olumba Obu of the Nigerian Brotherhood of the Cross and Star (Amadi 1996) insisted that he had never read the Bible since he had written it himself (Mbon 1992: 29).

Chapter 6

The Fringes of Christianity

During the Pentecost meeting of the Spirit Apostolic Church in the Gwembe Valley in May 2001, Rabson and his wife Derina were receiving patients to be healed in a shelter near the ceremonial grounds. Attending one of those patients while a church service was going on right beside her, Derina started to speak in tongues. After calming down she explained what causes of affliction had been revealed to her while she had been possessed by the Holy Spirit. The patient and her accompanying relatives were easily convinced, as it turned out maybe too easily, because upon leaving they declared: 'Your disclosures are identical to what the *mung'anga* we had attended last week told us'. This comment left Rabson and Derina in a state of distress. Hours later, they were still pondering what this unsettling sentence might have implied: how can the Holy Spirit reveal the same things as the demon of a 'traditional' healer (*mung'anga*)? Did the patient and her relatives actually know that they had just been consulting Christians and not *bang'anga* (plural of *mung'anga*)? The incident worried Rabson and Derina because they saw the Christian origins of the spirituality they professed being placed in serious doubt. By being compared to a *mung'anga*, they were ascribed a position near to, even beyond, the periphery of Christianity.

This incident suggests that the distinction between Christian and non-Christian practices is not always clear-cut. Determining the boundaries of Christianity in my area of research constituted a terrain of local controversies and recurrent negotiations. The respective assessments varied among people, and even one and the same person might voice different evaluations at different points in time.

Against this background, in what follows I shall first describe some exemplary points of intersection and criteria of distinction in the relationship between Christians (*bana baleza* – children of God) and *bang'anga* (cf. Schoffeleers 1989). In contrast to certain other scholarly treatments of African Christianity, which are more or less explicitly informed by normative ideas of what constitutes 'Christianity', I shall thus refrain from providing definitions myself, and shall instead concentrate on how my interlocutors drew religious boundaries or situationally blurred what at other times appeared to them to be different religious forms. One aspect that is of particular importance in this context is that use of the Bible did *not* in itself represent a mark of distinction between Christian and non-Christian practices. When dealing with the scriptural practices of (allegedly) non-Christian religious experts close attention must consequently be paid to the criteria employed in identifying a particularly 'Christian' use of the Bible.

Blurrings and Criteria

How different criteria for distinguishing Christian from non-Christian religious practices were utilized can aptly be demonstrated by examining the case of the prophet-diviner Sheal, who in 1994 had stopped attending the St Moses God's Holy Spirit Church, a Pentecostal-charismatic church belonging to the *mutumwa* movement, and had subsequently started to offer herbalist treatments.

Sheal received patients in his homestead and usually began his curative treatment with a divination that made use of the Bible. Sitting in front of the patient and skimming over the pages, Sheal explained the causes of the affliction and how it could be healed. The treatment itself consisted in the laying-on of hands, stretching out the patient's extremities and joints, and finally dispensing herbalist medicine. Sheal claimed that his knowledge of such cures was periodically revealed to him by the Holy Spirit in dreams. These procedures were almost identical to those I had witnessed in 1993, when he was still an active prophet and healer of St Moses God's Holy Spirit Church (Kirsch 1998). They also corresponded to a repertoire of healing methods that is widespread among the Pentecostal-charismatic churches of the Sinazeze area and among African-initiated churches in southern Africa in general.

Having once been a member of the St Moses God's Holy Spirit Church in Siankumba, Sheal was still being addressed in 1999 as '*mutumwa*' by some of his patients and neighbours. Literally translated, this term denotes 'the one who is sent'. In most cases, however, it connoted 'the one who is sent by God' and, moreover, implied a reference to the *mutumwa* movement for the majority of my interlocutors. Sheal himself justified being called *mutumwa* by stressing his former association with Siankumba and emphasizing that what he was pursuing was actually a *Christian* practice. This self-identification was pronounced correct by many of his patients and neighbours. For them, this attribution was not hampered by the fact that Sheal was actually no longer in contact with the congregation in Siankumba and that he had not been involved in the *mutumwa* branch founded in 1999 close to his homestead.

However, several of his patients and neighbours did not accept his representation of himself as a Christian healer; for them, Sheal was simply a *mung'anga*. They said that he had parted company with Christianity and had obtained healing powers by associating with spirits of a non-Christian kind. The disagreement thus revolved around the question of what constitutes the spiritual force behind the healing powers of the *bang'anga*. Some maintained that *bang'anga* were empowered by demons who would simply feign treatment while actually handing the patient over to Satan. In contrast to this interpretation, others insisted that *bang'anga* like Sheal, who had previous experiences with Christianity, would actually employ the power of God. According to this interpretation, it was God, not other types of spirit, who had created the herbs and roots that were used in the treatment of afflictions. They also assumed that Sheal was still endowed with the spirit he had obtained during his time in Siankumba. They thus considered that *bang'anga* like Sheal represented a specific type of manifestation of divine Christian spiritual authority.

Many African-initiated Pentecostal-charismatic churches, such as the Spirit Apostolic Church, also applied healing methods that resembled those of the *bang'anga* because, for instance, they made use of spiritually manipulated (sometimes salted) water for ingestion or for washing the body. Church leaders generally saw this method as akin to the healing and exorcising power of Christian baptisms. They distinguished between the positive materiality of water that had been prayed over, and the demonically infused materiality of the roots and herbs used by the *bang'anga*. My interlocutors from denominations with headquarters in a Western country, in contrast, usually declared the use of salt water in treating patients to be demonic. When pursuing a personal quest for therapy, however, and thus temporarily visiting prophet-healing churches, the same individuals would ostensibly accept propositions like those given by the leaders of the Spirit Apostolic Church.

Such shifting assessments of religious practices could also be found among the church leaders of African-initiated churches. Though they normally condemned the *bang'anga* as the 'devil's assistants', many of them had temporarily attended 'traditional' herbalists at some point in their lives. This recourse to religious practices

3. Spiritual healing, Simanzi village, 1999.

of a seemingly non-Christian kind was justified by pointing out that the respective *mung'anga* was a successful healer. According to this argument, success in healing was evidence of the *mung'anga's* divine power, since only God could effect a lasting improvement in health. Assessing whether a specific religious activity should be classified among Christian or non-Christian practices thus to some extent changed according to the circumstances of contact with the respective practice.

Furthermore, the categorization of a particular practice depended on the social relationships of those involved in any shared religious setting. In 1995, Ng'andu, at that time Bishop of the Spirit Apostolic Church, treated patients at his homestead by making them inhale the fumes of burning roots. This practice can also be found among *bang'anga* and in *masabe* possession cults. Ng'andu himself explained that inhaling such fumes differs from the ingestion of medicinal herbs and roots which, according to him, would only be practised by non-Christians. During that period, the other senior church leaders of the Spirit Apostolic Church knew what went on at Ng'andu's homestead and publicly affirmed that it had a genuinely Christian background. After Ng'andu had been demoted in 1996, however, their interpretation of his healing methods changed considerably. In 1999, they affirmed that inhaling was identical with ingestion and that their former bishop definitely had to be classified with the *bang'anga* or even amongst those who practised witchcraft. Conflicts within the church had led to a crucial reassessment of Ng'andu's religious practices that were subsequently no longer publicly supported but deemed to be a private and highly questionable practice of the former bishop.

In addition, the question of whether, and to what extent, a particular religious practice is socially embedded has an impact on the classification of Christian and non-Christian practices, as can be seen for the case of Sheal. Those who claimed that he was a *mung'anga* pointed out that Christianity is always integrated into a framework of essentially communal practice. Long-term associations and practices in the form of congregations, choirs and public sermons were for them distinctive marks of differentiation between the *bang'anga* and the Christian churches. The temporal encounters between a *mung'anga* and his patients, which usually do not result in an extended relationship after the herbalistic treatment is over, as well as the fact that *bang'anga* mostly pursue their practice alone, thus implied that *bang'anga* could not be counted as Christians. They thus rejected the idea that the designation *mutumwa* had any validity for Sheal and instead set about thinking what other *mung'anga* might actually have given him the power of some non-Christian spiritual entity.

Rabson's and Derina's disquieting encounter, sketched at the start of this section, can be interpreted in a similar vein. Since 1998, Rabson had been facing a severe crisis of legitimacy. The very fact that he and his wife Derina had not attended services on that particular day in 2001 was a clear indication that their position within the church had become precarious. Enacted as they were, without apparent backing by a religious community, the status of Derina's divinations thus became open to negotiation and speculation.

The controversies in the issue of Christianity versus non-Christianity even extended into the domain of what clearly appeared to be *church* communities. To outsiders, some denominations were not actually Christian, even though they represented long-term associations that assembled weekly to hear sermons based on the Bible. Many regarded the *mutumwa* congregations, for example, as being non-Christian because they provided herbalist treatments. The *mutumwa* congregations themselves justified this practice by referring to the Book of Revelation (22:1–2), which reads: 'On each side of the river stood the tree of life, bearing twelve crops of fruit, yielding its fruit every month. And the leaves of the tree are for the healing of the nations'. Nevertheless, others, especially members of other denominations, considered such biblical readings as misguided and misleading. They inferred that the *batumwa* (plural of *mutumwa*) were actually demonic *bang'anga* who were feigning Christianity. But similar reproaches were likewise voiced with respect to churches that showed no resemblance to the practices of the *bang'anga*, for example, the Jehovah's Witnesses in Sinazeze. In this case, the fact that this congregation contained a relatively high number of old men was occasionally seen as an indication that it actually constituted a 'community of witches'.

To complicate matters even more, the fringe of Christianity was at times even situated *within* a given church community. I was repeatedly told that Satan would occasionally make use of the Bible in order to win followers. Thus a preacher might become distracted by demons during a service and suddenly start to expound the Bible in a non-Christian undertone. Such instances, it was asserted, might occur to church elders who at other times were endowed with the power of the Holy Spirit and – more generally – in churches that were otherwise distinctly Christian. Being associated with a church, attending services and holding sermons thus did not automatically denote acceptance as a Christian.

As a whole, distinguishing Christian from non-Christian practices in my area of research meant engaging with and balancing a variety of criteria, of which three will be summarized here. First, the identification of 'genuine Christianity' involved the question of what spiritual force was employed by the religious expert, which in turn was linked to an evaluation of his or her religious biography. Secondly, it implied detailed assessments of the particular methods used for healing. Thirdly, it revolved around the question of whether, and to what extent, the particular religious practice was socially embedded. Rather than providing a stable and unambiguous set, however, these criteria were employed differently according to social relationships and to the circumstances of contact with the respective religious practice. Moreover, there were marked differences between the self-representations of religious experts and how they were perceived by others. Against this background, there was occasionally not even unanimity within a given denomination as to whether all of its church elders were genuinely Christian, or rather empowered by other, non-Christian spirits.

The latter point already suggests that even the association of Christianity with the Bible was not as crystal clear as plain common sense might have it. As was described in the previous chapter, local participants saw the Bible as an indispensable item for Christian religious practices. But importantly, they did not regard its use in a particular religious setting as constituting ultimate proof of genuine Christianity. In fact, the Bible was not only used in what were more or less undisputedly assumed to be Christian churches, but occasionally also in the religious practices of what people termed *bang'anga* or *masabe* possession cults.

Turning Letters Upside Down

Whenever a patient visited him for a consultation, the prophet-diviner Sheal opened his Chitonga Bible at a certain point in the proceedings.[1] Sitting in front of the patient and half closing his eyes, though also having them fixed on the Scriptures, he would slowly turn the pages. Previously, he would have silently intoned a song, which would have brought him into contact with the spiritual realm. The spirit (according to Sheal the Holy Spirit) then induced him to open the Bible at a particular page, even if it started in the middle of a sentence. He never skipped pages, nor did he jump back and forth; he leafed through the book with precision and in proper order. Yet he did not read in the sense of deciphering letters. Rather, he skimmed over the pages, looking (*kulanga*) at the middle of them using brief eye movements from left to right. In the course of this process, Sheal gradually articulated revelations about what had induced the patient's affliction. During the divinations I witnessed, his disclosures never quoted the Scriptures, and he never explicitly referred to the Bible as his object of perception. Although the Bible was fundamental to Sheal's divinations, it was not made a topic in itself or openly used as a source of oral discourses.

This practice of literacy was identical to the one that Sheal had pursued when acting as a prophet in the *mutumwa* congregation of Siankumba. Furthermore there were a number of *bang'anga* in my area of research who made use of the Scriptures in a similar way. Others had no Bible, yet still symbolically pursued 'readings' during their divinations. In August 1999, for example, one *mung'anga* from Sinazeze received an elderly patient who complained that she had been beaten by the spirit of her deceased husband at night and had found footprints in her house the next morning. Trying to determine who had induced this spirit to commit such malevolent acts (*kusonda*), at one point in the proceedings the *mung'anga* placed his hands in a mortar containing some dark coloured medicine (*musamu*) mixed with water. Then he looked at his drenched hands in a gesture that resembled the act of reading a book and started to disclose his findings. Besides the divinatory use of mirrors, 'readings' of this type were a common phenomenon among the *bang'anga* in my area of research.

Those patients who considered Sheal to be a *mung'anga* assigned no particular significance to the fact that he was using the Bible. They actually did not seem to care what kind of divinatory instruments a healer used, so long as they were effectively healed. Other patients, who called Sheal a *mutumwa*, reasoned that his use of the Bible was evidence of the Christian nature of his cures. To them, Sheal's skimming over the pages appeared no less powerful than deciphering them. Still others, however, who opposed Sheal's claim to be a *mutumwa*, maintained that he could hardly be a Christian, since a Christian would not merely look into the Bible (*kulanga mubbaibele*) but would actually *read* it (*kubala*) in order to understand and explain what was written within it. They distinguished between using the Bible merely as an object of perception and using it as a source of divine knowledge whose contents had to be made an issue in human communication. This critique of Sheal's literacy practice not only insisted that just looking at the pages of the Scripture was insufficient, it also condemned the fact that the oral discourse Sheal used during divination did not explicitly link up with biblical narratives.

The use of the Bible in *masabe* possession cults was another source of different views. In 2001, one of my female interlocutors from the Sinazeze area, who had attended a *masabe* cult some years ago, recounted:

> The healer was having a bible. She opened the Bible and I had to put some money inside, I think it was a thousand Kwacha, but I do not remember properly. Then she closed the Bible and opened it again. She was looking (*kulanga*) inside, but she was not reading it. It was impossible to read the Bible, because she was holding it upside down. And then she started to tell me about my problems.
>
> TK: Do you know why she was holding the Bible upside down?
>
> I do not really know. But I think that when she opened the Bible the second time, the spirit (*muya*) was entering the Bible and simultaneously the healer. There was a connection between these two. And this made her see (*kubona*) all my problems; she could even have told me about the future, if I had wanted to.

This description surely does not constitute a representative account of the divinatory procedures in *masabe* possession cults. In most cases, disclosing the causes of afflictions in *masabe* cults involves intoning songs, especially by playing drums. Elizabeth Colson (1969) and Ute Luig (1992, 1993b) have shown that each *masabe* has its own particular song. The effort to find out which *masabe* is afflicting a patient thus usually entails playing different *masabe* songs. If the patient manifestly reacts to the song, for example, by dancing or other bodily signs, the particular type of *masabe* can be recognized. There are also other divinatory methods among the *masabe* possession cults (like ringing hand bells in the case of the *masabe* spirit called *mungelengele*) which cannot be elaborated on in detail here. What is noteworthy for our concerns with literacy practices, however, is that even *masabe* healers occasionally use the Bible.

In the quotation above, the Bible is initially described as being used by the patient to make monetary payments to the healer. Such usage of the Bible as a depository for money can also be found among some African-initiated churches in my area of research. During the Sunday services of the *mutumwa* congregations, for example, an open Bible was usually employed as a vessel for churchgoers' offerings. Placing the Sunday collection in the sacred book of Christianity thus meant converting worldly money into a religiously devoted gift (cf. Kiernan 1988). By using the Bible as a deposit for fees, the *masabe* cult described above took part in this symbolism. As with the *mutumwa* congregations, here it was stressed that the money required did not serve solely the material benefit of the *masabe* healer. The healer's pocket was replaced by a Bible as a symbol of the 'common good'.

The account also describes how, after the Bible was opened the second time, the spirit entered (*kunjila*) it as well as the healer. Although my interlocutor could not provide an elaborate interpretation of this, she claimed that the spirit therefore induced a connection between the two. The book as a medium and the healer as a medium were infused with the same spirit.[2] This in its turn made spiritual visions possible. Whereas the healer's act of looking into the Bible was termed *kulanga* (i.e., to look around, to perceive rather diffusely), the spirit now enabled her to see in a more focused manner (*kubona*), that is, to envision the cause of the patient's affliction. We shall return to such connections between the Bible, the spirit and the human medium in Chapter 11, when discussing the literacy practices of the Spirit Apostolic Church in detail.

By holding the Bible upside down, the *masabe* healer indicated that her religious knowledge was of a spiritual kind. She demonstrated that she was not reading the Bible in the sense of deciphering its letters. Her revelations did not emanate from the Bible as a source of information, but were disclosed to her by a spirit. A Bible turned upside down gave the biblical letters the form of undecipherable cryptic signs. Nevertheless, the *masabe* cult leader was obviously 'reading' them. This literacy practice is linked to Christianity while at the same time marking a crucial difference from it: the *masabe* healer made use of the Bible, yet appropriated it in a manner that diverged decisively from how it was generally used in church communities.

As might be expected, the procedures outlined above were deemed unacceptable by those of my interlocutors who understood *masabe* possession cults to represent satanic assemblies. For them, turning the Bible upside down was a demonic practice comparable to overturning the cross. Yet even among churchgoers, this use of the Bible by *masabe* leaders was not interpreted as unanimously as might have been expected. I came across members of African-initiated churches who, besides going to church services, also attended sessions of a particular *masabe* cult that dealt with the *mungelengele* spirit. My interlocutors among these participants understood the Holy Spirit and *mungelengele* to be related spiritual entities, and therefore approved of the *masabe* cult leader's use of the Bible.

For example, Delis, a middle-aged female member of the Nanyenda congregation of the Spirit Apostolic Church, suffered from a severe illness until she started to attend a *masabe* cult close to her village. Her description of the use of the Bible by *masabe* healers differs from the above account. During the first session, Delis said, the cult leader opened the Bible without turning it upside down and leafed through it up to the particular page where the name of the *masabe* causing the affliction was noted. The healer did not mention the respective verses or chapters of the Bible, but all the same read aloud which song would provide an appropriate treatment for Delis' affliction. And when, later on, drums were played, Delis had actually started to dance at that specific song. Since then, she recounted, more and more types of *masabe* had started to enter her. At the time of our interview, Delis was recurrently possessed by *chelele*, *mangelo* and *mungelengele*. Each of these *masabe* had certain demands which she had to fulfil if she wanted to remain healthy and go on being helped by the spirits. Her first *masabe*, *chelele*, for example, required her to possess white and red cloth as well as beads in white, black and red. She was also required to dance *masabe* regularly. Whenever she heard drumming, Delis asserted, she would feel an urge to join the group and dance.

Nevertheless, Delis continued attending church services. She was a regular member of the Spirit Apostolic Church and sometimes even sung in the choir. Delis conceded that her simultaneous membership in a church and a *masabe* cult was not approved of by most other churchgoers, especially the senior church elders. Yet, she herself did not see this concurrent membership as being contradictory. She claimed that the *masabe* would provide protection against witchcraft resembling the protection of the Holy Spirit. Whenever someone tried to bewitch her, dreams would reveal the hiding places of harmful magical items. Though she admitted not being endowed with the power of the Holy Spirit herself, Delis emphasized that most of what she had learned about this divine being would fit or at least resemble the characteristics of *masabe*. She understood the Holy Spirit and her *masabe* to be 'spiritual brothers'. And because of this relationship, she said, she never fell into a trance when attending a church service.

Since they considered *masabe* to be demons, the senior church elders and most members of the Spirit Apostolic Church expected those associated with *masabe* spirits to evince convulsions in the presence of the Holy Spirit. For them, the struggle between the Holy Spirit and demons like *masabe* would inevitably lead to the exorcism of the latter. Delis, in contrast, assumed that the two types of spirit were engaged in corresponding kinds of activities. Certainly she never fell into a trance during the church services I witnessed. A similar situation related to the former wife of the Vice-Bishop of the Spirit Apostolic Church. Besides visiting the Mazwange congregation, she was a serious-minded member of a *mungelengele* cult, which she attended almost every fortnight.[3]

Delis' account of the use of the Bible by *masabe* cult leaders differs from the account above. The healer of the *masabe* cult she attended was described as holding the Bible upright and as disclosing the name of the afflicting *masabe* while reading it. She also knew of cases where a *masabe* cult leader had held the Bible upside down, yet she explained that this was not the rule: in turning the Bible on its head, Delis assumed, the healer was attempting to confuse the spirit of the afflicted. After being cured, patients of *masabe* cults occasionally come to act as a healer in relation to their particular *masabe* spirit. The established *masabe* healers, however, would not want all their patients to become cult leaders like them. Thus by turning the Bible upside down, Delis maintained, they would prevent some of those afflicted from receiving the knowledge required to become a healer. Only when treating those whom the cult leaders wanted to have as their future colleagues would they hold the Scriptures the proper way. Then the patient's spirit would be able to make a link with the Bible.

Other members of the Spirit Apostolic Church decried the practice of not giving the Biblical verses and chapters as definitely being a non-Christian practice, since there was no possibility to check whether the Biblical readings were accurate or not. They especially opposed the claim that *masabe* names could be found somewhere in the Bible. Delis, however, accepted the particular literacy practice pursued by her *masabe* healer, while at the same time expecting the Spirit Apostolic Church to pursue a different kind of literacy practice. When I interviewed her about how the Bible should be used in churches, she stated that giving the biblical references used during a sermon was important, since otherwise one would not be able to read the verses oneself. Her criteria for the proper use of the Bible thus differed according to context.

This already indicates that one and the same person occasionally appreciated divergent literacy practices as having a religious impact. Most of my interlocutors had experienced different ways of using the Bible, and some of them shifted with ease between various literacy practices when changing the setting or reference of worship. In the case of Delis, she accepted the literacy practice of the *masabe* healer for some occasions while advocating the literacy practice of the Spirit Apostolic Church for others. She alternated between the two, neither of them constituting an absolute principle for her.

Talking about religions of the book in general, Jack Goody has rightly stated that it is not 'always easy to tell who is a Muslim, a Jew, a Christian, a Buddhist, a Hindu; the boundary is often far from clear' (1986: 5). And yet, depicting literate religions as 'religions of conversion', he asserts that: 'Literate religions have some kind of autonomous boundary. Practitioners are committed to one alone and may be defined by their attachment to a Holy Book, their recognition of a Credo, as well as by their practice of certain rituals, prayers, modes of propitiation' (ibid.: 4–5). In contrast to this latter statement, the foregoing account has made clear that, in my area of research, first, Christianity as a literate religion is part of a wider religious field that makes the identification and definition of 'Christianity' an object of continuous controversies and negotiations; and secondly, that in actual religious practice there are no insurmountable boundaries for either religious practitioners or books.

Given that the Bible was referred to by a variety of religious experts from different sorts of background, the question of what constitutes 'Christian' use of it has been demonstrated to be crucial in this context. What was debated concerned not only questions of biblical hermeneutics, but also ways of physically handling the Bible, and how religious experts should relate to the Scriptures. At the same time, people were acquainted with different types of religious literacies that were ascribed value according to circumstance and context. It is in this sense that many people in my area of research, although themselves not being very well versed in reading and writing, can be said to be 'multi-literate'.

Notes

1. For a comparative analysis of text-based divination, see Zeitlyn (2001).
2. This resembles what H. Behrend has said about the healing practices of the Kenyan prophetess Mary Akatsa: 'Persons and things – Mary Akatsa as healer, the book, the picture, and finally the child as addressee – were connected with one another in a media chain by the power of God' (2003: 137).
3. This possession cult, which originated in Zambia's Western Province, was locally called *kutwelve* because the participants usually started their meetings at twelve o'clock on Saturdays. In contrast to other *masabe* cults, to some extent its organization resembled that of Christian churches. The regional headquarters of the cult was situated close to Batoka. Each year in June a General Meeting was held where different 'branches' attended, such as those from Monze, Kafue, Choma, Pemba, and Maamba. In these 'branches' some members held posts like Treasurer, Secretary and Chairman.

Chapter 7
Thoughts about 'Religions of the Book'

The preceding chapter dealt with several aspects of literacy practices in a pluralistic religious field that is characterized by, first, a great variety of different religious experts who all relate to the Bible; and secondly, divergent definitions of what it means to make religiously adequate use of it. In view of this complex situation, what is involved when we talk about Christianity as a 'religion of the book'? What is the relationship between the status of the Scriptures as a sacred text and literacy practices? In what follows, therefore, I attempt to outline some analytical questions and conceptual frameworks that will prove useful later on in the present work for examining Pentecostal-charismatic literacy practices.[1]

Book People

It is quite usual to call Christianity a 'religion of the book', yet in trying to determine the particular characteristics of contemporary book religions, opinions often tend to rely on rather simplistic notions. One prominent position here is to maintain that Christianity is obviously a religion of the book because the beliefs of its adherents correspond with scriptural doctrines as expressed in the Bible. Yet, by relying on an abstract and idealized notion of texts, this view neglects important issues concerning the materiality, availability and accessibility of religious writings, as outlined in a previous chapter, which often limit the possibility of such correspondence between belief system and biblical doctrines. In addition, this proposition is based on the questionable idea of there being a general homology between text and person: here, both are understood as representing clearly demarcated and contiguous entities that constitute containers for meaning. Thus, when it is based on implicit assumptions about structural similarities between belief systems and textuality, the analysis of religious communities mostly exhibits a pattern in which beliefs come to be systematically graded and ordered according to a presumed model of the text. It does not need stressing that such a line of thought is highly debatable from a number of perspectives. Nevertheless, as Rosalind Shaw has shown in respect of research on African traditional religions, the idea of 'religion as text' is still very influential (Shaw 1990; see also Buckland 1996).

The supposition of a homology between scriptural content and the religious thoughts of the believers simultaneously individualizes and collectivizes the members of a religious community. It individualizes, because here the individual participant is regarded as the locus of belief. However, such a precept runs the danger of being unduly slanted towards a Western, ethnocentric notion of 'belief' as a set of internalized convictions and commitments.[2] Furthermore, in tending to equate 'belief' with 'knowledge', the participatory, performative, experiential and interactional dimensions of religion remain disregarded (cf. Brenner 1989; Kapferer 1986; Turner 1969). To depict a religion of the book as being analyzable in terms of an analogy with what is assumed to be the inherent characteristics of books thus represents a biased, somewhat abstract and intellectualist systematization of what is involved.

As well as individualizing, the supposition outlined above also collectivizes in that all members of the religious community are defined as holding more or less the same beliefs. What the cover is for the book, the book appears to be for the religious community – it is a bookbinding for unity. Yet as James Fernandez (1965) and Peter Stromberg (1981) have succinctly demonstrated, participants within a given religious community usually display a substantial variety of beliefs and interpretations. It is certainly undeniable that those who adhere to a religion of the book may have shared ideas of why and how their particular practices do reflect (or must aim to reflect) scriptural tenets, and there is also no question that these apprehensions often constitute a unifying frame for their religious practice. Nevertheless, such affirmations should not be parallelled by any sort of analytical presupposition that religions of the book mirror scriptures. Rather, religious discourses about textual congruency must be seen as self-representations that are continuously produced and reproduced in and by social practices relating to written matters.

In trying to avoid the pitfalls associated with the idea that there is a homology between scriptural content and religious thoughts, the analytical focus on social practice is of the utmost importance. Developing a first (basic) idea as regards the conceptual framework for the ethnographic examination in the following chapters, it can thus be argued that Christianity as a religion of the book involves, among other things, the use of writings as 'boundary objects' (Star and Griesemer 1989) for the interactional construction of realities in which 'beliefs' and 'texts' are put into dialectical relationships with each other.

Scriptural Inerrancy and Authority

A related characterization of Christianity holds that the belief in the fundamental infallibility of the Bible is one of the major features defining it as a religion of the book. The notion of 'inerrancy', which is mostly invoked in studies of so-called Protestant fundamentalist churches, stands for the claim that the Scriptures are 'wholly without error, whether doctrinal, historical, scientific, grammatical or clerical' (Boone 1989: 13; see also Crapanzano 2000).

The term 'inerrancy' thus refers to the ascribed status of the Bible. For religions of the book, the attribution of superhuman sanctity is certainly indispensable if the

Scripture is to be assigned the status of supreme religious authority. Yet it remains to be asked how such a prominent position can be grasped analytically. As J. Barnhard (1993) has demonstrated for Protestant fundamentalists in the United States, the notion of biblical inerrancy is empirically ambivalent and conceptually pliable because different types of infallibility can be distinguished. Whereas 'extended inerrancy' denotes the premise that 'when Scriptures affirm something as true, it is true exactly and precisely as it is stated' (Barnhard 1993: 139), the idea of 'limited infallibility' implies that an interpretative accommodation to minor contradictions in biblical accounts does not entail a complete renunciation of the truths of the latter. Finally, a commitment to 'appropriate inerrancy' implies that the apprehension of Biblical texts distinguishes between essential truths (i.e., those deemed to be without error) and non-essential truths (i.e., those reflecting cultural peculiarities).

What we can see here is that, although all three types of 'inerrancy' would mainly touch on the idea that the Bible as a whole is authoritative and exempt from error, two types would simultaneously allow for the possibility of assigning different weights to its different parts. In fact, such differentiation of scriptural contents goes back to early Christianity. Ever since the endeavours of Philo (approx. AD 205–270) to reconcile the tensions between the Old and the New Testaments by demonstrating that the Old foreshadows the New in an allegorical way, the question of which hermeneutical principles should be employed in the exegesis of the Bible has played a crucial role in the history of theology. And while defining how the Scriptures should be understood, the exegeses often concentrate on particular passages of the Bible, namely those that demonstrate the reasoning involved most clearly.[3]

Such interpretative procedures highlight the fact that, although Christian exegetes share an appraisal of the Bible's unquestioned supreme status, differentiations between parts of the Scripture can be found that effectively give a different status to its varied components. For Martin Luther, for example, some New Testament writings, like James, Hebrews, Jude, and Revelation, could not be counted among the 'rechten, gewissen Hauptbüchern' – among 'the right and sure principal books' (cited in Adriaanse 1998: 319). He thus defined what the dogmatist Alexander Schweizer in the nineteenth century called a 'canon in the canon'. Likewise, in contemporary Christian practices not all passages of the Scripture are referred to equally. Though the canon links together a multiplicity of components, some of the latter are given prominence.

Thus we find situations in which a scripture is deemed to be sacred as a whole, yet only certain passages of it are made relevant for the effective practice, that is, are actualized. The remaining passages are held in a certain latency in that they are not used but still attributed the status of being sacred *in potentialis*.[4] Therefore, although the assumption of scriptural infallibility is essential to religions of the book, this at first sight obvious assessment eventually turns out to represent a rather complicated picture that inhibits simple equations between 'sacredness' and 'book'.

In addition to the analytical focus on social practices and the role of writings as boundary objects mentioned above, it can therefore be suggested that, in Christianity as a religion of the book, the ascription of superhuman sanctity to religious texts involves an interplay between scriptural latency and actualization. The Bible is ascribed intrinsic value, and yet continuously has to be made valuable for religious practitioners by actualizing its otherwise latent potency.

Canonization and the Bridging of Realms

It is only possible to talk about scriptural inerrancy, however, if the confines of the Scripture concerned have previously been demarcated. When seen from a historical perspective, religions of the book can be described as religious forms operating in relation to written materials that underwent interconnected processes of canonization and authorization (Goody 2000: 119–31; van der Kooij and van der Toorn 1998). Canonization thus implies an authoritatively marked selection of texts that are commonly defined as having a divine source, or at least as entailing spiritual truths and rules. As such, the selection of texts puts these written materials somewhat out of time and space. The selection is defined as immutable and as beyond human negotiability – nothing should be added to it, and no part of the canonized scripture should be omitted.

This claim to the socio-historically unbound nature of scripture eventually creates the necessity of repeatedly putting it back into time and space. Having postulated a substantive and distancing difference between the scripture and the world – a gesture that is indispensable if the texts are to represent an authoritative spiritual source – the gap has to be bridged continually, because otherwise the simultaneous assertion of an essential significance of the scripture for the world could not be sustained. Book religions thus form an assemblage in which scripture and the world must be bridged by mediation. The pivotal question now remains of how this sort of bridging is accomplished in particular religious communities.

In his renowned work on the role of literacy in the formation of 'cultural memory' in historical Egypt, Jan Assmann (1997, 2000) argues that this intermediation is usually accomplished by canonizations that involve the institutionalization of interpretational practices (*Sinnpflege*) through the establishment of social institutions and textual experts that continuously guarantee the authoritative interpretations of the scripture. In his view, the essential decontextualisation of canonized books makes for the necessity of continually and contextually retrieving – or rather establishing – the meaning expressed in them. By thus emphasizing processes of signification, Assmann depicts interpretative practices as mediating devices between the divine scriptural realm and the worldly laity.

These arguments are undoubtedly important, as is Assmann's awareness of issues of authority when he is dealing with the canonization and interpretation of scriptures. Yet he also differentiates between religions of the book that make use of sacred texts by iterating recitations, and those that are characterized by the interpretation of canonized scriptures. In doing so he explicitly situates the practice of textual recitation in the realm of rituals, while assigning interpretational practice the status of representing something like the full potency of literate culture.[5] Such differentiation appears debatable because in most book religions both textual recitations and interpretations play a decisive part in the particular practice (Coward 1988). Rather than separating these two forms of literacy practice categorically, we must ask how they are actually combined with each other in particular social, cultural and historical settings.

Related to this point is the fact that Assmann's prominent focus on 'interpretation' exposes the limitations of his analysis. Using a hermeneutical model, Assmann maintains that religions that refer to canonized books – in contrast to those based on the recitation of texts – mainly centre on questions of scriptural 'meaning' in the sense of 'propositional content'. Through such an assertion, meaning and cognition are given priority over experience and spirituality. Although Assmann bases his reasoning on the premise that canonized books are placed outside time and space by being declared spiritually authoritative, in the course of his argument this spiritual potency that is attributed to scriptures somehow gets lost.

Still, stressing mainly 'interpretation' makes it almost impossible to deal with religious communities that see their canonized scriptures as 'containing' significations and simultaneously as representing something inexpressible. These two dimensions of sacred books – the scripture as an object of interpretation, and the scripture as the token or promise of an unquestionable spiritual presence – have up to now mostly been considered separately. Whereas the hermeneutic model takes 'the Book' to be a vessel for meaning, interpretations that seek to understand the spiritual potency of books tend to take the vessel for a 'fetish' endowed with superhuman power. So the analytical challenge is to consolidate two dimensions of sacred books – 'the Scripture' as an object of interpretation, and 'the Scripture' as a token of a presence *sui generis*.

In developing some general thoughts about Christianity as a religion of the book, I have argued for an analytical emphasis to be placed on social practices that takes account, first, of the role of religious writings as boundary objects; secondly, of the interplay between scriptural latency and actualization; thirdly, of the importance of authoritative processes of intermediation between the divine scriptural and the worldly realms; and lastly, of the need to consolidate the interpretative and non-interpretative dimensions of sacred books.

These considerations will prove useful when, in the following chapters, I provide a 'thick description' of African Christian literacy practices in my area of research. In this trajectory, particular attention will be paid to the question of what, in specific religious-textual communities, are assumed to be the essential prerequisites – what I call 'enablements' – for a divinely ordained, and thus authoritative, reading and intermediation of the Bible.

Notes

1. I should emphasise that my considerations below concern Christianity as a 'religion of the book' rather than as a 'literate religion'. Since the latter expression has often been associated with normative ideas of what 'full literacy' is, I shall avoid using it. My use of the term 'religion of the book', in contrast, in being a much broader category, allows us to identify analogies, connections and differences between various religious practices relating to writings which would otherwise remain unnoticed.
2. For a critique of 'belief' as a category of anthropological analyses, see Needham (1972), Ruel (1982), Southwold (1979). See also Kirsch (2004).
3. In his 'Preface to Romans', for example, Martin Luther declares: 'This letter is truly the most important piece in the New Testament. It is purest Gospel'. And he continues: 'Therefore it seems that St Paul, in writing this letter, wanted to compose a summary of the whole of Christian and evangelical teaching which would also be an introduction to the whole Old Testament. Without doubt, whoever takes this letter to heart possesses the light and power of the Old Testament'. Retrieved 20 August 2007 from *Christian Classics Ethereal Library*, http://www.ccel.org/ccel/luther/romans/files/romans.html
4. By the term 'latency' I do not mean any inherent characteristics of the Scriptures, but rather instances of social ascriptions which assume the Bible to be sacred in all its parts, even if some of them are actually not referred to by the respective religious community.
5. Two exemplary statements of J. Assmann: 'It is not the sacred, but only the canonical text that requires interpretation and thus becomes the starting point for interpretational cultures' (1997: 93; my translation); 'The sacred text requires no interpretation, only ritually protected recitation with a careful observance of the rules concerning place, time, purity etc. A canonic text, on the other hand, represents the normative and formative values of a community, the "truth"' (1997: 94; my translation).

PART III

WAYS OF READING

Chapter 8

Texts, Readers, Spirit

As we have seen in Chapter 2, Western Protestant missionaries in southern Africa had regarded literacy as promoting 'the ascendance of the reflective, inner-directed self' (Comaroff and Comaroff 1991: 63). As regards literacy, this self was conceived as resulting from dyadic interactions between readers and texts. Yet, what has also become clear is that many churchgoers in southern Zambia took it for granted that their activities could at times be supported or controlled by an agency beyond their personal human faculties, namely the Holy Spirit (*muya usalala*). This chapter thus sets out to examine reading practices among members of Pentecostal-charismatic churches that were not based on the idea of a dyadic interaction between reader and text, but were expected to rely on a triad of text, reader, and Spirit (cf. Harding 2000: xi). Therefore, before dealing with performative aspects of scriptural readings during church services in Chapter 11, the present chapter describes how the Holy Spirit was assumed to assist readers in, for example, overcoming language-related problems arising from Bible translations, establishing the meanings of biblical phrases, and assessing the relevance of supplementary publications.

Bibles, Versions, Origins

Among members of Pentecostal-charismatic churches in my area of research, the Bible was accorded the high status of representing the Word of God as witnessed by the early prophets and the Apostles of the New Testament. These 'authors' were mostly ascribed the status of 'divine secretaries': since their writings had been guided or even dictated by God, the contents and phraseology of the Bible were not of human but of divine origin. And since even the historical narratives of the Scriptures were assumed to have been devised with the help of God, the Bible as a whole was deemed to be infallible. Mistakes in the interpretation of the Scriptures could thus only be due to human failings.

The commonest version of the Bible was the vernacular *Ibbaibbele – Ibbuku Lymajwi aa-Leza*, which had first been issued by the Bible Society of Zambia in 1963. During the first decades of the twentieth century, representatives of the Primitive Methodist Missionary Society had begun the translation of parts of the Bible while residing in a mission station in the Gwembe Valley. This work was continued in the 1940s and 1950s by Cecil Hopgood, who prepared the first comprehensive translation of the Bible into Chitonga. Yet this extended translation into a dialect spoken in the Gwembe Valley, which became the basis of the printed and published Bible, occasionally posed language problems for present day Christians on the Plateau because they were not familiar with this particular dialect and the rather old-fashioned expressions used. Some of them had come across the new version of the Bible in Chitonga issued in the mid-1990s, but although they would have preferred this translation, which used the contemporary dialect from around the district capital of Monze, they simply could not afford to purchase new Bibles.

The vocabulary in their own copies of the Scriptures accordingly made reading (*kubala*) and understanding the Bible a considerable challenge.[1] The meaning of certain phrases had to be inferred from their linguistic context, a procedure that could only be achieved with the help of the Holy Spirit. Their spiritualistic approach to the Bible, which will be explored in more detail below, thus coincided with practical difficulties in using the actual language of the available Bibles.

The 'old' Chitonga Bible, which reflected the language of a particular region in the Gwembe Valley at a particular point in time, repeatedly evoked retrospective views concerning the ethnic origins of the Tonga. I was told by churchgoers on the Plateau that even their families originally came from the Gwembe Valley. Their attempts to spiritually elicit the meaning of idiomatic biblical phrases therefore implied making an Arcadian gesture in retrieving the language of the past with the assistance of the Holy Spirit. This claim to a specific ethnic origin, however, was characterized by a marked degree of ambivalence: while people from the Plateau maintained that the former way of life on the banks of the Zambezi represented something like the essence of being a 'Tonga', they simultaneously asserted that since then the Gwembe Tonga had declined and fallen behind those Tonga who lived on the Plateau. The efforts of indigenous Christians on the Plateau to retrieve the 'archaic' language with the help of the Holy Spirit and to evangelize the 'heathenish' Gwembe Tonga thus to a certain extent reflected their desire to revive earlier ways of living by means of this linguistic retranslation. The regional origin of the vernacular Bible, which as a sacred scripture describes the origin of the world as a whole, was correlated with images of primordial scenes of what it means to be a 'Tonga'.

For the Christians in the Gwembe Valley, on the other hand, this particular translation of the Bible did not pose as many problems. They were, admittedly, also faced with difficulties in understanding some of its expressions, but living close to Mweemba area and being generally acquainted with the present day dialect of this region made understanding easier. In contrast to the headquarters of the Spirit Apostolic Church (SAC) in Siamujulu village on the Plateau, the congregations in the Gwembe Valley accordingly used spiritualistic discourses less when it came to decoding the Bible linguistically. In an almost paradoxical reversal, those who, in the eyes of headquarters, were in continuous danger of lapsing back into heathenism were able to pursue their studies of the Bible with a literalness that could not be attained by the church leaders on the Plateau.

Besides vernacular Bibles, some churchgoers had English versions of the Scriptures. In Siamujulu village, for example, one church elder of the SAC had a copy of the King James Version, whose phraseology still attests to its original date of publication in 1611. Another church elder was in possession of an Easy-to-Read Version, which was published in the 1970s to meet the demands of children, the deaf and those with difficulties in reading. This version, as well The Living Bible – A Thought for Thought Translation, which two of the members possessed, is a paraphrase, whereas the King James Version is a word for word translation. Moreover, one of the church elders had the Roman Catholic edition of the Good News Bible, which contains the Deuterocanonicals and Apocrypha. These books, however, were not included in the copies of the New International Version owned by two of the church elders, which had been prepared by Protestant translators, including, for example, Episcopalians, Lutherans, Mennonites, Methodists and Presbyterians.

This brief account shows that the English versions of the Bible in Siamujulu village differed in theological outlook, as well as in the readership that the particular translation was aimed at. The format and wording of the translations accordingly differed to a high degree. Yet none of these versions was accorded any authoritative status over any of the others. Rather, the four versions were used in alternation at different times and by different people in the course of a religious practice. And even those church elders who personally owned various versions of the English Bible did not make a deliberate choice between them. Which version was used in a particular situation was actually a matter of chance. There was only one church elder in Siamujulu village who would sometimes sit down and compare his vernacular copy of the Bible with some of the English versions; we shall return to him in a following section.

The existence of different versions of the Bible, however, was not generally a source of prolonged irritation among church members. One of the rare instances of such irritation occurred during a discussion in 1999, when a group of church elders of the SAC realized that the first sentence of the Book of Genesis in the King James Version read, 'In the beginning God created the heaven and the earth', whereas the New International Version put the word 'heaven' into the plural: 'In the beginning God created the heavens and the earth'. While at first expressing a certain uneasiness about this discovery, they eventually resolved the discrepancy by agreeing that different versions do not present problems if one's reading is substantiated by the Holy Spirit. Only those readers who are endowed with spirituality, it was claimed, would be able to understand the single meaning behind the two different versions. In the case of Genesis, the plural form 'heavens' was interpreted as being a metaphorical expression for 'an *eternal* heaven'.

The indifference with regard to conflicting versions of the Bible, which could also be found among other Pentecostal-charismatic churches in southern Zambia, was therefore connected with the spiritual orientation of these churches. The reception of the Bible by a spiritually endowed person was said to require guidance by the Holy Spirit, which would function as a corrective spiritual power by redressing any faults in the Bible translation in the very act of reading it.

Pamphlets and Eclecticism

This combination of spiritual orientation and indifference to some extent also related to other Christian publications, such as pamphlets, booklets or tracts. Far from being concerned about the denominational origins of unknown religious publications, people generally ignored all such indications. Newly arrived publications were read with unlimited interest. If the publication then proved to contain assertions that could be recognized by a reader who was endowed with spirituality as having a divine origin, the publication was accorded religious significance, regardless of denominational origin. The eclectic appropriation of religious publications by members of Pentecostal-charismatic churches in my area of research was thus not considered inconsistent.[2] The apparently indiscriminate reception of heterogeneous publications was balanced by stressing the readers' spiritual apprehension of religious adequateness, which did not use institutional boundaries as a criterion for evaluation.

In Siamujulu village, for example, one of the members of the Spirit Apostolic Church (SAC) possessed a copy of a booklet entitled *Strength for Today*, issued by the Salvation Army in 1964; a tract entitled *Holy Spirit: The Force Behind the Coming Order*, issued by the Watch Tower Bible and Tract Society of Pennsylvania; a Christian novel by Anna Kuhn, which, according to a stamp on the flyleaf, had previously been owned by the Jesuit Canisius College in Chikuni (cf. Charmody 1992, 1999); and pamphlets by various other denominations, like the United Church of Zambia, the Gospel Outreach Mission and the Christian Missionary Fellowship. Another member had a booklet entitled *Why Tongues* by the Rhema Bible Church in the USA; a copy of the book *Meeting Excuses in Soul Winning*, whose author, Waddy A. Shibemba, was the founder of the Mindolo and Kalulushi Baptist Congregations in Zambia; a small tract called *Just a Minute*, which gives Christian instructions without any hint as to its denominational origin; a copy of the magazine *Light of Hope* by the Apostolic Faith Church; and a book entitled *Junior Folks at Mission Study: China*, published by the General Mission Board of the Church of the Brethren, Illinois, which according to an Asian-style ex-libris label, was originally purchased in January 1921.

None of these church members actually cared about the denominational backgrounds of their publications. They read them out of a keen interest in religious progress. If the origin of publications was of any importance at all, it related to the question of how the particular piece of literature had been acquired. When Alaster, the district superintendent of the SAC in Siamujulu, showed me a newspaper-sized pamphlet describing the religious activities of the American preacher William Branham, he could not say who William Branham was, and only stressed that the pamphlet had been given to him by a leaseholder of the adjacent commercial farm where he had formerly been employed.[3] He also emphasized that this leaseholder was a reliable person and that the pamphlet should therefore not be dismissed too readily.

These pamphlets and booklets were considered important enough to keep them for the purpose of *reading*; they had not been used as notebooks or toilet paper. However, this certainly did not mean that these publications were beyond contestation by other churchgoers. On one occasion, when I was sitting together with Alaster and talking about the William Branham publication, another elder joined us. After Alaster had left, the latter dismissed the religious relevance of the pamphlet by remarking that it had the same trim size as a newspaper. This, he insisted, was evidence that the pamphlet's value was only ephemeral.

Among further arguments that might be adduced against the Christian literature owned by others, one is of particular relevance for us here. While a publication's denominational origin was not significant for those who wanted to accord it religious relevance, it was referred to condescendingly by those who wanted to dismiss its religious value. This contrast is significant, because criticism of this sort was usually also rooted in discourses about spiritualism. Making reference to the denominational origin of a particular publication was mostly linked to an assertion that the denomination concerned lacked spirituality. Whereas those readers of a publication that approved it acknowledged that the Holy Spirit allowed one to bridge different denominations, those who criticized the same publication made reference to the Holy Spirit in order to stress institutional boundaries between denominations.

On another level, this contrast referred to differences between 'readers' and 'authors'. Those who agreed with the general position taken in a particular religious publication assigned responsibility to the *reader* by stressing that it was the reader's own spirituality that enabled him or her to judge good from bad, and even to discern something of importance in an otherwise possibly second-rate piece of writing. Those who dismissed a publication a priori placed the responsibility on the *author* by claiming that nothing divine could be retrieved from a publication that had not been contained in it from the outset. Such views represented different descriptions of the relationship between the author, his or her writing and the reader. They had in common the allocation of a pivotal role to the Holy Spirit, but this spiritual being was positioned at different points in the literacy process, namely as a precondition either at the source or at the endpoint.

What is most noteworthy for us here is that, in the SAC, one's own claim to spirituality was never connected with any supposition that the author of a Christian denominational publication also had spirituality. If the attitude towards a publication was positive, it was the reader's spirituality that was necessary in order for it to be bestowed with religious significance: the source of the publication was of secondary interest and was generally neglected. When taking a negative position with respect to a particular publication, its origin was denied any spirituality, while it was simultaneously claimed that it was the power of the Holy Spirit that had made evaluation of the publication possible. In the final analysis, both cases thus entailed making a claim to personal spirituality while rejecting the authorial role through either neglect or dismissal. This asymmetric perspective marks a difference from those churches in my research area whose religious practice revolved around the communal use of denominational publications. Among the Jehovah's Witnesses and in the New Apostolic Church – denominations that will be discussed in Chapter 12 – authorship was a criterion for positive selection.

Selections and Combinations

As has been demonstrated in the above sections, members of Pentecostal-charismatic churches assumed the Holy Spirit to play a crucial role in making old-fashioned expressions comprehensible, in consolidating different translations of the Bible, and in assessing the religious value of denominational publications. In a previous chapter, similarly, it was argued that the Holy Spirit was regarded as an indispensable aide in deciphering damaged copies of the Scriptures, where missing letters or words had to be extrapolated.

But even 'ideal' instances of scriptural understanding were deemed to necessitate close contact between the reader and the Holy Spirit: since the biblical text was considered to be extremely allegorical (i.e., characterised by indirect [*masendelela*] speech) and thus confusing, the appropriate selection (*kusala*), interpretation (*kumvwa*) and combination of biblical passages (*kubika amwi mavesi*) was considered to be possible only when one was inspired – 'enabled' – by the Holy Spirit.[4] Where to start reading the Bible, how to proceed with it and how to understand a given scriptural verse thus presupposed that one possessed spirituality.

Given this notion of spiritual guidance, the selection and interpretation of Bible verses developed with marked flexibility and without official dictates. Indeed, interpretations differed even within one and the same congregation. During religious debates, these disagreements then led to the construction of different textual connections being made, even when all participants took the same verse as the starting point for their Bible reading. For example, it was widely agreed among the elders of the SAC that a certain passage in the first letter of Paul to the Corinthians included authoritative instructions on the question of whether women should be allowed to hold speeches in public or not. Those male participants in a small informal discussion group in Siamujulu village in April 1999, who opposed public statements by women in church, referred to 1 Corinthians 14:34–35, where it says: 'Women should remain silent in the churches. They are not allowed to speak, but must be in submission, as the Law says. If they want to inquire about something, they should ask their own husbands at home; for it is disgraceful for a woman to speak in the church'.

They then referred to 1 Corinthians 14:39: 'Therefore, my brothers, be eager to prophecy, and do not forbid speaking in tongues'. Using this combination of texts, they tried to prove that women should not be allowed to speak publicly during church services, though they were allowed to prophesy and to speak in tongues. Others, who advocated women being allowed to speak in public, criticized this particular selection of Bible verses as misguided and maintained that there was no reason to skip the verses in between (1 Corinthians 14:36–38), which read: 'Did the word of God originate with you? Or are you the only people it has reached? If anybody thinks he is a prophet or spiritually gifted, let him acknowledge that what I am writing to you is the Lord's command. If he ignores this, he himself will be ignored'.

They thus opposed this separation of Bible verses and instead suggested that 1 Corinthians 14:34–35 and 1 Corinthians 14:36–38 should be read as a dialogue between men and women. Then the first verses ('Women should remain silent in the churches...') would represent a common statement of the men, whereas the later ones ('Did the word of God originate with you? Or are you the only people it has reached? ...') would represent the response of the women. And since this reply was included in the Bible, they concluded, women should be allowed to address the congregation publicly. They accounted for 1 Corinthians 14:34–35 by pointing out that, in this context, a public speech did not mean preaching in front of the congregation but merely speaking to the congregation while standing in it.

The controversies concerning the making of textual connections thus related not only to the selection of Bible verses, but also to how selected passages should be combined. In the second argument reproduced above, two successive passages were understood as representing a dialogue; in other cases, these consecutive passages were interpreted as a simple monologue. The possibilities in combining different passages in the Bible were inexhaustible. Verse A could be linked to verse B through additions like 'and', 'because', 'then', 'simultaneously, 'although', 'which means in detail' etc. These conjunctions were the object of repeated and partly conflictual negotiations. Nevertheless, church elders agreed that determining the correct starting points for a reading of the Bible and deciding one's movements between different parts of the Scripture required the guidance of the Holy Spirit.

Private Readings, Implicit Influences

Reading the Bible during the week and in solitude in one's homestead was rather unusual among members of Pentecostal-charismatic churches. Quiet scriptural readings were normally confined to the periods shortly before Sunday services. On the other days of the week, the Bible was usually stored away in one's homestead.

The church elders of the SAC, for example, met on Sundays in front of the church building, where they started to engage in silent biblical studies. It was at this time that they decided what scriptural passages they would use to preach from during the service. However, since they did not make their choices known to one another, the preachers in charge never knew in advance what his colleagues would be dealing with during the service. This lack of knowledge, as well as the subsequent interaction with the congregation – which will be described in Chapter 11 – frequently required some preachers to revise their initial selections during the course of the service. Yet whenever a final decision of what to preach on had been made, the actual selection of passages from the Bible was always explained as originating as a spontaneous inspiration by the Holy Spirit. No preparations, like praying, were said to be necessary for such spiritual guidance.

What were read in solitude, however, were personally owned pamphlets and Christian publications. As already noted, many members of Pentecostal-charismatic churches appreciated Christian publications of different kinds – if they could get hold of them – and some adolescent churchgoers made great efforts to obtain Christian literature. It was also mentioned earlier that reading such literature was

4. Preachers preparing for Sunday service, Mazwange village, 1999.

nevertheless not publicly acknowledged as having any religious value. In 1999, the senior elders of the SAC even officially dismissed the use of any publications apart from the Bible. They maintained that nothing should be added to the Scriptures, and that the denominational publications of other churches represented undesirable 'supplementary scriptures'. Using such publications, it was asserted, would make preachers lazy and weak, since they would be tempted to rely on them completely.

Given the tone of this dominant discourse, pamphlets and Christian publications were mostly read in private, practically hidden from public view. In contrast to sermons on cassettes, which adolescent members obtained by post and which were generally listened to in small groups, Christian publications did not become the object of any communal practice. This contrast will prove significant when compared to practise among Jehovah's Witnesses, which will be examined below.

Although private readings of these publications certainly informed later sermons, this influence developed only implicitly. In September 1999, for example, Philimon of the SAC congregation in Sanangula village got hold of a copy of the *Higher Way* magazine of the Apostolic Faith Church. Having read an article entitled 'Confidence in God', he expounded on this topic during one of his sermons, without, however, indicating that the general tone of the sermon was based on a published source. Instead, he represented his preaching as being stimulated by and based on revelations by the Holy Spirit. Nonetheless, he had partly appropriated the selection of Bible verses and the textual links from the *Higher Way* magazine by proceeding from Hebrews 10:35 to Psalm 40 and then to Mark 4:37–40.[5] Other church members of the SAC made use of Christian publications in the same way. But while privately using Christian publications to provide inspiration for sermons, this fact was generally concealed in public. Moreover, the scriptural inspiration was converted into an official demonstration of spiritual inspiration.[6]

In the congregation in Siamujulu village of 1999 were two church members who made use of Christian publications in a rather unusual way. One junior church leader, Javan, generally based his sermons on a Bible commentary entitled *Opening up God's Word: the Compact Survey of the Bible*.[7] When preparing a sermon, he first skimmed through the pages of the commentary in order to obtain ideas on what to preach. *Opening Up God's Word* is arranged according to the books of the Bible and explains them under the headings 'Introduction', 'An Outline', 'The Main Message', 'An Application' and 'Key Themes'. Having found a topic for his sermon, Javan would go through the particular chapter of the commentary and then open the Bible to follow the indicated cross references. His textual shifts thus proceeded from the Bible commentary to the Scriptures, so that the commentary crucially shaped his understanding of the Bible.

This practice reflected certain biographical legacies as well as Javan's personal goals for the future. He had recently moved into his father's homestead in Siamujulu village after attending a secondary school in Livingstone. He had temporarily attended the adjacent New Apostolic Church and had then joined the SAC, where he soon became a junior church leader. Javan's explicit aim was to attend a theological college, for which purpose he was seeking support. He was one of the main protagonists in attempts to obtain Christian literature through correspondence with Western denominations, and he had made contact with a Lutheran priest in Choma. Javan's use of the biblical commentary in 1999 accordingly echoed a literacy practice that he had become acquainted with in secondary school, namely gradually approaching difficult subjects (Bible verses) by means of written explanatory devices (the Bible commentary). And it also reflected his anticipation that a similar literacy practice would be pursued in theological college.

The second rather unusual case in the congregation of Siamujulu village was Alaster, the district evangelist of the SAC. He had worked for some years as a storekeeper on an adjacent commercial farm and had previously been a member of the Brethren in Christ, where he had acted as a Sunday school teacher. Alaster took pride in having completed a business correspondence course and two courses offered by the Bible Way Correspondence College of the Baptist Mission of Zambia. The certificate for the latter stated that he had memorized sixty Bible verses. In preparing a sermon, Alaster made use of the written materials of these Bible correspondence courses and also examined different translations of the Scriptures. Since having been a working employee, he owned a New International Version and a King James Version of the Bible, as well as a copy of the Bible in Chitonga. For him, planning a sermon meant not only deliberately comparing these different translations, but also making use of the concordance that was included in the New International Version and of the cross references in the margins of the Chitonga Bible.[8] During his actual preaching, however, the comparison remained implicit, because he never openly commented on his particular literacy practice. And since the public Bible reading in the course of the church services relied only on the Chitonga Bible, a peculiar convergence occurred:

the passages of the Bible that were read aloud obviously referred to the Chitonga version, while Alaster's subsequent explanations concerning particular Bible verses were informed by his earlier understanding of other versions of the Bible.

In light of the spiritualistic discourse that prevailed within the SAC, neither Alaster nor Javan publicly disclosed their respective literacy practices. Sitting among the other church elders on a Sunday morning shortly before the service, they behaved just like all the others. Alaster left all but his Chitonga Bible at home, and Javan never brought his Bible commentary to church services.

Although these two cases demonstrate an unusual degree of formality regarding literacy practices, they nevertheless highlight some procedures that – to a considerably lesser extent – also informed the Bible reading of other church leaders of the SAC. While preparing their sermons in front of the church building, most church elders made use of the cross references in the page margins of the Chitonga Bible, where, for example, Matthew 1:1 is cross referenced to Luke 3:23–38, to Mark 17:11, to Genesis 5:1, and to Genesis 22:18. From this latter verse, one is referred to nine other Bible verses – and so on.

The paratextual devices of the Chitonga Bible thus hint at particular textual connections. And although the church elders of the SAC stressed the necessity of inspiration by the Holy Spirit during Bible reading, to a certain extent they followed the selections and combinations suggested. In contrast to Javan's *Opening Up God's Word*, however, these cross references in the Chitonga Bible do not indicate how concretely the Bible verses should be combined. Whereas the arguments of the Bible commentary model particular conjunctions between the verses – for example, the proposition in verse A 'is because of' the proposition in verse B – the cross references in the Chitonga Bible represent mere indicators. How the respective Bible verses eventually came to be combined thus depended entirely on the combinatory facility of the reader, – or, according to the Church's members, on revelation by the Holy Spirit.

Bible Studies

That the right combination of Bible verses was considered to require intervention by the Holy Spirit can also be seen with respect to the Bible studies (*kwiiya bbaibele*) and Sunday school lessons of the SAC. The elders of most congregations emphasized the importance of religious instruction for children and neophytes. Generally, however, Bible studies and Sunday school lessons hardly existed at all during my periods of field research. When Cephas from the congregation in Nanyenda re-established a Sunday school in April 1999 after a prolonged period of inactivity, his 'school' in the church building remained almost empty; shortly afterwards it was closed. There was no particular interest on the part of the laity to have religious teachings in the form of 'lessons', and the church elders did not make substantial efforts to urge the laity to attend Bible classes or Sunday schools. This indifference towards formal religious teaching had to do with the distinction mentioned earlier between 'religious education in school' and 'religious practice in church'.

What is significant for my argument here, however, is how the religious lessons of the SAC actually proceeded. One of the rare instances of a Sunday school I was able to witness took place during a church meeting in Siamujulu in July 1999. The religious instruction, which was led by Alaster, was attended by nine junior church leaders from different congregations and constituted official training in how to conduct the Sunday schools of the SAC. The lessons started by memorizing Bible verses: for about half an hour, Alaster recited short verses like Proverbs 3:5–6, which were then repeated by the participants. Then individual passages from the Bible were read aloud and discussed by the members of the group. In the course of this process, Alaster acted as the moderator and provided corrections whenever he considered it necessary. Nonetheless, the different interpretations that emerged were not subsumed under his authoritative reading. The debates frequently ended before a consensus about the interpretation of a Bible verse was agreed upon. Moreover, the scriptural readings and discussions were restricted to clearly demarcated passages from the Bible. There was no attempt to cross reference or combine one verse with another. Even during this most prominent example of formal religious training, therefore, there was no instruction concerning how individual Bible verses should be interpreted or interlinked to form particular arguments.

In the triad of texts, readers and Spirit, therefore, the Holy Spirit played a crucial role in how readers in Pentecostal-charismatic churches related to religious writings. The Holy Spirit was assumed to assist in overcoming difficulties in understanding the language of the Bibles available, in assigning value to other Christian literature, and in enabling readers to select, combine and interpret biblical verses in a divinely ordained way.

In contrast to common scholarly understandings, therefore, the Holy Spirit was not opposed to the use of writings, but instead represented an essential prerequisite for dealing with them. At the same time, two interrelated aspects are particularly noteworthy with relation to this literacy practice. First, as we observed, and *pace* Jan Assmann, interpretational practices were not institutionalized, and no official rules were laid down by church leaders regarding how certain biblical passages should be interpreted. In addition, though some members of Pentecostal-charismatic churches used standardized Bible commentaries and other Christian literatures that instructed readers in how to interpret the Scripture, such publications were not made part of the communal religious practice but were read in private. The prevailing spiritualistic discourse inhibited public acknowledgement that such literature might have any religious value. Secondly, this spiritualistic literacy practice empowered readers over authors: claiming to be assisted by the Holy Spirit while reading a religious text entailed making a claim to personal spirituality while rejecting the authorial role through either neglect or dismissal. This asymmetric perspective marks a difference from those churches in my research area whose religious practice revolved around the communal use of denominational publications: among the Jehovah's Witnesses and in the New Apostolic Church – churches that will be discussed in Chapter 12 – it was authorship that was a criterion for positive selection.

Notes

1. For the unintended consequences of missionary translations of the Bible in Ghana, see Meyer (1992, 1999).
2. The eclectic usage of different sorts of writings by African Christians has repeatedly been observed. H. W. Turner (1960), for example, examines the (seemingly indiscriminate) choice of literature by a West African churchgoer. In the Zambian context, R. Serpell (1993: 168–70) lists those writings that were usually read by his interlocutors, namely schoolbooks, novels, exercise books, religious booklets, letters and the Bible.
3. William Branham (1909–1965) was an influential American minister and one of the initiators of the healing and charismatic revival that started in 1947. In 1951 he held meetings in Durban (South Africa), which were sponsored by the Apostolic Faith Mission, the Assemblies of God, the Pentecostal Holiness and the Full Gospel Church of God.
4. This bears a close resemblance to what is articulated by Western proponents of a Pentecostal theology. According to S. Ellington, it is 'the transformative action of the Holy Spirit which persistently intrudes on Christian experience and prevents our interpretations from becoming simply a process of reading our own needs and wants into the text' (1996: 22). Therefore, he continues, apart from the 'active participation of the Spirit, the mere words of the text have no power to transform us' (ibid.: 28).
5. This magazine was *Higher Way: the Magazine for Spiritual Growth* (Portland, USA: Apostolic Faith Church; vol. 91, no. 6; 1998).
6. This resembles what A. Roberts has observed regarding Alice Lenshina's Lumpa Church, where the deacons of the church actually 'sought to give the impression while preaching that they too were divinely inspired; they preferred to consult the Bible in the privacy of their own homes' (1970: 15).
7. Originally published as *The Bible in Outline* in Great Britain and as *The Compact Survey of the Bible* in the USA, Javan's copy of the book was a special edition published by the Billy Graham Evangelistic Association (Minneapolis: Bethany House Publishers; 1985).
8. The New International Version also has footnotes indicating alternative translations, which occasionally give explanations concerning names, flora and fauna; in some passages, other Bible verses are cross-referenced. Javan's King James Version, in contrast, has no footnotes; at the end of the book, however, is a 'Bible Word List', which alphabetically lists phrases which are then explained and cross referenced to some verses.

Chapter 9

Evanescence and the Necessity of Intermediation

In most Pentecostal-charismatic churches, there were just a small number of Bibles available. This undoubtedly had to do with the fact that many participants could not afford to buy their own copy of the Scriptures. What is surprising at first glance, however, is that those churchgoers who might have been able to afford to buy a Bible often chose to spend spare cash on other items, and not always those required by the material needs of their subsistence economy. Such investment preferences might well be interpreted as indicating a lack of commitment on the part of these particular churchgoers. However, I would suggest that the widespread reluctance to purchase personal copies of the Bible emphasizes another crucial dimension in the literacy practice of these churches: the perceived need for scriptural mediation. Although many of my interlocutors among the laity hoped to acquire their own copies of the Bible someday, which would equip them for scriptural studies at home, the possibility of reading the Bible in private actually appeared rather unimportant to them. Instead, they placed a priority on scriptural mediation through the church elders (see also Cannell 2006: 18).

Thus, having outlined the triad of texts, readers and Spirit in the preceding chapter, this assemblage will now be supplemented by considerations concerning a fourth element, namely spiritualized social intermediation, which was assumed to be crucial for all those churchgoers who were not ascribed any privileged relationship with the Holy Spirit. As we shall see, an examination of this fourth element requires resuming the discussion of the relationship between objects and spiritual forces, as well as between the latter and human beings.

The Impossibility of Storing the Holy Spirit

There was common agreement among my interlocutors of all denominations that the private and uninstructed Bible reading of a non-Christian would not make him a Christian. This apparently simple view had far-reaching implications. First, it was argued that uninstructed and irreligious readers would be confused by the complexity and metaphorical language of the Bible, would not know how to proceed in their scriptural readings, and would be even less capable of interpreting it. Secondly, it was implied that there was nothing *in* the Bible which by itself told the reader how the Scriptures should be read.

The latter point is of particular relevance for our consideration here. According to a general tenet of Christians in my research area, it was not possible to achieve immediate contact with God or the Holy Spirit by reading the Bible. I was repeatedly told that there was nothing mystical about the letters of the Bible and that in their material form the scriptural verses did not 'contain' the Holy Spirit. Not even touching the Bible was assumed to have any healing power, unless touching was mediated by a spiritually endowed religious expert. The Bible as a physical object was thus not ascribed any spiritual power or agency by itself.

This finding is in marked contrast to Stanley Tambiah's analysis of Sinhalese Buddhist sacra. Discussing the concept of charisma, Tambiah rightly points out that Max Weber, 'who was so alive to the routinization and objectification of charisma in institutional structures', had neglected 'the objectification of charisma in talismans, amulets, charms, regalia, palladia, and so forth' (1984: 335). Linking this to Marcel Mauss' discussion of *mana* and to Karl Marx' treatment of fetishism, Tambiah explains that particular Buddhist sacra are treated as: 'enduring sedimentations, objectifications of power and virtue. Possession of them is a guarantee of legitimacy. But these sedimentations of virtue and power will remain with the possessor for as long as he is virtuous and deserving' (1984: 241). This ascription of charismatic agency to a religious object was not made in my research area where the Bible or any other Christian writing was concerned. This explains why physical objects of writing were not used here as 'fetishes' or protective 'talismans' (cf. Bledsoe and Robey 1993; Goody 1968b; Janzen and MacGaffey 1974: 11–13); why 'literacy power' was not internalized through the ingestion of written words as, for example, James Smith (1998) has described for Mau Mau insurgents; and why, as already noted, the everyday physical manipulation of the Scriptures did not differ from the rather casual handling of any other written material. Here there was no 'agent-ification' (Pels, Hetherington and Vandenberghe 2002: 4) of physical objects of writing.

A comparison between the Bible and other material objects connected with religious practices in my research area is significant in this context (cf. Engelke 2005). The *mutumwa* congregations held that knowledge of herbalist medicine (*musamu*) was a gift from God (*cipego caleza*): the knowledge about which type of *musamu* to use for the treatment of a particular affliction, where to find the appropriate medicine in the bush and how to apply the herbs and roots were all said to be revealed in dreams and to be guided by the Holy Spirit. This notion apparently corresponds to the idea, examined in the previous chapter, that only a divinely guided reader could find the right starting point for a reading of the Bible and would thus know how to interpret and combine the different verses. Similarly, expertise in herbalist medicines among *bang'anga* was mostly regarded as requiring the assistance of spiritual entities. Even the use of destructive magic items by witches was considered impossible if it was not supported by the corresponding malevolent spirits.

Nonetheless, there were strong disagreements among my interlocutors concerning how particular material objects actually worked. Some maintained that spiritual aid was only needed in finding the medicine, making the magic item and correctly using or placing it. Once this was done, it was claimed, the material object would develop a particular power by itself. For them, there accordingly remained a certain transformative power in the medicines (*bukali bwamusamu*) themselves, which could act independently of the co-presence of either spiritual beings or a healer. An extraordinary example of such 'objects with a power of their own' were allopathic tablets sold in stores, like malaria tablets or painkillers. They were bought like ordinary commodities and on the basis of a self-diagnosis by the afflicted. It was clear to everybody that such tablets had been manufactured and produced by worldly agencies, and that the storekeeper had no influence on the healing process.

In almost all other cases of medical treatment, however, the person who supplied the medicine, as well as its particular mode of procurement, were considered to be of pivotal importance. Herbalist medicine could not be given by just anyone, nor obtained just anyhow. Expertise, which mostly meant spiritual knowledge, experiences, and activities, was considered a precondition for a material object to develop healing powers. One of the reasons for the decreasing reputation of the *mutumwa* congregation in Siankumba village in 1999, for example, was the widespread rumour that healers in this congregation had stopped looking for herbs and roots themselves, and that they were getting children to look for them instead. Given this way of obtaining medicines, the overall conclusion was that the *musamu* provided by the particular *mutumwa* congregation did not have any power to heal, even though the same roots were being used as the healers had previously employed. The spiritual ability to know and physically to find a medicine was thus seen as prerequisite to the healing power of the *musamu*. The identification and procuring of a material object had to be intimately linked to a religious expert and – by extension – to the spiritual realm if it was to be attributed the power to heal.

The disagreement just mentioned among my interlocutors concerned the question of what actually empowered the medicine to heal once it had been identified and obtained. When, for example, herbs and roots were taken home after attending a *mutumwa* healer, why did they cure? Some of my interlocutors stated that the Holy Spirit was not connected with the medicine. For them, the very fact that a particular medicine had been spiritually discovered as something to provide treatment for the affliction was enough to account for its healing power. The material object was thought to contain substances capable of developing transformative power, provided the Holy Spirit had previously endowed the object with it. Others stated that the Holy Spirit maintained a connection with the medicine; the combination of substance and spirit would then ensure the cure. The Holy Spirit was thus either seen as a precondition for the medicine to develop a healing power or as somehow 'surrounding' or 'being attached' to the material object. None of my interlocutors, however, thought that the Holy Spirit was actually *in* the medicine. Even in those cases in which *mutumwa* congregations supplied items for continual protection against witchcraft, like charms worn on the body (*citumwa*) or items hidden in the homestead (*kuchinga munzi*), the Holy Spirit was generally understood to be close to the object, not within it.[1]

This finding is noteworthy when compared with how the relationship between objects and non-Christian spirits was repeatedly conceived. With regard to non-Christian spirits, many people also suggested that the power of the object resulted from its spiritually guided procurement and employment; some insisted that such material substances then evolved a healing potency or, in the case of witchcraft, destructive effects similar to poison. In contrast to the discourse on the Holy Spirit, however, the view that non-Christian spirits dwelt in an object was more prevalent. Some types of magic items used in witchcraft – especially the *insengo*, *chifunda*, and *chinaile*, mentioned earlier – were repeatedly said to contain malevolent spirits. The witches were said to posit spirits in the objects, which would then – when, for example, located at the homestead of the victim – lead to illness or death. Many 'traditional' herbalists (*bang'anga*) possessed paraphernalia, which they presented as 'containers' for their spiritual assistants (*kuyobola madaimona* – to store demons). A *mung'anga* in Sinazeze, for example, during his treatments of 1999 made use of two calabashes which he had stored in his house. The pear-shaped gourds had openings in the top, one of them decorated with beads, the other with a small piece of fur. In the course of a divinatory session, the *mung'anga* conversed with the spirits of two dead people which he described as living in the calabashes, and which he occasionally made leave in order to travel to the homestead of the afflicted person to discover the cause of the disease. This 'storing' of spirits was common among *bang'anga* and was also presumed to be essential to the practices of witches. In the latter case, keeping malevolent spirits was thought to be of particular importance, because 'free-ranging' spirits might turn against their own master.

The relationship between non-Christian spirits and objects was described in two other ways. Some of my interlocutors stated that spirits could serve a witch by conveying destructive magic items (like *insengo*) to their destination. Others felt that most magic items used in witchcraft should be understood as landmarks for the orientation of spirits: an *insengo* would thus represent a point of return for spiritual beings. As regards the Holy Spirit, on the other hand, the idea of spiritual transportation was completely absent. Distributing the Bible and other Christian paraphernalia was considered to require human carriers, although the Holy Spirit was understood to be a prerequisite *movens*. Likewise, there was no notion of Christian objects being 'landmarks' for the orientation of the Holy Spirit. The Holy Spirit was generally assumed to approach people, not objects. I encountered only one case in which the objects of a Christian denomination were interpreted as being landmarks for spirits. The leader of a Pentecostal-charismatic church near Sinazeze compared the denominational publications of the Jehovah's Witnesses with the witches' *insengo*, claiming that their publications are distributed in order to provide demons with points of orientation concerning whom to approach with their malevolent activities. It is very obvious, however, that this view denied the Jehovah's Witnesses the status of a *Christian* church; he interpreted their dissemination of material objects, in the form of publications, as behaviour reflecting non-Christian practices.

Objects, Bodies and Spiritual Evanescence

In view of these considerations, a crucial difference between non-Christian spiritual beings and the Holy Spirit can be suggested. Whereas it was repeatedly claimed that the 'physical' keeping of non-Christian spirits was possible, this possibility was rejected as far as the Holy Spirit was concerned. It was unthinkable to my interlocutors that anyone could succeed in keeping the Holy Spirit in some type of material vessel. Instead, the Holy Spirit was conceived as an inevitably unbound and evanescent entity, which human beings could not control in its movements.

Against this background, the Holy Spirit was presumed never to reside permanently at any particular material location, whether in the Bible or in any other object of Christian practice. And although the buildings of Pentecostal-charismatic churches were often said to be infused with divine powers, this did not mean that the Holy Spirit lived there perpetually.[2] When a new shelter for the Sanangula congregation of the Spirit Apostolic Church (SAC) was constructed in 1999, it was not anticipated that the Holy Spirit might occupy the site itself, not even after a Christian altar had been installed. Prayers and sermons were needed to introduce the new building to the Holy Spirit, which would then periodically take on a protective role towards it. There was no guarantee for a Christian congregation that their site of worship would be protected permanently. It was thus religious practice that was required in order to come into contact with the Holy Spirit. By themselves Christian symbols and objects could not secure the presence of divine powers. This could only be obtained through the proper use of objects by actors who were already endowed with the power of the Holy Spirit.

The unbounded nature of the Holy Spirit also related to its association with human beings. The Holy Spirit would select its human mediums by itself; it would approach appropriate persons, remain attached to them and occasionally enter their bodies, as well as leaving mediums at any time.[3] In general, interpretations differed concerning the actual relationship between the Holy Spirit and human bodies. Some, like the members of *mutumwa* congregations, maintained that the body of an ordinary human person in its normal state would resemble a *tabula rasa*. If one led a proper Christian life, however, the Holy Spirit would start to be close to one's body and to surround it. And by means of communal efforts, like the singing of spiritual hymns, the Holy Spirit could be induced to enter the body (*kunjila mumubili*) of the person concerned. Then, spiritual activities like witchfinding, prophesy or the exorcism of demons (*kungusya madaimona*) were to be expected. For members of *mutumwa* congregations, this spiritual invasion of the body caused a loss of bodily control on the part of the human medium, who would stumble around in a seemingly undisciplined manner.

The members of most other Pentecostal-charismatic churches in my research area, however, saw such loss of control as a clear indication of possession by demons. They agreed with the *mutumwa* congregations that the Holy Spirit would occasionally enter a human body, but insisted that possession by this divine being would not cause the medium to stumble around. Yet others opposed the claim that the normal state of a human body might be compared to a *tabula rasa*. Rabson, Bishop of the SAC in 1999, for example, insisted that everyone is endowed already at birth with some minor divine spirit and that this basic spirituality was essential to exist. The Holy Spirit in a stronger form could all the same enter the body and would then increase spiritual empowerment. Bishop Rabson asserted that having an interior *tabula rasa* would mean death and explained that invasion of the body by demons would also result in the person concerned dying. According to him, demons generally never entered humans but instead surrounded their bodies: the interior of a human being was reserved for divine beings. This view was admittedly rare, however, and was not even unanimously shared by the other church elders of the SAC.

In whatever way the relationship between the Holy Spirit and the human body was actually depicted, however, my interlocutors in Pentecostal-charismatic churches all agreed that people who had attained a close relationship with this divine entity could be distinguished from those who had not. For the latter group, it was asserted, the spiritualized social intermediation of the Scripture was required.

Taken together, the considerations in this and the previous chapter demonstrate three main points that will be important in the subsequent examination of processes of scriptural mediation in the Spirit Apostolic Church. First, the Bible was not considered to be a 'fetish' in the sense of it inherently containing spiritual powers. Second, proper use of the Bible presupposed a close relationship with the Holy Spirit. And third, the relationships of human beings with the Holy Spirit were assumed to be impermanent. The second and the third aspect refer to the previously developed idea that proper use of the Scriptures depended on spirituality. As the Bible was understood to be highly allegorical and obscure, it was felt that the appropriate selection, combination and interpretation of biblical passages were only possible when one was inspired by the Holy Spirit. The first point, on the other hand, that which highlights the 'non-fetishization' of the Bible, makes it seem rather insignificant in questions of spirituality. Yet it should be recalled that making ostensible reference to the Bible was considered indispensable for an authoritative Christian discourse: preaching without a Bible, it was commonly maintained, would entail the danger of the preacher deviating from the proper Christian track. Here, therefore, we are confronted with a use of the Scriptures based on two essential preconditions that must be combined: the Bible and the Spirit.[4]

The declared necessity of the mutual interaction of spirituality and scriptural usage implied that reading the Bible without assistance from someone who had a close relationship to the Holy Spirit would lead one astray. In other words, for those who were not regarded as having spirituality, the mediation of the Scripture was of the utmost importance if they were to understand the Bible properly. We have already seen, however, that Bible study groups and Sunday schools were almost absent in the SAC. Neither the laity nor the church elders attempted to achieve scriptural mediations based on modes of religious instruction resembling formal schooling. What was considered significant in scriptural mediation were church services, that is, those social events at which religious experts offered a public, spiritually guided and authoritative reading of the Bible. These events will now be examined by combining insights from the 'ethnography of reading' (Boyarin 1993) and the 'ethnography of speaking' (Bauman and Sherzer 1974) with what, borrowing a term from Regina Bendix (2000), can be called the 'ethnography of listening'.

Notes

1. The notion of the Holy Spirit being 'attached' to some object while not 'entering' it (*kunjila*) has certain parallels in the previously mentioned practice of 'attaching' the spirit of a deceased person (*kwanga muzimu*) to an heir of the matrilineage.
2. Such assessment differs from how many Central and Southern African 'land shrines' and 'places of power' (Colson 1997) are conceptualized. In territorial cults, for example, particular locations are assumed to be endowed with spiritual powers. They may be man-made shrines, but also naturally occurring phenomena like trees, hills, groves, or pools (cf. Schoffeleers 1978).
3. Processes of social negotiation concerning the human loci of spirit mediumship in the *mutumwa* congregation of Siankumba are analysed in Kirsch (1998). One of the case studies discussed there refers to a female churchgoer whose status changed from prophetess to patient in the course of a church service.
4. Comparable notions of an indispensable complementarity are also known from other religious practices in Central and Southern Africa. With regard to a particular type of Congolese *mung'anga* regalia, for example, namely the *nkisi*, a practitioner stated that the 'medicines placed in an *nkisi* are ... forces in its body to help it to work. The *nkisi* is as it is, but if it lacks medicines, it cannot do a thing. So the *nkisi* has medicines, they are its strength, and its hands and feet and eyes; medicines are all these' (cited in MacGaffey 1974: 106). It is interesting to note in this context that *nkisi* have occasionally been compared to 'the Europeans' books' (Andersson 1958: 44).

Chapter 10

Setting Texts in Motion

In his book *Beyond the Written Word: Oral Aspects of Scripture in the History of Religion*, William Graham cautions that we should not ignore the 'prominent but rarely emphasized oral function – in ritual, reading, recitation, devotions, and song – of all religious texts' (1987: 5; see also Coward 1988). This perspective is pivotal in the present case, since it shifts the focus in studies of 'religions of the book' from an emphasis on hermeneutics and religious doctrines to performativity and the experiential dimensions of textual reception. At the same time, however, the emphasis on the 'oral dimension of the written scriptural text' (Graham 1987: 7) runs the danger of reintroducing a certain asymmetry: whereas many studies privilege the written text over its oral performance, those that concentrate on oralization often tend to blank out the materiality of the textual source.

As the medievalist Joyce Coleman points out, this asymmetry has to do with the scholarly inclination conceptually to align empirical findings on the side of either 'orality' or 'literacy'. In contrast to this, J. Coleman makes a strong claim for the existence of a conceptual middle space, namely 'aurality', which she defines as 'the reading aloud of written literature to one or a group of listeners' (1996: 1). J. Coleman continues: 'Aurality is distinguished from "orality" – i.e., from a tradition based on the oral performance of bards or minstrels – by its *dependence on a written text as the source of the public reading* … this written form would visibly dominate the group experience, in a way that no oral or memorial author's text could do' (1996: 28; my italics).

She demonstrates that, in late medieval England and France, such public readings were not just performed for the illiterate or because of a shortage of reading materials, but that even the literate members of the upper classes, who had personal collections of books, often chose to listen to texts rather than reading them themselves in private.

J. Coleman interprets the physical presence of written sources during public readings as bringing forth 'an increased awareness of the fixity and authority of the text' (1996: 28). A similar point has been made by another medievalist, Paul Zumthor, who remarks: 'When the poet or his interpreter sang or recited … voice alone conferred authority on the text. But when the poet gave an oral recitation from a book, the authority came rather from the book' (Zumthor 1991: 35, cited in Nichols 1991: 138). According to Zumthor, whereas the performer's voice organically connects the oral poet and the audience, recitation from a written source entails an alienating interposition of the book between the performer and the listeners.

When, in the following, these perspectives are related to the examination of public scriptural readings in a Pentecostal-charismatic church in southern Zambia, the focus on the oral performance of religious writings and the concept of 'aurality' are helpful.[1] Since scriptural oralization in this church depends on the physical presence of the Bible and therefore is comparable to what J. Coleman has described for medieval Europe, I shall replace the term 'oralization', commonly used in anthropology, with 'auralization'. However, depicting the physical presence of the written source as merely increasing awareness of the authority of the book tells only half of the story. In many cases, the auralization of religious writings also means that the performer confers authority on the text by transforming scriptural latency into relevance for the audience. Publicly 'performing' the Bible therefore relies on a particular dialectical movement: grounding one's authority as a religious leader on the written authority of the Bible, while simultaneously constituting the authority of the Bible by auralizing an authoritative actualization.

As we shall see, the aural performance of the Scriptures in the Spirit Apostolic Church entailed what Stephen Nichols elsewhere has called a certain 'transgressive gesture intended to counter prevailing orthodoxy founded on written authority' (1991: 146). But this did not mean dismissing the Bible as a written, objectified reference point altogether. Instead, as Carol Muller has noted for the Church of the Nazarites (*Ibandla lamaNazaretha*), it meant that here the Bible was involved 'as both object and performance' (2003: 93). Moreover, rather than interposing the book between performer and audience, as Paul Zumthor would have it, an interactional setting was actually created in which the Scriptures and spiritualized oral performers came to be positioned symmetrically vis-à-vis the audience, while at the same time a (spiritual plus scriptural) connection was established with the audience, which both provided religious authorization to the church elders and empowered the laity.

Deciphering and Preaching

The Sunday services of the Spirit Apostolic Church (SAC) normally started at around ten o'clock in the morning and usually involved different types of prayers, singing and dancing, a series of sermons, divinations and healing sessions, a collection, and short speeches by the laity, in which they thanked God. For churchgoers, attending the services obviously promised to enhance their religious knowledge and to enable them to fulfil their duties as Christians, as well as providing a degree of entertainment. An additional and encompassing motivation, however, lay in the striving to achieve direct experience of God. Most activities during communal religious practice can thus be described as attempts to prepare oneself for personal contact with God, or as actually enabling such contact. As will become evident in the following, this was also true for sermons delivered by spiritually endowed church elders.

A service in the SAC normally included three to four sermons, which together formed a clearly structured sequence, starting with the most junior church elder, who was followed by those of a higher status in rank order (cf. Jules-Rosette 1975a: 107). Since no preacher knew in advance what the other preachers would be dealing with, this assured that church elders who held higher positions could refer to, as well as implicitly change, what had been said by those who had spoken earlier. Without openly commenting on or rejecting the contents of the preceding sermons, those who preached later were therefore in a position to resolve what had been said earlier according to their own ideas and interests. The sequence of sermons came to an end when the last preacher in charge – that is, the one with the highest position – gave a sermon that implicitly rearranged but simultaneously also comprised all the sermons given on that particular Sunday. Despite the existence of a structured sequence, services were therefore characterized by an 'emergent quality of performance' (Bauman 1977).

There is a marked difference between this liturgical order and that found in the New Apostolic Church (*Neuapostolische Kirche*), which will be examined in the next chapter. In the latter church, the highest-ranking church leader began the preaching and in doing so made use of written guidelines, the authoritative 'circulars' sent out beforehand by denominational headquarters. The services of the New Apostolic Church thus developed in an order that more or less remained in line with the circular and only allowed minor deviations. In the SAC, by contrast, the liturgical sequence started with relatively unrestrained and – at least in the eyes of the superior church leaders – therefore potentially deviant statements and suggestions of the junior church leaders. In the course of the service, these were then altered little by little in order finally to lay down a discourse that had authority. Since the authoritative circulars of the New Apostolic Church were available before the communal religious practice, the sequence of preachers proceeded down the hierarchy. The existence of authoritative written guidelines thus informed the denomination's liturgical sequences. Since, conversely, it was impossible for the senior church leaders of the SAC to provide comparable authoritative guidelines for the sermons of the juniors, preaching proceeded up the hierarchy instead.

To be accepted as a preacher in the SAC, one had to submit oneself to the process of having one's sermons revised in a series of services, until one's own religious discourse had reached a high degree of convergence with that of one's superiors. Yet before being allowed to preach at all, aspirants had to go through a prolonged period of making religious speeches in public: giving thanks to God during church services was the main training ground for preaching. Many younger church leaders had started their careers in the SAC by giving thanks to God in a way that impressed the established church leaders as being of outstanding quality. After a time, aspirants were then given church posts and requested to give sermons at the altar. There was widespread disagreement, however, as to what actually constituted the difference between thanking God in a suitable manner and giving a 'proper sermon'. Some maintained that the difference was mainly a question of spirituality – the non-spiritual ordinary church member versus the spiritually endowed church elder.

Others insisted that giving thanks to God differed from sermons only in that the latter should refer to, and quote from, the Bible. There was actually great variation between the different congregations of the SAC, and even between the different services of one and the same congregation concerning whether ordinary church members were allowed to use the Scriptures during their speeches. Those cases in which use of the Bible was restricted to the sermons of the church elders suggest that the latter had some fear of losing their authority over the congregation and fear that the boundaries between themselves and the latter would become blurred. Whereas it was difficult to control the public ascription of someone as being endowed with the Holy Spirit, it was easier to control the second component of the two prerequisites for a proper Christian discourse, namely use of the Bible. By restricting references to the Bible, the elders therefore tried to retain a contrast between their own religious discourses and those of the laity.

Sermons developed in such a way that the Bible reader and the preacher took turns (cf. Dillon-Malone 1978: 79–80; Jules-Rosette 1975a: 101, 108). Shortly before each sermon, the preacher (*mukambausi*) quietly told the reader (*mubazi mabbaibele*) which passages of the Bible were to be read out. Then both stood up in front of the congregation and the first passage was read out loud. Each reading usually consisted of a verse or a part of a verse and tended to be rather slow, sometimes even spoken in a stuttering way, because of the dim light in the church building, which made reading difficult, but also because of the lack of literacy skills on the part of most readers.

In general, the reader strictly followed the reading instructions given by the preacher; regarding the detail, however, he had considerable liberty with respect to when to interrupt his reading. Sometimes, the reader paused at a particular point, for example, in the middle of a verse, where the preacher was not expecting him to do so. Yet whenever the reader stopped, the preacher had to follow, repeating the previously uttered words more or less identically to how they had been read, but this time in a more fluent, intense, louder voice. Then the preacher would call for another reading from the reader. After a series of such alternations, in which biblical passages were first read out loud and then repeated almost exactly word for word, the preacher started to expound on some of the details. It was at this point that the sermon was expanded to cover explanations and interpretations, or the congregation called upon to follow Jesus Christ's example. Occasionally the preacher then called for another biblical passage, so that the whole procedure of scripture reading, verbal reiteration and exposition was repeated.

In order to illustrate this procedure of textual auralisation, let me give the example of a sermon delivered on 23 May 1999 during a service which was held at the headquarters of the SAC. In the course of this service, a preacher by the name of Kiran told one of the other church elders, Lyson, which Bible verses he wished to be read during his sermon. Then Kiran stood up and after exclaiming 'Halleluiah', which the congregation responded to using the same word, started to preach:

Kiran: 'Reader, you read 1 Corinthians, chapter 2, verse 12 to 15'.

Lyson: [reading] '1 Corinthians, chapter 2, verse 12 says: "We have not received the spirit of the world but the Spirit who is from God (*muya uuzwa kuli leza*), that we may understand what God has freely given us"'.

Kiran: 'We have not received the spirit of the world, but the Holy Spirit (*muya usalala*); so that we know what is given freely to us by God. Reader, continue!'

Lyson: [reading] 'This is what we speak, not in words taught us by human wisdom but in words taught by the spirit, expressing spiritual truths in spiritual words'.

Kiran: 'Listen to me! This is what we speak, not in words taught us by human wisdom but in words taught by the spirit! Halleluiah! [Congregation: 'Halleluiah'] We speak spiritual truths in spiritual words!'

While taking turns with the reader, the preacher occasionally altered the sentence structure, sometimes using synonyms for words from the Bible, and making short interjections. In general, however, he repeated the biblical wording almost word for word. Whereas the reader spoke in a calm voice, the preacher's utterances were loud and passionate. This interweaving of scriptural recitation and verbal reiteration (cf. Presler 1999: 198–205) was continued with respect to the next verse. At 1 Corinthians 2:15, however, the reading developed in a way that the preacher had not expected:

Lyson: [reading] 'The spiritual man makes judgements about all things –' [pause]

Kiran: [apparently irritated and hesitating briefly] '... Halleluiah! [Congregation: 'Halleluiah'] The spiritual man makes judgements about all things! He knows what to say about it; and he is right in doing so. Halleluiah! [Congregation: 'Halleluiah'] Who else would be in the position to know things?! Only the prophet! [about five minutes of further exposition] Reader continue!'

Lyson: [reading] '...but he himself is not subject to any man's judgement'.

Kiran: '... but he himself is not subject to judgement. Nobody should oppose the prophets! Such person would be a liar'.

In reciting this verse, the reader split it into two fragments. Although the actual verse connected 'making judgement about things' with 'being judged' the reading separated these two issues. The reader thus influenced what the preacher actually repeated and simultaneously endowed the particular passages with an emphasis of his own.

There also existed another way of influencing sermons, which did not occur during this particular instance of Kiran's preaching, but was nonetheless common in SAC services. Some member of the congregation might spontaneously start singing a hymn, which was then usually taken up by the rest of congregation, drowning out the sermon.

These songs gave the congregation a means of indirectly expressing disapproval of what the preacher was expounding (cf. Jules-Rosette 1975b; Kirsch 2002). When this happened, the preachers in charge generally joined in the singing and indicated their pleasure with it. The elders were well aware that the singing was usually intended to silence a sermon, and most of them admitted that in some cases this might really be a good thing, because occasionally they too would disagree with the content of a particular sermon. However, the explicit discourse represented these interruptions rather as spiritual support for the preacher. This made it possible to represent the interruption not as a humiliation but as a confident expression of affirmation of the preacher's spiritual power. Thus, even after being interrupted in this way, the preachers usually continued their sermons, although in most cases with clear changes. These interruptions by means of singing, as well as the reader's freedom to decide when to pause in the reading – through which he could influence what elements of the biblical verses were stressed – clearly point to the fact that to some extent sermons in the SAC were a joint performance involving the reader, the congregation and the preacher.

Sediments of the Spirit

In order to analyse the idea of the spiritual impact of sermons, mentioned above, we must first examine local ideas about the difference between readers and preachers. Interestingly enough, those who read from the Bible (*mubazi wabbaibele*) usually acted as preachers (*mukambausi*) on other occasions. The difference between these two functions therefore cannot be described as a difference concerning church offices or spirituality; rather it is a difference in function and practice. The act of reading (i.e., the deciphering of scriptural letters) was commonly held to have no spiritual potency in itself, even when the reading was done out loud by someone otherwise assumed to be spiritually endowed. Preaching (i.e., the act of successively repeating and expounding Bible verses), on the other hand, was understood to require an existing state of spiritual power, as well as simultaneously enhancing this power already on display on the part of the preacher.

The notion of the spirituality of preaching thus assumed that the preacher was able to free himself from the materiality of the letters without – in the first step – deviating from the message they contained: as we have already seen, the preaching initially consisted of a more or less pure reiteration of what the reader had just read out. Through this 're-oralization', the preachers continually produced a convergence between their own utterances and those in the Bible. The convergence was enhanced by particular strategies used by the preachers: in some cases, the preacher loudly chimed into the recitation of the *mubazi mabbaibele* by uttering exactly those words that the reader was simultaneously voicing, thus creating an overlap in unison between the biblical words as read out loud and his own sermon. It was only in the second stage of their sermons that the preacher started expounding on what had just been read out. Starting from a convergence with the Scripture, therefore, the Bible was now explained, contextualised and expanded. This development was supposed to require spirituality on the part of the preacher, while at the same time it was assumed to be an immediate consequence of his earlier convergence with the words of the Bible. The Bible and the preacher who was endowed with spirituality thus developed a relationship of mutual influence, which determined the effective course of the sermon.

Two different words were usually used by those listening to a sermon to describe the preacher's utterances, *kupandulula* and *kuzuzikizya*. The word *kupandulula* denotes 'to explain' in the sense of 'to clarify' or 'to elaborate'. *Kuzuzikizya*, on the other hand, has a wider range of connotations, meaning 'to put on top', but also 'to fulfil'. Thus, when after a sermon people talked about the preacher as having *kuzuzikizya* the Bible, this either alluded to him adding to the Bible – for example, by narrating stories – or to him actually 'fulfilling' the Bible in the sense of 'making it come true' or 'making it happen'.[2] This idea of fulfilment, however, could also be taken the other way round: preachers who were highly versed in biblical knowledge occasionally ended a passage of their exposition by uttering a sentence that, when the next passage of the Bible was read out shortly afterwards, turned out to be the exact wording of that particular verse. In these situations, the preacher put himself before the Bible in the sequence of events. In a certain sense, the Bible then became the fulfilment of the preacher's spirituality.[3]

Against the background of these findings, it is clear that sermons in the SAC cannot be understood as merely an interpretative mediation of the contents of the Scriptures. They had something more to them, which must be dealt with in detail. Exposure to the elders' sermons was mentioned as one of the means of achieving a closer relationship with the Holy Spirit. I was repeatedly told that this connection between preaching and the achieving of spirituality on the part of the audience had to do with the process of auralisation outlined above: whereas the reader would stick closely to the letters and read in a low tone, the preacher's reiteration of the verse would add spirituality and intensity to the words. By being uttered through the medium of the Holy Spirit, a powerful motion was imparted to previously fixed letters. Some of my informants put it metaphorically by saying that the sermon of an inspired preacher (*kukambauka anguzu zyaleza* – to preach with the power of God) is like a river that is suddenly released. According to this same metaphor, aural mediation was seen to convey a fertile substance, which, if received with an open mind, would settle within the listener like 'sediments of the spirit'. In this metaphor, the Bible was interpreted as constituting the river bed that ultimately controlled the movement of the preacher.[4] Thus when talking about sermons in the SAC, some members alluded to the Chitonga proverb '*mulonga watakazyolwa, wakabula makoba*' ('A river that is not controlled brings no sediments/manure').[5] The idea expressed in such associations must certainly be taken metaphorically, because none of my informants would have accepted that these sediments of the spirit have a physical materiality within the body of the listener.

Yet, even when understood as a metaphor, these notions have some interesting connotations. First and foremost, there was assumed to be a difference between these 'sediments of the spirit' and the process of memorizing Bible verses. Whereas the latter was associated with private reading, formal schooling and learning verses for Sunday school lessons (*kwiiya bbaibele* – to study the Bible), the former was said to be obtainable only during services. Furthermore, simple memorizing (*kubikilila mumizezo*) could not increase a person's spirituality: even the servants of Satan, it was said, would sometimes memorize the Bible in order to get followers. Thus, although the act of memorizing was generally regarded as a significant Christian practice, at the same time it was seen as being quite a mundane affair, sometimes even a means of deception. What is most important for us here, however, is that memorizing was considered different from the sediments of the spirit that were acquired by listening to inspired sermons.

In using the metaphor of 'sediments of the spirit', my informants were expressing their view that, if the sermon was given by a preacher who had spirituality, something empowering happened to the laity, something that could not be described solely in terms of absorption through memory or the interpretation of the words uttered. This 'something' was said to be transported by the spiritualized voice of the preacher and to enter the listeners' bodies, where it would settle down like fertile manure and induce sensory experiences (cf. Bendix 2000; Graham 1987: 162–65). Yet all my informants maintained that it was impossible for them to describe exactly what took root in the body in this way: they could not say whether they were, for example, utterances or biblical phrases. All the same, they asserted that it was not the Holy Spirit in its totality, but rather some spiritual fragment of it, which later made it possible for the Holy Spirit to obtain easier access to the person concerned. The fragments filled some part of the individual and could thus develop a certain protective power. By somehow 'occupying' the interior of the person, the spiritual fragments would reduce the possibility of demons entering the person's body.

It is in this latter sense that sermons in the SAC in 1999 were widely assumed to have perlocutionary force (Austin 1962; see also Tambiah 1968). The auralization of biblical words was ascribed performative power through the spiritual immediacy of the uttering. At the same time, however, this performativity did not preclude a referential 'interpretation' of the words being uttered. In the case of the sermon held on 23 May 1999, for example, described above, Kiran's preaching was intended, and widely considered, to have had a spiritual impact on the congregation. His utterances thus constituted a kind of socio-religious action. Nevertheless, the spiritual aspect did not prevent the listeners from simultaneously trying to grasp the substantive message (*bupanduluzi*). As I became aware after the service, members of the congregation discussed the propositional contents of Kiran's sermon in great detail.

But there is another crucial point concerning the idea of 'sediments of the spirit': they were claimed to represent only fragments, not the totality of the Holy Spirit. This aspect is closely linked to processes of self-authorization through scriptural mediation. Being fragments, the 'sediments of the spirit' were not assumed to be sufficient by themselves for a person to acquire full spirituality. Even more so, they were said to provoke a longing for further contact with sermons that conveyed spirituality and to require such contacts if they were to be revived. Alluding to another metaphor, some of my informants explained that 'sediments of the spirit' are like a dried-up river bed, which throughout most of the year simply left an empty mark in the landscape that needed to be filled with vitalising water. They went on to explain that these river beds were a good thing, because they provided somewhere to wait for the water. And sometimes, if one were lucky, water could even be found beneath the dried-out sand at the bottom. The 'sediments of the spirit' are thus both a symbol of hope and a place of potential fulfilment. All the same, they were not sufficient by themselves but required 'water', that is, repeated exposure to the inspired sermons of the church elders. These associations make it clear that the notion of spiritual fragments actually developed in a context in which one case of spiritual 'infusion' was claimed to require repeated linkage to succeeding acts of a similar kind.

The prevailing idea of scriptural mediation in the Spirit Apostolic Church can be summarized as follows. A preacher sets the biblical words into motion by freeing them from their materiality and instilling them with his spiritual power. His utterances then enter the congregation, where they settle down like 'sediments of the spirit'. These spiritual fragments in turn imply a demand for further inspired preaching if they are to be revived.

In this way, the discourse concerning 'sediments of the spirit' framed the continuous reproduction of an interactional network that placed the mediation of the church elders at its centre. Being seen as closely associated with the power of the Holy Spirit, the church elders cultivated a two-pronged performance in which the Scriptures and the congregation were connected. The Bible was an essential but, in itself, insufficient condition for scriptural practice. Only when it had been orally infused with the power of the Holy Spirit could it develop its empowering spiritual potential. And only when it was verbally and repeatedly exposed to such inspired preaching would the laity be able to receive 'sediments of the spirits', which were not to be equated with the 'deposit' of merely propositional messages.

We should recall in this context that the metaphor of a river bed was used in respect to both the 'sediments of the spirit' and the Bible. Both of these, the Scripture and the active members of the church, were accordingly held to have the potential to be spiritually connected and fulfilled through the mediation of the church elders. Taken together, the church elders thus strove to establish and maintain their religious authority, first, by commingling orality and literacy, and secondly, by providing fragments of a scripturally bound spirituality, which had to be continuously reproduced through interactional connections in which they themselves were the obligatory passage points.

The theme of these connections made by means of written materials will be taken up again in the next chapter, which attempts to trace the prevailing literacy practices of two denominations in my research area that crucially depended on printed and spatially distributed written materials. This will provide an interesting basis for a comparison with the Pentecostal-charismatic reading practices that have been discussed so far.

Notes

1. On the relationship between orality and literacy in sermons, see also Besnier (1991, 1994, 1995), Heath (1983: 201–11).
2. In other more mundane contexts, *kuzuzikizya* also refers to fulfilling a promise. In a similar vein, S. Noakes (1993) interprets St Luke's scene of reading as reflecting a procedure in which Jesus established his religious authority by establishing a particular way of reading the Old Testament, which he was able to do by presenting himself as the fulfilment of earlier prophecies: 'And he said to them: "Today this scripture has been fulfilled in your hearing"' (Luke 4:21).
3. Similar overlaps are described in N. Besnier's intriguing examination of sermons on Nukulaelae atoll, where 'intonation does not necessarily distinguish biblical quotes from the preacher's comments and elaborations' (1994: 357) so that 'the voice of the preacher and the voice of divine authority are essentially blurred' (ibid.).
4. A comparable, though much more modernist, idea has been expressed by a follower of the South African prophet Paulo Nzuza: 'The Bible line is like a railway line, and the Spirit is the engine' (cited in Sundkler 1976: 99).
5. This represents the adoption of a proverb, which to some extent departs from its usual interpretation in the area of my research. E. Wendtland and S. Hachibamba give the following translation and explanation: 'A river that does not wind [in its course] does not have steep banks (i.e., a person who is not prepared to receive, and act upon, good advice often goes astray / is unstable)' (2000: 540). The adoption of the proverb by members of the SAC, which formed the basis for my translation above, has two main elements: a) it was the Bible that was seen as 'giving advice' and whose neglect would 'lead astray'; b) the term *mukoba* was explained as denoting not 'steep banks' but a certain type of organic material that settles on the steep banks of a winding river.

Chapter 11

Missions in Writing

Exploiting the potential of the newly invented printing press, the Protestant reformation movements of the sixteenth century set new standards for Christianity as a 'religion of the book'. According to Elizabeth Eisenstein, the symbiosis of religious agencies, discourses and printed matter not only enhanced a hitherto unknown spatial spread of religious ideas, it also created novel organizational forms that revolved around the production, distribution and consumption of an ever-increasing output of typographical letters. 'Within a few generations', Eisenstein points out, 'the gap between Protestant and Catholic had widened sufficiently to give rise to contrasting literary cultures and lifestyles' (1979: 312; see also Edwards 1994). Putting the words 'cultures' and 'lifestyles' into the plural thus seems advisable even beyond the division between Protestant and Catholic. The increased availability of vernacular Bible translations, the controversies called forth by editions of older theological and philosophical texts, and the simultaneous evolution of theological disputes through pamphlets and printed books were accompanied by a growing diversification in Christian communities, which, among other things, developed a variety of 'literacy cultures'.

The use of writings for Christian teachings was certainly not newly created by print culture: the Pauline Epistles represent the prime example of early Christian encouragement and instruction through literacy. Yet, since these letters were canonized and reprinted in innumerable copies of the Scriptures, later missionary societies made sure that they would not only reach Corinth or Ephesus but also the rest of the world. Wherever such societies came to settle, the Bible represented an indispensable item in the missionaries' baggage, and organizations in the home countries of the missions, like the British and Foreign Bible Society, endeavoured to supply as many cheap copies of the Scriptures as possible (Howsam 1991; Schaaf 1994).

However, when looking at the scholarly literature on mission societies, it becomes evident that the role of printed publications for the worldwide spread of these societies and the processes of their reception in local religious settings have up to now not been addressed sufficiently. Scholars from different disciplines and theoretical backgrounds agree that communication media are enablers of, and powerful agents in, transformations that, on an increasingly global scale, affect how people see themselves and others, make meaning and act in the world. Yet, most of the recent literature on global media and media consumption in a globalizing world refers to electronic and broadcast media, like television, radio and the Internet. Thus, surprisingly, there is a certain tendency among the literati of global academia to disregard the medium of the printed word, despite the fact that in many domains and regions of the world 'glocalization' (Robertson 1995) is mediated through reading and writing.[1]

This neglect has arisen possibly because, following Benedict Anderson, many contemporary social scientists associate print with the historical rise of nationalism and thus with the demarcation of spatially bounded national territories. In his widely acclaimed book *Imagined Communities: Reflections on the Origin and Spread of Nationalism*, first published in 1983, Anderson argues that 'nationality, or, as one might prefer to put it in view of that word's multiple significations, nation-ness, as well as nationalism' (2006: 4), was made possible, among other things, by print capitalism, in which novels and newspapers 'provided a technical means for 're-presenting' the *kind* of imagined community that is the nation' (2006: 25). For Anderson, communication through print media accordingly represents an essential precondition for 'nation-ness' (see also Wogan 2001).

But empirical cases like the Watch Tower Bible and Tract Society of Pennsylvania (hereafter referred to as 'Jehovah's Witnesses') – with which, among other things, this chapter is concerned – indicate that the dissemination and consumption of printed writings in a multiplicity of languages has long been a thoroughly globalized phenomenon. Having started publishing in the late nineteenth century, the Jehovah's Witnesses nowadays translate their publications into 410 languages, many of which are vernacular languages whose usage is not confined to one nation-state and that do not represent national 'official languages'. Disregarding this denomination's other publications, the average twice-monthly printing of the Jehovah's Witnesses' two main periodicals (*Watchtower* and *Awake*) alone amounts to almost 50 million copies distributed worldwide. Because of this extensive circulation, as well as the contents of these periodicals – which can be said to raise awareness of 'global interconnectedness' by regularly addressing issues from all around the world – the publications of the Jehovah's Witnesses represent an example of what, in a modification of Anderson's term 'print nationalism', might be called 'print globalization'.

Similar to 'print nationalism', in the kind of print globalization addressed here, the printed word helps to construct 'imagined communities' in that members of globally active Christian denominations 'will never know most of their fellow-members, meet them, or even hear of them, yet in the minds of each lives ... the image of their communion' (Anderson 2006: 6). In contrast to Anderson's theory, however, this imagined (global) communion takes the form of socio-religious networks that cut across national boundaries and, without being based on a shared 'sacred language' (cf. Anderson 2006: 12–19), therefore evolve a connectivity that differs from how 'print nationalism' is usually described.

Against this background, in this chapter I argue that churches engaged in the global distribution of religious print media seek to ensure a homogenous interpretation of their publications by standardizing literacy practices. By making their publications 'obligatory passage points' (Callon 1986) for socio-religious advancement and determining particular ways of dealing with them, the leaders of these churches attempt to establish power over the laity. At the same time, the question of whether such regulations concerning literacy practices are adhered to or not depends on whether those subject to them consider them to facilitate personal socio-religious empowerment.[2] Once successfully established, therefore, networks created through religious print media evolve as a twofold process where the construction of power by media producers and distributors and their audiences' seeking of socio-religious empowerment form an integrated whole. In this trajectory, literacy practices bridge local and global realms by enabling extensive religious networking based on the shared use of print media.

Literacy Networking

Nowadays, apart from the Bible, most globally active churches disseminate a wide range of additional publications in the form of hymn books, devotional tracts, circulars, wall calendars with prayers, denominational magazines, catechumen instructions, etc. Taken together, these widely dispersed publications form a certain crisscrossing layer of what Arjun Appadurai calls 'mediascapes' (1990: 9). Some of them can be found in even the remotest parts of the world without there being any organizational connection to a particular church's headquarters. On the whole, however, the publishing activities of these churches tend to be linked to the hope that they might provide an incentive to join that particular religious community. From the perspective of these churches, it is certainly salutary to read their publications even if one is not associated with the church, but it seems still more beneficial if such reading takes place in the context of a shared religious practice. The freewheeling use of denominational publications by people who are not linked organizationally to a particular church might even lead to criticism from the official headquarters: the use of Watchtower literature by early African Christian movements in Northern Rhodesia, mentioned in a previous chapter, which were otherwise uncontrolled by the American Watchtower Bible and Tract Society, was forcefully rejected by official church representatives as misleading because it was not informed by proper instruction (Fields 1985).

Let me dwell on this point for a moment. In this case, the denominational magazines and booklets, ostensibly printed and disseminated in order to explain the Bible seem – astonishingly enough – to be in need of explanation themselves. 'Proper instruction' might mean spiritual guidance or theological advice. But it might also refer to the question of *how* the respective publications are to be used within the religious practice. Taking the 'literacy cultures' referred to above to be 'literacy practices', it can be argued that the proliferation of a globally active church crucially depends on its success in establishing obligatory ways of dealing with its publications. This is not to under-emphasize the importance of other features of these organizations' activities or the (potential) influence of the propositional contents of the published works. Rather, the aim is to stress a hitherto rather neglected aspect of Christian churches as global organizations: when distributing and exploiting publications to supplement the Bible or to explain the church's doctrines and rules, the churches on the one hand propagate authoritative interpretations of the propositional contents, while on the other hand, also having to make sure that their publications are integrated into their communal religious practice. Only when they manage to institute more or less compulsory literacy practices do publications develop a centripetal effect among the members of the church. It is thus not enough to distribute publications: if they are to stabilize or increase the denominational network, their circulation has to be accompanied by regulations on how to use them. Are they to be read alone or in a group? If interactional reading is the aim, what marks the internal social differentiations within the group? What is the proper relationship between denominational publications and the Bible? And is each publication to be read as a whole, or are they rather reference books to be consulted sporadically?

Although these questions are certainly not exhaustive, they can give some idea of what might define denominational literacy practices. Since they coordinate organizational means, denominational literacy practices partake in the construction of the churches' complex organizations. Without having to resort to presumptions of an all-pervading and homogenous belief system within the particular church or to ground the analysis on a sketch of an allegedly fixed organizational structure, the focus on denominational literacy practices thus promises to provide an interesting clue concerning what binds the different congregations of a church located in various parts of the world together: Globally active churches evolve particular ways of distributing and allocating their publications and, most importantly, construct extensive networks of literacy practices that form a consolidating framework for religious practice, even when local discrepancies can be detected in the interpretation of otherwise shared denominational texts.

This theme will be elaborated in analysing the following case studies. Using the example of two congregations in southern Zambia, that is, 'endpoints' of denominational literacy networks, I shall examine and compare how denominational publications are incorporated into the religious practice of the New Apostolic Church (*Neuapostolische Kirche*), as well as by Jehovah's Witnesses. By describing the particular literacy practices that are applied to the respective publications, it can be shown how their appropriate use is constructed to form an 'obligatory passage point' for spiritual and social progress within these two churches. My analysis will have to refrain from describing local textual interpretations or discussing concrete social contexts of textual reception, and will concentrate rather on the social interactions and procedures that revolve around denominational publications as exemplified by the *Watchtower* magazine among Jehovah's Witnesses and by the 'circulars' of the New Apostolic Church.

The Jehovah's Witnesses: Questions and Answers

Among the Jehovah's Witnesses in Sinazeze, most interactions revolved around the church's magazines, pamphlets and books.[3] The members of the church purchased these reading materials on a regular basis and could be seen openly reading the pamphlets. Moreover, to some extent the church's services were characterized by practices that resembled those of a school in that some sequences during the liturgical routine were devoted to the communal reading of the monthly magazine, *Watchtower*.

This reading, however, meant neither privately studying nor publicly reciting the magazine. Rather, the reading was graded into a highly structured form of questions and answers: the church's headquarters prescribed a particular chapter of the magazine for each week to be read during services (cf. Keller 2005, 2006). Most of the members present during the service were in possession of a current copy of *Watchtower* and readily opened it at a particular point in the proceedings. Then one of the church elders would start posing to the congregation the questions that were arranged at the bottom of the particular page in the form of footnotes. These questions referred to the contents of the chapter under discussion and were gradually answered by the members of the church, who scanned the pages of the magazine to find the right answer. If an answer was not considered correct by the church elder, he briefly corrected it and then handed the question over to the next member until finally the correct answer was given and the congregation proceeded to the next question.[4]

Describing the complete course of services conducted by the Jehovah's Witnesses would exceed the scope of this chapter. As it is, however, the procedures described so far provide some interesting clues to other literary practices within this denomination. As mentioned above, the Jehovah's Witnesses purchased and read the magazines in their everyday lives. The actual process of this private reading usually developed in accordance with the procedures carried out during the services. Whenever I was able to observe the private reading practice of a Jehovah's Witness, comprehension of the *Watchtower* magazine began by reading the questions. Then the reader would go through the text and, using a pen, underline those passages of the chapter that seemed to contain the right answers. It was only then that the reader would open the Bible to read those verses that were given in the cross references in the magazine.

Starting with the questions, proceeding to the text of the magazine and finally looking at the Bible itself forms a sequence that represents a particular hermeneutical practice aiming at the apprehension of divine truth. Understanding the Bible was pre-structured by the questions and answers given in the magazine.[5] Becoming a Jehovah's Witness and attaining socio-religious empowerment through this church thus meant learning how to proceed in one's reading, as well as, to a certain extent, how to make productive use of markings for orientation in a text.

Underlining passages in the *Watchtower* magazine helped members display their knowledge during the services' question-and-answer sessions. This acquaintance with the correct usage of magazines, pamphlets and books also proved to be of the greatest importance with respect to other activities undertaken by Jehovah's Witnesses. When 'going into the field', that is, when approaching non-members in order to win them over to the church, after a short prelude of purely verbal exchange, interaction was supposed to revolve around the church's written materials as soon as possible. Even the introductory words of the evangelists frequently started with a reference to writings. When a Jehovah's Witness who belonged to the congregation in Sinazeze conducted a field ministry in May 1999, he approached neighbouring villagers by asking, 'Do you believe in the Bible?' He explained to me that the question, 'Do you believe in God?' might provoke unintended controversies and opposition, whereas his own question would be more likely to produce a positive response.

Creating an interest in the Jehovah's Witnesses meant interesting people in its publications. In this way, an attempt was made to build up relationships that centred on communal preoccupations with the questions and answers as formulated by the church's headquarters and on a shared practice of how to come up with answers by means of particular textual procedures. By thus constructing a network of particular literacy practices, the Jehovah's Witnesses crucially relied on the accessibility of their written materials. It was the extent of circulation of these materials and of the interactions that revolved around them that defined the boundary of the church. Although the Bible was assigned the status of supreme authority, and although all the magazines ultimately dealt with Biblical issues, it was the church's books, magazines and tracts that were actually given priority in religious practice.

One of their most distinctive characteristics is the fact that the Jehovah's Witnesses' publications can be seen as an attempt to anticipate all imaginable questions.[6] Limiting the range of possible questions means indirectly defining those that are permitted. Seeking socio-religious empowerment by becoming a Jehovah's Witness thus entailed an admission that the headquarters of the church is the only body that can ask the right questions. Moreover, when proceeding from these questions to the process of looking for answers within a particular publication, actual hermeneutic practice is continually linked to the publication. The answers have to be underlined in the text; they cannot be found anywhere outside it. This ultimately creates a need to refer back to the publication constantly.

The New Apostolic Church: Mediation via Circulars

Other churches strongly disapproved of such widespread use of devotional publications. The New Apostolic Church was an interesting example of a church that also developed its religious activities with reference to written materials from its headquarters, while in the process stressing a completely different, because more restricted, literary practice.[7]

During the services of the New Apostolic Church, the congregation used no denominational publications. The ordinary members were even discouraged from bringing their Bibles into the church. They were told by the church elders that reading or consulting the Bible during the services would distract them from the sermons. Thus many members scribbled the numbers of the Bible chapters and verses read out during the service on small pieces of paper, so that they could read these passages later at home. Use of the Bible during services was therefore confined to the church elders, thus creating a difference between the public mediation of the Scriptures and the practice of private and devotional reading.

Yet, in the course of the services the church elders made extensive use of circulars published by the denominational headquarters in Switzerland that provided guidelines concerning which scriptural passages should be preached, when and how, for the whole world. These circulars were handed down from the Zambian headquarters in Lusaka via a system of personal networks and were treated in an almost conspiratorial manner upon reaching their destination at Sinazeze. Only the church elders had access to these papers, and I never came across an ordinary member who had had an opportunity to read one of the current circulars.[8]

There was an elaborate hierarchy of reference regarding these circulars in the services of the New Apostolic Church. The sermons followed a chronological order in which the church elder of highest rank preached first. During the services I attended, this first sermon routinely linked all propositions to the current circular, which was also ostensibly displayed in front of the congregation. The substantiating remarks and interpretations of the preacher and the references to the Bible were thus tied to the stipulations found in, and presentation of, the circular. All the following subordinate preachers, however, referred less to the circular than to the propositions that had been made in the preceding sermons. Referentiality therefore evolved in several steps. It started with the first preacher's explicit reference to the circular and his substantiations, which to some extent transcended the circular by voicing particular readings of it. Then it continued with subsequent sermons, during which transcending substantiations – often explicitly quoting previous preachers – were adopted and made the starting point for further elaborations.

Here, the circular represented a highly treasured source of knowledge and innovation, acquiring its exceptional status from the very fact that it was not accessible to ordinary members, even though it was simultaneously linked to a network of a higher order that promised socio-religious empowerment. By constructing a hierarchy of referentiality, different and possibly antithetical readings of the denominational guidelines were prevented. All sermons were more or less linked to the circular. The sermon of the first preacher exemplified this connection most directly and explicitly, as it oscillated between agreement with the circular and interpretative or biblical annotations. The sermons of the subsequent preachers, on the other hand, were linked to the circular in so far as they definitely reflected the earlier sermons. Here, oscillations developed between agreements with authoritative readings of the circular and further interpretative annotations.

Though access to its publications was highly restricted, the New Apostolic Church thus also represented a church in which additional writings came to inform religious practice to such an extent that use of these writings amounted to an obligatory passage point for anyone who wanted to acquire a religiously empowering understanding of the Bible or an advanced position within the Church.

Supplements as 'Obligatory Passage Points'

What these two case studies have in common is the fact that their scriptural practices situate additional written materials in the space between the congregation and the Bible. These materials were reckoned to be merely subsidiary to the Holy Writ, since in both churches the Bible was considered to be the ultimate source of Christian truth. Yet, by situating denominational publications as 'obligatory passage points' in reaching a proper understanding of the Bible, the Bible became what these publications made of it. Among the Jehovah's Witnesses, pre-set questions and subsequent cross references to the Bible came to define the perspective of the members' reading and thus moderated particular actualizations of the Scripture.[9] In the New Apostolic Church, on the other hand, the actualization of biblical passages was accomplished by preachers using denominational circulars that determined authoritative selections and readings.

In both cases, the Bible to some extent became a promise that was perpetually being postponed, one in which the additional publications added up to small advances in the possibly unending passage to fulfilment. This gesture of postponement to some extent resulted from the intervals between the denominational publications. The magazines and circulars periodically introduced novelties to the local congregation, who therefore, in endeavouring to be socio-religiously empowered through such publications, continually had to keep up with new developments. Each new publication or circular showed participants that there was still much to learn on one's way to a proper understanding of the Bible. Among the Jehovah's Witnesses, the movement from question to answer was revelatory. As it was the headquarters of the movement that both posed the questions and simultaneously provided the answers, the members of the church were repeatedly placed in a position of ignorance when faced with the questions contained in a new publication. And, in being instructed in the 'right' answers afterwards, this provision came close to being an act of revelation that was contained in the publications and mediated authoritatively by the church elders during the services.

But the periodicity of the publications also suggested that spiritual authority in the New Apostolic Church and among the Jehovah's Witnesses developed in the form of a timely structured continuity: novel publications and circulars could be expected each week or month. Such regularity marked a difference from the Pentecostal-charismatic churches in my research area, where spiritual revelations could not be anticipated: they could occur spontaneously at any time.

As might be expected from the foregoing, the likelihood of achieving religious authority within these two churches depended crucially on acquiring expertise in dealing with their respective publications. Given the high level of availability of most of its magazines and pamphlets, the literacy practice of the Jehovah's Witnesses developed on a participatory basis, in which it was compulsory for all the members to achieve a certain familiarity with the church's written materials. After some time, neophytes in the congregation in Sinazeze had to undergo an examination, during which they were asked questions about a denominational book they had been given to read. If they failed to answer, they were not baptized. Since, therefore, the particular hermeneutic practice to some extent took the form of a shared stock of knowledge among the participants, this practice was a fundamental but in the end insufficient basis for claims to religious authority. Rather, achieving a prominent position in the church entailed a need to outbid others in one's involvement with the publications. Only when one had worked through the 'lessons' in more detail than others and minutely followed up cross references to the Bible and to other publications of the Jehovah's Witnesses was one able to display the degree of knowledge during the meetings of the church that was essential if one was to be recommended by the established church elders for promotion within the hierarchy.

Being 'ahead of others' was thus based on a prolonged, private, studious preoccupation with the church's publications. Moreover, one's status within the congregation also depended on one's efforts at evangelization. Field ministry was a highly valued activity, and each instance of it was carefully recorded in special lists that were later sent to the national headquarters in Lusaka, where they were incorporated into the yearly statistics of the church. As these evangelizations were crucially concerned to distribute denominational publications, achieving a distinguished position within the church thus presupposed success in expanding the denomination's scriptural network.

In contrast to this, the literacy practice of the New Apostolic Church was characterized by the highly restricted access to denominational guidelines, as well as by a marked distinction between public and private scriptural readings. The exclusion of Bibles from the laity during services and the fact that the circulars were only accessible to church elders both encouraged the development of religious settings that located the elders at the centre of any legitimate public use of the written materials. This use, however, did not necessitate a protracted occupation with the circulars. Whereas, among the Jehovah's Witnesses, a superior religious status could only be reached by outstripping others through exceptionally intense private studies, the restriction of access to the circulars in the New Apostolic Church allowed the elders to hold relatively non-competitive positions. Because the elders monopolized the circulars, there was no need for them to defend their readings against possible objections from the laity. For the ordinary members, reading the Bible privately was assumed to be of importance. Yet, having studied the Bible in this way did not decisively increase the chance of attaining a superior position within the church. As the only admissible interpretation of the Bible was that voiced within the public church services and mediated by the circulars, a private reading could never lead to a superior understanding of the Scripture itself. To be mediated properly within the New Apostolic Church, the Bible had to be linked to an authoritative reading of the circulars. Thus, the evolution of religious authority was ultimately bound to those instances in which the circulars were referred to publicly. Consequently becoming a church elder in the New Apostolic Church crucially implied learning how to reproduce the above-mentioned system of referentiality during the services. One's overall status within the church defined whether one was permitted to read the current circulars and how directly one was allowed to relate to them publicly.

Increases in religious expertise took the form of a process of apprehending how to ornament the superior church elders' readings of the circulars. Only when one became skilled in this type of referentiality was one allowed to refer directly to the circulars, which in their turn were held to be indispensable for a proper understanding of the Bible.

Besides their textual expertise, the superior status of the church elders in both churches was also based on the fact that it was they who represented the logistical connections of the local community with the wider denominational sphere. In Sinazeze, the publications of the Jehovah's Witnesses were only available in the small shop of one of the main elders of the congregation, so that each member had to go there regularly. The church elders could therefore identify who actually bought the publications. And, when returning from visits to the national headquarters in Lusaka or to denominational meetings in other parts of Zambia, the leaders of the congregation occasionally introduced newly released publications into the area. These publications were then openly displayed and talked about in a highly appreciative manner. For members of the congregation, in turn, the fact that such denominational publications originated from a place far away had a decisive influence on how they were perceived. The USA, where the world headquarters of the Watch Tower Bible and Tract Society of Pennsylvania are situated, for these members being a vague and almost mysterious idea, the perception of the nebulous yet appreciated spatial origin of the publications to a certain extent converged with local notions of indefinite yet highly valued transcendence, the latter notion used in the sense of a condition of being characterized by divine 'sublimeness' that remains unknowable to ordinary human beings.[10]

In the New Apostolic Church, the church elders' position as the source of denominational knowledge in the form of the circulars went beyond even the practices seen among the Jehovah's Witnesses. Ordinary members usually never had a chance to read the circulars, which actually had a status that paralleled the Pauline Epistles of the New Testament: the Apostle Paul sent letters to distant congregations in order to spread Christian instruction and encouragement. And since the overall leader of the New Apostolic Church, at present the Chief Apostle Wilhelm Leber in the Swiss headquarters, was regarded as the successor of the New Testament Apostles, his directives – for example, in the form of circulars – were compared to these early epistles.[11] The system of referentiality to the circulars outlined above thus restaged the historical passage of Christian messages that started with the Apostles. The pronouncements of the Chief Apostle were handed down within a highly structured hierarchy (cf. Gifford 1998: 196) in which each point in this chain of translation derived its authenticity and authorization by referring to those superior to him. The personalized actualization of circulars by local church elders thus represented the concretization of a religious righteousness that was ultimately linked to the early church fathers. Here, the idea of 'transcendence' converged not only with notions of 'global space', but also with a temporal *longue durée*.

Enablement through Denominational Publications

In this chapter, I have shown that the dissemination of denominational publications by globally active churches is associated with the determination of particular practices concerning how they should be dealt with. The comparison between the Jehovah's Witnesses and the New Apostolic Church showed that, in what I call print globalization, the wide availability of such publications is not a prerequisite for them to have an impact on local audiences. The circulars of the New Apostolic Church shape the religious practice of this church, even though – or maybe precisely because – their accessibility is highly restricted.

By linking the congregations to networks of a higher order in the global realm, the publications of both churches come to represent an empowering source of religious truths in the local sphere. For members, learning how to engage with them promises not only spiritual advancement but also promotion within the church hierarchy. The literacy practices therefore form an essential cornerstone in the organization of these churches. In order to achieve homogeneity in the interpretation of their publications and, by extension, the Bible, both churches encourage their members to follow certain literacy practices. The standardizations of modes of reading consequently represent attempts to construct 'interpretative communities' (Fish 1980) authoritatively at a distance. In this sense, the Jehovah's Witnesses can be described as a widely branching network of particular hermeneutic procedures that is sustained and extended by circulating publications and by instructing neophytes how to engage with them. The New Apostolic Church, on the other hand, is characterized by a literacy practice based on restricted access to the church's doctrinal guidelines; here, an interactional network is constructed in which the circulars are situated as a detached but highly valued vanishing point for any aspirations to increased religiosity or promotion within the church. The circulars are made present in the local sphere through a perpetual system of referentiality.

These two types of literacy practice have in common the fact that they link the respective local congregations to highly venerated, but otherwise rather aloof headquarters. However, the particular modes of such connections differ crucially. Whereas the Jehovah's Witnesses of Sinazeze construct these connections through congruence in literacy methods, the members of the New Apostolic Church are connected to their headquarters through chains of referentiality in the form of textual quotations. Here, therefore, we find two different attempts by local religious participants to keep up with what they consider to be a promising perspective in terms of life improvement.

Making the publications an obligatory passage point for any advancement within the respective church simultaneously meets local *and* wider organizational requirements in processes of authorization. For the denominational organization in general, the publications guarantee its headquarters a presence in different parts of the world. But the concrete impact of the publications depends on the readiness of local participants to become involved with them in a manner that is always tied to their respective headquarters. In the final analysis, local aspirations for religious leadership form an essential basis for the status of the publications. Here, a twofold gesture can be observed. On the one hand, the church elders base their authority on particular uses of the publications and on efforts to position themselves as obligatory passage points in the circulation and comprehension of the publications. On the other hand, this dependence on publications continually gives rise to public assurances that these denominational publications are of a superior religious status. If the authority of the church elders is to be backed up by the use of written materials, the authority of these materials must be stabilized too. The success of the denominational publications of a globalized church thus depends on their acceptance by local people as a means of personal socio-religious empowerment.

There is one final point to be made here, which links up with my observations in Chapter 7 concerning 'multi-literate' competences. From the perspective of the laity, such denominational networking through literacy practices does not have to be exclusive: in my area of research, most members of the Jehovah's Witnesses and the New Apostolic Church do have both knowledge and experience of other denominations and 'traditional' religious practices. Occasionally visiting other churches or *bang'anga* is nothing unusual, especially where the treatment of illnesses is concerned. And since these other religious experts pursue literacy practices that differ from those of the New Apostolic Church and the Jehovah's Witnesses, most members of the two denominations being analysed here are simultaneously acquainted with a range of alternative literacy practices. Yet, this does not inevitably subvert the particular literacy practice of the church one normally attends. As long as the religious practice of a church continues to be based on an authoritatively marked and shared literacy practice, possible alternatives will run placidly alongside it. All the same, these alternatives might be conjured up by the participants according to context and necessity. Only when literacy practices come to be questioned *within* the denominational setting do the alternatives start to undermine that particular form of literacy networking. Any interruption to the chain of referentiality in the New Apostolic Church or, among the Jehovah's Witnesses, an interrogation of the headquarters' right to pose questions and answers would thus undoubtedly mean exiting that particular literacy network connecting the local and global realms.

There are pronounced differences between the literacy practices described above and those examined previously. In contrast to the Pentecostal-charismatic churches, for example, which basically subscribed to the idea of empowerment through the Holy Spirit, the notion of empowerment in the local branches of globally active churches, such as the Jehovah's Witnesses and the New Apostolic Church, mostly related to their respective denominational publications. The comparison between these religious literacies in the next chapter can thus help us add some important analytical points to the general discussion of 'religions of the book'.

Notes

1. Exceptions to this are Isabel Hofmeyr's (2004, 2005) fascinating analysis of the transnational circulation of John Bunyan's book *The Pilgrim's Progress* and studies in which the production of newspapers is addressed in the context of globalization, such as U. Hannerz's *Foreign News: Exploring the World of Foreign Correspondents* (2004) and M. Pedelty's *War Stories: The Culture of Foreign Correspondents* (1995).
2. Since, in my case studies below, the two prevailing dimensions of empowerment – increased participation in encompassing religious truth and/or of promotion within the church hierarchy – cannot be treated separately from each other, I use the term 'socio-religious' when referring to church members' overall striving for empowerment.
3. As already mentioned, writing, printing and disseminating Christian literature, as well as pursuing religious practices that revolve around the study of such literature, have always been characteristic features of the Jehovah's Witnesses since the founding of this American denomination in the nineteenth century (cf. Beckford 1975; Curry 1992; Holden 2002; Penton 1985). At present, the Jehovah's Witnesses have a membership of more than 15 million and congregations in 235 countries. For the Jehovah's Witnesses in Zambia, see Cunnison (1951), Epstein (1986), Long (1968). This denomination has been active in my area of research since 1969; in mid-1999, the services of the Jehovah's Witnesses in Sinazeze were attended by congregations of about 80 to 120, of whom 35 had been baptized.
4. For a similar description of these procedures, see Bayerl (2000: 54).
5. Structuring texts in the form of 'questions-and-answers' was already known in early Greek philosophy and has become a standard form of written religious instruction among innumerable Western denominations. Martin Luther's *Small Catechism* is an example of such structuring in early European print culture.
6. A good example of this is the denomination's book *Reasoning from the Scriptures* (New York: Watchtower Bible and Tract Society of Pennsylvania; 1989), which comprises 438 pages of possible questions and recommendations concerning how to answer them.
7. The New Apostolic Church originated in nineteenth-century England (Burklin 1978; Fincke 1999; Obst 1996). With a current membership of more than 10 million, it has established congregations in 184 countries and therefore represents one of the largest international religious bodies worldwide. The first southern African congregation north of the Zambezi was established in the mid-1920s. According to Henkel (1989), it represented the fourth largest denomination in Zambia in 1989. In contrast to the Jehovah's Witnesses, however, the history of this denomination has not yet been dealt with adequately. For a short historical overview of its development in Zambia, see Henkel (1989: 86). The congregation of the New Apostolic Church in Sinazeze was started in 1975 by a local businessman. In mid-1999 this congregation comprised about 500 registered members, attendance at the Sunday services typically being between 200 and 350.
8. An anthology of circulars by the New Apostolic Church for the year 1994 has a paragraph entitled 'How to use the year-book', in which one can read: 'Dear brothers, this book is exclusively for the ministers of the New Apostolic Church. Please read the articles carefully at home. You are not to read from this book during the services. The 'Word of Life year-book' remains the property of the New Apostolic Church and must be returned on request. The articles in this book cover a whole year; the priestly ministries are to base the sermons on the texts issued by the chief apostle' (*Word of Life for Missionary Areas, III.*; Zürich: Verlag Friedrich Bischoff; 1994: 4).
9. In a booklet called K*nowledge That Leads to Everlasting Life* (New York: Watchtower Bible and Tract Society of Pennsylvania; 1995: 12–13), one can read, for example: 'The Bible fills all our needs for wise direction. True, many are overwhelmed when they first look through the Bible. It is a big book, and some portions of it are not easy to understand. But if you were given a legal document outlining what you had to do in order to receive a valuable inheritance, would you not take the time to study it carefully? If you found certain parts of

the document hard to understand, likely you would get the help of someone experienced in such matters. Why not approach the Bible with a similar attitude? (Acts 17:11) More is at stake than a material inheritance. As we learned in the previous chapter, the knowledge of God can lead to everlasting life'. At the bottom of the same page, the following question is raised regarding this paragraph: 'How should we approach a study of the Bible?'

10. A similar appreciation of non-local religious knowledge among the Gwembe Tonga can be found in 'traditional' religious forms, where non-local religious experts are frequently preferred to those living in the vicinity (cf. Colson 1966b: 222). For an interpretation of 'missions in Africa as sites for inventing "the world"', see Hofmeyr (2005).

11. The Internet homepage of the New Apostolic Church introduces the Chief Apostle as follows: 'Since Pentecost 2005, Wilhelm Leber has been the chief apostle of the New Apostolic Church. As such he leads the Church from its headoffices in Zurich, Switzerland. Wilhelm Leber is a German national, and the eighth chief apostle since the founding of the Church. *His position can be compared to the one Peter had 2,000 years ago in the circle of the apostles*' (New Apostolic Church International; 'Structures and Ministries'; Retrieved 20 August 2007 from http://www.nak.org/en/about-the-nac/structures-ministries/; my italics).

Chapter 12

Enablements to Literacy

As has become clear in the preceding chapters, the difference between African-initiated Pentecostal-charismatic churches, as discussed using the example of the Spirit Apostolic Church, and churches with headquarters in a Western country, such as the Jehovah's Witnesses and the New Apostolic Church (*Neuapostolische Kirche*), is not a difference between churches in which writings are used and those in which they are absent: it is not, in other words, a contrast between 'literate' and 'oral' cultures. Instead, both types of church have in common the fact that they make objects of writing a quintessential component in chains of socio-religious interaction that are continuously reproduced, in this way establishing complex relational configurations between church elders, laity, religious writings and God. Moreover, by constituting hierarchies and dependencies while also being seen as a means of socio-religious life-improvement, these chains of interaction simultaneously serve the self-authorization of the church leaders and the empowerment of the laity.

Nevertheless, besides highlighting commonalities, a comparison between the reading practices of these churches also allows us to discern crucial differences. Having the Bible surrounded, commented on and backed up by additional publications, the Jehovah's Witnesses and the New Apostolic Church both construct networks of writings. Writings are connected to one another and simultaneously refer to the originating authority of the Scriptures and to the supplementary materials. Religious progress thus depends on retracing the inscribed textual movements until the reader's understanding reaches a certain point of convergence with the 'intention' of the divine or divinely guided 'author'. In the Pentecostal-charismatic Spirit Apostolic Church, by contrast, such convergence between divine authorship and comprehension through reading is not assumed to require retracing inscribed textual movements. Instead, the Holy Spirit instantaneously blurs the boundary between spiritualized readers and the spiritually authored Scriptures.

Moreover, there is a crucial difference in how supplementary publications are used. Members of the Spirit Apostolic Church study pamphlets and other Christian writings besides the Bible. In contrast to the two other churches, however, such reading is not a communal affair but is generally pursued in an almost clandestine degree of privacy. There is no social networking using supplementary denominational publications. If pamphlets do exert an influence on religious practice, this is mostly concealed or declared officially to be of a spiritual kind; in public, no explicit reference is made to the publications.

Finally, and most importantly for the present chapter, the churches differ in what they consider to be the essential preconditions for a proper Christian reading of texts. For the members of the Spirit Apostolic Church, reading the Bible in a divinely ordained way requires 'enablement' through the Holy Spirit. For the members of the Jehovah's Witnesses and of the New Apostolic Church, by contrast, this 'enablement' is intricately linked to their own denomination's publications.

The difference between these two types of church in my area of research therefore consists, first, in how Christian publications are used and integrated into social interaction and, secondly, in what is considered to be an essential precondition for a divinely ordained reading of religious writings. In order to generalize from these ethnographic findings and develop analytical terms that promise to be useful for studies of 'religions of the book', this chapter discusses the notion of 'enablements to literacy' in greater detail and with regard to two types of reading practices in the Western history of Christianity, which I have chosen because they are 'good to think with'.

Rumination and Scholarship

In the Western history of Christianity, there have been a range of alternative discourses about how the Bible should be approached. In the *Rules of Saint Benedict*, for example, which the founder of Western monasticism drew up around AD 530, and which are still used in some Roman Catholic monasteries today, the monk's daily duties include periods of silent reading: 'Idleness is the enemy of the soul. Therefore, the brothers should have specified periods for manual labour as well as for prayerful reading (*lectione divina*)' (Rules of St. Benedict 48: 1). The *lectio divina* represents a slow perusal of the Bible, which is not undertaken in order to obtain information but rather in order to use the text as a means of accomplishing union with God (Leclerq 1974). As a contemplative praying of the Scriptures, therefore, the *lectio divina* mostly encompasses four subsequent steps: reading (*lectio*), meditation (*meditatio*), prayer (*oratio*) and contemplation (*contemplatio*). Since many readers of this book might be unfamiliar with this particular reading practice, I shall now quote an extended passage in which instructions for practising *lectio divina* are given. And in order to avoid giving the impression that the *lectio divina* is an archaic and extinct phenomenon, these instructions are taken from the contemporary homepage of a Roman Catholic Benedictine monastery in California (USA):

> Choose a text of the Scriptures that you wish to pray. Many Christians use in their daily *lectio divina* one of the readings from the Eucharistic liturgy for the day; others prefer to slowly work through a particular book of the Bible. It makes no difference which text is chosen, as long as one has no set goal of 'covering' a certain amount of text: the amount of text 'covered' is in God's hands, not yours.

Place yourself in a comfortable position and allow yourself to become silent. Some Christians focus for a few moments on their breathing; others have a beloved 'prayer word' or 'prayer phrase' they gently recite in order to become interiorly silent. For some the practice known as 'centering prayer' makes a good, brief introduction to *lectio divina*. Use whatever method is best for you and allow yourself to enjoy silence for a few moments.

Then turn to the text and read it slowly, gently. Savor each portion of the reading, constantly listening for the 'still, small voice' of a word or phrase that somehow says, 'I am for you today'. Do not expect lightening or ecstasies. In *lectio divina* God is teaching us to listen to Him, to seek Him in silence. He does not reach out and grab us; rather, He softly, gently invites us ever more deeply into His presence.

Next take the word or phrase into yourself. Memorize it and slowly repeat it to yourself, allowing it to interact with your inner world of concerns, memories and ideas. Do not be afraid of 'distractions'. Memories or thoughts are simply parts of yourself which, when they rise up during *lectio divina*, are asking to be given to God along with the rest of your inner self. Allow this inner pondering, this rumination, to invite you into dialogue with God.

Then, speak to God. Whether you use words or ideas or images or all three is not important. Interact with God as you would with one who you know loves and accepts you. And give to Him what you have discovered in yourself during your experience of *meditatio*. Experience yourself as the priest that you are. Experience God using the word or phrase that He has given you as a means of blessing, of transforming the ideas and memories, which your pondering on His word has awakened. Give to God what you have found within your heart.

Finally, simply rest in God's embrace. And when He invites you to return to your pondering of His word or to your inner dialogue with Him, do so. Learn to use words when words are helpful, and to let go of words when they no longer are necessary. Rejoice in the knowledge that God is with you in both words and silence, in spiritual activity and inner receptivity.

Sometimes in *lectio divina* one will return several times to the printed text, either to savor the literary context of the word or phrase that God has given, or to seek a new word or phrase to ponder. At other times only a single word or phrase will fill the whole time set aside for *lectio divina*. It is not necessary to anxiously assess the quality of one's *lectio divina* as if one were 'performing' or seeking some goal: *lectio divina* has no goal other than that of being in the presence of God by praying the Scriptures.[1]

These instructions are surely not identical with the practices of *lectio divina* in medieval times, yet they exhibit certain general patterns in respect of 'praying the Scriptures'. They include instructions about the inner attitude and bodily condition that should be sought, the preparations one should make, and how meditative interaction between reader and text should be accomplished. This interaction is defined as interaction with God; the textual procedure of the *lectio divina* accordingly represents a spiritual exercise under the guidance of God. Although the reader is required to 'ponder' and to 'ruminate' on biblical verses, and although God is depicted as 'teaching' the reader, the *lectio divina* does not aim at a cognitive interpretation of the Bible but rather at grasping scriptural meanings on an experiential level.

It is noteworthy that the instructions of the Benedictine monastery in California – similar to medieval treatises on *lectio divina* – state that it 'makes no difference which text is chosen' from the Bible. There are, furthermore, no prescriptions concerning how much textual material should be covered during a *lectio*: a person can linger over just a single word or phrase for an indefinite period of time. Thus, the instructions relate to a particular literacy procedure, irrespective of the actual content of the Bible reading.

The *lectio divina* is assumed to be an aid to spiritual advancement through experiencing the immediacy of God. It thus represents an important means of achieving an outstanding spiritual capacity in the monasteries. In this sense, ascriptions of religious authority are linked to a specific confluence of the Scriptures and particular literacy procedures, as well as to certain prerequisites on the part of the scriptural reader. In its general pattern, the *lectio divina* involved 'reading', 'prayer', 'meditation' and 'contemplation'. Yet even before the first step – the act of reading – certain preparatory activities are named. The Benedictine instructions advise the reader to place himself bodily in a comfortable position, to seek meditative silence, or to recite a prayer. The document can thus be understood as formulating requirements concerning prerequisites and the framing of the *lectio divina*. Whoever strives to undertake a *lectio divina* should, for example, look for solitude and be willing to meet God. Crowded and noisy places, as well as the wish to obtain cognitive knowledge from the Bible, are detrimental to a *lectio divina*. Not even a university degree in theology would give one any advantage over an 'ordinary' practitioner.

In contrast to this, the approach to the Bible advocated by the Dutch scholar, Erasmus of Rotterdam (1466/9–1536), presupposed the existence of libraries. The establishment of schools of theology in the course of the twelfth century had increasingly led to formalizations and systematisations that restricted the spiritual impact that had formerly been experienced in *lectio divina*. About two hundred years later, Erasmus was among the first to ground his exegesis of the Bible on a philological-historical basis. Erasmus' hermeneutic principles sought to determine the meaning of a biblical passage in that the interpreter:

> should weigh not only what is said but also by whom it is said; ... should observe to whom the words were said; ... should see what words were used at what time and on what occasion; ... should note what precedes and what follows the words under consideration, that is, the historical and literary context must be known; ... should have a knowledge of Hebrew, Greek and Latin as well as the disciplines of dialectic, arithmetic, music, natural science, history and especially grammar and rhetoric; ... should handle the

ambiguities and apparent contradictions by textual emendation and knowledge of grammar (Dockery 1995: 13).

There are obviously crucial differences between these hermeneutic principles and the *lectio divina*. Though the two share a perspective that places a solitary and silent form of interaction between reader and scripture at the centre of the hermeneutic practice, the tradition of *lectio divina* emphasizes the experiential and mystical dimensions, whereas Erasmus stresses an intellectually and critically based approach. The *lectio divina* represents a practice that, in the course of beholding the Scripture, locates the reader outside worldly time and space. It thus aims at the apprehension of the spiritual (i.e., allegorical) senses of the Bible. In contrast to this, Erasmus' hermeneutical principle stresses the *sensus literalis* of the Scriptures. Such emphasis on literalism significantly links biblical exegesis to other written sources besides the Bible. Erasmus strove to determine the Scripture's message by tracing cross references within the Bible or between it and the works of historians or previous theologians. The exegete should be acquainted with several languages and different historical circumstances, and should thus possess knowledge that emanates from a somewhat formal and canonized training. According to Erasmus' judgment, being able to approach the Bible properly presupposes being a scholar. The two approaches thus differ in what they consider to be the essential preconditions on the part of the reader. Whereas in the *lectio divina* antecedent prayer and a certain degree of faith are deemed necessary to acquire experience of God, Erasmus's reader is expected to have a certain standard of canonized knowledge.

As has been demonstrated in the previous chapters, while such preconditions for a divinely ordained reading of the Bible among the Jehovah's Witnesses and in the New Apostolic Church crucially involved the readers' proficiency in supplementary publications, in the Pentecostal-charismatic Spirit Apostolic Church the immediate presence of the Holy Spirit was the enabling factor. By drawing these findings together and invoking the considerations on 'religions of the book' developed in Chapter 8, it now becomes possible to specify on a more general level what this notion of 'enabling' might involve.

Scripture and Enablement

The scriptural approaches sketched out above and in the previous chapters have in common the fact that they regard the Bible as an indispensable religious authority. Yet, in order to actualize the Scripture – which, if not actualized, remains in a state of ascribed spiritual latency – certain preconditions have to be brought into scriptural practice by participants. Thus, it is the tightly interlinked combination of scripture and a certain 'enablement' which is of utmost importance in developing a religious capacity.

It can therefore be suggested that religions of the book are characterized by particular practices of referring to authoritatively marked written materials, in which these materials represent an essential, yet insufficient prerequisite for the particular religious community. Those participating in the religious practice continually refer to the Scriptures and thus treat them as an essential cornerstone of practice. The actual potency of the Scripture, however, crucially depends on its being employed properly. Though the status of the Scripture is placed beyond doubt – outside time and space – only its proper use guarantees that the gap between the scriptural and the worldly realms will be bridged.

What I have termed 'literacy enablement' relates to those activities, qualities and devices which, in a particular socio-religious field, are seen as those that are required when attempting to bridge the divine-scriptural sphere and the worldly realm. My definition of the term comprises 'action or means of enabling' and in particular: a) 'the process of rendering able competent, or powerful'; b) 'something by which one is enabled, a qualification'; c) 'support, sustenance, maintenance'; and d) 'an equipment, implement' (*Oxford English Dictionary* 1989, Vol. 5: 202).

On the one hand, therefore, 'enablement' encompasses literacy *procedures*, that is, the routines and operations concerning how a book should be approached and how one's reading of it should proceed. Literacy procedures thus raise a number of questions, like: a) how to prepare an act of reading; b) how to hold and physically handle a textual object; c) where to start reading; d) how to make selections within the text, if at all; and e) how to move from one selected passage to the next.

On the other hand, the term 'enablement' as used in this context evokes those *qualities* on the part of the reader that are considered essential in order to carry out the particular literacy procedure successfully. In the case of *lectio divina*, for example, a certain degree of faith is considered necessary; in the Spirit Apostolic Church, it was the notion of the reader as a medium of the Holy Spirit; while in the case of Erasmus, knowledge of different languages – among other things – was seen as a prerequisite for biblical hermeneutics. This connotation of the term therefore ranges from the reader's beliefs, to spirituality, to learned scholarship.

Finally, the term 'enablement' also refers to *auxiliary material devices* that are assumed to be necessary in any divinely ordained approach to the Bible. As has been elaborated, scriptural practices among Jehovah's Witnesses and in the New Apostolic Church, for example, presuppose a use of supplementary texts that comment on the Bible or give instructions relating to how it should be read. Studying the Scriptures without such devices is thus considered potentially misleading.

Such literacy procedures, qualities and devices are mostly seen as being secondary to the actual beholding or interpretation of the Bible, appearing to constitute mere auxiliaries for scriptural mediation. Yet, as I argue here, the particular form of 'enablement' involved is essential for and highly influential on scriptural readings and processes of religious authorization. How one approaches and moves through the text, and what is considered a precondition in doing so, shapes ruminations, reading experiences and interpretations – it informs whatever one takes from the Bible in order to do whatever. And since a successful scriptural mediation depends on 'enablement', the right to define and specify it constitutes a crucial cornerstone of authority in religions of the book.

Enabling Supplements

The objection might well be raised that the Protestant Reformation, with the dictum of *sola scriptura* (the Bible only), the print revolution (Eisenstein 1979) and the rise of mass literacy since the seventeenth century (Vincent 2000) instituted literacy procedures of a rather neutral technological type that did not require any particular form of 'enablement'– indeed, nothing more than a copy of the Scriptures, the ability to read and something like 'common sense'. An argument of this kind has been put forward by, for example, Robert Moffat of the London Missionary Society, who ends his book *Missionary Labours* and *Scenes in Southern Africa* by expressing his conviction that 'the simple reading and study of the Bible alone will convert the world. The missionary's work is to gain for it admission and attention, and then let it speak for itself' (1842: 618).

However, as I have suggested in the previous chapter with regard to what I call 'print globalization', it is rare for the notion of an autonomous agency of texts – where the Bible 'speaks for itself' – to be unaccompanied by the hope that the texts provide an incentive for people to join the religious community that has issued and distributed them. But once the reception of such texts has become part of a shared socio-religious practice, conditions are usually specified for how the textual agency can develop its 'full potential'. Among other things, this is because the idea of an autonomous agency of the Bible makes it impossible to explain and legitimize the existence of denominational boundaries. If the Bible, as an expression of God's unitary will, simply has to be distributed and then 'does the rest' (cf. Howsam 1991: xiv) by itself, why is it that different churches and Christian practices exist? Thus, even when a Christian community subscribes to the notion of an autonomous textual agency, there has to be some argument for why it is this specific community and not others that is able to make use of the Scripture in a divinely ordained way.

Such conditionality does not have to be formulated explicitly. As Jean and John Comaroff point out with reference to Robert Moffat, the Nonconformist missionaries in South Africa 'sought to reconstruct the inner being of the Tswana chiefly on the ... humble ground of everyday life' (1991: 202). This involved a 'long conversation between the missionaries and the Africans [that] reshaped the "heathen" world not by winning souls in spiritual or verbal battles but by inculcating the everyday forms of the colonizing culture' (1991: 251). In the context of my argument, the latter statement can also be phrased differently: by inculcating particular forms of everyday life, the missionaries sought to endow Africans with new 'Protestant selves'. These new subjectivities, in turn, promised to 'win the souls' of the Africans by preparing them to receive God's word as contained in the Bible and as mediated through their evangelizing activities. Thus, although many missionaries like Moffat expressly subscribed to the idea of an autonomous agency of the Bible, they still engaged in a range of activities more or less implicitly aimed at enabling Africans to make divinely ordained use of the Bible.

My argument, accordingly, is that even claims to 'neutral' or 'universal' literacy practices in most cases presuppose particular types of 'enablement'. For clarification, let me discuss this with regard to an author who, in the history of Christian theology, stands paradigmatically for the doctrine of *sola scriptura*. Martin Luther (1483–1546) held the Bible to be its own interpreter ('*scriptura sui ipsius interpres*') and the final and sufficient authority for an understanding of God's words, regardless of any ecclesiastical authorities.[2] He therefore expected Christians to study the Scriptures in their everyday lives. In his 'Preface to the Letter of St. Paul to the Romans', for example, he stated:

> This letter is truly the most important piece in the New Testament. It is purest Gospel. It is well worth a Christian's while not only to memorize it word for word but also to occupy himself with it daily, as though it were the daily bread of the soul. It is impossible to read or to meditate on this letter too much or too well. The more one deals with it, the more precious it becomes and the better it tastes.[3]

In this passage, Luther mentions three different methods of approaching the Bible, namely 'memorizing', 'reading', and 'meditating'; he also alludes to the imagery of 'ingestion'.[4]

In general, Luther combines the principle of *sola scriptura* with the principles of *sola fide* (belief only) and *solus Christus* (Christ only),[5] as well as with a call for catechist instruction:

> The first requisite in the German system of Divine Worship is a good, plain, simple, and substantial Catechism. A Catechism is a form of instruction by which heathens, desirous of becoming Christians, are taught and shown what they are to believe, to do, to leave undone and to know in Christianity. … This instruction or information I know no better way of putting than that in which it has been put from the beginning of Christianity till today: I mean, in those three articles of the Ten Commandments, the Creed, and the Lord's Prayer. In those three articles is contained, plainly and briefly, all that a Christian needs to know (cited in Kidd 1911: 199).

Luther's *Small Catechism* of 1529 and his *Large Catechism* of the same year constitute attempts to place such instructions in writing. In an extension of the three articles mentioned above, the *Small Catechism* is subdivided into sections on 'The Ten Commandments', 'The Creed', 'The Lord's Prayer', 'Holy Baptism', 'Confession', and 'The Sacrament of the Altar', and it also contains two prayers. This catechism starts in part with quotations from the Bible, which are then discussed in the form of questions and answers:

> The First Commandment: You must not have other gods.
> Q. What does this mean?
> A. We must fear, love, and trust God more than anything else.[6]

The question, 'What does this mean?', represents the most anticipated interjection. Other questions are, for instance, 'How does this happen?' or – when dealing with baptism – 'How can water do such great things?' In several passages, it is also asked, 'Where is this written?', a question that is subsequently answered by biblical quotations.

The outline of the *Small Catechism* thus takes the Bible as its starting point, then proceeds to sequences of an imaginative dialogue, before frequently anticipating a movement back to the Scriptures. This configuration was devised in order to provide neophytes with a Christian 'enablement'. Each section is headed with an instruction like 'The Ten Commandments: The Simple Way a Father Should Present Them to His Household', or 'The Confession: How One Should Teach the Uneducated to Confess'.

In the introductory address to the 'Preface' of Luther's *Large Catechism* (1529), such striving for 'enablement' is even more explicit: 'A Christian, Profitable, and Necessary Preface and Faithful, Earnest Exhortation of Dr. Martin Luther to All Christians, but Especially to All Pastors and Preachers, that They Should Daily Exercise Themselves in the *Catechism*, which is a Short Summary and Epitome of the Entire Holy Scriptures, and that They May Always Teach the Same'.[7]

Here, it is recommended that the *Large Catechism* should be studied by the general Christian public. Furthermore, mediating activities by religious experts are mentioned which should rely on a 'Short Summary and Epitome of the Entire Holy Scriptures' – the written *Catechism*. Despite grounding his scriptural practices on the principles *sola scriptura, solus Christus* and *sola fide*, Luther thus introduces a literacy setting in which intermediaries and auxiliary writings are inserted into the space between the Bible and the laity.

As Holger Flachmann (1996) points out, Luther evaluated supplementary Christian literature according to how clearly it referred to, and 'led' to, the Bible. In general he advocated using books for purposes of religious education, yet voiced disapproval if – according to his view – the reference to the Bible was not explicit enough. He also stressed that the reading of supplementary literature should generally not be used as a substitute for studying the Scriptures. All the same, he attributed the *Small* and *Large Catechisms* a special status. Because of 'their unquestioned material affinity to, and even textual correspondence with, the Holy Writ, studying the Catechism can be a substitute for reading the Bible, maybe not in its variety, but certainly with regard to its central content' (Flachmann 1996: 155; my translation). As such, the *Catechisms* come to represent the Bible; learning the Bible can be replaced by learning the *Catechisms* (Flachmann 1996: 165). The diligent study of the *Large Catechism* is thus said to promise religious advancement:

> If they manifest such diligence, then I will promise them, and they shall also perceive, what fruit they will obtain, and what excellent men God will make of them, so that in due time they themselves will acknowledge that the longer and the more they study the Catechism, the less they know of it, and the more they find yet to learn; and then only, as hungry and thirsty ones, will they truly relish that which now they cannot endure because of great abundance and satiety. To this end may God grant His grace![8]

The *Large Catechism* continues by stating that 'this sermon is designed and undertaken that it might be an instruction for children and the simple-minded' and that 'we must have the young learn the parts which belong to the *Catechism* or instruction for children well and fluently and diligently exercise themselves in them'. As such, the *Catechism* represents the 'Bible for the laity' (cited in Flachmann 1996: 162; my translation). His notion of laity in this context, however, even encompasses Luther himself, who pointed out that '[I] remain a child and pupil of the Catechism and would like to remain such' (cited in Flachmann 1996: 161; my translation).

Male parents are invested with the status of religious experts: 'Therefore it is the duty of every father of a family to question and examine his children and servants at least once a week and to ascertain what they know of it, or are learning and, if they do not know it, to keep them faithfully at it'. Certain features – the Ten Commandments, the Lord's Prayer, the Articles of Faith – are stressed as being the essential and obligatory constituents of religious instruction:

> These are the most necessary parts which one should first learn to repeat word for word and which our children should be accustomed to recite daily when they rise in the morning, when they sit down to their meals, and when they retire at night; and until they repeat them, they should be given neither food nor drink. Likewise every head of a household is obliged to do the same with respect to his domestics, man-servants and maid-servants and not to keep them in his house if they do not know these things and are unwilling to learn them.

Subsequent to further instructions relating to the issues of baptism and sacraments, the father is instructed to proceed as follows: 'When these parts have been well learned, you may, as a supplement and to fortify them, lay before them also some psalms or hymns, which have been composed on these parts, and thus lead the young into the Scriptures, and make daily progress therein'.

This now represents the time when the Bible is opened: the 'young' are led 'into the Scriptures'. Before coming to this immediate reading of the Scriptures, however, the Christian neophytes had to undergo a protracted period of study on the basis of the *Catechism*. And as mentioned above, such studies are depicted as obligatory: unwilling children should be given no food, and unwilling servants should be pushed out of the house.

The literacy procedure as outlined in Luther's *Large Catechism* thus suggests a sequence that makes training in the *Catechism* an obligatory passage point for certain aspects of social life, as well as for what is understood to represent an adequate reading of the Bible. Proficiency in the *Catechism* is said to be an indispensable 'enablement' for religious advancement.

At first glance, compared to other types of enabling prerequisites like spiritual guidance, such supplementary writings do not appear to be 'enablements' in the sense defined above. They seem to constitute mere commentaries to the Bible. Yet, as I have tried to demonstrate above, such supplementary writings are mostly embedded in particular literacy practices that define specific relationships between religious experts, the laity, the Bible, the written commentary and God. The 'enablement' in respect to the Scriptures is here linked to an 'enablement' in respect to other writings. The latter seems more profane than the former and is generally considered subordinate to it. In many religious communities, however, the attainment of such 'literacy enablement of the second order' is actually obligatory in achieving an 'enablement' in scriptural reading.

Having up to this point discussed a variety of religious *reading* practices and described, among other things, how they were contextualized and what were deemed to be the prerequisites for a divinely led beholding of the Scripture, the remainder of the present book will now turn to *writing* practices in African-initiated Pentecostal-charismatic churches and thus to an examination of 'bureaucracy in the Pentecostal-charismatic mode'.

Notes

1. Dysinger, L. 'The Practice of Lectio Divina'. Retrieved 20 August 2007 from http://www.valyermo.com/ld-art.html. The author belongs to Saint Andrew's Abbey, Valyermo/California where two *lectio divina* are scheduled for each day.
2. In contrast to widely held presumptions, the doctrine of *sola scriptura* was not 'invented' by the Protestant reformation. Some early church fathers advocated a comparable position. A Greek bishop of Alexandria in the fourth century, Athanasius, for example, writes: 'The holy and inspired Scriptures are fully sufficient for the proclamation of the truth' (cited in Volz 1983: 147). And Cyril, the bishop of Jerusalem at about the same time, remarks: 'For concerning the divine and sacred Mysteries of the Faith, we ought not to deliver even the most casual remark without the Holy Scriptures' (Catechetical Lectures, Lecture 4.17).
3. 'Preface to Romans'. Retrieved 20 August 2007 from *Christian Classics Ethereal Library*, http://www.ccel.org/ccel/luther/romans/files/romans.html
4. Luther partly advocated a *meditatio* of texts – even of non-Christian literature – that resembled the *lectio divina*. Thus he occasionally prayed before reading (Flachmann 1996: 21–27).
5. By taking up a Christological perspective which, for example, understands Jesus Christ as representing the speaker, the 'I', in the Old Testaments' Psalms, Luther made the *sensus literalis* the foundation of his scriptural exegesis without associating it with a mere grammatical-historical sense (Ebeling 1964: 40–41).
6. 'The Small Catechism of Martin Luther'. Retrieved 20 August 2007 from *Christian Classics Ethereal Library*, http://www.ccel.org/ccel/luther/smallcat.txt
7. 'The Large Catechism of Martin Luther'. Retrieved 20 August 2007 from *Christian Classics Ethereal Library*, http://www.ccel.org/l/luther/large_cat/large_catechism.htm
8. This and the four subsequent quotations, apart from Flachmann's (1996), have been retrieved on 20 August 2007 from *Christian Classics Ethereal Library*, http://www.ccel.org/l/luther/large_cat/large_catechism_c.htm

PART IV

BUREAUCRACY IN THE PENTECOSTAL-CHARISMATIC MODE

Chapter 13
Offices and the Dispersion of Charisma

In my area of research, churches of all types engaged in some sort of organizational writing, through which the particular religious practice was more or less planned, administered, monitored and, in some cases, linked to a wider denominational framework. The importance attributed to such writing practices was connected with specific model conceptions of how churches should be organized. In contrast to 'traditional' herbalists and possession cults, churches (*bachikombelo*) were generally perceived to require a formal organizational structure that, according to my interlocutors, had to be specified in written form and in the English language. Thus, all churches had formally defined offices such as 'Treasurer', 'Secretary' or 'Pastor', most had a written church constitution, and many kept registers, composed agendas and reports, or issued membership cards. These bureaucratic features were the product of a transnational diffusion of organizational models that in southern Africa had originated with colonial administrations and historical mission Christianity and had subsequently led to a variety of local appropriations and adjustments.

Dealing with such bureaucratic practices in the following chapters means taking up an issue which has been widely neglected in anthropology so far (or merely treated in a rather dismissive and thus analytically problematic manner) (see, for example, Herzfeld 1992). As Martin van Creveld (1999: 137) has pointed out, right from its initial coinage by the French philosopher Vincent de Gourmay in the eighteenth century, the term 'bureaucracy' has had highly pejorative connotations in the Western history of ideas. 'Bureaucracy', David Beetham observes, 'is something we all love to hate' (1993: 1). Being linked to ideas of dehumanizing formalism, estrangement and loss of personal autonomy, this negative image of 'bureaucracy' has unjustifiably informed how many anthropologists have approached the study of 'formal organizations'. When seen from the perspective of works in the field of organization studies, one of the most surprising aspects of this is that anthropologists have long tended to overlook the fact that the 'formalism' of formally organized institutions is not a structural given that lies beyond human agency, but is constantly being made and remade through what Karl Weick (1979) has called 'organizing practices'. Bureaucracy as 'formal organization' must therefore be seen as a precarious and ambiguous *process* revolving around the social construction, maintenance and re-construction of 'formalized' organizational realities.

Adopting this approach naturally implies a shift away from normative discourses on bureaucracy and an attempt to go beyond descriptions of abstract administrative structures. In short, what are needed are not generalizing (and disparaging) claims about bureaucracy per se, but detailed ethnographic studies of the making of bureaucracies which take account of situated social practices, discourses and sense-making interpretations (Weick 1995) that involve, yet cannot be reduced to, 'power-wielding' (Heyman 2004). In the remainder of this book, this aim is pursued by making a thick description of bureaucratic practices in the Spirit Apostolic Church. I shall demonstrate that the bureaucratic aspects of this Church are accommodated to local conceptions of religious power. Since positions of authority depend here on ascriptions of spiritual capability, this accommodation creates a configuration in which bureaucratic procedures are conflated with discourses and practices of a Pentecostal-charismatic type. Thus, what emerges is a 'bureaucracy in the Pentecostal-charismatic mode'.

This chapter begins by offering some theoretical considerations about research on bureaucracies by drawing on, among other things, approaches from organization studies. Then the groundwork for the examination of bureaucratic writing practices in the Spirit Apostolic Church, pursued in the subsequent chapters, will be set out, first by sketching the (historical) role of bureaucratization in this church; secondly by outlining how the dispersal of charisma and the allocation of church offices led here to personal unions of officeholders and spirit mediums; and thirdly by delineating how spiritual and rational-legal hierarchies between church elders were acted out in practice.

Bureaucracy as Social Practice

Max Weber's ideal type of 'bureaucracy' (1968d: 66–77), which he developed against the background of Prussian politics and administration in the nineteenth century, encompasses a set of characteristic features: a) each member of the organization has a specialised domain of responsibilities; there thus exists a division of labour with fixed areas of jurisdiction; b) the different offices are arranged in a hierarchy that forms a particular chain of command and structure of supervision; c) the organization is based on established and prescribed regulations; d) due to his impersonal role, the officeholder should act according to these institutional regulations; clients of the organization should thus be treated as 'cases' and not as individuals; e) the activities of the organization are to be communicated and registered in writing, which provides a permanent record to guide future action; f) the allocation of offices depends on technical competence and qualification, which are also the crucial prerequisites for a career within the organization; and g) the existence of an administrative staff supporting the operation of the organization without being connected to its explicit goals (e.g., accountants). Finally, Weber understood bureaucracies to be goal-oriented organizations designed according to rational principles in order to efficiently attain their goals.

In general, Weber's model of bureaucracy has been highly influential in the social sciences, first because it provided a detailed analytical vocabulary and framework for the examination of formally organized institutions, and secondly because it could be taken to represent an ideal-typical endpoint of socio-historical processes that have variously been described as 'rationalization', 'formalization', 'depersonalization' or 'disenchantment'.

In the decades following its publication, however, Weber's work on bureaucracy has also been criticized and reworked. In a renowned article by Don Handelman, for example, it is suggested that the idea of formal organization represents an 'ideational construction' (1981: 6) of Western culture and that 'Weber's conception of a rational-legal bureaucracy bears a strong logical resemblance to the ideas of social or scientific taxonomy of the Classical Age' (1981: 9). Taking up ideas of Michel Foucault's, Handelman argues that:

> The most elementary premise of bureaucratic epistemology is that of taxonomy. There is no bureaucracy without classification, without the invention of categories of inclusion and exclusion. This premise is integral to bureaucracy whether it is viewed from within or from without, whether it is perceived to be rooted in metaphysics or rationalism, whether it is created in history or positioned situationally. The classification of target populations to elicit certain behaviors from them is the exercise of control. Bureaucratic classification impacts the social orders that generate this kind of organization of information. This impact is the exercise of power (1995: 280).

In the following chapters, the issue of this taxonomic enterprise will be taken up again. In analysing bureaucracy as a social practice, however, the observable ambiguities and problems of classification – for example, the question of who is to count as a church member – call into question Handelman's identification of bureaucratic categorization with the exercise of power. The performance of bureaucracy certainly entails a striving for taxonomy, but this does not automatically mean that there is also an authoritative 'taxonomic impact' on society. Putting power in the anthropology of bureaucracy – to paraphrase the title of an article by Josiah Heyman (1995) – thus requires not only examining closely how bureaucratic practices are actually enacted in order to exert power but also how such attempts are subverted by 'the administered' as well as by contradictions within these practices themselves (cf. Czarniawska-Joerges 1992).

Another element of criticism regarding Weber's ideal type of bureaucracy is that it implies a strict distinction between 'formal' and 'informal' social behaviour. The principles of organizational formalism here seem detached from any socio-cultural context (Wright 1994: 18). For example, summarizing the contributions to the volume *Hierarchy and Society: Anthropological Perspectives on Bureaucracy*, Gerald Britan and Ronald Cohen point out that the essays 'share a belief in the importance of *informal* organization in *formal* bureaucratic process' (1980: 2; my italics). This distinction also occurs in Larissa Lomnitz's article, 'Informal Exchange Networks in Formal Systems' (1988), which Richard Rottenburg comments on as follows:

> Lomnitz understands the formal system of society as something rational in itself and legitimate simply for this reason, without reference to political and cultural processes. By assuming that when the formal system fails, the actors tactically resort to informal relation patterns from the sphere of the reciprocity ethic, she creates the impression that only this frame of reference is politically and culturally constructed. As a result, she logically only endeavours to explain this part of the story, while omitting the rest from analysis. ... She takes it for granted that the flagstones do not need to be explained, only the grass in between (1996: 208).

Rottenburg also points out that Lomnitz 'ignores the fact that the formal structures are built up intentionally by people' because they strive to strengthen 'their role in the informal network via a role in the formal system' (1996: 209). With regard to the 'formal' and 'informal' systems, he rightly concludes that they 'are not so much a matter of two separate worlds as of two types of discourse which are continually intersecting and traversing each other: one cannot exist without the other and vice versa' (1996: 209).

This perspective is of crucial importance in any attempt to examine bureaucracy as social practice. Instead of treating 'informal' relationships as 'communicational noise' in an otherwise abstractly principled 'formal' framework, the two dimensions will be seen here as intersecting. We shall therefore concentrate on practices through which 'formal structures' are constructed, maintained, altered and contested.

Lastly, Max Weber's emphasis on 'bureaucratic rationality' has also been criticized for its treatment of organizational 'rationality' and 'effectivity' as neutral categories. Paul DiMaggio and Walter Powell, for example, have pointed out that today:

> structural change in organizations seems less and less driven by competition or by the need for efficiency. Instead, we contend, bureaucratization and other forms of organizational change occur as the result of processes that make organizations more similar without necessarily making them more efficient. Bureaucratization and other forms of homogenization emerge, we argue, out of the structuration (Giddens 1979) of organizational fields (1991: 63–64).

This neo-institutionalist argument, which will be discussed in more detail in Chapter 17, thus treats organizational 'rationality' or 'effectivity' as socio-culturally informed 'myths' (Meyer and Rowan 1977) that are ceremonially enacted in order to obtain legitimacy within particular organizational environments.

In combination with the focus on organizational practices, mentioned above, the neo-institutional perspective allows us to distance ourselves from certain otherwise prevailing scholarly notions concerning 'Third World bureaucracies', which to a certain extent represent a legacy of Max Weber's modernist position. As far as Africa is concerned, Wim van Binsbergen has recently pointed out that:

the most powerful and most amazingly successful social technology implanted on African soil in the course of the 20th century, has been the formal, voluntary or bureaucratic organization as defined along Weberian lines, which ... within a century has almost completely transformed all spheres of African life ... and which particularly has come to provide the dominant model of religious self-organization (2004: 87).

However, in contrast to these insights, until now examples of African bureaucratization have mostly been portrayed as either *caricatures* or *facades*. In the former case, the actual practices of organizational formalization in Africa are measured against the Weberian ideal type of bureaucracy. With regard to processes of 'modernization', it is thus noted that African bureaucracies do not fulfil the scholar's normative expectations, because their practices can be shown to involve informal procedures or patronage. This observation is then mostly explained with reference to a lack of adequate training in bureaucratic procedures or to the long-term persistence of tradition. Given the obvious serious-mindedness of many African bureaucrats, however, such judgements ultimately amount to caricaturing these bureaucracies: they surely would act as such if they only could. Bureaucracy is thus depicted as something that is basically alien to African culture, but that will increasingly be acquired and/or perfected in Africa's march towards modernization. In contrast to this scholarly tendency, the second approach interprets the informal and patronage aspects of African bureaucracies as representing more or less deliberate strategies. The bureaucratic apparatus is accordingly described as an intentionally presented facade disguising something fundamentally different from whatever is being put on public display: they do, but they only seem to do. And what is concealed is something that lends itself to being judged negatively, like corruption or political intrigue. In this view, African bureaucratic practices are not taken seriously since they are depicted as a merely outward, chimerical form concealing an authentic substantial (negative) core.

I certainly do not want to deny that organizational formality in most parts of southern Africa is a relatively recent development and that bureaucracy often serves the goals of political and economic exploitation. However, I would suggest that we can get more insights into processes of African bureaucratization if we acknowledge that bureaucratic practices are a widespread and 'authentic' phenomenon in contemporary Africa, if we take seriously the African bureaucrat's serious-mindedness, and if we likewise accept that there is no 'formal organization' imaginable which does not produce its own contradictions and tensions by the simple fact of its being part of, and informed by, dynamic socio-cultural relationships.

Keeping these general points in mind, the remaining sections of this chapter will introduce some organizational aspects of the Spirit Apostolic Church that will prove important for the ethnographic analysis of bureaucratic writing practices pursued in the next chapters.

Organizational Formalization as a Founding Myth

While returning, some time between 1959 and 1961, from a mining town in Southern Rhodesia (nowadays Zimbabwe) to his home village of Siasalala in the hilly escarpment between the Gwembe Valley and the Plateau, Enock, a Tonga labour migrant, started to form a church on the basis of his experience with the Full Gospel Church of God in Southern Rhodesia, which he initially said was the headquarters of his congregation.[1] In 1999 some of the earliest members of the church in Siasalala recalled that there had been a close association between the Northern Rhodesian branch and the headquarters in Southern Rhodesia for several years. Others insisted that there had been no contact between Siasalala and the headquarters after Enock's return to his home village. They maintained that Enock had ended the connection because he did not want to be subordinate, wanting to become the bishop himself. Therefore, after some time Enock did not hesitate to split from the Full Gospel Church of God in Southern Africa, naming his congregation the Full Gospel Church of Central Africa instead. According to a different account, Enock's passport had expired in 1973, so he could no longer travel to Southern Rhodesia.[2] At about the same time, the congregation ran out of printed baptism certificates headed: 'Full Gospel Church of God in Southern Africa'. Enock had initially brought a bunch of these forms from Southern Rhodesia, but now saw no way of obtaining new ones. Nonetheless, the forms were felt to be urgently required in order for the congregation to grow. So they looked around for a typist and had him draft new baptism certificates, though this time with the heading: 'Full Gospel Church of Central Africa'.

These accounts of the separation of the congregation in Siasalala from the church in Southern Rhodesia stress two different causes. One version described the separation as having been due solely to Enock's self-centred striving for power and to have been achieved by taking advantage of the headquarters' problems in controlling distant branches. The other version declared church growth to be dependent on bureaucratic necessities and concluded that a breakdown of bureaucratic control led to church autonomy. It thus pursued a form of logic in which whoever drafts and multiplies written forms like certificates can call his congregation 'headquarters'.

According to my interlocutors in 1999, the Full Gospel Church of God in Central Africa (FGCGCA) had flourished in the period from the early 1960s up to the 1980s. However, the future founders of the Spirit Apostolic Church (SAC), who at that time occupied the middle level of the church hierarchy in the FGCGCA, had increasingly become dissatisfied with the overall performance of the FGCGCA, and especially with the authoritarian and dominating attitude of its Bishop. During church meetings, when different branches gathered together to celebrate – for instance, on Good Friday or at Pentecost – Bishop Enock would allocate responsibilities and duties to his subordinates spontaneously and apparently arbitrarily. Nobody knew in advance what would happen at a particular point in the meeting. For example, services started without a written agenda, which meant that none of the preachers who were participating could tell whether they would be obliged to deliver a sermon at some point in the proceedings. Certainly this spontaneity was a by-product, even an essential component, of the denomination's spiritual practices. Referring to their religious practice in 1999, the elders of the SAC asserted that a spiritually able preacher could act at any time and without preparation. Yet during their time in the FGCGCA, they insisted, the Bishop had used his authoritative spontaneity improperly, because he had maliciously sought to prove their own 'incompetence' against his spiritual superiority. The Bishop's autocratic style of leadership had placed them in the awkward position of constantly being forced to keep up with his impulsive decisions. This in turn had brought them into a precarious situation with regard to the congregations: since mistakes were likely to occur under such conditions, their own authority as church elders was being publicly undermined.

In the course of the developing conflict, a particular narrative emerged, which was later used as one of the main justifications for the subsequent separation from the FGCGCA, namely the accusation that its leader had failed to establish effective organizational structures and procedures. The significance of bureaucratic practices in the FGCGCA had decreased over the years. The actual separation, which occurred towards the beginning of 1990, was thus not justified by referring to controversies on the spiritual level, but by a reference to the lack of organizational formality. There were no obvious disagreements about religious doctrines or spiritual matters between the Bishop of the FGCGCA and the rebellious junior leaders, some of whom were already then ascribed an outstanding spiritual capability. Instead, it was bureaucratization that became one of the bases of the founding myths of the Spirit Apostolic Church.

Taken together, this development contradicts common scholarly notions about charisma and institutionalization. Whereas charisma is usually depicted as an innovative, temporary, personified moment breaking with an institutionalized past, organizational formality is the epitome of institutionalization, involving a comparatively *longue durée* of objectified (written) rules and depersonalized social positions. The transition from the Full Gospel Church to the Spirit Apostolic Church, by contrast, was presented in 1999 as *continuity in spirituality* (charisma) and an *innovation in organization* (institutionalization).

By actually bureaucratizing the SAC in the years following its separation from the FGCGCA, an attempt was being continuously made to fulfil what had been promised at the outset. All the same, at the beginning of 1999 – that is, at the time when I collected the ethnographic material presented in the following chapters – the Spirit Apostolic Church was in disarray. By that time, Rabson had been acting as the bishop of the church for four years. Yet his term in office had been overshadowed by repeated and prolonged bodily afflictions, which were partly explained as having been caused by witchcraft. The resulting quest for therapy had involved hospitals, 'traditional' herbalists and a *mutumwa* congregation. For many members of the SAC, this participation in non-Christian religious practices gave rise to the suspicion that Rabson had lost his relationship with the Holy Spirit, or even that he had started to associate himself with another, perhaps evil, spiritual being. In 1998, moreover, he lost his job as a driver. Being deprived of his previous mobility, it was now impossible for him to continue with his regular visits to outlying branches. However, the Bishop's physical inability to tour the Church's branches had not been replaced by any corresponding commitment by the other elders. The Church's eight branches and its overall membership of about 1,200 participants had thus suffered from a disruption in communications. In 1998, there had been no church meetings held that had brought together all the Church's congregations; each branch had pursued its religious practice more or less separately.

Against this background, 1999 can be characterized as a period of denominational reconsolidation. When Rabson regained his health in March 1999, he and the other senior church leaders set out to reintegrate the branches and re-establish their authority. This involved them making efforts to rehabilitate their positions as the leaders of the church. The discourses of the senior leaders emphasized more strongly than in previous years how they had obtained and maintained their personal spirituality, which often involved explicit references to those parts of their biographies in which they had been 'initiated' into spirituality by the church elders of the Full Gospel Church of Central Africa. At the same time, the process of re-consolidation expressly exploited the founding myth of the Spirit Apostolic Church mentioned earlier, namely bureaucratization, which also meant that the senior leaders tried to strengthen their bureaucratic control over the branches.

Dispersing Charisma, Allocating Offices

How, then, were spirituality and church offices related to each other in practice? A first answer to this question can be obtained by examining those interactions which led to the formation of new congregations. Here, we find an extended 'dispersion of charisma' (Shils 1958) that went along with a 'dispersion of church offices'.

According to the accounts of the senior leaders of the SAC in 1999, the FGCGCA set up twenty-eight branches in the period from the early 1960s until 1973. Most of these congregations were located close to the church headquarters in Siasalala village on the escarpment between the Gwembe Valley and the Central African Plateau, but some others were established in the Gwembe Valley. In general, the founding of these branches was presented as a spin-off of healing activities: elders of the FGCGCA toured different places to preach and to heal the afflicted, and some of those who received successful spiritual treatment subsequently opened a branch. In other cases, a patient was treated at the homestead of the Bishop of the FGCGCA, Enock, and this healed patient then went on to found a new congregation after returning to his village. In both cases, the actual founding of the branch was accomplished without the assistance or control of the church elders in Siasalala. Prayer groups were formed and named themselves 'Full Gospel Church', their status only later being confirmed by Enock.

Let us consider the establishment of new congregations in the FGCGCA with a view to providing an example. One day in 1980, Bishop Enock passed through Mazwange village in the Gwembe Valley in order to sell tin-ware like pots and buckets. Aspin, who at that time was living in Mazwange and who in 1999 was acting as the Vice-Bishop of the SAC, related how he experienced this first encounter:

> It all started with his beard. He had a beard and I was still a young man, I did not show much respect to old people at that time. So I asked him, 'Why do you have this long beard?' and he answered, 'Because I am a bishop'. We started to chat, and he said that he could heal the sick and exorcize demons. Initially we did not believe him, but we nonetheless thought that it might be great fun to watch him perform. So we came together. First he taught us a song which was easy to learn because it consisted only of a few words. We still have this song in our church today [He sings some lines]. Then we brought a lady to him whom we knew to be afflicted by demons because she sometimes attended *masabe* meetings. It was like a joke for us; actually we wanted to ridicule him. He made her sit down and laid his hands on her head, with a slightly rubbing movement. And suddenly this lady started to roll on the ground and to make funny noises. We were surprised. Shortly afterwards, the lady calmed down and declared, 'The demons are out'. BaEnock asked her to point with the hand to heaven and after she did so, he said, 'You are truly healed now'. We were amazed by the power of the old man, yet we were still a bit doubtful. The next morning, after BaEnock had left our village, we thought, 'We have to test him. Maybe he is just cheating'. That time I was a member of the Pilgrim Holiness Church and I had never seen such things before. So we went to the home of this lady and started to beat *masabe* drums. But nothing happened, she just remained seated.

Aspin and his friends assumed that the spirit possession would persist even after Enock's treatment and had expected the demons to reveal themselves when they performed the type of drumming associated with the *masabe* possession cult that the afflicted woman had attended previously. But when this drumming did not make her dance, which would have been clear proof of spirit possession, they became convinced and wrote a letter to Enock asking him to visit Mazwange village for a second time.

When Enock eventually acceded to their request, some people in Mazwange had already formed a prayer group and now wanted spiritual and organizational advice. During this second encounter, Enock said that, as an outsider, he could not allocate church offices. They themselves should elect (*kusala*) their leaders, namely a pastor, a secretary, a deacon and a treasurer. Aspin became the deacon, his wife the church treasurer, and friends of his the pastor and the secretary. They were all baptised by the Bishop. Enock also demanded that a shelter for Sunday services should be built and that the new members should stop attending other churches. Most of the participants in the new congregation had previously been members of the Seventh-day Adventist Church, the New Apostolic Church (*Neuapostolische Kirche*) or the Pilgrim Holiness Church. Aspin insisted that their interest in the FGCGCA mainly resulted from their wish to be protected against afflictions and to have a place to go where they could be healed. Some time after this second meeting, however, it became increasingly clear to the church members of Mazwange that they were entirely dependent on the healing powers of Enock, whose homestead was about seventy kilometres away, so they made a request to be given healing powers as well. Aspin recalled:

> At that time, the Bishop was a healer and a prophet. And when he came, he observed us for some time and then selected the Pastor and said, 'Let us try with you. Maybe you can be a healer'. He laid his hand on the Pastor's head and prayed for him. ... But at first, the Pastor did not succeed in healing other people. He tried again and again, Saturday and Sunday morning, but there was no result until at last he exorcized the demon of a young girl. From then onwards, we knew how it worked. After BaEnock was gone again, the Pastor successively mediated his power to others (*kupa zyamuya usalala*) and many of us started to heal. At last there were four healers in our congregation and I was among them.

In this narrative of the founding of the branch in Mazwange village, the spiritual growth of the local participants is depicted not so much as a by-product of Enock's efforts in healing than as the consequence of a deliberate act of intermediation. The congregation developed under the patronage of a superordinate religious authority that represented its originating source of spirituality. At the same time, however, a further centre of spiritual origination was said to have evolved: the newly elected pastor was the first member of the congregation to receive the Holy Spirit, and it was he who henceforth provided others in his area with spiritual powers for healing and prophecy. Aspin continued his narration of the development of this branch as follows: 'The Pastor and the other church elders visited surrounding villages, preaching and healing patients like BaEnock had done before us. After some time, people came to realize that there was the power of God working in our church and they joined us. Eventually they started to call the Pastor 'father' (*bataata*) and 'chief' (*mwami*)'.

Having attained an initial association with the Holy Spirit through Enock's mediation and carried out a series of successful healings, the pastor came to be seen as a medium of the Holy Spirit. Enock visited Mazwange only rarely in the years following the establishment of the branch, but the pastor remained. Now not only the Bishop of Siasalala was regarded as a healer and a prophet, but also one of the local residents. And eventually the pastor achieved a local standing, which to some extent corresponded to that enjoyed by Bishop Enock: one of respect and of being regarded as a centre of spiritually originating activities. This attainment of local spiritual authority, however, did not induce the pastor and his congregation to break with the church in Siasalala. Rather, they subordinated themselves to what was regarded as the spiritually originating headquarters, while at the same time emphasizing their own potential for spiritual origination. They thus attributed two origins to the spirituality of the congregation: the spatially distant headquarters *and* the local manifestations of the Holy Spirit.

This account of the establishment of a branch of the FGCGCA in Mazwange village in 1980 shows how most senior church elders of the SAC had initially experienced the temporal sequence of spiritualization and of the allocation of church offices. The people from Mazwange were particularly interested in attaining the spiritual power they had witnessed during Enock's visit. The first step, however, consisted in the allocation of church posts. These appointments were made by the prospective church members themselves, not by the Bishop of the FGCGCA. The allocation of church posts thus depended on personal interests and feelings of vocation, as well as on highly contextualized knowledge of applicants' reputations. By assigning church offices, responsibilities were allocated and addressees for future communication determined. A continuation of religious practices that was distinct from other collateral church communities and that had its own permanent place of worship was thus secured. Subsequent baptism by Enock endowed these appointments with an authoritative signature. Yet neither baptisms nor church offices provided the hoped-for spiritualization. The members of the newly established branch thus called on the mediation of the power of the Holy Spirit, which Enock had not offered himself. And when the Bishop of the FGCGCA actually arranged this spiritualizing intermediation, it was the officeholders who were tested for this and who eventually received spiritual powers. Moreover, the success of the intermediation was judged according to the same criteria as Enock's first activities, namely effectiveness.

As a whole, this sequence, which was also characteristic of the further development of the Spirit Apostolic Church, can therefore roughly be described as follows: a) spirituality was the essential aim; b) church offices provided a certain stabilization of religious practice and authority; c) spiritualization was achieved only after the religious community had been set up in a rudimentary way; and d) what evolved in this process was a church leadership characterized by personal unions in which 'officeholders' also acted as 'spirit mediums'. Therefore, in 1999 officeholders in the Spirit Apostolic Church were still for the most part assumed to have received 'gifts of God' (*cipego caleza*) and consequently to be endowed with spiritual capacities for, among other things, healing, preaching and/or prophecy.

Charisma, Hierarchies, Variations

For Weber, as already mentioned, charisma is an inherently unstable phenomenon, which in its pure form 'may be said to exist only in the process of originating. It cannot remain stable, but becomes either traditionalized or rationalized, or a combination of both' (1968a: 54). He therefore describes an inevitable process of routinization in which charisma loses its innovative impact by being transformed into institutionalized types of authority. Weber concedes, however, that charisma might attain continuity through conversion into 'inherited charisma' or a 'charisma of the office'.

These two forms of 'domesticated' charisma cannot be found in the church being discussed here. In contrast to many other African-initiated churches, there was no trace of 'inherited charisma' in the Spirit Apostolic Church (SAC). Succession in terms of charismatic leadership followed neither matrilineal nor patrilineal descent. Most of the children and nephews of church leaders belonged to the laity. Some were invested with minor church posts like conductor of the choir, which, however, did not mean that they had any hereditary prerogatives or that they were automatically ascribed spirituality. It was actually a common view among my informants that it was impossible to obtain the Holy Spirit through inheritance within the family. Whereas it was assumed that other spiritual beings, like *masabe* spirits or the evil spirits used in witchcraft, could be handed down from generation to generation, this transference was regarded as impossible in the case of the Holy Spirit. Furthermore there existed no distinct 'charisma of the office' in the SAC. Being invested with the church office of 'Bishop', for example, did not automatically mean that all members supposed that the person holding the office actually represented the highest spiritual authority. The first Bishop of the SAC, Lameck, was generally assumed to be less spiritual than his Vice-Bishop. The second Bishop, Ng'andu, was initially attributed the status of a 'great prophet' but was then, while still in his post, increasingly accused of being a witch. And the third Bishop, Rabson, was widely felt to have lost his spiritual potency during prolonged bodily afflictions; in 1999, he was still holding on to the post while struggling to restore confidence in his spirituality. Thus, the existence of personal unions of officeholders and spirit mediums did not mean here that charisma was inherent in the church offices themselves.

In general, acquiring a church post (*chuuno*) was highly desired in the area of my research, since it was seen as an indication of having been delegated responsibility, representation and authority within a social community that was based on voluntary association and that stuck to principles different from those of kinship relations or local political affiliation (e.g., the village (*munzi*) or neighbourhood (*cisi*)). Holding a church office was often seen as an expression of personal action, sociability and success. At the same time, the allocation of church offices was also considered to be a product of human arbitration and thus to be potentially arbitrary. It was occasionally suspected that holding a church office actually reflected pretentiousness, egoism and material interests. Generally, however, very few church elders in my area of research profited financially from their religious activities. It was purely voluntary work. None of them received a salary; and only some of those who offered herbalist treatment actually charged their patients for the treatment.

In 1999, the 'main board' (*basololi* – the leaders) of the SAC consisted of the Bishop (*mupati wachikombelo*), the Vice-Bishop (*mucilizi wachikombelo*), the General Secretary (*mulembi mupati*) and the General Treasurer (*muyobozi wamali*). Three officeholders resided in Siamujulu village on the Plateau, while the Vice-Bishop lived in Intema village on the escarpment between the Gwembe Valley and the Plateau. Most members of the 'main board' thus lived in close and neighbourly contact with one another, while at the same time being spatially separated from the branches that were located in the Gwembe Valley. The distance between Siamujulu and the most distant branch in Keela village, for example, was about seventy kilometres. This distance posed severe logistical problems for the Church's leadership because journeys by minibus or on the back of pickups and lorries were costly; they were therefore only undertaken when absolutely necessary.

Moreover, the members of the 'main board' had all been among the prominent founders of the denomination (*bajani wachechi*), and since the SAC had been set up, the highest church offices had been distributed among them. Although the church constitution restricted the terms of office to a three year period, actual incumbencies did not always follow this regulation. Among other things, this had to do with the fact that it was considered inappropriate for senior church leaders to remove incumbents. Degrading an officeholder, it was feared, would inevitably lead to open conflict, which all the church leaders continually attempted to avoid. They feared that those who had been degraded might resort to witchcraft in revenge, that their own involvement in degrading a colleague might be seen by the public as antisocial behaviour, and that the whole church community might break apart due to such quarrels. Those who had reached a particular level were accordingly never forced to step down from the hierarchy; they either stuck to their church posts for an extended period of time, or they alternated between more or less equivalent offices. This practice obviously had its drawbacks. Since the 'main board' was permanently occupied by the same people, the promotion of junior church leaders was clearly restricted, and indeed, in 1999, they could not hope for such promotion. These restrictions nourished feelings of alienation and schismatic tendencies.

At the level of the local congregations, there existed seven church offices for male members: pastor, local preacher, deacon, secretary, treasurer, doorkeeper, and choirmaster. In some congregations, not all of them were occupied; in others one of the church elders held several at once. The respective duties and responsibilities of these posts were not always clearly defined, and there were notable differences between congregations in how the offices were carried out. The posts of pastor and local preacher were difficult to distinguish, although the pastor was officially superior to the preacher, since he represented the overall leader of the branch. With the exception of the choirmaster and the doorkeeper, who had to make sure that silence was observed during services and meetings, all male officeholders were potentially allowed to preach, and all of them occasionally took on the role of conducting services, that is, the role of managing the proceedings of a service. If the secretary or treasurer were absent on any particular day, other officeholders simply took over their tasks. The internal workings of a congregation were thus characterized by a high degree of variation and flexibility, so that it was sometimes difficult for outsiders to discover who was responsible for what. The senior leaders' attempts to pin down accountabilities and duties by means of allocating church offices was undermined by day-to-day contingencies within the congregations.

Ignorance and Mutual Recognition

As has been noted above, at the beginning of 1999, the senior leaders of the Spirit Apostolic Church (SAC) sought to re-establish their authority by reintegrating the church's branches bureaucratically while simultaneously emphasizing their own spirituality. We have also seen that the spatial distance between the headquarters and branches of the Church posed logistical problems, that there existed feelings of alienation among junior leaders because their options for promotion were restricted, and that the internal workings of a congregation were usually contingent and flexible. As the following demonstrates, these factors together formed a complex configuration in which the relationship between senior and junior leaders was characterized by both ignorance and mutual recognition (cf. Jules-Rosette 1979: 119–22).

In mid-1999, the senior church elders from Siamujulu village were visited by a junior church leader called Kedrick from the Gwembe Valley. They had not been in contact with each other for almost five months, but now Kedrick wanted to talk about the organization of the projected Pentecost meeting in his home village of Mazwange. During the discussion, he informed the 'main board' that two new branches had recently been founded in villages adjacent to Mazwange, namely Bululami and Keela. The senior leaders were obviously surprised by this development, yet they were also excited about it, and declared it to be a clear indication of the imminent success of the church. The founders of the new congregations had written introductory letters, which Kedrick handed over to Bishop Rabson. Having read them silently, Rabson voiced his appreciation and then put the letters away without giving anybody else the chance to read them. Some days later I joined Kedrick on his way back to Mazwange village. The next Sunday, the church elders from Mazwange, Bululami and Keela met to conduct a church service. In the course of this, the leaders from Bululami and Keela, who were introduced to me as 'pastors', 'secretaries' and 'deacons', publicly read out the letters that Bishop Rabson had sent through Kedrick. In them, Rabson gave his approval for the new branches and encouraged their leaders to attract as many members as possible. During the following weeks, the two congregations pursued their religious practice without interference or instructions from the headquarters of the SAC. Yet when the Pentecost meeting was held in July 1999, at which different congregations were present, the leaders of the new branches were summoned by the 'main board'. Some of them were not even known personally to the senior church elders. After a short introduction, they received religious instructions from the members of the 'main board', which were confined, however, to general remarks about proper Christian behaviour and the responsibilities of church elders. Then the names of the new leaders were written down in a list by the general secretary and certificates were issued to the new officeholders indicating their offices. The senior leaders also prayed publicly for the new elders. From then on, the SAC officially consisted of two more branches.

This case is of interest in the present context for several reasons: first, the range of the SAC had increased outside the control of the Church's headquarters; second, the local leadership had set itself up and was only confirmed a posteriori by the 'mainboard'; third, the headquarters assimilated the new branches in a rather indiscriminate and yet especially bureaucratic manner; and fourth, despite such assimilation, the relationship between the headquarters and the branches was generally characterized by a certain ignorance, since none of the parties involved had any detailed knowledge of the others.

The literacy practices associated with the exchange of letters also demonstrate an apparently trivial but in fact significant difference: whereas the letters from the new branches were given to the overall leader of the Church, who read them himself without informing the others of their contents, the Bishop's letters in reply were made public by the leaders of the local branches. What is worth noting here is the following detail: although the new branches had been established independently and were already active, the leaders of these congregations sought the authoritative backing of the headquarters of the SAC. Reading aloud the letters and the subsequent official acknowledgement of their positions in the Church provided the church elders in Bululami and Keela with legitimacy that was additional to the retrospective authority they required to set up their congregations. In the physical absence of the senior leaders, this authority was provided by the Bishop's letters and subsequently through the certificates that were issued. The reference to de facto absent superior elders thus implicitly made them present and linked the religious status of the junior leaders to the Church's chain of spiritual transmission.

This latter finding brings up the important question of 'presence' and 'absence' in the organizational structure of the SAC. The junior leaders of congregations in which members of the 'main board' ministered faced the problem that they always had to subordinate themselves to those of a higher rank. They could only preach or act during services when the senior leaders allowed them to do so. The co-presence of different hierarchical levels in the form of church offices thus represented a certain impediment to their religious careers. Whereas the pastor of a congregation that had no higher ranking church elders (as in Bululami and Keela) could locally attain a status that to some extent resembled that of a bishop, the pastors of those congregations in which superordinate officeholders attended regularly usually remained mere pastors in the eyes of the laity. In the former case, a pastor's reputation was occasionally increased by attributions of outstanding spirituality. People then said that although he might just be a 'pastor', in truth he behaved like a bishop. In the latter case, however, the impediment to the junior leaders also involved questions of spirituality, since the presence of superior officeholders frequently prevented the public demonstration of spiritual activities by junior members. It was almost impossible for them to obtain a reputation for spirituality that would have added substantially to their respective church posts and increase their personal standing within the community. In the absence of superior leaders, junior officeholders could upgrade and reshape the contours of their particular church posts by achieving a reputation for outstanding spirituality. In the presence of their superiors, such upgrading was impossible, since each elder was then seen in his or her institutional and hierarchical relation to the others. Periods of physical absence by senior leaders were thus necessary if the junior leaders wanted to advance their personal religious careers.

Yet at the same time, a certain 'presence' by them was indispensable. As demonstrated in the preceding sections of this chapter, religious authority in the SAC evolved in the form of an extended dispersion of charisma. All the church elders in 1999 had achieved their association with the Holy Spirit through an act of intermediation involving someone who had previously achieved a reputation for spiritual capacity. In the case of the senior elders, this mediation was traced back to the Full Gospel Church. In the case of the junior leaders in the branches, the mediation of the Holy Spirit was said to have been carried out by the senior members of the SAC. In this way, authorization by the church elders was related to previous instances of spiritualization, that is, to centres of origination where the particular dispersion of charisma was supposed to have started. This referentiality did not necessitate co-presence: most congregations were visited by the superior leaders of the church only rarely. When they came, they were celebrated and treated in a highly respectful manner by the members and junior leaders of the branches. Obviously close contact with the senior leaders was prestigious and deemed to have a spiritualizing effect. During the long periods of the senior leaders' absence, however, the branches resorted to making discursive references to its headquarters, thus also endowing it with a certain presence.

The members of the 'main board' were well aware of the significance of occasional visits to the branches (*kuswaya mbungano*). Some of the conflicts within the Church were actually considered to result from their own failure to tour them regularly. Yet at the same time, the elders tried to ensure that the congregations did not see them too often. During church meetings, there were grass shelters near the grounds for worship where the senior leaders spent most of their time. Members of the laity were not allowed to enter these shelters, which were deliberately built in such a manner that they prevented their being seen into from outside. Even during their visits, the senior leaders therefore sought to present themselves as something extraordinary and as rarely to be seen. The grass shelters had been built by the local junior leaders, who during the meeting served as the intermediaries between the laity and the senior elders. Although the senior leaders provided the agenda, it was the junior leaders who moderated and arranged the proceedings and who appeared in public, thus allowing the senior leaders to remain in a more elevated background. The performative construction of authority was thus based on a balancing of presence and absence. An attempt was made to create an aura by the immediacy of the aloof. This served both the junior and the senior leaders: while the junior leaders tried to present themselves as proficient mediators between the laity and the representatives of an allegedly outstanding spirituality, the senior leaders acted with authority over the junior leaders, while at the same time trying to maintain an unbridgeable distance from the laity.

The division of labour between the junior and senior leaders during church meetings entailed moments of mutual instrumentalization. A process evolved in which both groups publicly displayed recognition of the other (cf. Wallis 1982). During the meetings, the junior leaders benefited from the presence of their superiors, who provided them with an authority that could be extended into the branches' everyday religious practices. In order to achieve this end, the junior leaders propagated the authority of the superior church elders, elevating the latter in order to be elevated themselves. Religious authority evolved in a chain of translation (Callon and Latour 1981) in which the authority of the senior leaders was constructed by the junior leaders' instrumentalizing and self-authorizing references to it. The religious authority of the senior leaders thus relied crucially on the willingness of the junior leaders to use them for their own empowerment. At the same time, the senior leaders instrumentalized the junior leaders by allowing them to perform on the public stage at religious practices. By having the junior leaders deal with the minor activities of the meeting, the senior elders' own spirituality and religious activities were endowed with outstanding importance. Each of the groups had a certain influence over the other, while simultaneously being dependent on it.

This mutual recognition was staged in public. During meetings of the leaders themselves and in private discussions, however, it became all too clear that the relationship between the elders was often conflictual and to a certain extent mutually ignorant. It is thus possible to discern two dimensions: whereas the elders at different hierarchical levels demonstrated unanimity, friendship and reciprocal respect when acting in front of the laity, their relationship was otherwise characterized by dissension and ignorance of one another.

The distinction and the movements between 'presence' and 'absence' informed the religious and organizational practices of the Spirit Apostolic Church and must be kept in mind in the following analysis, where I shall argue, among other things, that bureaucratization in this church served as a 'facade', which – while being enacted with much commitment – actually *enabled* spiritual practices rather than constrained them. Before elaborating on this point, however, the following two chapters will deal with various aspects and dimensions of 'bureaucracy in the Pentecostal-charismatic mode', first by discussing attempts to constitute 'file persons' (Harré 1984: 69), and secondly by addressing the contradictions and conflicts that arose from the written scheduling and documentation of spiritual practices.

Notes

1. Due to the lack of historical knowledge and of records documenting Enock's early church affiliation, we cannot be certain about the identity of this earlier denomination. It is highly probable, however, that Enock had attended a branch of the Full Gospel Church of God, which originated in South Africa. In 1909, an American missionary named George Bowie came to South Africa, where he formed the Bethel Pentecostal Assembly. He was soon joined by a former preacher from the African Faith Mission, Archibald H. Cooper (see also Sundkler 1976: 52, 86–87). After conflicts, Cooper separated from the Bethel Pentecostal Mission and founded the Church of God. In April 1910, however, the two denominations joined up again under the name of the Full Gospel Church of God in Southern Africa. These early developments were part of the Pentecostalist revival in South Africa, which also involved the revival of the Reformist churches of the Western Cape in the early 1860s and John Alexander Dowie's Zionist movement. At present, the Full Gospel Church of God is one of the largest denominations in South Africa and has a comparatively large percentage of English-speaking members, as well as covering all sections of South Africa's multi-racial population. For an official history of the Full Gospel Church of God, see du Plessis (1984).
2. This was also a time when the relationship between Zambia and Zimbabwe (then Rhodesia) was strained because Rhodesian independence fighters sought refuge in Zambia. Enock's failure to return to Zimbabwe could thus also be due to wider political conflicts.

Chapter 14

Positions of Writers, Positions in Writings

In his book *Discipline and Punish* (1977), Michel Foucault attributes to 'writing' a crucial role in the interrelated processes of producing knowledge, exerting disciplinary power and subjectification. Referring to a number of different relationships in European history, like priest–confessor and doctor–patient, he highlights how surveillance, normalizing judgement and examination brought about the subjugation and inscription of 'subjects' into existing power relations. This inscription, according to Foucault, was bound to particular literacy practices:

> The examination that places individuals in a field of surveillance also situates them in a *network of writing*; it engages them in a whole *mass of documents* that capture and fix them. The procedures of examination were accompanied at the same time by a system of intense registration and documentary accumulation. A 'power of writing' was constituted as an essential part in the mechanisms of discipline (1977: 201; my italics).

While Foucault never expanded further on these insights and has been criticized for failing to take into account the importance of print for modern forms of disciplinary power (Luke 1989: 3), administrative 'technologies of person production' – that is, 'methods of collecting, constructing, compiling, and storing ... information about individuals' (Cahill 1998: 141) – have in recent years received heightened attention in the anthropology and sociology of the state. Anthony Giddens, for example, points out that the capacity of the modern state is linked to its use of written documents, and that 'administrative power can only become established if the coding of information is actually applied in a direct way to the supervision of human activities' (1987: 47). Scholars have therefore examined, for instance, the connection between written registration and population control (Greenhalgh 2003), or the documentary control of citizens' identities and movements (Browne 2005; Caplan and Torpey 2001; Torpey 2000). These works more or less explicitly take up Max Weber's stress on 'files' in bureaucracy, while concentrating on the state in action and also showing great awareness of issues of power. Generally speaking, they have made it clear that a state-issued document 'legalizes and authorizes the citizen, making him/her visible, liable to control, and legitimate for the state' and that it consequently '*makes* the citizen in performative and obligatory terms' (Peirano 2002: 8).

In this chapter I shall examine how bureaucratic inscriptions in the form of religious certificates, identity cards and registers were used in the Spirit Apostolic Church in an attempt to establish durable relations between the different levels of the church leadership on the one hand, and between leaders and members of the church on the other. As with the documentary state just referred to, here bureaucratic measures were undertaken to stabilize socio-religious positions and hierarchies by identifying and legalizing individuals. Nonetheless, Foucault's 'disciplinary writing' differs crucially from the bureaucratizing practices of the Spirit Apostolic Church (SAC). Although the leaders of this church struggled to produce authoritative inscriptions, their efforts were hampered by a series of factors, like difficulties in classification and the subversive practices of the churchgoers themselves. I argue that these difficulties must largely be seen in the context of spiritualistic discourses and practices, as well as against the background of how – as outlined in the previous chapter – rational-legal and spiritual church hierarchies were played out in practice.

Certifications of Authority

When senior leaders attended the church meeting in Mazwange village in May 1999 (mentioned in the previous chapter) they incorporated the leaders of the newly established branches by registering them and issuing them with certificates. They thus acknowledged them in their function as officeholders, not as prophets or healers. Although they had been told that divinations and healings were conducted in Bululami and Keela and had assembled for a Pentecost meeting, the senior leaders did not officially sanction the branch leaders' spiritual activities. Instead they incorporated them into a hierarchy and taxonomy of church offices that were regulated by the constitution of the church. Obligations and forms of accountability were allocated as in a contract, and the relationships between the church leaders became formalized.

These activities of registration and regulation were carried out by church leaders, whose prominent position during the meeting was based especially on the attribution of an outstanding degree of spirituality, and who used their additional roles as officeholders to institutionalize the religious authority of their subordinates. Or, to put it in Weberian terms, charismatic leaders constituted an authority of legal-rational type. In attempting to control the junior church leaders, the senior elders officially invested them with authority, while simultaneously channelling this authority in a particular direction: the junior leaders were merely incorporated into the hierarchy of structural positions. Since spirituality, which posed a greater threat to the church leadership than church offices, was not officially acknowledged, the senior leaders signalled a difference between the junior leaders' and their own claims to spirituality, without, however, denying altogether spirituality to the branch leaders. Whatever spiritual power they might have, the junior leaders were unmistakably shown that they were merely 'officeholders' in the eyes of the superior leaders.

Positions of Writers, Positions in Writings

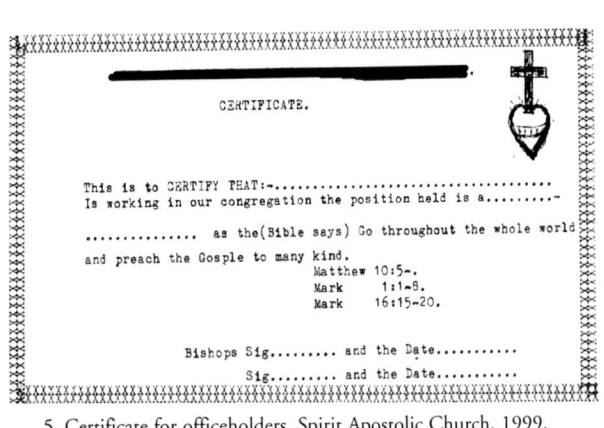

```
                    CERTIFICATE.


    This is to CERTIFY THAT:-.................................
    Is working in our congregation the position held is a........-

    ............. as the (Bible says) Go throughout the whole world
    and preach the Gosple to many kind.
                               Matthew  10:5-.
                               Mark     1:1-8.
                               Mark     16:15-20.


              Bishops Sig......... and the Date...........
                      Sig......... and the Date...........
```

5. Certificate for officeholders, Spirit Apostolic Church, 1999.

The certificates were written (*kulemba*) in English, the official language of the Zambian state and the lingua franca throughout Zambia. It was therefore thought that the activities of the church leaders might range beyond the local branches and even involve interactions with people from other language groups and administrative agencies of the Zambian state. The certificates were expected to be particularly useful when travelling to distant regions and in encounters with bureaucratic institutions, that is, when moving in social realms other than the BaTonga. At the same time, however, use of English and the specific bureaucratic form of the certificates incorporated this wider realm into the practices of the SAC. They were intended to represent the Church officially towards the 'outside' world, while, in a gesture of self-authorization, being employed to represent this 'outside' within the church. These functions were even given priority over local concerns and circumstances: a number of the branch leaders, who had never learned English, could not read what was written on their own certificates.

The certificate also contained blank lines for the date and the signatures of the bishop and the respective officeholder. They resembled legal contracts in which the parties concerned signed a mutual agreement that henceforth – that is, from the date of signing – laid down mutual obligations and forms of accountability. Lastly, the certificates contained references to Bible verses: the authority conveyed by the certificates was thus backed up by their being linked to the authority of the Scriptures. After specifying the name of the officeholder and his or her church office, the officeholder's main task was introduced by the sentence, 'As the (Bible says), "Go throughout the whole world and preach the Gospel to many kind"'. This provided an indication of how these passages in the New Testament that were drawn up in a reference list should be understood. The practice of citing these Bible verses without reproducing their wordings assumed either that they were common knowledge or that the respective reader would have to consult the Bible after reading the certificate.

During the Pentecost meeting of 1999, it was not only the leaders of the newly founded branches who received certificates, but also those from already established congregations. In previous years, the SAC had not issued certificates due to a lack of funds for photocopying. Certificates were thus not obligatory or indispensable for a person to act as an officeholder. All the same, once they had been made available, they were used as a device to prove one's position within the church by reference to an objectified form of authority.

Taken together, therefore, the certificates helped stabilize socio-religious authority while simultaneously being employed by the senior church elders to signal a difference between their own (spiritual plus rational-legal) authority and that of the junior leaders, which was only acknowledged formally to be of a rational-legal type. We shall come back to this double-edged function of the church's bureaucratic products in Chapter 17.

What is significant at this point in my argument, however, and what will be demonstrated in the following section, is that – almost paradoxically – the senior church elders' efforts to channel the authority of the junior leaders by bureaucratically reducing them to 'officeholders' went along with elaborate spiritualistic discourses concerning the activities and personal qualities of officeholders. This is suitably demonstrated by a paradigmatic position in the church's bureaucracy, namely church secretaries.

God's Secretaries

All congregations of the SAC in 1999 had church secretaries (*balembi*). Most of them had been selected from among the ordinary church members and had then received brief instructions from the former secretary or one of the other church elders. In some cases, they had merely been shown samples of previous secretarial work so that they could understand its overall pattern. Henceforth they were left alone with the task, for none of the branch members usually cared how the secretary carried out his job. Only once a year did the branch secretaries receive any supervision from the general secretary of the Church. Having collected the service reports for a whole year, the secretaries sent them to the headquarters in Siamujulu village, where they were examined with a view to their accuracy, handwriting and formal organization. During the General Meeting, which was normally held in Siamujulu village in July of each year, the secretaries were then given feedback and further instructions on how to improve their work.

The selection and training of secretaries was thus an apparently unremarkable and mundane affair. The initial instructions in secretarial tasks were given by the way, and supervision by the main board only evolved on a long-term basis. All the same, the question of who might be an appropriate person to act as a secretary involved a series of locally important issues. My interlocutors agreed that some basic literacy skills were indispensable for anyone to be invested with the office. They differed, however, in the extent to which they emphasized reading and writing: whereas some insisted that secretaries should be proficient readers and writers right from the start, others maintained that rudimentary literacy skills would suffice at the beginning and that the Holy Spirit would subsequently improve their skills while they did the job. The latter view agreed with the suggestion made by some that literacy might be acquired through divine guidance. Several of my interlocutors knew of cases in their neighbourhood where somebody who had never attended school suddenly developed the ability to read and write after joining a Christian congregation. In such cases, it was stated, the Holy Spirit had assisted them in becoming proper Christians by providing them with the ability to read the Bible themselves (cf. Hofmeyr 2002: 449–50; MacGaffey 1983: 114). A similar idea was voiced concerning the church secretaries of the Spirit Apostolic Church. If someone was truly willing to serve God as a secretary, the Holy Spirit would not let him fail because of a lack of literacy skills: God would rather help him to *become* a secretary.

6. Church Secretary, Siamujulu village, 1995.

In describing the criteria for proper secretarial work, my interlocutors also disagreed over whether, and to what extent, secretaries should be endowed with spirituality from the start. Some suggested that the office of church secretary was too low in rank to presuppose spirituality: thus anyone could initially be invested with the post. The very activity of documenting the religious practices of spiritually able church leaders, however, would itself bring the secretary closer to God. Observing and recording spiritually inspired activities would thus increase his personal association with the Holy Spirit and make the incumbent a proper – that is, divinely ordained – secretary. Others saw spirituality as a prerequisite for being appointed a church secretary, asserting that only a spiritually able secretary would be able to appreciate the main points (*makani mapati*) of an ongoing religious practice. Ordinary secretaries, I was told, would either write down too much or simply choose the wrong aspects. In order to know what exactly had religious importance at any particular point of time, one had to be endowed with divine power.

There are some parallels here with local discourses on the need for spirituality if one is to preach, as described in Chapter 11. Those who interpreted the secretary's career as representing spiritual evolution induced by observing and documenting religious proceedings compared them to members of the laity attentively witnessing sermons and other religious activities in order to be spiritualized themselves. The other view, which understood spirituality as a prerequisite for proper secretarial work, drew a parallel with the activities of preachers and prophets. Similar to preachers, who had to be spiritually able in order to select the right Bible verses, selective observation and documentation by church secretaries presupposed the assistance of the Holy Spirit. And since this task required one to proceed from a rather diffuse perception of the whole (*kulanga*) to a concentrated focusing (*kubona*) on the significant aspects, the secretary could also be compared to the prophet. This assessment to some extent corresponded with the locally prevailing notion of the verbal inspiration of the Bible. Like the 'authors' of the Old and New Testaments, it was assumed, what the secretary wrote had to be divinely guided.[1]

Other debates in my area of research concerned the topic of God's book in heaven. God was depicted as the primordial bookkeeper, dwelling in heaven with a large bound volume close beside him. There were disagreements, however, concerning, first, whether God had already written down everything that would happen in the future, or whether he was continuously taking written records of what he observed, and second, how the relationship between God's book and the secretaries' writings might adequately be described. Some members of the SAC insisted that God's book was *closed*, that is, that God had written down everything that would happen on earth a long time ago. The church secretaries thus produced nothing other than an exact copy of what had previously been projected in God's book. God knew beforehand what would happen and how the secretaries would record it. Other members of the SAC considered God's book to be still *open*, that is, God was said to be continuously monitoring and recording human activities. This interpretation led to two further but different conclusions. For some of my interlocutors, there was an invisible connection between God's book in heaven and the writings of spiritually able secretaries. With the assistance of the Holy Spirit, it was assumed, such secretaries would produce identical documentation to what God was producing in heaven. The monitoring and recording were thus depicted as evolving simultaneously in heaven and on earth. And since the writings in these two dimensions were identical, one knew what was written in God's book by reading the writings of a spiritually endowed secretary. The other conclusion was that the secretaries and their writings were themselves among the objects of God's monitoring. According to this interpretation, God observed and documented how the secretaries were carrying out their task. Whereas the first explanation assumed that spiritually able secretaries would work side by side with God, the latter made the commitment and accuracy of secretaries a criterion upon which they would be judged by God on the Last Day of Judgement. God's book would thus differ from a secretary's writings by including judgements on it.

However, even those of my interlocutors who assumed that the office of church secretary presupposed spiritual ability did not consider the material products of secretarial work to be endowed with any divine power in themselves. The agendas, reports and lists they drew up were treated like mundane writings. They were not shown any particular reverence, and the reading or consultation of such documents was generally undertaken with a view to their pragmatic value.

Identifications and Registries

While the senior elders of the SAC endeavoured to institutionalize the authority of the junior leaders by granting 'certificates', an attempt was simultaneously made to institutionalize church membership by issuing 'identity cards' and keeping membership registers.

The identity cards, which formed part of Bishop Rabson's attempts to reconcile the church through bureaucratic means, resembled the certificates of the church elders in that they too referred to a Bible verse without reproducing its wording. Instead of containing blank lines for signatures, however, the identity cards only provided a space for the church member's name, the headquarters of the SAC being indicated in the form of a postal address. In contrast to the certificates, therefore, the identity cards did not resemble legal contracts. A depersonalized institution was mentioned as the contact address. None of the senior elders signed the certificate of membership. The relationships between senior and junior church leaders, on the one hand, and between church elders and laity, on the other, were thus based on different premises. The relationship enshrined in the certificates of the church elders not only had legalistic connotations, it was also based on the inscription of an interaction – in the form of the two signatures – and a highly personalized transfer of authority from 'above' to 'below'. This transfer thus had parallels with the dispersion of charisma. By contrast, the relationship between the church elders and the laity as inscribed in the identity cards did not presuppose any interaction. The forms had no blank spaces for signatures that could be construed as indicating mutual agreement. The elders could therefore not be made responsible for the particular church member's conduct. Instead of referring to an identifiable religious leader, church affiliation was to a depersonalized institution.

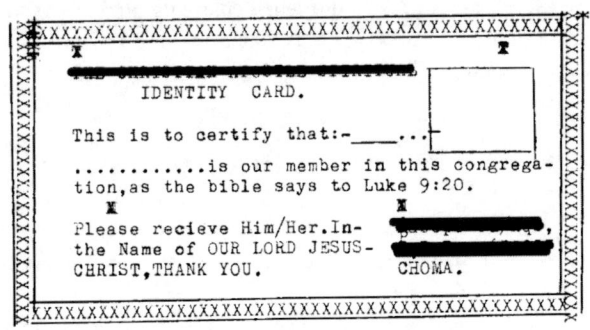

```
IDENTITY   CARD.
This is to certify that:-_____...
............is our member in this congrega-
tion,as the bible says to Luke 9:20.
Please recieve Him/Her.In
the Name of OUR LORD JESUS-
CHRIST,THANK YOU.                CHOMA.
```

7. Identity card, Spirit Apostolic Church, 1999.

This kind of affiliation with an abstract institutional entity had certain parallels with citizenship in the Zambian nation state. Some features of the identity cards actually resembled Zambian 'registrations cards' in, for example, having a space for a photograph. They also contained a request by the church leadership that those persons or institutions to whom the document was presented should receive the holder of the identity card as a Christian. Identity cards were devised for situations in which the particular church member encountered people from beyond his normal and immediate social context, elsewhere in Zambia or the English-speaking world, perhaps, as well as in problematic settings where some form of documented identity might prove useful. Since many church members did not have Zambian 'registration cards' or any other document formally certifying their personal identity, the identity cards issued by the SAC on the basis of membership provided a certain substitute.[2] Being designed for use in a wider social space, they also suggested that any interactions that developed should be of a *Christian* kind.

Besides the identity cards, branch leaders also registered the members of their respective congregations.[3] There were, however, no explicit rules about when and how such an 'inventory of persons' (Goody 1977: 80) should be created. Each congregation therefore registered members in its own way: whereas some registers merely recorded the names of churchgoers, others also included information about gender, age, and/or village of residence. They also differed in what they regarded as the proper age for membership. In some branches – mostly in those of smaller size like the one in Intema village – even babies were put on the membership lists, because otherwise it would hardly have been worthwhile to start registration at all. In others, being of marriageable age was a precondition for registration.

That the identity cards and membership registers of the SAC did *not* inscribe the churchgoers into 'networks of writing' was connected, among other things, with the fact that these two types of documentation were not linked to any other occasion of writing outside the church: instead, they constituted singular instances of inscription which occasionally did not even accord with one another. When, in June 1999, the choirmaster of Siamujulu village decided to adopt the name of his mother's family, he was able to do so without constraint. He had neither a passport nor a registration card issued by the Zambian state and was not even registered as a voter, something that would have to be taken into account when changing one's name. In the end, his name on his SAC identity card, which was issued in May 1999, differed from how it was entered in the membership register in August 1999.

Fixing Polyvalent Rites of Passage

One of the main problems in allocating identity cards and registering members was the floating membership that characterized the SAC: who were actually to be counted as 'members' was difficult to determine. Some of the participants in its forms of religious practice had started attending the church services to obtain treatment for an affliction, and there was never any guarantee that they would continue participating. Terminating one's church attendance after successful treatment in a prophet-healing church was common in my research area (cf. Kirsch 1998: 40–46). Others attended church services only sporadically. Yet others did not show up in church for many months but still identified themselves as members of the SAC. Should they be registered as members, and should they be given identity cards?

There were, moreover, no clearly defined criteria for the transition from mere participation to church membership. During church meetings, the leaders of the SAC baptized anyone who requested it. No religious instruction or examination by the church leadership was considered necessary before baptism. In any case, in the SAC – as in other Pentecostal-charismatic churches in my area of research – baptism was not seen to be necessarily a single event in the life of a Christian. It undoubtedly represented a significant symbol of religious devotion and affiliation with the church. Yet, since baptism was also related to the cleansing of sins and the exorcizing of demons, most church members had been 'baptized' more than once. Similarly, for some casual visitors to church meetings, baptism meant being spiritually cleansed; after being 'baptized', they never attended the church again. Baptism in the SAC thus represented a polyvalent rite of passage (van Gennep 1922) from a sinful to a Christian way of life, from demonic possession to being freed from evil spirits, and from being an outsider to being an insider within the church. Given such polyvalent meanings, baptism provided no clear indication of membership.

Against this background, it was almost impossible for the church elders to identify who among the congregation could actually be counted as members at any given point of time. Since there was no unambiguous rite of passage, and since the church's own headquarters had not laid down binding standards for membership, the secretaries of the different branches used different criteria in registering the names of 'members' and allocating identity cards. All the same, there had been attempts in the history of the SAC to institutionalize baptism as a rite of passage. In 1997, the senior church elders issued 'baptism tickets'. These documents at first sight resembled the certificates for officeholders issued in 1999. Yet in contrast to the latter, which the incumbent and the bishop both had to sign, the baptism tickets provided a blank space for the baptizer's signature. They were not contracts between the baptized person and the church leadership, but rather documents that certified that one had gone through a rite of passage. Describing the document as a 'ticket' thus underlined the idea that baptism punctuates and even constitutes the transition from a non-Christian to a Christian way of life. By issuing baptism tickets with signatures representing two levels of the church hierarchy (the baptizer and the bishop), the church elders sought to link this transition officially to formal church affiliation. They thus provided the rite of passage with the institutional stamp of bureaucratic certification. However, because of the difficulties mentioned above in laying down formal criteria for church membership and the polyvalent connotations of baptism among church members, this attempt was deemed to have failed by 1999.

In general, the difficulties in stabilizing socio-religious positions by identifying 'church members' were related to the particularities of the wider religious field. As discussed in Chapter 3, religious practice in my area of research was generally characterized by a high degree of selectivity and flexibility. It was considered a truism by my interlocutors that church leaders might easily fail to contact God due to their human fallibility, the evanescent character of the Holy Spirit or the workings of evil spirits. They accordingly stressed that one should always be sceptical of claims to absolute religious authority. Therefore, although bureaucratic inscriptions in the form of 'identity cards' or 'baptism tickets' were taken seriously once they had been issued, they ultimately represented portrayals of the momentary that, in the final analysis, did not confine people's movements between different forms of religious practice.

Portrayals of the Momentary

Difficulties in generating membership registers also had to do with the fact that many Christians in my research area tended to be rather indiscriminate when it came to registering their names. Church secretaries complained that some people were entered simultaneously in the membership registries of different denominations. This practice of multiple registration, they explained, was due to the widely held supposition that, on Judgement Day, only one Church would prove to have been authorized and guided by God. In this view, the members of all the other churches would subsequently have to suffer for having made a wrong choice on earth. Only those who had registered with the right denomination would immediately go to heaven, since the membership register of 'the genuine church' would be identical with God's heavenly registry of proper Christians (cf. Droogers 1980: 193; Hofmeyr 2002: 448–49; Muller 1997; see also Wogan 2004). Being entered in several church registers at once thus increased one's chance of being placed among the chosen on Judgement Day.[4]

Using these explanations, the church secretaries tried to account for their difficulties in conveying to the religious participants a sense of the exclusiveness of membership: one name, one church, one register. However, churchgoers' actual practices and the religious framework of the SAC inhibited such exclusive arrangements. Registers did not coincide with the actual social boundaries of particular congregations. And even when someone's name was recorded in the register, the inscription did not commit him or her to anything. Raising donations – for example, to hire a lorry for a church meeting – and recruiting volunteers for the maintenance of church buildings were arranged without recourse to the membership registry. In fact, the church elders had as few opportunities to exert compulsion on the registered members as on the non-registered participants.

Given that there were no rights or duties associated with being registered, at first sight it seems astonishing that the branches of the SAC kept membership registers at all. The branch leaders' endeavours to institutionalize the membership of their congregations certainly represented an attempt to demarcate the boundaries of the community by encouraging unequivocal statements of religious affiliation. Yet, as we have seen, being entered in such registers did not imply stabilizing social positions and roles in the long-term. Being registered had no actual consequences. The registers themselves – i.e., the material entries – were not used for administrative purposes. Whatever decisions had to be made within the Church were negotiated without consulting the membership registers. Registration was therefore not made to correspond to objectified social positions. Instead, it was the *act* of registering that was important: in assenting to being registered, participants in the religious practice of the SAC were making a declaration of intent. And this declaration was momentary, a spontaneous expression of volition concerning the participant's affiliation to the church. Membership registration through the secretaries accordingly represented an effort to ascertain the degree of commitment at a certain point in time. And since this could not be objectified, the registers had to be continually updated, each up-date providing a fresh picture of each congregation's current position.

Branches also registered their members because the headquarters of the SAC obliged them to do so. Copies of the membership registers had to be handed over to the main board each year and were then kept in the homestead of the General Secretary. For many branch members, the existence of this particular 'archive' provided an incentive to have themselves registered. Since they assumed that the headquarters of the church must be a place of outstanding spirituality, storing the registers in Siamujulu village implied that their names were closer to God. In contrast to the assumption mentioned earlier that the register of 'the genuine church' would have its identical double in heaven, this idea was based on the assumption that membership registers had to be passed on within the church hierarchy so that God would finally notice them. Such conjectures could also be found in other denominations: members of the New Apostolic Church (*Neuapostolische Kirche*), for instance, knew that the membership registers proceeded through a number of hierarchical steps until they were eventually archived in the national headquarters of the denomination. Some of my interlocutors thus took pride in the fact that – in the words of one of them – 'our names are written in Lusaka'. Here again, a spatially distant realm with positive connotations of success and a prosperous lifestyle was equated with closeness to God.

This chapter has dealt with bureaucratic inscriptions of socio-religious identity in the form of 'certificates', 'identity cards', 'baptism tickets' and 'registers'. I have shown that, although these written inscriptions were taken seriously by church elders and church members as a means of capturing and/or signalling socio-religious identities, they were involved in a complex configuration which, for the most part, undermined efforts to construct a 'network of writings'. On the one hand, bureaucratic inscriptions were used in an attempt to constitute and maintain institutional authority over the church laity and – in the case of the senior elders – over the junior leaders too. In the latter case, the (potentially subversive) Pentecostal-charismatic authority of the junior leaders was ignored by the official stress on their rational-legal authority. On the other hand, as has been demonstrated with regard to church secretaries, the formal institutionalization of church offices went along with elaborate Pentecostal-charismatic discourses concerning the activities and personal qualities of officeholders. Spirituality was therefore used to give meaning to and legitimize the church's bureaucratic work. Finally, the bureaucratic stabilization of church membership represented a challenge to the church leadership because people in my research area were generally sceptical of claims to absolute religious authority. Being registered by a church was religiously significant for them, but this did not mean that their movements between different forms of religious practice were restricted.

Notes

1. The notion of 'divine secretaries' is well known from the history of European Christianity. H. Adriaanse gives an example from the Lutheranism and Calvinism of the sixteenth and seventeenth centuries. Here, a new conception of divine inspiration had been introduced, which referred less to the inspired contents of the Bible than to 'the way in which Scripture had been written down. The humans who had played a role in this putting-on-record had by no means acted for themselves. God was the causa principalis of Scripture; they were merely its causa instrumentalis' (1998: 322).
2. The distribution of membership cards certainly goes back to the practices of Western missionaries. Jean Comaroff, for example, points out that the members of Nonconformist Methodist missions in South Africa were 'issued with "tickets", whose renewal on a quarterly basis was subject to an assessment of moral standing' (1985: 141).
3. Seen in a historical perspective, devising registers was first pursued in my area of research by colonial administrators when collecting taxes or distributing famine relief (Read 1932: 21), and it also reflected a common practice among early Western missions (e.g., Comaroff 1985: 141; Garvey 1994b: 66; Scarnecchia 1997: 93).
4. These positive connotations of being registered are probably a relatively recent phenomenon. E. Andersson (1958: 41) points out, for the early history of Christianity in the Lower Congo: 'The Europeans were also thought to be able to take possession of the souls of natives by writing their names. When the school at Madzia was founded in 1910–11, the children accordingly dared not tell their own or their parents' names, "because", as they said, "if we reveal our names to him, we will die at once"'. A similar reluctance was voiced by those of my interlocutors who had been among the first school children of Sinazeze area. They stressed that registration during colonial times was associated with taxation, forced labour, and the fear that a child might forcibly be taken away from its parents.

Chapter 15

Outlines for the Future, Documents of the Immediate

The word 'organization', it has been argued, 'is a noun and it is also a myth. If one looks for an organization one will not find it. What will be found is that there are events, linked together, ... and these sequences, their pathways, their timing, are the forms we erroneously make into substances when we talk about an organization' (Weick 1979: 358). While having in the preceding chapter addressed Pentecostal-charismatic attempts to establish bureaucratic inscriptions of socio-religious positions and hierarchies, this chapter takes up Karl Weick's emphasis on the processual character of organizing practices. Dealing with the bureaucratic coordination of religious activities through agendas and reports, I demonstrate, first, what contradictions arose through the written planning and documentation of Pentecostal-charismatic practices and, secondly, that these contradictions and the concomitant conflicts between church elders did not lead to an institutionalization of charisma but to demands for a re-spiritualization of bureaucratic practices instead.

Agendas as Revelations

For each Sunday service at the Spirit Apostolic Church (SAC), a written agenda was prepared by one of the junior leaders of the congregation. These agendas were usually sketched out briefly before the event according to the instructions of the superior church elders, who earlier in the morning had discussed the seating plan and the order of sermons. The drafts thus usually contained lists of names in a certain order and sometimes a plan of the seating arrangements of the church elders. Later on, the junior leader used this outline as a mnemonic aid in conducting the service and announcing the names of those who were to preach. During the course of the service, it was usually another junior officeholder who took notes of the proceedings. In some cases, however, the person conducting the service simultaneously acted as secretary. The written agenda then occasionally provided a structural framework into which the details of the documentation were simply inserted. This procedure, which was mostly due to a shortage of paper, progressively transformed the 'agenda' into a 'service report'.

Agendas for church meetings, on the other hand, were drawn up in more detail. Some days prior to the meeting the Bishop of the SAC usually retreated into the wilderness in order to pray, fast and write the agenda. It was thus usually claimed that the agenda had been divinely inspired, that is, the Holy Spirit had revealed how a particular church meeting should be conducted. The Bishop's initial handwritten draft was then usually copied on a typewriter. Occasionally, the typist used carbon paper, so that there might be four or five copies available. All the same, these copies were never sent out before the meeting but always remained with the Bishop until he himself arrived at the particular meeting ground. This sometimes meant that the agendas reached their destination after the religious service had already started.

The agendas generally consisted of several pages headed by the name of the church, the purpose and place of the meeting, and the date.[1] The rest of the page gave a simple chronology of the proceedings, divided into periods that were usually rounded up or down to the nearest quarter of an hour. The agendas specified obligatory times for daily routines like waking up in the morning, cooking, eating, and going to sleep. For the most part, however, the programme outlined in the agendas referred to members' and church elders' activities during religious services, which were held several times each day. Some procedures were laid down in a detailed manner. The early morning hours of 28 July 1999 of the General Conference Meeting in Siamujulu, for instance, were specified as follows:

05:00 hrs   All women should wake up so that they wake up all the people, from there everybody should go in church so that they can have morning opening prayer. While singing when leaders get inside the church all the people should stand up. Then just after that all the leaders/elders should kneel down to pray in their hearts. After than then a song of prayer and all the people should kneel down and pray to God also.

05:30 hrs   Then time will be given to the speaker to enlighten the members of the church what is to be done. He is to tell them, what is to be done, while others go and wash their faces and eat breakfast. Just after the service still the sick people should remain in church to be prayed for.

Some parts of this programme obviously corresponded with the usual procedures for commencing a service in the SAC. Although all the Sunday services of all the branches more or less exactly followed these routines on their own, the particular sequence of interactions and activities was here specified in minute detail, as if it were a novel procedure. In addition, this elaborate sequence was usually contained in the written schedules for each day of a meeting.

This redundancy of repetition is the first noteworthy feature of the agendas of church meetings. It has already been mentioned that the senior church elders tended to adopt a certain attitude of aloofness during church meetings. They refrained from walking around in public and most of the time shunned overt visibility by staying in a grass shelter. Nor did they usually come to all the religious celebrations of a meeting. Some services were only attended by the junior leaders, and even when senior elders were present, the junior leaders were responsible for managing the proceedings. This placed the senior leaders in a certain position of dependence on their subordinates. By devising a detailed agenda, an attempt was therefore made to control the proceedings even in the absence of the overall leadership of the church. And by articulating the descriptions in a redundant form, account was also taken of the fact that the written agenda of a meeting mostly consisted of loose papers: since pages occasionally went missing, it seemed inadvisable to make references between pages. Instead of simply inserting an indication in the schedule for a particular time on a particular day that the same procedures had been described for the previous day, each page was treated as an independent unit.

Another noteworthy feature of the agendas for church meetings was their emphasis on solemn and ritualized courtesies. Besides specifying the activities of the choirs, those conducting services and the preachers, a lot of space was devoted to descriptions of the appropriate behaviour of the laity towards the church elders. The evening service on 28 July, for example, was scheduled to start as follows: 'All the choir members must be inside the church and start singing as they wait for the members to get in. Then the elders will come in and still the people will stand up giving respect to them'. Such descriptions are surprising at first sight, because they project forms of conduct – the laity's reaction in terms of 'giving respect' (*kulemeka*) – that cannot be 'scheduled' by the church leadership. They nonetheless represented prescriptions regarding what the senior church elders saw as the formally correct behaviour in their presence. In the hands of the junior leaders, who were responsible for managing the movements of the congregation, laying down proper behaviour thus assisted them in 'staging' the senior church elders' exceptional status and importance.

A comparison between what was included in the agendas of church meetings and what was not is revealing. Let us return to the agenda for 28 July:

13:45 hrs   This time all the choir members will be inside the church as they wait for other people of the church to come in. Then one choir will go out and bring the elders of the church, while the other choir continues to sing. As the elders reach the door the choir which is outside stops singing and the singing inside choir takes the place. Then all the elders in front will kneel down and pray in their hearts, but before that as the elders enter the church all the people should stand up. Then the song of prayer will be sung and still all the people will kneel down and then one person in front will pray for all the members in church.

This passage articulates a complicated choreography of movements and interactions. There is no indication, however, concerning which particular groups should act as choirs and which hymns should be sung. Nor were the names of those who were to pray for the congregation or the contents of their prayers determined in advance. In some parts of the agendas, however, blank spaces were provided where the relevant person's name could be filled in: '(12:30 hrs) This will be to close the morning service. The one person will be given time to close the word of prayer. The prayer was led by ………………… and then all the people will leave the church'.[2] Such blank spaces were also available for preachers. The timetable for the morning service of 27 July, for instance, was as follows:

09:30 hrs	This will be time for the choir so that they make stand up the preacher man. The preacher man is …………… and he has opened the book of ……………….
09:45 hrs	The choir will sing a song to make the second preacher to stand up: He has preached and opened the book of ………………… He is ……………………

Such blank spaces for the names of the acting preachers and for chapters of the Bible are significant in the analysis being pursued here for two reasons. First, the fact that these blank spaces had been created when drawing up the agenda indicates that the author intended the written schedule to be used by others as some sort of framework for recording the service, similar to the aforementioned literacy practice during the Sunday services in the branches. The form of the 'agenda' could thus be transformed into a 'service report'. Slight modifications would turn a schedule for the future into a record of the past. The phrasing of the above quotation in the past tense might therefore not just result from the author's lack of proficiency in English: it might also be interpreted as having a certain programmatic character about it.

Secondly, the blank spaces stood for two kinds of unpredictable situation. On the pragmatic level, it was actually impossible to know in advance which church elders would be present during a church meeting and which choirs would attend. Inserting blank spaces into the agenda thus promised organizational flexibility. At the same time, however, the blank spaces reflected another essential unpredictability: the in-pouring of the Holy Spirit. As in Sunday services, sermons presented at church meetings were said to require the guidance of the Holy Spirit. Whoever acted as the preacher on a particular day and what his sermon would contain were not always considered predictable. The same applied to prayers, which were assumed to be a matter of spontaneous inspiration that could not be scheduled or scripted in advance. The vacant spaces in the lines of the agenda thus represented blank spaces for the Holy Spirit, which had to be filled with what could not be known in advance.

Reports of the Unpredictable

Besides being scheduled in writing, the SAC's weekly services were also documented in 'Service Reports'. To some extent, these reports resembled the agendas for church meetings. Headed by the relevant date, the words 'Sunday Service Report' and occasionally the name of the branch, these reports outlined the course of the service in chronological order. The Sunday service in Siamujulu village on 5 May 1999, for example, was documented as follows:

10:16	Choir songs
10:48	Opening song
	~~Gondingo~~
10:55	Prayer.
10:54	Gondingo[3]
10:57	Thanking time. Only three people given chance to thank our Lord.
11:50	The time was given to Mr [Alaster] the D. Evangelist, who opened the book of Issaiah 66:10.
12:15	The time was given to Mr [Kiran] our G. Secretary who opened the book of second Corinthias 4:1
12:57	The time was given to our General treasurer Mr [Esnart]. And he opened the Book of 2 Corinthias 9:1 and verse 8 and verse 9. And the service was ended by G. Secretary.
13:48	The service ended at 13:48
	Attendance is 138
	Money offering is K 1,290

The report was arranged according to the exact times when something occurred. Whereas the scheduling of agendas for church meetings was usually rounded up to the nearest quarter of an hour, in the service reports an attempt was made to record the time accurately. In some cases, the reports had minor inconsistencies in the temporal order: for example, in the case above the 'prayer' is noted before the '*gondingo*', although the time indicated suggests that the order had actually been other way round. Such inconsistencies were mostly due to the secretaries' difficulties in simultaneously participating in the service and recording it in writing. If the secretaries tried to keep pace with social time, 'mistakes' were almost unavoidable and (idiosyncratic) abbreviations often indispensable. Yet although the reports of Sunday services were therefore provisional in form, they were not corrected or rewritten later on. This is in contrast to the service reports of church meetings, which were occasionally subjected to a considerable post hoc reworking.

The crossed-out word '~~Gondingo~~' in the above report at first glance appears to represent another instance of secretarial 'error'. Yet seen in light of the actual proceedings of the service and of widely shared views of the secretary's role, the peculiarity of this 'mistake' becomes evident. After the opening song had been sung, one of the choir members initiated a *gondingo* by singing the first lines of a popular hymn, soon followed by some other members joining him and dancing. Sitting beside the secretary, I noticed that he wrote down the word 'Gondingo' at this point. It shortly afterwards emerged, however, that a majority of the churchgoers were reluctant to join in. Two minutes later, the *gondingo* faded away, and everyone returned to his place. Before starting the next paragraph of his report, the secretary crossed out the word 'Gondingo', which he had previously written down. After the service, a group of church elders assessed the event. They explained to me that this first attempt to start a *gondingo* had lacked the inspiration of the Holy Spirit. The fact that the secretary had eventually omitted it from his report on the service, they asserted, clearly indicated his personal spiritual capacity: any ordinary secretary would not have recognized that this had not been a properly spiritual *gondingo* and would have accordingly recorded it in writing. Knowing what to include and what not to include in a report on a service thus presupposed that one had spirituality.

At their briefest, the Sunday service reports of 1999 took the form of chronological lists in which the kind of activity was merely indicated by one or two words. In other reports – like the one above – some parts of the service were described in complete sentences that reproduced conventionalized formulae (e.g., by starting with the phrase 'Time for…' [*Chiindi*…]). Both types of documentation had in common the fact that they usually did not give any indication concerning who had written them. Although the reports frequently mentioned the church offices and personal names of the main actors in the service, those who kept records of the proceedings did not usually record their own names. This self-negation was mostly connected with the view mentioned earlier that secretaries were guided by the Holy Spirit. Since reports of services were widely assumed to be authored by this divine being using the secretaries as its vessel, any secretary adding his own signature would have been dismissed as having made a narcissistic and misguided gesture.

All the same, this conception of spiritual authorship was not shared by everybody. As already described in the previous chapter, opinions differed when it came to the question of the secretaries' spirituality. Some church elders maintained that being endowed with the powers of the Holy Spirit was no prerequisite for being a secretary. A former General Secretary of the SAC, for instance, clearly distinguished between 'gifts of God' (*cipego caleza*) and secretarial tasks. What is remarkable here is that, in contrast to most other secretaries, he included personal comments when writing reports of church meetings. In May 1993, when describing a baptism, he commented: 'That was a nice day to see those who were sick that they are okey and the began to praise God singing together. The praising of God was forward because some were born again all their deferent dieseses finished'.[4] These personal additions are unusual when compared to the rather depersonalized tone of most other service reports. In imbuing his report with a sermonizing gesture, the former General Secretary was using writing as a means of worshipping God. Occasionally, he even concluded a report of a meeting with the words: 'The End. Amen. Good Night', before placing his signature at the bottom of the page.

These annotations of 1993 were admittedly made in reports of church meetings which in subsequent years were also generally more elaborate than the routine Sunday service reports of individual congregations. During church meetings in 1999, it was the General Secretary who was in charge of the reporting. Since he usually did not attend all the services at a meeting, he was assisted at times by some of the branch secretaries, who alternated in making records in their own personal school exercise books. At the end of each day, the General Secretary collected the different records in order to collate them into one official report. This process entailed making considerable alterations: hastily taken-down drafts were transformed into carefully phrased stories about what had happened on that particular day. As well as modifications in wording and graphic layout, the initial record of the proceedings was frequently recast so that it approximated to an ideal version of 'how it should have been'.

Whether the former General Secretary's reports of meetings in 1993 had been generated by this sort of (collaborative) writing cannot be determined in retrospect. Yet, a comparison between the service reports of the former General Secretary and those of most later secretaries is telling: whereas the former General Secretary often imbued his reports with a personalized undertone, the reports of 1999 tended to be depersonalized. At first sight, this seems to suggest that the SAC had undergone a process of increased formalization in the form of 'institutionalization'. I would argue, however, that there is another way of interpreting this. Denying that secretarial work presupposed spirituality, as the former General Secretary did, went along with claims to authorship and a rather personalized style of writing. Linking secretarial activities to the works of the Holy Spirit, on the other hand, as most later secretaries did, implied a denial of authorship and brought about a rather depersonalized style of writing. Conceptions of spirituality on the one hand, and conceptions of organizational institutionalisation on the other, therefore agreed in their particular effects, namely the formalized appearance of reports of services.

What was actually depicted in the reports of 1999 thus followed highly formalized and apparently conventionalized patterns. Framed by specifications concerning the beginning and the end of the event, the reports of the weekly services usually recorded the singing of the choir, the 'thanking time', the prayers and sermons, the collection, and the *gondingo* dancing. The reports of meetings of the SAC contained the same features while also dealing with those parts that were only enacted during the meetings, such as baptism and the allocation of certificates. In addition, both types of reports indicated how many churchgoers had been present during a particular event, as well as the amount of money in the collection. When the service reports were checked by the General Secretary, it was especially these latter features and the themes of the sermons that were examined.

The attendance number for the service was taken as an indication of the evangelical success or failure of the respective branch leaders. If, over time, there was a noticeable falling-off in attendance, the senior church elders usually increased their supervision. Figures for the amounts received in the collections were added up in Siamujulu village in such a way that the amount that had to be passed on from the branches to headquarters was specified. And lastly, the themes of the sermons were checked by the General Secretary in order to determine whether the teaching of the branches was in line with the senior church leaders' expectations.

In most reports, however, the themes of the sermons were merely indicated by mentioning the Bible verses that they had dealt with. The Sunday service report of the 14 March 1999 for the congregation of Siamujulu, for example, stated: 'Time was given to Mr. [Obed] the deacon who opened the book of Mathew 16:24' and 'Time was given to Mr. [Alfeo] Branch Secretary who opened the book of Issaiah 59:2'. It was not recorded how in particular the preachers had interpreted these Bible verses. Only in rare cases was additional information given. This mostly took the form of short summaries: 'Time was given to the District Evangelist [Kedrick] him he gave ... the book from Deut 30:11 to 18. This book says obeying these commandments is not something beyond your strength and reach'.[5] Others repeated the headline of the respective chapter in the Chitonga Bible: A preaching was 'from the book of Mat 26:26 which the headline says The paska of Jesus'.[6] Such commentaries represented short annotations rather than detailed descriptions. What was actually said during a sermon was not recorded in detail.

The monitoring of the branches' sermons through the General Secretary thus related almost entirely to the Bible verses indicated, not to how they had been interpreted and commented on. As with attendance numbers and money collected, supervision of preaching was reduced very nearly to a list of Bible verses. This had certain parallels in how other religious activities were documented, since it was also unusual to describe the contents of prayers and of the hymns sung by the choirs. The headquarters of the SAC accordingly did not attempt to overcome their (relative) 'ignorance' with regard to the religious practices of the branches. Bible verses served as shorthand symbols that effectively prevented potential conflicts in matters of Biblical interpretation.

Of particular importance to the present work here, however, is the fact that some features of the services and meetings were omitted altogether. In going through the 'archived' documents for the years 1991 to 1999, I found only rare references to glossolalia or prophesying. Although all the Sunday services of the SAC I attended in 1993, 1995, 1999, and 2001 had been characterized by such Pentecostal-charismatic manifestations of spirituality, they were generally not recorded in the service reports, nor were divinations or cases of spiritual healing. In the case of the Sunday services, this certainly had to do with the fact that these latter activities only took place after the public event had ended, that is, after most participants had left the church. To some extent, divination and healing thus appeared detached from the public part of the Sunday services. All the same, such activities presupposed the presence of patients, as well as of several witnesses and church elders. They were also considered to be activities of the utmost importance in terms of weekly religious practice and for the church in general. It therefore seems surprising that they were omitted from the Sunday reports, and even more surprising that prophesies uttered in the course of the services were also not mentioned.

In general, these reports of religious practice in the SAC thus reveal an interesting constellation: while the secretaries' activities were mostly assumed to require spiritual guidance, spiritual activities like prophecy and healing were generally left out of the records. In other words, the Holy Spirit was understood to inspire secretarial reports in a highly formalized manner that ruled out the Holy Spirit actually manifesting itself in the writings.

Agendas, Reports, and the Holy Spirit

The importance assigned to spiritual guidance in whatever religious activity was pursued in the SAC produced unavoidable paradoxes when it came to church meetings. It was shown above that the production of divinely ordained agendas for church meetings was assumed to require a spiritual capacity on the side of the writer. It has also been shown that some features of religious practice were similarly deemed to be spiritual, for example, in *gondingo* dancing, or when spiritual revelations were being disclosed. Such highly valued spiritual activities were essentially characterized by their unpredictability. Only the unexpected and unscheduled was ascribed the status of a spiritual event. *Gondingo* dancing was initiated in an impromptu manner, and prophecies were attributed to spontaneous spiritual impulses.

In terms of the chronological sequencing of agendas and religious practice, therefore, it was not feasible to schedule everything that ought to occur during services. Worshipping in the SAC meant anticipating and hoping for the unforeseen. Ultimately this implied that if a given religious practice turned out to be identical with what had been scheduled in advance, it was assumed to lack spirituality. The agendas for church meetings were thus characterized by in-built shortcomings. Paradoxically, both the agenda *and* the subsequent religious practice were regarded as being informed by the Holy Spirit. If they were more or less congruent, it was assumed that the Holy Spirit had not been involved at all. Yet if the agenda and the religious practice as experienced exhibited differences, only one of the two elements was attributed spirituality, which conversely was denied to the other. In such cases, conflicting perspectives were brought to bear on the question of whether it had been the bishop's agenda or the whole religious practice that had lacked inspiration by the Holy Spirit.

One example of such conflicts is the case of the General Meeting in Siamujulu village in July 1999. One week before the meeting, Bishop Rabson had retreated into the wilderness in order to pray in solitude and to ask God to reveal a divinely ordained schedule for the meeting. When he came back, he drafted the agenda and then asked me to copy it on his typewriter and to produce several carbon copies. The meeting was scheduled to start on 25 July in the afternoon. Due to transport problems, however, the congregations who were expected to come from the Gwembe Valley were delayed and only arrived late on the afternoon of 26 July. Even before the opening service had commenced, the first three pages of the agenda had thus already become waste paper. The same evening, the church elders met in order to discuss the agenda of the meeting, and Rabson handed out the copies of the written schedule. Shortly after this discussion, however, he demanded the copies back and declared that they would only be accessible in the senior church elders' shelter. The other church leaders protested and stated that proper planning was essential in the SAC. Without a written agenda, they maintained, the whole church meeting would be as disorganized as those they had experienced in the Full Gospel Church of God. They demanded clear directions concerning the order of activities. Rabson kept arguing for some time that he did not see their problem since, after all, written agendas existed. But when the junior leaders insisted that the agendas would not be of any use if they could not be taken to the ceremonial grounds, he grudgingly gave in and distributed some of the copies. In the following days, the junior leaders could be seen studying the written agenda, while the deacons used it to orient themselves while conducting the services. Yet, it actually proved impossible for them to follow the agenda precisely. The agenda for the evening service of 27 July, for example, was as follows:

19:45 hrs	All the people should go in the church and start singing as they wait for the elders to come in. As the elders came in all the people should tand up given respect to the elders. Then the elders in front should neel down and pray in their hearts. From there one is to pray for all the people while they are neeling down.
20:00 hrs	It is time when all the people should praise God, starting the highest to the youngest, so that we hear how people praise their God and to be examed on how they thak their God. As this praising of God will be there still songs from the choir should continue.

On the day itself, it took the local junior leaders until nine o'clock to assemble their congregations at the meeting grounds. The subsequent singing, the entry of the church elders and the prayers all conformed to the agenda, until Jason, a junior church leader, suddenly approached the person conducting the service and asked for a few minutes to make a public speech. He then addressed the participants by telling them about his journey from Intema village to the meeting in Siamujulu. Talking about the difficulties at home, he described how the Holy Spirit had helped him overcome his problems. He also explained that even this very act of addressing the congregation had been induced by the power of the Holy Spirit. He had suddenly felt an urgent desire to praise God and to encourage the congregation to do likewise. About twenty minutes later Jason sat down again. After a brief period of obvious embarrassment at being confronted with Jason's request, the conductor announced the speech as a 'sermon'. After that there did not seem to be enough time to resume the schedule on the written agenda. The planned 'words of thanking God' by lay members were cancelled and the service continued with the choirs singing and with another 'sermon'.

The following morning, the branch leaders, and particularly the deacon who had conducted the service the previous evening, complained greatly about the unreliability of the written agenda. In confidential conversations, most of them agreed that a schedule that had proved 'false' could not possibly have been generated with the aid of the Holy Spirit. According to them, the Holy Spirit had obviously manifested itself during Jason's public address. This very manifestation made it evident that the agenda was wrong and of a rather profane nature. In these debates, Jason himself kept a low profile. Later he explained to me that his speech had been intended as an indirect reproach to the branches from the Gwembe Valley for their late arrival. Summarizing his address, he said that anyone who was empowered by the

Holy Spirit would be able to overcome all difficulties and reach a church meeting at the right time. Several senior church elders from Siamujulu, who backed Rabson's claim that the agenda had been inspired, confirmed this version and stated that the agenda had been right and that the divergence between agenda and religious practice was the branches' own fault, since their delayed arrival clearly demonstrated their lack of religious zeal and spirituality.

In these different versions, the written agenda and the religious practice as experienced were compared and their relationship with spirituality assessed differently. The conflicts that emerged during the General Meeting in Siamujulu were certainly due to other, latent frictions among the church elders. Nonetheless, it is interesting to note that the junior leaders expressed their opposition by making reference to Rabson's written agendas. These provided a way of bringing the Bishop's authority into question by demanding organizational predictability while simultaneously voicing expectations of unpredictable spiritual activities during the service.

The paradox and apparent incompatibility between writing agendas and pursuing a spiritual form of religious practice was aggravated by another factor: the reports. It was noted above that the agendas and the reports were usually assumed to require spiritual capacity on the part of the writer. Only in being guided by the Holy Spirit would the Bishop be able to produce an agenda according to God's wishes. Similarly, only the assistance of the Holy Spirit would enable the secretary to select the 'significant' features of a particular religious practice. When Jason held his speech during the evening service of 27 July 1999, the General Secretary, Kiran, made the report of the proceedings. He wrote:

21:00 hrs	This time is the time when all member were get in the church. After that the speaker start conducting the service, he first gave chance to [Mazwange] choir sing two songs reciewing the elders.
21:20 hrs	The speaker gave time to [Sanangula] choir two songs for [Jason] to give a preaching to the congregation. He first give his way from his home, telling people about matters on his village. His friend's child was passed away but him he manage to attend the conference meeting at [Siamujulu] Headquoters. He had nothing to say but only thancking God who gave him chance to attend the meeting and on his way journey.

The report gives a comparatively detailed summary of the District Secretary's public address. It also specified the exact time of the proceedings. This degree of accuracy was not always observed. When the General Secretary correlated the reports of the different secretaries into one unified report of the church meeting, he occasionally even consolidated the agenda. The written schedule was then used as an additional resource to provide information that was missing from the reports. At the same time, merging the agenda into the report frequently represented an effort to cover up inconsistencies between the schedule and the religious practice as actually experienced. The unified report was accordingly made to resemble the agenda.

Whatever had actually been experienced, the 'archived' official report then agreed with the similarly 'archived' official agenda.

In the report of the meeting in July 1999, however, the General Secretary did not eliminate 'contaminations'. He made no modifications in order to accommodate his report to the schedule but instead reported everything in a manner that appeared indifferent, like an outpouring of 'neutral' observations. This represented a withdrawal from solidarity with Bishop Rabson, with whom the General Secretary was in strong disagreement at that time. The junior church leaders' attempts to demonstrate inconsistencies between the written schedule and the religious practice as experienced were thus corroborated by the secretary's attitude, which denied responsibility for the 'schedules' and saw 'plain documentation' as the main secretarial task.

Re-spiritualizing Bureaucracy

What is of particular significance here is the fact that such inconsistencies were usually not seen as a problem. During most church meetings, the actual proceedings did *not* agree with the respective agendas. However, these disagreements were not referred to. Although the agendas and religious practices of most meetings were characterized by a similar slippage, the dissociation was not made an issue of conflict.

In general, attempts to resolve the paradoxical tensions between the three main elements in this constellation – schedules as revelations, unpredictable spiritual events during religious practices, and the documentation of scheduled yet unpredictable practices – mostly exploited two basic strategies: the withholding of agendas, and the prompt archiving of the reports, to which access was subsequently restricted. All the same, the commonly shared founding myth of the SAC did not make it feasible to monopolize or neglect bureaucratic products altogether. These paradoxes therefore represented an integral configuration of the SAC that continually had to be taken into account.

During times of (relative) unanimity among the church elders, the paradoxes were resolved by concentrating solely on the bureaucratic process of production, not on bureaucratic products. This approach disregarded anything that could be used as an 'objectification', and instead highlighted the intricate connection between spirituality and the performance of secretarial tasks. It presupposed that the church leaders had agreed among themselves which of them was spiritually endowed. During times of conflict, however, it was this very question that became the crucial object of contention.

Nonetheless, in the period from 1995 to 2001, criticism of the senior elders' bureaucratic practices never took the form of stressing an essential difference between spirituality and bureaucracy. Instead, these two dimensions were stressed as being interrelated, the complaint being about a lack of spirituality in bureaucratization. This line of reasoning was pursued by shifting the focus from the bureaucratic process of production to the bureaucratic products themselves. As 'objectifications', the bureaucratic products now constituted 'evidence' opposing claims to spiritual capability. Nonetheless, even this criticism was ultimately aimed at achieving a re-spiritualization of bureaucratic practices: it was not an attempt to substitute spiritual practices with more emphatic bureaucratic (or in a sense institutionalized) practices. Criticism by way of bureaucratic products rather strove for a re-consolidation of spirituality. Thus, it was not expected that the Bishop should refrain from composing written agendas or that the church secretaries should stop writing reports, nor were they expected to keep spirituality apart from their bureaucratic tasks. Instead, what was emphasized was that a divinely ordained church bureaucracy essentially depends on a spiritually endowed church leadership.

This chapter has discussed paradoxes in the written scheduling and documentation of spiritual practices. In the social sciences, comparable paradoxes have commonly been interpreted as validating the idea of an essential incompatibility between 'charisma' and 'institution'. The existence of bureaucratic features in Pentecostal-charismatic practices has consequently been seen as indicating the routinization or institutionalization of charisma. Yet, in contrast to this supposition, the detailed ethnographic analysis above has presented us with the example of a combination of Pentecostal-charismatic and bureaucratic practices, in which the conflicts revolving around such paradoxes did not induce demands either to de-bureaucratize the church or to de-spiritualize its bureaucracy. On the contrary, there was agreement among the parties involved in such conflicts that the basic aim was to strengthen the connection between spirituality and bureaucracy. For them, the crucial question was how this could be achieved, and who could guarantee this connection.

Notes

1. Both agendas and reports, which will be discussed in the next section, were frequently written in English. In 1999, this certainly represented a polite gesture towards me as a European visitor. Yet as the 'archived' writings make clear, many documents from previous years were also written in English, which was considered the most appropriate language for the Church's bureaucracy.
2. Agenda for the General Conference Meeting in Siamujulu, 28 July 1999.
3. *Gondingo* is a type of passionate dancing in front of the altar in which anyone present can participate.
4. Agenda for the Pentecost Meeting in Simanzi, 16 May 1993.
5. Report of the Service in Siamujulu, 9 May 1999.
6. Report of the Good Friday Meeting in Nanyenda, 3 April 1999.

Chapter 16

Bureaucracy In-between

In the preceding chapters, various dimensions of writing practices that took the form of a 'bureaucracy in the Pentecostal-charismatic mode' were analysed. Building on these findings, this chapter examines the role of bureaucracy, first in relation to the organizational structure of the Spirit Apostolic Church, and secondly with regard to the church–state relationship. I shall argue that bureaucracy here served as both an internal and an external 'facade', which actually enabled Pentecostal-charismatic practices, rather than constrained them.

Flows and Facades

As we have seen, the attempts by senior church leaders to restore their authority in 1999 and stabilize the Spirit Apostolic Church (SAC) brought about a complex combination of Pentecostal-charismatic and bureaucratic practices. On the one hand, the local branches expected the visitations of senior leaders to provide a spiritualizing input. Repeated acts of mediation were deemed necessary for the junior church leaders to achieve a close association with the Holy Spirit. When a branch leader visited headquarters, however, he was not expected to be capable of providing such input of spirituality. The organizational structure of the SAC thus embedded a unidirectional top-to-bottom flow of spirituality. On the other hand, this was parallelled by a bureaucratic institutionalization at branch level and a subsequent bottom-to-top flow of bureaucratic products.

By granting certificates to the officeholders, the top echelons of the church endeavoured to institutionalize their relationship with subordinate levels of the hierarchy in a form that resembled legal contracts. This particular form of authority officially allocated to the junior church leaders influenced how relationships and communication subsequently evolved. When approaching the senior church leaders, the branch leaders could either address them as mediums of the Holy Spirit – for example, as prophets or healers – or in terms of their function as incumbents. The senior leaders, by contrast, addressed the junior leaders solely as officeholders. Although several of them acted as prophets and healers in their respective branches, the senior leaders never officially acknowledged these roles. In contrast with the senior church elders, therefore, the branch leaders were not assumed to be speaking from the position of prophets or healers, but only from their prescribed position as officeholders.

As incumbents, the branch leaders were consequently obliged to communicate with headquarters mainly by means of formalized bureaucratic procedures: the secretaries of the branches had to record the proceedings of church services. In these service reports, the general course of the worship, attendance numbers and the amount of money collected were documented. Each year, these reports had to be handed over to the General Secretary at the headquarters in Siamujulu village, who would then examine the activities of the respective congregations. Furthermore, membership registers were sometimes demanded from the branches, which would also subsequently be checked by one of the senior church elders. Using such procedures, the branch leaders were made to account for their efforts in evangelizing and their supervision of their respective congregations' religious practices. The Sunday reports and the membership registers thus constituted examples of a bottom-to-top flow of bureaucratic products. Whereas headquarters – apart from occasional letters, individual instances of distributing membership identity cards, and sporadically issued agendas for church meetings – was very reluctant to deliver documents to the branches, the local congregations were expected to report regularly to the main board in writing.

The two prevailing flows – spirit from above and paper from below – contrast with the practices among the Jehovah's Witnesses and in the New Apostolic Church (*Neuapostolische Kirche*), already discussed. In these denominations, literacy products were exchanged almost symmetrically. The two headquarters expected their congregations to transfer registers and lists of different kind. Yet they themselves also engaged in producing writings – for example, in issuing pamphlets, tracts and circulars – that were disseminated among the branches and that, as described in Chapter 12, had a revelatory aspect to them when they reached the branches in my area of research. In the Pentecostal-charismatic SAC, on the other hand, revelations from headquarters were only deemed realizable if the senior church elders were physically present. Their letters, identity cards, certificates and agendas were generally not considered to have any kind of spiritual impact.

Such a lack of spirituality in literacy products was also characteristic of those documents that were delivered by the branches to headquarters. The membership registers represented mere lists in the eyes of the senior church elders. And the weekly reports of services in the branches were likewise devoid of any indications of spirituality. Whatever spiritual activities occurred during the services in the branches, like prophecies or the healing of afflictions, were not to be found in the secretarial documentation later on. If one had not witnessed these services, but only checked the reports, one would not know that any spiritual activities had taken place in that particular branch. This helps us recognize a further important dimension in the relationship between the headquarters of the SAC and its branches.

We have already seen that the senior church elders usually confined their recognition of the leadership of the local branches to the allocation of church offices.

They did not sanction claims to spiritual capacity on the part of the junior leaders, and actually ignored such claims, instead instituting formalized relationships by means of bureaucratic procedures. The junior leaders' acceptance of these prescribed roles certainly induced certain constraints. Yet it simultaneously provided them with an opportunity to pursue spiritual activities completely uncontrolled by their superiors. In fact, the senior church elders were often unaware of who in particular acted as a medium of the Holy Spirit in the branches, and in some cases they did not even know what kind of spiritual activities were pursued in which congregation. The branch in Sanangula village is an appropriate example of this.

When the Divine Church with its headquarters in Namwala disintegrated after the death of its bishop in 1992, one congregation in Sanangula village in the Sinazeze area was characterized by a strong group identity and therefore planned to go on worshipping together. Conceiving the need for a denominational framework, the members of this congregation started to look for new headquarters. In 1997, they eventually joined the SAC while still retaining a corporate identity that differed from that of the other branches of the same denomination. Among other things, the Sanangula congregation tended to treat certain religious practices positively, practices that were seen in a rather negative light by most other congregations. The doctrines of the Divine Church resembled those of the *mutumwa* churches, which meant that they treated patients by means of herbs and roots. After the Divine Church had been dissolved, some of the healers left the congregation and became herbalists working on a freelance basis and combining Christian discourses with practices that to many seemed similar to those of 'traditional' healers. Yet even those who remained in the congregation mostly supported the view that herbalist treatment was an inherently Christian practice. Some of the branch leaders accordingly continued to provide such treatment, even though they were aware that the senior church elders of the SAC would strongly oppose it. The Sanangula branch regularly handed in their Sunday service reports to be examined by the General Secretary, yet since the herbalist practices were not mentioned in these reports the Church headquarters never received information that one of its branches was actually pursuing spiritual activities of this type.

Thus not only did Pentecostal-charismatic leaders institutionalize subordinate (potentially) Pentecostal-charismatic leaders in order to control them – this very institutionalization and formalism even ensured that these subordinate leaders could pursue practices of a spiritual kind without restriction. Rather than being detrimental to their Pentecostal charisma, the formalized and bureaucratized relationships actually enabled uncontrolled Pentecostal-charismatic activities.

Against this background, a configuration can be identified that crucially determined why bureaucratic procedures were pursued in the SAC, despite the paradoxes and conflicts arising out of these practices that have already been mentioned. The junior leaders of the branches officially accepted the reductionist ascription of formal roles by headquarters. Their standing within the respective local congregations simultaneously benefited from their association with the senior church leaders, who presented themselves as prominent mediums of the Holy Spirit. In overtly acknowledging this claim and instrumentalizing it according to their interests, they presented themselves locally as spiritual intermediaries between the overall leadership of the church and the laity. Their own activities as mediums of the Holy Spirit, which evolved through the religious practice of the branches, was to some extent based on such links to headquarters. At the same time, however, the spiritual activities of the junior leaders only took place in the absence of the senior church elders, who were accordingly almost ignorant of the branches' spiritual activities. The junior leaders' positions of authority thus exhibited two different constellations: to the laity in the branches, they presented themselves as both officeholders and mediums of the Holy Spirit; to headquarters, they acquiesced in their roles as incumbents.

Such a constellation implied a mutually instrumentalized asymmetry between different levels of the church hierarchy. Realizing that their claims to spirituality had become debatable by 1998, the senior leaders made efforts to reconcile themselves with the congregations and to control the church through bureaucratic means. This was taken up by the junior church leaders in a manner that left important parts of their respective branches' religious practices, namely their spiritual activities, unaffected. Bureaucracy was situated at the centre of this constellation. The products of bureaucratization – the reports, agendas, lists, etc. – attained the status of 'boundary objects' that permitted each of the parties involved to pursue its own interests while at the same time being engaged in shared literacy practices. In this sense, the bureaucratization of the SAC can be understood as a shared effort in generating a 'facade' that simultaneously concealed and made visible, a facade that was enacted with playful sincerity, and that constructed social associations and detachments at the same time.

A similar constellation can be found in the relationship between the SAC as a whole and Zambian state agencies. As we shall see in the following sections, bureaucracy attained the status of a 'protective measure' against a wider political and administrative framework that was locally assumed to be (potentially) coercive. After some introductory remarks about Southern African church–state relations in general, I shall attempt to reframe some of the previous findings concerning the bureaucratization of the SAC. This reframing with a view to the wider social space must be understood as supplementing the foregoing analysis of interactional dimensions, not as forming some kind of superstructure.

African Christianity and the State

In studies of religion in sub-Saharan Africa, the relationship between Christian movements and state powers has always been one of the main areas of research.[1] Besides examining missionary societies and their associations with and dissociations from colonial and postcolonial agencies, such investigations have concentrated on indigenous churches and movements that have separated from their original mission bodies and become autonomous. The term 'African Independent Churches', which is often used for these movements, not only refers to their organizational and doctrinal independence from Western forms of Christianity, it frequently also connotes a detached or even antagonistic relationship between forms of Christianity that originated in Africa and dominant state structures.

In his review of 'Religious Movements and Politics in Sub-Saharan Africa', Terence Ranger comments: 'In too much of the literature "politics" has meant only the politics of relating in some way to colonialism or to the post-colonial state' (Ranger 1986b: 1–2). It can also be argued, however, that this quotation might productively be inverted: in too much of the literature on religious movements in sub-Saharan Africa, relating to colonialism or to the postcolonial state has predominantly meant 'politics', where the latter term has the sense of a striving for participation in power within the institutional confines of a state. By seeing African-initiated churches through the eyes of an anthropologically informed political theory, either they come to be analysed as 'protest movements' or 'counter-societies', or else they are said to have 'accommodated' themselves to outside forces.

It is certainly undeniable that the attitude of churches towards state agencies in Africa has always been politically charged, oscillating between different forms of resistance, disengagement, accommodation and collaboration. Yet it seems that, by concentrating mainly on the political dimensions of church–state relations, other dimensions have been rather neglected so far. In an important article on the 'organizational and legal aspect of church/state interaction', Wim van Binsbergen observes that social scientists working on Christianity in sub-Saharan Africa have 'failed to problematize the successful implantation, rapid spread, and creative adaptation and transformation of the imported model of the formal bureaucratic organization on African soil' (1993).[2] His analysis of postcolonial Botswana demonstrates how the institutional framework of church–state interactions increased the organizational formalization of African Independent Churches.

This perspective can productively be brought to bear on my analysis of bureaucratization in the SAC. In what follows I shall attempt to explore some aspects of church–state relationships that have evolved implicitly and on the basis of an organizational 'mimetic isomorphism' (DiMaggio and Powell 1983). I shall demonstrate how ideas and anticipations concerning a potentially coercive state lead to a mimetic incorporation of bureaucratization.[3] Against the background of the above considerations concerning the blending of bureaucracy and Pentecostal charisma in the SAC, this appropriation simultaneously represented an accommodation towards the Zambian state *and* a withdrawal from its ambit.

Formalizing Social Relations

In his study 'African Independent Churches and the State in Botswana', Wim van Binsbergen (1993) demonstrates how interactions with state agencies have stimulated African-initiated churches in postcolonial Botswana to formalize their organizations. Starting with the Societies' Act of 1972, state agencies in Botswana endeavoured to contain and control the proliferation and practices of these movements by incorporating them into a formalized procedure of church registration. On the basis of a quantitative analysis of documentary evidence held by the Registrar of Societies and of qualitative studies of cases like the Guta Ra Mwari church, van Binsbergen argues that such incorporation actually took the form of 'co-optation'. Christian idioms of expression came to be integrated into the discourses of state agencies and representatives, while the African-initiated churches were prompted to fulfil the bureaucratic requirements for being legally registered. By registering churches, the administration brought its influence to bear on, for example, the naming of denominations and their constitutions. According to van Binsbergen, formal registration thus enhanced accommodation:

> Names chosen for such good reasons as personal preference, a prophet's dreams, their time-honored emotional and symbolic power ..., distance from yet recognizable association with a parent body from which one has broken away, are put to the test of bureaucratic adequacy, ethnic and linguistic acceptability, juridically unequivocal identification. Offices, election to which is supposed to be governed by divine inspiration or hereditary succession, have to be re-defined so as to fit in with, e.g., 'the democratic spirit of the Botswana constitution'. Unspeakable conflicts which ought never to arise in a living, inspired church have to be considered and catered for long before they inevitably do arise (van Binsbergen 1993).

Such rethinking and reshaping of previous practices in the face of state-defined demands is certainly highly significant for any research on African Christian bureaucratization. But although van Binsbergen demands a close study of the 'implantation, rapid spread, and *creative adaptation and transformation* of the imported model of the formal bureaucratic organization on African soil' (1993; my italics), his own analysis tends to treat formalized organization as a 'logic' that is rather 'alien' to African Christian movements. Instead of devoting more attention to the question of how African Christians actually adapt and incorporate organizational formalism – thus making it inevitably part of their own practice, as has been demonstrated in the preceding chapters – van Binsbergen considers 'bureaucratic logic ... often irrelevant and alien to their original orientation'. If the term 'original' is here understood to mean 'previously held', this quotation helps us specify the cases van Binsbergen seems to be referring to, namely those churches that had no formalized organization before being confronted with state-defined bureaucratic requirements. The bureaucratization of the churches induced by the state, then, would at first actually represent something 'external' to such churches. Yet in most cases it appears questionable to me where this initial externality ought to be located. As argued above, the ethnography of both contemporary and historical Christian movements in Africa suggests that most churches have in some way or another had a formalized hierarchy and a variety of church offices since their very foundation: indeed, many of them outline and document their religious practice in texts such as constitutions, registers and reports. Formalized organization, after all, is a gradual matter, not something that can be said to be simply 'present' or 'absent' (cf. Zucker 1977: 726). And, as my analysis will show, organizational formalism does not only arise in situations of immediate contact with state agencies.

Van Binsbergen also argues that the practice of bureaucracy might impose 'demands upon the churches which run so much counter to their doctrine, liturgy and general orientation that they have to present an official *bureaucratic front*, a compromise to bureaucratic discourse, which may greatly deviate from *actual* church practice' (van Binsbergen 1993; my italics). Here, we have an 'official bureaucratic front', one which is depicted as a facade that shows itself but at the same time conceals something, namely 'actual church practice'. We have already encountered such a double gesture of presentation and concealment in the preceding section in dealing with the bureaucratic 'facade' that connects and simultaneously separates the different hierarchical levels of the SAC. Yet in both cases, whether located 'within' the church or whether directed towards the 'outside', we should be careful not to equate such a 'facade' or 'bureaucratic front' with mere 'simulation': the notion of a facade too often implies that there must be an authentic core somewhere behind the appearance. When bureaucratization evolves in the social practice of African Christians even without being immediately instigated by external forces, there is hardly any reason to argue that it is not an actual – 'authentic'? – part of their church practice.[4]

It has been demonstrated in the preceding chapters that bureaucracy was an integral and significant feature of religious practice in the SAC. In contrast to van Binsbergen, who deals with churches that are or become registered by the state and that therefore interact with the institutional context of the Botswana Registrar of Societies, in 1999 the SAC had never even applied for registration, even though it moulded its religious practices according to what was locally assumed to be the basic characteristics of state agencies. The analysis must thus concentrate on the question of how particular aspects of the social and organizational environments are implicitly incorporated.

Imagining the State

Like most people in my area of research, members of the SAC only rarely came into contact with representatives of the state. Even the denomination itself has remained rather unknown to Zambian government agencies, as it has never officially been registered since being founded in 1991. The leaders of the church did have some idea of the necessary procedures, but in fact never made raising the registration fees a priority.[5] This relative lack of connectedness between the SAC and the state can also be shown with regards to the daily religious practices of the church. The only moments of contact that arose during my fieldwork in 1999 concerned general meetings of the congregations on Good Friday and Pentecost. Knowing that public assemblies in Zambia require official permission, and fearing that their church meetings would be outlawed if they were not authorized by the police, the leaders of the church filled in the required forms and finally succeeded in obtaining the desired permits, with the condition that there would be 'no political speeches'. The second case of direct contact between the SAC and state agencies took the form of a police-authorized 'neighbourhood watch' during the Pentecost meeting in Mazwange village, which gave the event a slight feeling of being supervised by the state.

Nonetheless the permits for the assemblies were approved and in the second case the police-authorized 'neighbourhood watch' attended in a supervisory role, even though the SAC was not an officially registered society and was thus potentially an illegal association. The SAC, however, was not the only case of a Zambian church that had no entry in the national Registry of Societies but that still functioned with the tacit consent of local state agencies. In 1999, only a very few denominations were officially registered in my area of research, although eighteen denominations were active within a range of about forty-nine square kilometres. The considerable lack of information available to the Zambian state in respect of the existence and proliferation of local churches clearly resulted from the financial, bureaucratic and logistic problems it had in controlling its citizens, though it can also be seen as an expression of a certain laissez-faire attitude towards civil society associations, at least as long as they were not politically active.[6]

For many local churches, however, there was constant ambivalence and uncertainty. If, for example, they received official permission to hold a meeting, then they were somehow approved by the local state agencies. But knowing that they were not legally registered, many churches were in constant fear of being declared illegal some day by the state.[7] Because of such ambivalence, imaginings and expectations concerning possible state actions and expectations abounded. Thus, among the leaders of the SAC, the Zambian state was seen as a potentially repressive and coercive apparatus. Many of them vividly narrated how the followers of the Zambian prophetess Alice Lenshina had been crushed by state agencies in the early 1960s, an action in which over 700 people had been killed because of their alleged political resistance (cf. Bond 1979; Oger 1960; Roberts 1970). They also recalled how, in the mid-1990s, the police in Sinazongwe District had forced members of the African Apostolic Church of John Maranke to take vaccinations, despite the fact that, according to the doctrine of this church, taking medicine was a sacrilege.[8] They also remembered the problems some young members of the Watchtower movement had when they refused to salute the national flag in front of the school building.

Without ever having entered into conflict with the state themselves, the church leaders assumed that the state wanted to be appreciated, that there should be no public criticism of politics, and that politics and religion should be kept carefully separate. Although they were aware of the fact that Zambia had been declared a 'Christian Nation' by President Frederik Chiluba in 1991 (Phiri 2003), they concluded that Christian belief in itself meant nothing to the state and that the state followed its own laws. They also felt that the Zambian state might even use force to control its own subjects. In addition, the church leaders were acquainted with the problems some of the other churches and most 'traditional' witch-finders had in spiritually identifying witches. An accused witch might go before a magistrate, and then the witch-finder would be obliged to provide judicial evidence of his accusation, a kind of evidence that – in the eyes of the church leaders – contradicted the spiritual or magical source of the witch-finder's revelation and would thus be impossible to produce. Even though the leaders of the SAC did not themselves search for witches, knowledge of such occurrences led them to be concerned with the question of what might happen if the state were to demand that they account before the law for their own activities.[9] And lastly, like most people in the area, the leaders of the SAC preferred to approach the local headmen for settling disputes within their immediate social surroundings, rather than involving the nearest police station. In contrast to the police, who had a reputation for being rough in their dealings, the headmen's procedures were characterized by a certain negotiability, which kept the parties to the dispute in a continuous dialogue. With the police, conversely, there was assumed to be no dialogue, unless one had the money to bribe them.

These latter practices can help us discern what 'the state' actually meant to the members of the SAC. The Zambian state was assumed to be 'the government' (*mfulumende*) and its representatives, like the police, agents of the 'neighbourhood watch' and the district administrators. The Paramount Chief and the village headmen were not regarded as belonging to the *mfulumende*. Such discriminations are significant because they highlight and result from Zambia's dual legal system, which separates, yet at the same time combines, the jurisdiction of 'customary' leaders and the general law of the nation-state. Although the Paramount Chief and the village headmen acted in some respects as the delegates of the Zambian national state, they were classified differently. That the term *mfulumende* also reflected a particular colonial legacy can be seen in the fact that to this day old people occasionally greet whites by calling them *mfulumende*, regardless of whether they are tourists, development workers or researchers like myself. Voicing my irritation with such greetings, I was repeatedly told that 'in former times, all white men were in some form or the other part of the government'. So it appears that the practices of the postcolonial national state were to some extent equated with the articulations of colonial politics and administration.

Some imaginings and expectations concerning the state can now be summarized. In the eyes of the leaders of the SAC in 1999, the Zambian state was a potentially oppressive apparatus of a supra-local order that might call them to account at any time and that significantly refused to enter into negotiations or dialogue. Against this background, besides the variety of internal rationalities for bureaucratization discussed above, the bureaucratization of the SAC can be understood as an attempt by the leaders of the church to obtain a self-protective compatibility with state agencies by mimetically incorporating bureaucratic procedures like classification, registration, documentation and 'archiving' (cf. MacGaffey 1983: 115). Despite their seemingly remote and 'uncaptured' (Hyden 1980) position, the practices of the SAC were characterized by continual efforts to achieve compatibility with the institutions of the state. Although there were almost no points of contact between state-run agencies and representatives of the church, the leaders of the church mimetically reproduced what they understood to be one of the prominent features of the Zambian state, namely the bureaucracy.

Legacies and Isomorphism

Any assessment of such processes of incorporation must first address questions of historicity. It might well be argued that the bureaucratization of the SAC can be understood as a legacy of its earliest predecessor, the American Protestant Full Gospel Church of God in Southern Africa. Yet such an interpretation is hard to sustain in the face of the actual historical development of the church. As shown in Chapter 14, the separation of the SAC from the Full Gospel Church of Central Africa was mainly justified with reference to the claim that the bishop of this earlier denomination had failed to establish effective organizational structures and procedures. Bureaucratization thus became a cornerstone for the founding myths of the SAC. And by bureaucratizing the Church in the years that followed, a continuous attempt was made to fulfil what had been promised at the beginning, among other things as a strategy for distinguishing itself in those villages where a congregation of the SAC coexisted with a branch of the Full Gospel Church of Central Africa.

The historical development of the SAC thus makes it unlikely that its organizational formalism represented a legacy – the endpoint in a direct chain of transmission – that can be explained diachronically. As the degree of formalism of the earlier denomination had been quite restricted, the bureaucratization of the SAC must rather be accounted for synchronically. The strategies for distinguishing itself mentioned above thus provide us with our first clue to the fact that the SAC developed its organizational formalism mainly because of its contemporary institutional situation. Its bureaucratization distinguished it from the Full Gospel Church of Central Africa, but it also represented a policy of rapprochement towards other Christian denominations and towards state agencies.

The bureaucratization of the SAC admittedly manifested locally prevailing ideas of how a 'proper' church should work, thus perpetuating models that had been introduced to my area of research by Western mission societies from the early twentieth century. All the same, such legacies only had an indirect impact, via the observation of collateral churches. In being oriented towards other denominations, the SAC appropriated something of the cosmopolitan flair and high reputation that was generally enjoyed by denominations in the Gwembe Valley with extensive organizational networks. These denominations were well known to the members of the SAC, because most of them had attended other churches before joining the SAC and because they were repeatedly confronted with the alternative religious practices of friends and relatives. Some of the church elders had even been officeholders in the denomination they had previously attended. The skills for and the modelling of organizational formalism in the SAC was thus largely informed by this denominational field.

Yet, if one concentrates on the reasons given by the church leaders as to why the constitution, agendas, reports and registers were important for the church, a different picture emerges, because then one is repeatedly confronted with the assertion that bureaucratization was essential because of the state. The dominant discourse in the church was not a historical one and did not refer to collateral denominations either, but justified the bureaucratic practices with reference to the state as an outside force that was both absent and present at the same time. The undeniable presence of imaginings concerning an, in fact, absent state thus induced a mimetic incorporation of bureaucratization.

The importance of considering the synchronic social context in the case of such processes of organizational formalization has repeatedly been pointed out by proponents of the 'neo-institutionalist' perspective in organization studies (e.g., DiMaggio and Powell 1983; Meyer and Rowan 1977; Zucker 1977). In their article 'Institutionalized Organizations: Formal Structure as Myth and Ceremony', John Meyer and Brian Rowan observe: 'Institutional rules function as myths which organizations incorporate, gaining legitimacy, resources, stability, and enhanced survival prospects' (1977: 340). They criticize theories that treat organizational formalization as being inherently rational and suggest that 'organizations are driven to incorporate the practices and procedures defined by prevailing rationalized concepts of organizational work' (1977: 340). Through processes of adoption, such prevailing paradigms are disseminated through organizational fields that therefore evolve what has been called 'institutional isomorphism'. Although most scholars limit the scope of neo-institutionalist arguments to post-industrial societies, their concepts can fruitfully be applied to the case study of the SAC. Paul DiMaggio and Walter Powell (1983: 150–54) distinguish between: a) 'coercive isomorphism', which comprises instances of a dominant or superordinate institution exerting pressure on other organizations to adopt particular organizational models – most of the ethnographic cases in van Binsbergen's analysis (1993) certainly belong to this type; b) 'normative pressures', which lead to an adoption of organizational models through 'professionalization' and the proliferation of normative definitions of the conditions and methods of organizing – in the case of the SAC such normative pressures can be seen as stemming from collaterally existing churches that are known for their ideas on how denominations should 'properly' work; and finally c) 'mimetic isomorphism', which develops when 'the environment creates symbolic uncertainty', so that organizations 'model themselves on other organizations' (DiMaggio and Powell 1983: 151) that appear to have greater legitimacy. This latter type of isomorphism is the one that most fits the case of the SAC. By mimetically incorporating the features of formal organization, the SAC attempted to gain legitimacy in the otherwise rather uncertain 'environment' of the state.

Presentations and Concealments

In focusing on church–state relationships, some of our findings concerning the bureaucratization of the SAC can therefore be approached from another perspective, one that supplements our previous analysis. The lists of officeholders and the written constitution can then be seen as appropriate counterparts to Zambian constitutionalism. They satisfy the perceived need for clearly demarcated social positions whose relationships are based on legal–rational principles. For the church leaders they therefore provided a platform that promised that future contacts with the state would be made on a more or less shared basis. Moreover, the agendas represented an expression of 'good will': whatever unexpected events happened during a Sunday service or church meeting that might be taken as political by state agencies, the written agenda provided the church leaders with the means to demonstrate later that they never intended these. And finally, the reports of services, meetings and conferences were placed in an 'archive' intended to keep a record of the church's activities in recent years, just in case the police call it to account. By thus mimetically bureaucratizing their religious practice, the church leaders have ensured that they have achieved a degree of compatibility with what they regard as a potentially repressive state.

Despite this degree of convergence, however, the bureaucratic mimesis of the SAC was clearly neither a mere copy of the bureaucratizing procedures of state agencies, nor a faithful outline or documentation of the religious practice of the church. There were significant differences between what was bureaucratized and what actually characterized church life. Let us recall some of these aspects. A good example is provided by the minutes of conferences kept by the church leaders, where they discussed organizational matters. Whatever disputes and quarrels might have arisen during those conferences, they were usually not recorded in the minutes. During my fieldwork I was always surprised how what had actually been controversial conferences were bureaucratically documented as peaceful events characterized by unanimity. In this way, church leaders were assured that reports on the church had been 'archived' in order to provide the accountability that might be demanded by state agencies, while simultaneously reducing them almost to a level of vacuity that meant that they could never later be used as a legal document. The similar production of an empty space in bureaucratization can be seen with regard to the service reports: whatever the spiritual activities, like prophecies or healing, that occurred during a service or meeting, they were not found later in the report. The recorded proceedings of the services thus left the impression that there had been no spirituality in the church on that occasion. Here again, accountability through an 'incorporation of the state' is provided for, while at the same time a degree of disengagement is practised in which particular aspects of the church are obscured to ensure a certain autonomy. The bureaucratization of the SAC was thus not a passive or merely reactive mimesis of a wider bureaucratized realm, but rather an active creation that at the same time both *presented* and *concealed*.

The mimetic bureaucracy of the leaders of the SAC thus evolved in a threefold manner. First, expectations and imaginings of potentially repressive state agencies stimulated the incorporation of particular bureaucratic features of the state that promised to provide a degree of compatibility and thus a measure of protection against the threat of the church being outlawed by the state. Thus, the bureaucratization of the church can be depicted as creating a form of self-protective legitimacy towards the state. Second, the very practice of mimetic bureaucratization brought the church leaders into a position that, in the eyes of the laity, paralleled the powerful position of the state. Therefore, what initially appears to be simply a defensive policy on the part of the church leaders towards the state – namely bureaucracy – also turns out to enhance the legitimacy of the church elders within their own community. Third, in fashioning a bureaucratic formalism that accorded with local aspirations, the bureaucratization of the SAC was conflated with Pentecostal-charismatic practices. It evolved a 'bureaucracy in the Pentecostal-charismatic mode' whose bureaucratic products were implicitly linked to state agencies, while at the same time marking a resistant form of detachment from such agencies by means of spiritualistic discourses on bureaucratic procedures.

Although I have arranged these three points in alphabetical order, it should be stressed that they do not form a chronological sequence. It is not the case that the first point temporarily preceded the following one, for instance. The threefold aspect instead evolved as a simultaneity in which each aspect agreed with and was blended in with the others. My discrimination of 'mimetic bureaucracy' and 'Pentecostal-charismatic embeddedness', which will be dealt with in what follows, is thus purely analytical.

Bureaucracy as Pentecostal-charismatic Empowerment

It has already been mentioned that the dominant discourse within the church – which was mainly proposed by the church leaders – took bureaucratization to be a necessity required by the Zambian state. By emphasizing this, the discourse sharply distinguished between the local context of the church and another wider, powerful sphere in the outside world. The state was endowed with an air of arcanum. In the last instance, however, this powerful arcanum was continually made present by the church leaders when they visibly displayed their own bureaucratic practices. During most services and meetings, the church secretary was given a prominent seat in the church, so that his actions in documenting the proceedings could be witnessed by all. This public and sometimes almost theatrical representation of bureaucracy evoked two connotations that enhanced the authority of the church leaders. First, the latter presented themselves as being able to manage church–state relationships. It was they who were proficient in moving between the two worlds, between the local context and the wider, powerful sphere of the nation. Such self-representation accorded with the fact that, in contrast to the majority of the laity, most leaders of the SAC worked or had worked as truck drivers or long-distance traders. Thus, whereas many members of the church had never in their lives even left their own remote rural localities, they knew that most of the church leaders actually had experience of urban areas of Zambia. The first connotation of empowerment therefore implied that the leaders were able to act as an interface ensuring that an important but otherwise distant relationship was being bridged. Yet at the same time, by publicly representing and practising bureaucracy, the leaders of the church put themselves into the position of the arcanum. The second connotation of empowerment therefore consisted in making the absent present, that is, in somehow embodying the powerful outside. Thus, although most people agreed that the state (*mfulumende*) was something external to the immediate social context, bureaucratization integrated the practices of the *mfulumende* into the local sphere.

This empowerment of the church leaders through their representation of bureaucracy, however, is not an uncontested arena in itself. It must therefore be asked how the church leaders actually brought bureaucratization into religious practice in order to stabilize their authority. Here, they mainly faced two problems. First, they had to combine bureaucratization with their claims to be Pentecostal-charismatic leaders, especially since most church elders simultaneously held a church post and were ascribed spiritual capacity. Secondly, they also had to ensure that the products of their bureaucratization – that is, the written texts – could not be used as objectifications that could be turned against them, for example by a member of the church pointing out contradictions between the constitution or a report and the observable practices of the church. Having no means to force members to follow their own readings of such documents strictly, the church leaders had to control the negotiability of bureaucratic products if they wanted to continue using them to enhance their own authority.

These two processes, the imperative to combine bureaucracy with Pentecostal charisma and the urge to suppress the negotiability of the bureaucratic products, went hand in hand in the course of achieving empowerment through bureaucratization. The leaders of the SAC claimed that their practices of writing agendas and documenting services and meetings, as well as the origin of the written constitution, were inspired by the Holy Spirit. Even though bureaucratic products were finally treated as more or less profane objects, the source of these products was asserted to be spiritual. Writing agendas for church meetings, for example, was mostly done by the bishop in a spiritual retreat. In claiming bureaucratization to be inspired in this way, the church leaders both linked bureaucracy to their alleged Pentecostal charisma and suppressed attempts to criticize their writings. Since it was the Holy Spirit who was actually the author of bureaucratic documents, the latter were placed beyond any human negotiability. Nobody should try to counter suggestions made by the Holy Spirit. The suppression of negotiability was also accomplished by restricting access to the products of bureaucratization to a very limited number of individuals. The written agendas, reports and constitution were publicly revealed at a distance rather than distributed. In 1999, only the church headquarters was in possession of a written constitution, although the bishop had stored enough photocopies for all the congregations. Similarly, the 'archive' containing the reports and minutes existed but was not readily accessible.

This Pentecostal-charismatic mode of empowerment through bureaucratization might simply be seen as a masquerade for the suppression of the laity. This would involve distinguishing between 'charisma' and 'bureaucracy', and would either imply that the leaders of the SAC deceitfully pretended to be 'bureaucrats' when in fact they were 'charismatics', or else that they were actually 'bureaucrats' who were simulating being 'charismatics'. Yet, both presumptions would be wrong: although the church elders certainly used bureaucratic practices and performances for their own self-legitimation, again this does not imply that it is possible to distinguish 'appearance' from 'authentic core'. What the elders of the SAC actually did was to infuse bureaucratization with Pentecostal charisma and Pentecostal charisma with bureaucratization.

These findings force us to rethink what the bureaucratic products and practices of the SAC represented. We have already seen that the reports, agendas etc. were moulded in such a way that the religious practice of the SAC appeared to be devoid of spiritualism. By anticipation, the products of bureaucratization were directed at state agencies that were deemed to be incompatible with spiritual practices. Despite the idea that the secretaries' minutes were copies of God's book in heaven, these bureaucratic products were therefore treated like mere material objects, without any increase in reverence or circumspection. On the other hand, we have been compelled to notice that 'doing' bureaucracy was linked to Pentecostal-charismatic ideas, like the bishop going into a retreat to write agendas or the secretaries' connection with the Holy Spirit. Consequently, the bureaucratization of the SAC evolved a twofold aspect. Bureaucratic products were created which linked to dominant models of organizational formalization. These products were constructed in the course of religious practice whilst simultaneously exhibiting virtually no trace of practices that were deemed to be highly significant for the church: they appeared mundane, externalised, and depersonalised. At the same time, however, the actual work of bureaucracy was associated with the very phenomenon that was kept out of the records, namely spirituality. So it was not the product of bureaucratization (formalized organization) that was seen as being both empowered and empowering, but the ongoing process of producing bureaucracy (formalizing organization).

In relation to state agencies, the bureaucratization of the SAC therefore presented an intricate coming together of incorporation and transformation. The products created through bureaucratization were directed at the Zambian state, whereas the production of this bureaucratization exhibited those very features that the bureaucratic product attempted to conceal. Thus the actual practice of formalizing organization in the SAC represented a local withdrawal from state agencies while simultaneously moulding objectifying written materials whose form reproduced dominant bureaucratic models. And by spiritualizing the bureaucratizing practices of the church, a certain mystification was created, which for the local people was informed by a parallelism with the bureaucracy of Zambian state agencies. Like the latter, which during encounters was at once authoritatively displayed and made present, as well as actually seeming to conceal its real, but absent, locally unintelligible source of power, bureaucracy in the SAC was displayed at a distance and endowed with an arcanum of non-tangible authority. This is where conceptions of God and the source of bureaucratic power were made congruent.

Notes

1. For an excellent overview, see Ranger (1986b); more recent works on church–state relations in Southern Africa include Gifford (1998), Maxwell (2000), Phiri (1999), Smith (1999).
2. Van Binsbergen's article appeared in the volume *Power and Prayer: Essays on Religion and Politics* (Bax, M. and A. Koster, A. (eds); Amsterdam: University Press; 1993). An extended version of this article can be found on van Binsbergen's homepage (http://www.shikanda.net/african_religion/bots0.htm). This quotation and all forthcoming references to van Binsbergen (1993) are taken from this homepage.

3. For a fascinating analysis of the incorporation of bureaucratic forms among Kenyan Mau Mau insurgents, see Smith (1998); see also Rappaport (1987).
4. For an anthropological perspective that elaborates on the term 'facade' while dealing with organizations in Africa, see Rottenburg (1996: 232–40).
5. The former Zambian president, Kenneth Kaunda, actually banned the registration of new denominations in 1988, a ban that was removed in 1996 under the presidency of Frederik Chiluba (*Times of Zambia*, 15 August 1996). Yet, as I noted in 1993 and 1995, the church elders of the Spirit Apostolic Church were unaware of this ban. Thus, the anticipatory attempts of the church implicitly to construct a relationship with the state agencies happened against the background of the participants' quite uninformed position – which, however, made their attempts no less serious.
6. The financial and bureaucratic problems of the Zambian state became obvious when the Spirit Apostolic Church applied for permission to hold a church meeting in July 1999: the police station responsible expected four sheets of blank paper as payment for their administrative efforts.
7. This fear is not backed by substantial experience of cases of the actual banning of churches by contemporary Zambian state agencies. The *Annual Report on International Religious Freedom* of the U.S. Department of State for 1999 documents no serious infringement on the religious freedom of Zambian citizens.
8. In 1995 conflicts over inoculations almost led to the forced resettlement of one of this denomination's villages; fifteen unvaccinated people had died there of measles. Similar disputes occurred in February 1999 when the Zambian Ministry of Health started an immunization campaign against polio.
9. For the same reason, many 'traditional' herbalists (*bang'anga*) in the area keep a register or even short written records of their healing sessions.

Chapter 17

Epilogue

Johannes Fabian once noted that, by the mid-1990s, 'a generation of anthropologists [had] emerged which could no longer maintain the illusion of clear distinctions between literate and illiterate societies even if they wanted to. Almost all ethnographers ... now face people-writers: "natives" who use literacy for their own projects of survival' (1993: 84). The present book started with the observation that – surprisingly, and despite the insights above – situated literacy practices in contemporary sub-Saharan Africa have hitherto only rarely been made the object of anthropological investigation. The book therefore attempted to fill this gap by examining reading and writing practices among present day African Christians in Zambia.

More particularly, by adopting Brian Street's (1984) perspective on 'literacy practices', the present book inquired into reading and writing practices in Pentecostal-charismatic Christianity in order to challenge prevailing scholarly notions of the relationship between 'charisma' and 'institution'. I have presented empirical cases of church elders whose religious authority relies on the attribution of Pentecostal-charismatic extraordinariness, yet who also act as officeholders, make use of a variety of religious texts and engage in bureaucratic practices. With an analytical focus on social practices, the book thus asked how these religious practitioners resolved the (potentially) tense relationship between their ascribed spiritual extraordinariness and their concurrent use of objectifying writings.

In the course of my argument, the common notion that the 'fixity' of written materials intrinsically contradicts the fluidity of spiritualistic practices and the dynamism of charismatic authority has been questioned in relation to two different aspects.

First, I examined Pentecostal-charismatic *reading* practices and compared them to those of two non-Pentecostal and non-charismatic churches, the Jehovah's Witnesses and the New Apostolic Church. In the latter two cases, making and retracing connections between denominational publications and the Bible played a pivotal role. Here, a reader needed texts in order to understand texts. This notion coincided with a religious practice that located denominational writings at the centre of interactions, thus making them 'boundary objects' in the negotiation and construction of social realities and also for the religious empowerment of church members and the construction of authority. The reading practices in Pentecostal-charismatic churches, by contrast, were based on different premises. It was not that such churches refrained from reading the Bible or Christian pamphlets. As became evident, they were 'religions of the book' and at times advocated a 'literal' reading of religious texts. Yet, whereas among the other two denominations the Bible was basically defined by the supplementary publications of the denomination itself, reading practices in Pentecostal-charismatic churches were expected to rely on a triad of the text, the reader and the Holy Spirit. Spirituality here was seen as a prerequisite not only for healing or prophecy, but also for a divinely ordained understanding of the Bible. Where to open the Scriptures, how to overcome language-related problems arising from Bible translations, how to select and connect verses and how to interpret particular passages all required the inspiration of the Holy Spirit. Moreover, it was assumed that a spiritual reader could detect something divine in potentially any book or pamphlet. In contrast to prevailing scholarly understandings, therefore, the Holy Spirit was not opposed to the use of writings, but instead represented an essential epistemological prerequisite for dealing with them.

As regards reading practices, the difference between these denominations was thus a difference between neither 'orality' and 'literacy' nor 'allegorical' and 'literal' hermeneutics of the religious texts. Rather, the denominations differed in what was assumed to constitute a prerequisite for scriptural readings: enablement through supplementary publications versus enablement by the Holy Spirit. In the Pentecostal-charismatic churches, this also meant that the role of the (spiritualized) reader was given priority over that of the author. Relying on an *authoritatively* defined use of denominational texts would have been regarded as unacceptably replacing the Holy Spirit. Instead of moving within a bounded network of writing, as among the Jehovah's Witnesses or in the New Apostolic Church, the readers of Pentecostal-charismatic churches thus created their own textual networks, which crossed denominational boundaries. Nevertheless, religious texts were also used here for processes of religious authorization. As has been shown for public readings in Pentecostal-charismatic churches, here the Bible was considered an essential, but in itself insufficient, condition for scriptural practice. Only when it had been orally performed by a spiritually capable preacher, church members stated, could it develop its spiritually empowering potential for ordinary churchgoers. During sermons, interactional networks were therefore created, which placed the mediation of the church elders at its centre and eventually enhanced their authority within the church.

In terms of the dichotomies outlined in the introduction to the present book, therefore, this is not a case of role complementarity (between 'preacher' and 'prophet') or of strained relationships between either 'orality' and 'literacy', on the one hand, or 'scripturality' and 'spirituality', on the other. Instead, this is a case where role combinations in the form of personal unions prevailed, where textual source and oral performance coalesced, and where the conjunction of scripturality and spirituality represented an essential precondition for religious practice and empowerment.

The second aspect of my enquiry into this material has involved my challenge to commonly accepted notions about the relationship between 'charisma' and 'institution'; this challenge has been informed by my examination of *writing practices* in an African-initiated Pentecostal-charismatic church, the Spirit Apostolic Church. Just as reading the Bible was assumed to presuppose spirituality, here the process of producing bureaucratic writings was deemed to require divine guidance. The ensuing combination of Pentecostal-charismatic and bureaucratic practices thus led to what I called a 'bureaucracy in the Pentecostal-charismatic mode'. This combination certainly gave rise to paradoxical constellations and contradictions that were not always easy to resolve. As has been demonstrated above, for example, the administrative coordination of religious activities such as church meetings regularly produced paradoxical tensions between its three main elements: written schedules as revelations, unpredictable spiritual events during religious practices, and the documentation of scheduled yet unpredictable practices. Yet, in the final analysis, these tensions and the concomitant conflicts did not lead to an institutionalization of charisma, but to demands for a re-spiritualization of bureaucratic practices. Thus over the course of my eight years of recurrent visits to southern Zambia bureaucratization had not started to overshadow spiritual practices, nor were spiritual practices being privileged over bureaucracy. The conflicts did not induce demands either to de-bureaucratize the church or to de-spiritualize its bureaucracy. Instead, continuous attempts were made to keep the spiritual and bureaucratic dimensions in an intricate balance by foregrounding the connections between them.

As regards writing practices, moreover, the present book has shown that the bureaucratic practices of the ethnographic case study, the Spirit Apostolic Church, were influenced by translocally circulating ideas and models of how a Christian church should be organized. In this sense, its bureaucracy represented a mimetic incorporation. But this appropriation also entailed particular detachments. Although the process of producing bureaucratic writings was assumed to require spirituality, certain aspects of religious practice, namely spiritual practices such as healing and prophecy, were actually kept out of the records. By omitting indications of spirituality from the written products of bureaucracy, I suggested, the Spirit Apostolic Church precluded two potential fields of conflict. Within the church, keeping spiritual activities off the record represented an effort to ensure that the authority of Pentecostal-charismatic leaders could not be undermined by referring to bureaucratic writings. The prevailing bureaucratic form of interaction between charismatic leaders also guaranteed that spiritual revelations were not confronted with one another. Prophets disclosed revelations in their respective congregations, none of them being familiar with the prophecies of their colleagues. Spiritual activities thus evolved in a highly localized and diversified manner: they were not controlled through any denominational framework. A similar constellation existed in relation to Zambian state agencies. In the form of objectified writings, the bureaucracy of the Spirit Apostolic Church promised compatibility with the wider socio-political realm. Since the Zambian state was imagined to be potentially oppressive and to be opposed to spiritual activities, leaving spirituality out of writings seemed to guarantee protection against being outlawed by the state. In both cases, the bureaucratization of the church served as a facade by presenting and enabling certain social interactions, while simultaneously concealing certain other ones that were considered to be controversial and potentially dangerous. On the whole, therefore, the bureaucracy of the Spirit Apostolic Church enabled the existence of its seeming opposition, namely Pentecostal-charismatic practices. 'The Letter' protected empowerment by 'the Spirit'. In this sense, the bureaucracy represented not an illusory camouflage, but instead a supporting facade, which carried the social and religious organization of the church by means of its twofold aspect consisting of presentation and concealment.

My overall argument in this book, therefore, is that the reading and writing practices described above are based on specific Pentecostal-charismatic notions of religious power. In the churches concerned, spiritual empowerment is considered to be an essential means for successfully accomplishing a divinely ordained literacy practice. However, in contrast to what characterizes many contemporary mainstream churches in Western countries, for example, in principle there is no distinction here between 'spiritual' and 'bureaucratic' practices. Therefore, the same notion of spiritual empowerment is employed in different dimensions of church life. This empowerment presupposes the religious practitioners' close association with – and even incorporation of – the Holy Spirit. In the final analysis, therefore, divine immanence in the form of bodily incorporated empowerment in practice associated what in the scholarly literature has so far usually been treated as categorically separated. Therefore, instead of regarding 'texts as terror', for members of the Pentecostal-charismatic churches examined in this book, it is only the coalescence of 'the Letter' with 'the Spirit' that gives life.

Bibliography

Abasiattai, M. 1989. 'The Oberi Okaime Christian Mission: Towards a History of an Ibibio Independent Church', *Africa* 59(4): 496–516.
Adams, R. 1947. 'Oberi Okaime: A New African Language and Script', *Africa* 17(1): 24–34.
Adriaanse, H. 1998. 'Canonicity and the Problem of the Golden Mean', in A. van der Kooij and K. van der Toorn (eds), *Canonization and Decanonization*. Leiden: Brill, pp. 313–30.
Ahearn, L. 2001. *Invitations to Love: Literacy, Love Letters and Social Change in Nepal*. Ann Arbor: University of Michigan Press.
Amadi, G. 1996. 'The "New World Order": The Brotherhood of the Cross and Star's Perspective', in C. Fyle and A. Walls (eds), *Christianity in Africa in the 1990s*. Edinburgh: Centre of African Studies, pp. 149–59.
Anderson, A. 1993. 'Prophetic Healing and the Growth of the Zion Christian Church in South Africa', *NERMIC conference, 4 July 1993*. Johannesburg: University of the Witwatersrand.
———. 2001. 'Types and Butterflies: African Initiated Churches and European Typologies', *International Bulletin of Missionary Research* 25(3): 107–13.
———. 2004. *An Introduction to Pentecostalism: Global Charismatic Christianity*. Cambridge: Cambridge University Press.
———. 2005. 'New African Initiated Pentecostalism and Charismatics in South Africa', *Journal of Religion in Africa* 35(1): 66–92.
———. 2006. 'Exorcism and Conversion to African Pentecostalism', *Exchange* 35(1): 116–33.
Anderson, B. 2006. *Imagined Communities. Reflections on the Origin and Spread of Nationalism*. New York: Verso.
Andersson, E. 1958. *Messianic Popular Movements in the Lower Congo*. Uppsala: Almquist & Wiksell.
Appadurai, A. 1990. 'Disjuncture and Difference in the Global Cultural Economy', *Public Culture* 2(2): 1–24.
Aquina, M. 1967. 'The People of the Spirit: An Independent Church in Rhodesia', *Africa* 37(2): 203–19.
Assimeng, J. 1970. 'Sectarian Allegiance and Political Authority: The Watch Tower Society in Zambia, 1907–35', *Journal of Modern African Studies* 8(1): 97–112.
Assmann, J. 1997. *Das kulturelle Gedächtnis. Schrift, Erinnerung und politische Identität in frühen Hochkulturen*. München: C.H. Beck.
———. 2000. *Religion und kulturelles Gedächtnis*. München: C.H. Beck.
Austin, J. 1962. *How to Do Things with Words*. Cambridge, MA: Harvard University Press.
Barber, K. (ed.). 2006. *Africa's Hidden Histories: Everyday Literacy and Making the Self*. Bloomington: Indiana University Press.
Barnhard, J. 1993. 'What's All the Fighting About? Southern Baptists and the Bible', in N. Ammerman (ed.), *Southern Baptists Observed*. Knoxville: University of Tennessee Press, pp. 124–43.
Barrett, P. 1968. *Schism and Renewal. An Analysis of Six Thousand Contemporary Religious Movements*. Nairobi: Oxford University Press.

Bartelink, G. 1999. 'Die Rolle der Bibel in den Asketischen Kreisen des Vierten und Fünften Jahrhunderts', in J. den Boeft, J. van Poll-Van and M. de Liskonk (eds), *The Impact of Scripture in Early Christianity*. Leiden: Brill, pp. 27–38.

Barton, D. 1994. *Literacy. An Introduction to the Ecology of Written Language*. Oxford: Blackwell.

Barton, D., Hamilton M. and R. Ivanič. 2000. Situated Literacies: Reading and Writing in Context. London: Routledge.

Bauman, R. and J. Sherzer. 1975. 'The Ethnography of Speaking', *Annual Review of Anthropology* 4: 95–119.

Bauman, R. 1977. *Verbal Art as Performance*. Prospect Heights: Waveland.

Baxter, T. 1958. 'Notes on the Mission Presses of Northern Rhodesia', *Northern Rhodesia Journal* 3(6): 489–96.

Bayerl, M. 2000. Die Zeugen Jehovas. Geschichte, Glaubenslehre, religiöse Praxis und Schriftverständnis in spiritualitätstheologischer Analyse. Hamburg: Verlag Dr. Kovac.

Baynham, M. 1995. *Literacy Practices: Investigating Literacy in Social Contexts*. London: Longman.

Beckford, J. 1975. *The Trumpet of Prophecy: A Sociological Study of Jehovah's Witnesses*. Oxford: Blackwell.

Beetham, D. 1993. *Bureaucracy*. Buckingham: Open University Press.

Behrend, H. 1999. *Alice Lakwena and the Holy Spirits. War in Northern Uganda, 1987–97*. Oxford: James Currey.

———. 2003. 'Photo Magic: Photographs in Practices of Healing and Harming in East Africa', *Journal of Religion in Africa* 33(2): 129–45.

Bendix, R. 2000. 'The Pleasures of the Ear: Towards an Ethnography of Listening', *Cultural Analysis* 1: 33–50.

Berger, P. and T. Luckmann. 1966. *The Social Construction of Reality: A Treatise in the Sociology of Knowledge*. New York: Anchor Books.

Berman, E. 1974. 'African Responses to Christian Mission Education', *African Studies Review* 17(3): 527–40.

Besnier, N. 1991. 'Literacy and the Notion of Person on Nukulaelae Atoll', *American Anthropologist* 93(3): 570–87.

———. 1994. 'Christianity, Authority, and Personhood: Sermonic Discourse on Nukulaelae Atoll', *Journal of the Polynesian Society* 103(4): 339–78.

———. 1995. *Literacy, Emotion, and Authority: Reading and Writing on a Polynesian Atoll*. Cambridge: Cambridge University Press.

Biakolo, E. 1999. 'On the Theoretical Foundations of Orality and Literacy', *Research in African Literatures* 30(2): 42–65.

Bledsoe, C. and K. Robey. 1993. 'Arabic Literacy and Secrecy Among the Mende of Sierre Leone', in B. Street (ed.), *Cross-Cultural Approaches to Literacy*. Cambridge: Cambridge University Press, pp. 110–34.

Bloch, M. 1993. 'The Uses of Schooling and Literacy in a Zafimaniry village', in B. Street (ed.), *Cross-Cultural Approaches to Literacy*. Cambridge: Cambridge University Press, pp. 87–109.

———. 1998a. 'Literacy and Enlightenment', in M. Bloch (ed.), *How We Think They Think*. Boulder: Westview, pp. 152–70.

———. 1998b. 'Astrology and Writing in Madagascar: Anthropological Approaches to Cognition, Memory, and Literacy', in M. Bloch (ed.), *How We Think They Think*. Boulder: Westview, pp. 131–51.

———. 2003. 'Literacy: A Reply to John Postill', *Social Anthropology* 11(1): 101–2.

Böhringer-Thärigen, G. 1996. *Besessene Frauen. Der zar-Kult von Omdurman*. Wuppertal: Peter Hammer.

Bond, G. 1979. 'A Prophecy that Failed: The Lumpa Church of Uyombe, Zambia', in G. Bond, W. Johnson and S. Walker (eds), *African Christianity: Patterns of Religious Continuity*. New York: Academic Press, pp. 137–67.

———. 1987. 'Ancestors and Protestants: Religious Coexistence in the Social Field of a Zambian Community', *American Ethnologist* 14(1): 55–72.

Boone, K. 1989. *The Bible Tells Them So. The Discourse of Protestant Fundamentalism*. New York: State University of New York Press.

Boudieguy, Prince Birinda de. 1952. *La Bible secrète des noirs*. Paris: Omnium Litteraire.

Boyarin, J. 1993. *The Ethnography of Reading*. Berkeley: University of California Press.

Brenner, L. 1989. '"Religious" Discourses in and about Africa', in K. Barber and P. de Moraes Farias (eds), *Discourse and its Disguises*. Birmingham: Centre of West African Studies, pp. 87–103.

Britan, G. and R. Cohen. 1980. *Hierarchy and Society: Anthropological Perspectives on Bureaucracy*. Philadelphia: Institute for the Study of Human Issues.

Browne, S. 2005. 'Getting Carded: Border Control and the Politics of Canada's Permanent Resident Card', *Citizenship Studies* 9(4): 423–38.

Buckland, S. 1996. 'Culture and Religion as Text', *Studies in World Christianity* 2(1): 26–54.

Burklin, F. 1978. 'The New Apostolic Church', in D. Hesselgrave (ed.), *Dynamic Religious Movements: Case Studies of Rapidly Growing Religious Movements around the World*. Grand Rapids: Baker Book House, pp. 67–81.

Cahill, S. 1998. 'Toward a Sociology of the Person', *Sociological Theory* 16(2): 131–48.

Callon, M. and B. Latour. 1981. 'Unscrewing the Big Leviathan: How Actors Macro-Structure Reality and How Sociologists Help Them to Do So', in K. Knorr-Cetina and A. Cicourel (eds), *Advances in Social Theory and Methodology: Toward an Integration of Micro- and Macro-Sociologies*. Boston: Routledge & Kegan Paul, pp. 277–303.

Callon, M. 1986. 'Some Elements of a Sociology of Translation: Domestication of the Scallops and the Fishermen of St. Brieuc Bay', in J. Law (ed.), *Power, Action and Belief. A New Sociology of Knowledge?* London: Routledge, pp. 196–233.

Campbell, J. 1995. *Songs of Zion: The African Methodist Episcopal Church in the United States and South Africa*. Chapel Hill: University of North Carolina Press.

Canieso-Dornonila, M. 1996. *Landscapes of Literacy. An Ethnographic Study of Functional Literacy in Marginal Philippine Communities*. London: UNESCO.

Cannell, F. 2005. 'The Christianity of Anthropology', *Journal of the Royal Anthropological Institute* 11(2): 335–56.

———. (ed.). 2006a. *The Anthropology of Christianity*. Durham: Duke University Press.

———. 2006b. 'Introduction', in F. Cannell (ed.), *The Anthropology of Christianity*. Durham: Duke University Press, pp. 1–50.

Caplan, J. and J. Torpey. 2001. *Documenting Individual Identity: The Development of State Practices in the Modern World*. Princeton: Princeton University Press.

Carmody, B. 1991. 'Secular and Sacred at Chikuni, 1905–1940', *Journal of Religion in Africa* 21(2): 130–48.

———. 1992. *Conversion and Jesuit Schooling in Zambia*. Leiden: Brill.

———. 1999. *Education in Zambia: Catholic Perspectives*. Lusaka: Bookworld Publishers.

Caspary, G. 1979. *Politics and Exegesis: Origen and the Two Swords*. Berkeley: University of California Press.

Chau, W. 1995. *The Letter and the Spirit. A History of Interpretation from Origen to Luther*. New York: Peter Lang.

Chennells, A. 1977. 'The Image of the Ndebele and the Nineteenth-Century Missionary Tradition', in M. Bourdillon (ed.), *Christianity South of the Zambezi*, vol. II. Gwelo: Mambo Press, pp. 43–68.

Clark, S., et al. 1995. 'Ten thousand Tonga: A Longitudinal Anthropological Study from Southern Zambia, 1956–1991', *Population Studies* 49(1): 91–109.

Cliggett, L. 2000. 'Social Components of Migration: Experiences from Southern Province, Zambia', *Human Organization* 59(1): 125–35.

———. 2003. 'Gift Remitting and Alliance Building in Zambian Modernity: Old Answers to Modern Problems', *American Anthropologist* 195(3): 543–52.

———. 2005. *Grains from Grass: Aging, Gender, and Famine in Rural Africa*. Ithaca: Cornell University Press.

Cohen, A. 1985. *The Symbolic Construction of Community*. Chicester: Ellis Horwood.

Coleman, J. 1996. *Public Reading and the Reading Public in Late Medieval England and France.* Cambridge: Cambridge University Press.

Coleman, S. 1996. 'Words as Things: Language, Aesthetics and the Objectification of Protestant Evangelicalism', *Journal of Material Culture* 1(1): 107–28.

———. 2000. *The Globalisation of Charismatic Christianity.* Cambridge: Cambridge University Press.

———. 2002. 'The Faith Movement: A Global Religious Culture?', *Culture and Religion* 3(1): 3–19.

Collins, J. 1995. 'Literacy and Literacies', *Annual Review of Anthropology* 24: 75–93.

Collins, J. and R. Blot. 2003. *Literacy and Literacies. Texts, Power, and Identity.* Cambridge: Cambridge University Press.

Colson, E. 1948. 'Rain-Shrines of the Plateau Tonga of Northern Rhodesia', *Africa* 18(4): 21–68.

———. 1949. *Life among the Cattle-Owning Plateau Tonga.* Livingstone: Rhodes-Livingstone Museum.

———. 1951. 'The Plateau Tonga of Northern Rhodesia', in E. Colson and M. Gluckman (eds), *Seven Tribes of British Central Africa.* London: Oxford University Press, pp. 94–162.

———. 1955. 'Ancestral Spirits and Social Structure among the Plateau Tonga', *International Archives of Ethnography* 47(1): 21–68.

———. 1960. *The Social Organisation of the Gwembe Tonga.* Manchester: Manchester University Press.

———. 1962a. 'Trade and Wealth among the Tonga', in P. Bohannan and G. Dalton (eds), *Markets in Africa.* Evanstone: Northwestern University Press, pp. 601–16.

———. 1962b. *The Plateau Tonga of Northern Rhodesia. Social and Religious Studies.* Manchester: Manchester University Press.

———. 1963. 'Land Rights and Land Use among the Valley Tonga of the Rhodesian Federation', in D. Biebuyck (ed.), *African Agrarian Systems.* London: Oxford University Press, pp. 137–56.

———. 1965. 'Marketing of Cattle among Plateau Tonga', *Human Problems in British Central Africa* 37: 42–50.

———. 1966a. 'Land Law and Land Holdings among Valley Tonga of Zambia', *Southwestern Journal of Anthropology* 22(1): 1–8.

———. 1966b. 'The Alien Diviner and Local Politics among the Tonga of Zambia', in M. Swartz, V. Turner and A. Tuden (eds), *Political Anthropology.* Chicago: Aldine, pp. 221–28.

———. 1969. 'Spirit Possession among the Tonga of Zambia', in J. Beattie and J. Middleton (eds), *Spirit Mediumship and Society.* London: Routledge & Kegan Paul, pp. 69–103.

———. 1970. 'Converts and Tradition: The Impact of Christianity on Valley Tonga Religion', *Southwestern Journal of Anthropology* 26(2): 143–56.

———. 1971a. 'The Impact of the Colonial Period on the Definition of Land Rights', in I. Duignan and V. Turner (eds), *Colonialism in Africa.* Cambridge: Cambridge University Press, pp. 193–215.

———. 1971b. *The Social Consequences of Resettlement. The Impact of the Kariba Resettlement upon the Gwembe Tonga.* Manchester: Manchester University Press.

———. 1977. 'A Continuing Dialogue. Prophets and Local Shrines among the Tonga of Zambia', in R. Werbner (ed.), *Regional Cults.* London: Academic Press, pp. 119–39.

———. 1979. 'In Good Years and in Bad: Food Strategies of Self-Reliant Societies', *Journal of Anthropological Research* 35(1): 18–29.

———. 1980. 'The Resilience of Matrilineality: Gwembe and Plateau Tonga Adaptations', in L. Cordell and S. Beckerman (eds), *The Versatility of Kinship.* New York: Academic Press, pp. 359–74.

———. 1997. 'Places of Power and Shrines of the Land', *Paideuma* 43: 47–57.

———. 2000. 'The Father as Witch', *Africa* 70(3): 333–58.

Colson, E. and T. Scudder. 1975. 'New Economic Relationships between the Gwembe Valley and the Line of Rail', in D. Park (ed.), *Town and Country in Central and Eastern Africa.* London: Oxford University Press, pp. 190–210.

Bibliography

———. 1980. *Secondary Education and the Formation of an Elite. The Impact of Education on Gwembe District, Zambia*. New York: Academic Press.

Comaroff, Jean. 1985. *Body of Power, Spirit of Resistance: The Culture and History of a South African People*. Chicago: University of Chicago Press.

———. 1996. 'Reading, Rioting and Arithmetic: The Impact of Mission Education on Black Consciousness in South Africa', *Bulletin of the Institute of Ethnology, Academia Sinica* 82: 19–63.

Comaroff, Jean and John Comaroff. 1989. 'The Colonization of Consciousness in South Africa', *Economy and Society* 18(3): 267–96.

———. 1991. *Of Revelation and Revolution, vol. I. Christianity, Colonialism, and Consciousness in South Africa*. Chicago: Chicago University Press.

———. 1997. *Of Revelation and Revolution, vol. II: The Dialectics of Modernity on a South African Border*. Chicago: University of Chicago Press.

Cook-Gumperz, J. 1986. 'Literacy and Schooling: An Unchanging Equation?', in J. Cook-Gumperz (ed.), *The Social Construction of Literacy*. Cambridge: Cambridge University Press, pp. 16–44.

Cooper, F. 1994. 'Conflict and Connection: Rethinking Colonial African History', *American Historical Review* 99(4): 1516–45.

Cooper, F. and A. Stoler. 1989. 'Tensions of Empire: Colonial Control and Visions of Rule', *American Ethnologist* 16(4): 609–21.

———. 1997. *Tensions of Empire: Colonial Cultures in a Bourgeois World*. Berkeley: University of California Press.

Coward, H. 1988. *Sacred Word and Sacred Text: Scripture in World Religion*. Maryknoll: Orbis Books.

Cox, H. 1994. *Fire from Heaven: The Rise of Pentecostal Spirituality and the Reshaping of Religion in the Twenty-First Century*. London: Cassell.

Crapanzano, V. 2000. *Serving the Word: Literalism in America from the Pulpit to the Bench*. New York: The New Press.

Cross, S. 1970. 'A Prophet Not Without Honour: Jeremiah Gondwe', in C. Allen and R. Johnson (eds), *African Perspectives*. Cambridge: Cambridge University Press, pp. 171–84.

———. 1977a. 'Social History and Millennial Movements: The Watch Tower in South Central Africa', *Social Compass* 24(1): 83–95.

———. 1977b. 'The Watchtower Movement in Southern Central Africa, 1908–1945', Ph.D. dissertation. Oxford: Oxford University.

Crumbley, D. 2000. 'On Being First: Dogma, Disease and Domination in the Rise of an African Church', *Religion* 30(2): 169–84.

Csordas, T. 1997. *Language, Charisma, and Creativity: The Ritual Life of a Religious Movement*. Berkeley: University of California Press.

Cunnison, I. 1951. 'A Watchtower Assembly in Central Africa', *International Review of Missions* 40: 456–69.

Curry, M. 1992. *Jehovah's Witnesses: The Millenarian World of the Watch Tower*. New York: Garland Publishing.

Czarniawska-Joerges, B. 1992. *Exploring Complex Organizations. A Cultural Perspective*. Newbury Park: Sage.

Dagenais, J. 1991. 'That Bothersome Residue: Toward a Theory of the Physical Text', in A. Doane and C. Pasternack (eds), *Vox Intexta: Orality and Textuality in the Middle Ages*. Madison: University of Wisconsin Press, pp. 246–59.

Daneel, M. 1971. *Old and New in Southern Shona Independent Churches*, vol. I. The Hague: Mouton Publishers.

———. 1987. *Quest for Belonging: Introduction to a Study of African Independent Churches*. Gweru: Mambo Press.

———. 1988. *Old and New in Southern Shona Independent Churches*, vol. III. Gwelo: Mambo Press.

Davis, J. 1982. 'Introduction', in J. Davis (ed.), *Religious Organization and Religious Experience*. London: Academic Press, pp. 1–8.

Derrida, J. 1976. *Of Grammatology*. Baltimore: John Hopkins University Press.
Devisch, R. 1985. 'Perspectives on Divination in Contemporary Sub-Saharan Africa', in W. van Binsbergen and M. Schoffeleers (eds), *Theoretical Explorations in African Religions*. London: Routledge & Kegan Paul, pp. 50–83.
De Witte, M. 2003. 'Altar Media's Living Word: Televised Charismatic Christianity in Ghana', *Journal of Religion in Africa* 33(2): 172–202.
———. 2005. 'The Holy Spirit on Air in Ghana', *Media Development* 42(2): 22–26.
Dillon-Malone, C. 1978. *The Korsten Basketmakers: A Study of the Masowe Apostles*. Manchester: Manchester University Press.
DiMaggio, P. and W. Powell. 1983. 'The Iron Cage Revisited: Institutional Isomorphism and Collective Rationality in Organizational Fields', *American Sociological Review* 48 (2): 147–60.
———. (eds). 1991. *The New Institutionalism in Organizational Analysis*. Chicago: University of Chicago Press.
Dirks, N. 1992. 'Introduction: Colonialism and Culture', in N. Dirks (ed.), *Colonialism and Culture*. Ann Arbor: University of Michigan Press, pp. 1–25.
Dockery, D. 1995. 'The Foundation of Reformation Hermeneutics: A Fresh Look at Erasmus. *Premise* 2(9): 6–19.
Doke, C. 1945. *Bantu: Modern Grammatical, Phonetical and Lexicographical Studies Since 1860*. London: International African Institute.
Draper, J. (ed.). 2003a. *Orality, Literacy, and Colonialism in Southern Africa*. Atlanta: Society of Biblical Literature.
———. 2003b. 'The Closed Text and the Heavenly Telephone: The Role of the Bricoleur in Oral Mediation of Sacred Text in the Case of George Khambule and the Gospel of John', in J. Draper (ed.), *Orality, Literacy, and Colonialism in Southern Africa*. Atlanta: Society of Biblical Literature, pp. 57–89.
Droogers, A. 1980. 'Kimbanguism at the Grassroots', *Journal of Religion in Africa* 11(3): 188–211.
Du Plessis, I. 1984. *Pinkster-panorama. 'n Geskiedenis van die Volle Evangelie Kerk van God 1910–1983*. Irene: Volle Evangelie Kerk.
Dumont, L. 1985. 'A Modified View of Our Origins: The Christian Beginnings of Modern Individualism', in M. Carrithers, S. Collins, and S. Lukes (eds), *The Category of the Person*. Cambridge: Cambridge University Press, pp. 93–122.
Ebeling, G. 1964. 'The New Hermeneutics and the Early Luther', *Theology Today* 21(1): 34–46.
Edwards, M. 1994. *Printing, Propaganda and Martin Luther*. Berkeley: University of California Press.
Eisenstadt, S. 1968. 'Introduction', in S. Eisenstadt (ed.), *Max Weber: On Charisma and Institution Building*. Chicago: Chicago University Press, pp. ix–lvi.
Eisenstein, E. 1979. *The Printing Press as an Agent of Change. Communications and Cultural Transformations in Early-Modern Europe*. Cambridge: Cambridge University Press.
Elbourne, E. 2002. *Blood Ground: Colonialism, Missions and the Contest for Christianity in the Cape Colony and Britain, 1799–1853*. Montreal: McGill-Queen's University Press.
Ellen, R. 1987. 'Fetishism', *Man* 23(2): 213–35.
Ellington, S. 1996. 'Pentecostalism and the Authority of Scripture', *Journal of Pentecostal Theology* 9: 16–38.
Engelke, M. 2004. 'Text and Performance in an African Church: The Book, 'Live and Direct'. *American Ethnologist* 31(1): 76–91.
———. 2005. 'Sticky Subjects and Sticky Objects: The Substance of African Christian Healing', in D. Miller (ed.), *Materiality*. Durham: Duke University Press, pp. 118–39.
———. 2007. *A Problem of Presence: Beyond Scripture in an African Church*. Berkeley: University of California Press.
Englund, H. 2003. 'Christian Independency and Global Membership: Pentecostal Extraversions in Malawi', *Journal of Religion in Africa* 33(1): 83–111.
Epstein, L. 1986. 'The Millenium and the Self. Jehovah's Witnesses on the Copperbelt in the '50s', *Anthropos* 81: 529–54.

Bibliography

Errington, J. 2005. *Colonial Linguistics: The Story of Language, Culture and Power*. Oxford: Blackwell Publishers.
Etherington, N. 2002. 'Outward and Visible Signs of Conversion in Nineteenth-Century Kwazulu-Natal', *Journal of Religion in Africa* 32(4): 422–39.
———. 2005. 'The Missionary Writing Machine in Nineteenth-Century KwaZulu Natal', in J. Scott and G. Griffith (eds), *Mixed Messages: Materiality, Textuality, Missions*. New York: Palgrave Macmillan, pp. 37–50.
Ezeogu, E. 1998. 'Bible and Culture in African Christianity', *International Review of Missions* 87: 25–38.
Fabian, J. 1971. *Jamaa. A Charismatic Movement in Katanga*. Evanston: Northwestern University Press
———. 1979. 'The Anthropology of Religious Movements: From Explanation to Interpretation. *Social Research* 46: 4–35.
———. 1985. 'Religious Pluralism: An Ethnographic Approach', in W. van Binsbergen and M. Schoffeleers (eds), *Theoretical Explorations in African Religion*. London: Routledge & Kegan Paul. pp. 138–63.
———. 1986. *Language and Colonial Power: The Appropriation of Swahili in the Former Belgian Congo, 1880–1938*. Cambridge: Cambridge University Press.
———. 1991. 'Text as Terror: Second Thoughts about Charisma', in J. Fabian (ed.), *Time and the Work of Anthropology*. Amsterdam: Harwood, pp. 65–86.
———. 1993. 'Keep Listening: Ethnography and Reading', in J. Boyarin (ed.), *The Ethnography of Reading*. Berkeley: University of California Press, pp. 80–97.
———. 1994. 'Jamaa: A Charismatic Movement Revisited', in T. Blakely (ed.), *Religion in Africa: Experience and Expression*. London: James Currey, pp. 257–74.
Fernandez, J. 1965. 'Symbolic Consensus in a Fang Reformative Cult', *American Anthropologist* 67(4): 902–29.
———. 1982. *Bwiti. An Ethnography of the Religious Imagination in Africa*. Princeton: Princeton University Press.
Field, M. 1960. *Search for Security*. London: Faber & Faber.
Fields, K. 1985. *Revival and Rebellion in Colonial Central Africa*. Princeton: Princeton University Press.
Fincke, A. 1999. *Die Neuapostolische Kirche im Umbruch*. Berlin: Evangelische Zentralstelle.
Finnegan, R. 1970. *Oral Literature in Africa*. Nairobi: Oxford University Press.
Firth, R. 1970. *Rank and Religion in Tikopia: A Study in Polynesian Paganism and Conversion to Christianity*. London: Allen & Unwin.
Fish, S. 1980. *Is There a Text in this Class? The Authority of Interpretive Communities*. Cambridge: Harvard University Press.
Flachmann, H. 1996. *Martin Luther und das Buch. Eine historische Studie zur Bedeutung des Buches im Handelns und Denken des Reformators*. Tübingen: J.C.B. Mohr.
Foucault, M. 1977. *Discipline and Punish*. New York: Pantheon Books.
Fuchs, S. 2001. *Beyond Agency*. Sociological Theory 19(1): 24–40.
Garvey, B. 1994a. 'Colonial Schooling and Missionary Evangelism: The Case of Roman Catholic Educational Initiatives in North-Eastern Zambia, 1895–1953', *History of Education* 23(2): 195–206.
———. 1994b. *Bembaland Church. Religious and Social Change in South Central Africa, 1891–1964*. Leiden: Brill.
Gerth, H. and C. Mills. 1948. 'Introduction', in H. Gerth and C. Mills (eds), *From Max Weber: Essays in Sociology*. London: Routledge & Kegan Paul, pp. 3–74.
Giddens, A. 1979. *Central Problems in Social Theory: Action, Structure, and Contradictions in Social Analysis*. Berkeley: University of California Press.
———. 1987. *The Nation-State and Violence*. Berkeley: University of California Press.
Gifford, P. 1990. 'Prosperity: A New and Foreign Element in African Christianity', *Religion* 20(4): 373–88.

———. 1998. *African Christianity: Its Public Role*. London: C. Hurst.
———. 2004. *Ghana's New Christianity: Pentecostalism in a Globalizing African Economy*. Bloomington: Indiana University Press.
Goody, J. and I. Watt. 1963. 'The Consequences of Literacy', *Comparative Studies in Society and History* 5(3): 304–45.
Goody, J. 1968a. *Literacy in Traditional Societies*. Cambridge: Cambridge University Press.
———. 1968b. 'Restricted Literacy in Northern Ghana', in J. Goody (ed.), *Literacy in Traditional Societies*. Cambridge: Cambridge University Press, pp. 198–264.
———. 1977. *The Domestication of the Savage Mind*. Cambridge: Cambridge University Press.
———. 1982. 'Alternative Paths to Knowledge in Oral and Literate Cultures', in D. Tannen (ed.), *Spoken and Written Language*. Norwood: Ablex Publishing Corporation, pp. 201–15.
———. 1986. *The Logic of Writing and the Organization of Society*. Cambridge: Cambridge University Press.
———. 1987. *The Interface between the Written and the Oral*. Cambridge: Cambridge University Press.
———. 2000. *The Power of the Written Tradition*. Washington: Smithonian Institution Press.
Graff, H. 1979. *The Legacies of Literacy. Continuities and Contradictions in Western Culture and Society*. Bloomington: Indiana University Press.
Graham, W. 1987. *Beyond the Written Word. Oral Aspects of Scripture in the History of Religion*. Cambridge: Cambridge University Press.
———. 1989. 'Scripture as Spoken Word', in M. Levering (ed.), *Rethinking Scripture: Essays from a Comparative Perspective*. Albany: State University of New York Press, pp. 129–69.
Gray, R. 1990. *Black Christians and White Missionaries*. New Haven: Yale University Press.
Greenhalgh, S. 2003. 'Planned Births, Unplanned Persons: "Population" in the Making of Chinese Modernity', *American Ethnologist* 30(2): 196–215.
Grimes, R. 1990. *Ritual Criticism*. Columbia: University of South Carolina Press.
Gunner, E. 1988. 'Power House, Prison House: An Oral Genre and Its Use in Isaiah Shembe's Nazareth Baptist Church', *Journal of Southern African Studies* 14(2): 204–27.
———. 1989. 'Orality and Literacy: Dialogue and Silence', in K. Barber and P. de Moraes Farias (eds), *Discourse and its Disguises*. Birmingham: Centre of West African Studies, pp. 49–56.
———. 2000. 'Hidden Stories and the Light of the New Day: A Zulu Manuscript and Its Place in South African Writing', *Research in African Literatures* 31(2): 1–17.
———. 2002. *The Man of Heaven and the Beautiful Ones of God: Writings from Ibandla lamaNazaretha*. Leiden: Brill.
———. 2006. 'Keeping a Diary of Visions: Lazarus Phelalasekhaya Maphumulo and the Edendale Congregation of Amanazaretha', in K. Barber (ed.), *Africa's Hidden Histories*. Bloomington: Indiana University Press, pp. 155–79.
Guy, J. 1994. 'Making Words Visible: Aspects of Orality, Literacy, Illiteracy and History in Southern Africa', *South African Historical Journal* 31(3): 3–27.
Hackett, R. 1995. 'The Gospel of Prosperity in West Africa', in R. Roberts (ed.), *Religion and the Transformations of Capitalism*. London: Routledge, pp. 199–214.
———. 1998. 'Charismatic/Pentecostal Appropriation of Media Technologies in Nigeria and Ghana'. *Journal of Religion in Africa* 28(3): 258–77.
———. 2003. 'Discourses of Demonization in Africa and Beyond', *Diogenes* 50(3): 61–75.
Halverson, J. 1992. 'Goody and the Implosion of Literacy Thesis', *Man* 27(2): 301–17.
Hammond-Tooke, W. 1986. 'The Aetiology of Spirit in Southern Africa', *African Studies* 45(2): 157–70.
Handelman, D. 1981. 'Introduction: The Idea of Bureaucratic Organisation', *Social Analysis* 9: 5–23.
———. 1995. 'Reply to Josiah Heyman', *Current Anthropology* 36(2): 280–81.
Hannerz, U. 2004. *Foreign News: Exploring the World of Foreign Correspondents*. Chicago: University of Chicago Press.
Harding, S. 2000. *The Book of Jerry Falwell. Fundamentalist Language and Politics*. Princeton: Princeton University Press.

Bibliography

Harré, R. 1984. *Personal Being*. Cambridge: Harvard University Press.
Harries, P. 2001. 'Missionaries, Marxists and Magic: Power and the Politics of Literacy in South-East Africa', *Journal of Southern African Studies* 27(3): 405–27.
Hastings, A. 1996. *The Church in Africa, 1450–1950*. Oxford: Clarendon Press.
Hau, K. 1961. 'Oberi Okaime Script, Texts and Counting system', *Bulletin de l'Institute Français d'Afrique Noire* 23(1–2): 291–308.
Hawkins, S. 2002. *Writing and Colonialism in Northern Ghana: The Encounter Between the LoDagaa and the 'World on Paper'*. Toronto: University of Toronto Press.
Heath, S. 1982. 'Protean Shapes in Literacy Events: Ever-Shifting Oral and Literate Traditions', in D. Tannen (ed.), *Spoken and Written Language*. Norwood: Ablex, pp. 91–118.
———. 1983. *Ways with Words: Language, Life, and Work in Communities and Classrooms*. New York: Cambridge University Press.
Henkel, R. 1989. *Christian Missions in Africa: A Social Geographical Study of the Impact of Their Activities in Zambia*. Berlin: Reimer.
Herzfeld, M. 1992. *The Social Production of Indifference: Exploring the Symbolic Roots of Western Bureaucracy*. Chicago: University of Chicago Press.
Hexham, I. 1994. *The Scriptures of the AmaNazaretha of Ekuphakameni*. Calgary: University of Calgary Press.
———. 1997. 'Isaiah Shembe, Zulu Religious Leader', *Religion* 27(4): 361–73.
Hexham, I. and G. Oosthuizen. 1996. *The Story of Isaiah Shembe: History and Traditions Centred on Ekuphakameni and Mount Nhlangakazi*. Lewiston: Edwin Mellen Press.
Hexham, I. and R. Pappini. 2002. *The Catechism of the Nazarites and Related Writings*. Lewiston: Edwin Mellen Press.
Heyman, J. 1995. 'Putting Power in the Anthropology of Bureaucracy: The Immigration and Naturalization Service at the Mexico-United States Border', *Current Anthropology* 36(2): 261–87.
———. 2004. 'The Anthropology of Power-Wielding Bureaucracies'. *Human Organization* 63(4): 487–500.
Hinfelaar, H. 2004. *History of the Catholic Church in Zambia 1895–1995*. Lusaka: Bookworld Publishers.
Hobsbawm, E. and T. Ranger. 1986. *The Invention of Tradition*. Cambridge: Cambridge University Press.
Hodgson, J. 1980. *Ntsikana's Great Hymn: A Xhosa Expression of Christianity in the Early 19th Century Eastern Cape*. Cape Town: Centre for African Studies.
Hofmeyr, I. 1991. 'Jonah and the Swallowing Monster: Orality and Literacy on a Berlin Mission Station in the Transvaal', *Journal of Southern African Studies* 17(4): 633–53.
———. 1993. *'We Spend Our Years as a Tale that is Told': Oral Historical Narrative in a South African Chiefdom*. Johannesburg: Witwatersrand University Press.
———. 1995a. '"Wailing for Purity": Oral Studies in Southern African Studies', *African Studies* 54(2): 16–31.
———. 1995b. 'The Letter and the Law: The Politics of Orality and Literacy in the Chiefdoms of the Northern Transvaal', in G. Furniss and L. Gunner (eds), *Power, Marginality and African Oral Literature*. Cambridge: Cambridge University Press, pp. 35–46.
———. 2002. 'Dreams, Documents and "Fetishes": African Christian Interpretations of The Pilgrim's Progress'. *Journal of Religion in Africa* 32(4): 440–56.
———. 2004. *The Portable Bunyan: A Transnational History of The Pilgrim's Progress*. Princeton: Princeton University Press.
———. 2005. 'Inventing the World: Transnationalism, Transmission and Christian Textualities', in J. Scott and G. Griffiths (eds), *Mixed Messages: Materiality, Textuality, Missions*. New York: Palgrave Macmillan, pp. 19–35.
Holden, A. 2002. *Jehovah's Witnesses. Portrait of a Contemporary Religious Movement*. London: Routledge.
Hooker, J. 1965. 'Witnesses and Watchtower in the Rhodesias and Nyasaland', *Journal of African History* 6(1): 91–106.

Hopgood, C. 1950. 'Conceptions of God amongst the Tonga of Northern Rhodesia', in E. Smith (ed.), *African Ideas of God*. London: Edinburgh House Press, pp. 61–77.

Hoppers, W. 1980. 'The Aftermath of Failure: Experiences of Primary School-Leavers in Rural Zambia', *African Social Research* 29: 709–39.

Howsam, L. 1991. *Cheap Bibles. Nineteenth-Century Publishing and the British and Foreign Bible Society*. Cambridge: Cambridge University Press.

Hunter, C. and D. Harman. 1979. *Adult Illiteracy in the United States*. New York: McGraw-Hill.

Hyden, G. 1980. *Beyond Ujamaa in Tanzania: Underdevelopment and an Uncaptured Peasantry*. London: Heinemann.

Irvine, J. 1982. 'The Creation of Identity in Spirit Mediumship and Possession', in D. Parkin (ed.), *Semantic Anthropology*. London: Academic Press, pp. 241–60.

Iser, W. 2000. *The Range of Interpretation*. New York: Columbia University Press.

Jackson, M. and I. Karp. 1990. *Personhood and Agency: The Experience of Self and Other in African Cultures*. Washington: Smithsonian Institution Press.

Janzen, J. and W. MacGaffey. 1974. *An Anthology of Congo Religion: Primary Texts from Lower Zaire*. Lawrence: University of Kansas Press.

Janzen, J. 1978. *The Quest for Therapy in Lower Zaire*. Berkeley: University of California Press.

———. 1985. 'The Consequence of Literacy in African Religion: The Kongo Case', in W. van Binsbergen and M. Schoffeleers (eds), *Theoretical Explorations in African Religion*. London: Routledge & Kegan Paul, pp. 225–52.

Johnson, D. and D. Anderson. 1995. *Revealing Prophets: Prophecy in Eastern African History*. London: James Currey.

Jules-Rosette, B. 1975a. *African Apostles*. New York: Cornell University Press.

———. 1975b. 'Song and Spirit: The Use of Songs in the Management of Ritual Contexts'. *Africa* 45(2): 150–66.

———. 1979. 'Prophecy and Leadership in the Maranke Church', in G. Bond, W. Johnson, and S. Walker (eds), *African Christianity: Patterns of Religious Continuity*. New York: Academic Press, pp. 109–36.

Kapferer, B. 1986. 'Performance and the Structuring of Meaning and Experience', in V. Turner and E. Bruner (eds), *The Anthropology of Experience*. Chicago: University of Illinois Press, pp. 188–203.

Katulushi, C. 1999. 'Teaching Traditional African Religion and Gender Issues in Religious Education in Zambia', *British Journal of Religious Education* 21(2): 101–11.

Keane, W. 2006. 'Epilogue: Anxious Transcendence', in F. Cannell (ed.), *The Anthropology of Christianity*. Durham: Duke University Press, pp. 308–23.

———. 2007. *Christian Moderns: Freedom and Fetish in the Mission Encounter*. Berkeley: University of California Press.

Keller, E. 2005. *The Road to Clarity. Seventh-Day Adventism in Madagascar*. New York: Palgrave Macmillan.

———. 2006. 'Scripture Study as Normal Science. Seventh-Day Adventist Practice on the East Coast of Madagascar', in F. Cannell (ed.), *The Anthropology of Christianity*. Durham: Duke University Press, pp. 273–94.

Kelly, M. 1999. *The Origins and Development of Education in Zambia: From Precolonial Times to 1996*. Lusaka: Image Publishers Limited.

Keyes, C. 2002. 'Weber and Anthropology', *Annual Review of Anthropology* 31: 233–55.

Kidd, B. 1911. *Documents Illustrative of the Continental Reformation*. Oxford: Clarendon Press.

Kiernan, J. 1976. 'Prophet and Preacher: An Essential Partnership in the Work of Zion', *Man* 11(3): 356–66.

———. 1982. 'Authority and Enthusiasm: The Organization of Religious Experience in Zulu Zionist Churches', in J. Davis (ed.), *Religious Organization and Religious Experience*. London: Academic Press, pp. 169–79.

———. 1988. 'The Other Side of the Coin: The Conversion of Money to Religious Purposes in Zulu Zionist Churches', *Africa* 23(3): 453–68.

Bibliography

Kilson, M. 1966. *Political Change in a West African State.* Cambridge: Harvard University Press.

Kirsch, T. 1998. *Lieder der Macht. Religiöse Autorität und Performance in einer afrikanisch-christlichen Kirche Zambias.* Münster: Lit-Verlag.

———. 2002. 'Performance and the Negotiation of Charismatic Authority in an African Indigenous Church of Zambia'. *Paideuma* 48: 57–76.

———. 2003. 'Church, Bureaucracy and the State. Bureaucratic Formalization in a Pentecostal Church of Zambia'. *Zeitschrift für Ethnologie* 128(2): 213–31.

———. 2004. 'Restaging the Will to Believe. Religious Pluralism, Anti-Syncretism, and the Problem of Belief'. *American Anthropologist* 106(4): 699–711.

———. 2007. 'Ways of Reading as Religious Power in Print Globalization', *American Ethnologist* 34(3): 509–20.

Krüger, G. 2006. *Die Verbreitung der Schrift in Südafrika. Zur Praxis des Schreibens in alltags- und sozialgeschichtlicher Perspektive, 1830–1930.* Köln: Böhlau-Verlag.

Kubera, U. 1998. *Frauen in der Missionierung Sambias: 'ich will ein Beweis für meine Religion sein'.* Nettetal: Steyler Verlag.

Kulick, D. and C. Stroud. 1993. 'Conceptions and Uses of Literacy in a Papua New Guinean Village', in B. Street (ed.), *Cross-Cultural Approaches to Literacy.* Cambridge: Cambridge University Press, pp. 30–61.

Langworthy, H. 1996. *'Africa for the African'. The Life of Joseph Booth.* Blantyre: Claim.

Leclerq, J. 1974. *The Love of Learning and the Desire for God.* New York: Fordham University Press.

Lehmann, D. and J. Taylor. 1961. *Christians of the Copperbelt. The Growth of the Church in Northern Rhodesia.* London: Charles Birchall and Sons.

Livingstone, D. 1857. *Missionary Travels and Researches in South Africa.* London: Ward, Lock & Co.

Lomnitz, L. 1988. 'Informal Exchange Networks in Formal Systems: A Theoretical Model'. *American Anthropologist* 90(1): 42–55.

Long, N. 1968. *Social Change and the Individual. A Study of the Social and Religious Responses to Innovation in a Zambian Rural Community.* Manchester: Manchester University Press.

Luig, Ulrich. 1997. *Conversion as a Social Process. A History of Missionary Christianity among the Valley Tonga, Zambia.* Münster: Lit-Verlag.

Luig, Ute. 1992. Besessenheit als Ausdruck von Frauenkultur. *Peripherie* 47/48: 111–28.

———. 1993a. 'The Bacape Movement between Local Identity and Transregional Practices', Conference *'Symbols of Change: Transregional Culture and Local Practice'*, 7 January 1993. Berlin: Free University Berlin.

———. 1993b. 'Besessenheit als historische Charta', *Paideuma* 39: 343–55.

———. 1993c. 'Gesellschaftliche Entwicklung und ihre individuelle Verarbeitung in den affliktiven Besessenheitskulten der Tonga', *Tribus* 42: 100–20.

———. 1994. 'Gender Relations and Commercialization in Tonga Possession Cults', in M. Reh and G. Ludwar-Ene (eds), *Gender and Identity in Africa.* Münster: Lit-Verlag, pp. 33–49.

———. 1997. 'Wanderarbeiter als Helden: Zwischen kolonialer Entfremdung und lokaler Selbstvergewisserung', *Historische Anthropologie* 4(3): 359–82.

———. 2000. 'Der Kampf der Regenmacher: Geistbesessenheit, Macht und Magie in einer Tonga-Familie (Zambia)', in G. Best and R. Kößler (eds), *Subjekte und Systeme: soziologische und anthropologische Annäherungen.* Frankfurt am Main: IKO, pp. 13–34.

Luke, C. 1989. *Pedagogy, Printing, and Protestantism.* Albany: State University of New York Press.

Lungwangwa, G. 1987. 'Basic Education in Zambia: A Study in Educational Policy Development', Ph.D. dissertation. Chicago: University of Illinois.

MacGaffey, W. 1983. *Modern Kongo Prophets. Religion in a Plural Society.* Bloomington: Indiana University Press.

———. 1986. 'Ethnography and the Closing of the Frontier in Lower Congo, 1885–1921', *Africa* 56(3): 263–79.

Malungo, J. 2001. 'Sexual Cleansing (*kusalazya*) and Levirate Marriage (*kunjilila mung'anda*) in the Era of AIDS: Changes in Perceptions and Practices in Zambia', *Social Science and Medicine* 53(3): 351–82.

Maxwell, D. 1997. 'New Perspectives on the History of African Christianity', *Journal of Southern African Studies* 23(1): 141–48.
———. 1998. '"Delivered from the Spirit of Poverty?": Pentecostalism, Prosperity and Modernity in Zimbabwe', *Journal of Religion in Africa* 28(3): 350–73.
———. 1999. 'Historicizing Christian Independency: The Southern African Pentecostal Movement, c. 1908–60', *Journal of African History* 40(2): 243–64.
———. 2000. '"Catch the Cockerel before Dawn": Pentecostalism and Politics in Post-Colonial Zimbabwe', *Africa* 70(2): 249–77.
———. 2001. '"Sacred History, Social History": Traditions and Texts in the Making of a Southern African Transnational Movement', *Comparative Studies in Society and History* 43(3): 502–24.
———. 2006. *African Gifts of the Spirit: Pentecostalism and the Rise of a Zimbabwean Transnational Religious Movement.* Oxford: James Currey.
Maxwell, K. 1983. B*emba Myth and Ritual: The Impact of Literacy on an Oral Culture.* New York: Peter Lang.
Mbiti, J. 1987. *Bible und Theologie im afrikanischen Christentum.* Göttingen: Vandenhoeck & Ruprecht.
Mbon, F. 1992. *Brotherhood of the Cross and Star. A New Religious Movement in Nigeria.* Frankfurt am Main: Peter Lang.
Meyer, B. 1992. '"If You Are a Devil, You Are a Witch and, if You Are a Witch, You Are a Devil". The Integration of "Pagan" Ideas into the Conceptual Universe of Ewe Christians in Southeastern Ghana', *Journal of Religion in Africa* 22(2): 98–132.
———. 1995. 'Magic, Mermaids and Modernity. The Attraction of Pentecostalism in Africa', *Etnofoor* 8(2): 47–67.
———. 1998. '"Make a Complete Break with the Past": Memory and Post-Colonial Modernity in Ghanaian Pentecostalist Discourse', *Journal of Religion in Africa* 28(3): 316–49.
———. 1999. *Translating the Devil: Religion and Modernity among the Ewe in Ghana.* Edinburgh: Edinburgh University Press.
———. 2004a. 'Christianity in Africa: From African Independent to Pentecostal-Charismatic Churches'. *Annual Review of Anthropology* 33: 447–74.
———. 2004b. '"Praise the Lord...": Popular Cinema and Pentecostalist Style in Ghana's New Public Sphere'. *American Ethnologist* 31(1): 92–110.
———. 2006. 'Impossible Representations. Pentecostalism, Vision, and Video Technology in Ghana', in B. Meyer and A. Moors (eds), *Religion, Media and the Public Sphere.* Bloomington: Indiana University Press, pp. 290–312.
Meyer, J. and B. Rowan. 1977. 'Institutionalised Organisations: Formal Structure as Myth and Ceremony', *American Journal of Sociology* 83(2): 340–63.
Miracle, M. 1959. 'Plateau Tonga Entrepreneurs in Historical Inter-Regional Trade', *Human Problems in British Central Africa* 26: 34–59.
Mitchell, C. 1991. 'Preface', in C. Mitchell and K. Weiler (eds), *Rewriting Literacy: Culture and the Discourse of the Other.* New York: Bergin & Garvey, pp. xvii–xxvii.
Moffat, R. 1842. *Missionary Labours and Scenes in Southern Africa.* London: John Snow.
Msiska, A. 1986. Early Efforts at Creating African Literature: Its Distribution, Local Authorship and Library Service in Northern Rhodesia (Zambia) and Nyasaland (Malawi)', *Libri* 36(3): 240–46.
Muller, C. 1997. '"Written' into the Book of Life": Nazarite Women's Performance Inscribed as Spiritual Text in "Ibandla LamaNazaretha"', *Research in African Literatures* 28(1): 3–14.
———. 2003. 'Making the Book, Performing the Words of Izihlabelele ZamaNazaretha', in J. Draper (ed.), *Orality, Literacy, and Colonialism in Southern Africa.* Atlanta: Society of Biblical Literature, pp. 91–110.
Murphree, M. 1969. *Christianity and the Shona.* London: Athlone Press.
Needham, R. 1972. B*elief, Language, and Experience.* Oxford: Blackwell.
Newell, S. 2002. *Literary Culture in Colonial Ghana.* Manchester: Manchester University Press.

Bibliography

Nichols, S. 1991. 'Voice and Writing in Augustine and in the Troubadour Lyric', in A. Doane and C. Pasternack (eds), *Vox Intexta: Orality and Textuality in the Middle Ages*. Madison: University of Wisconsin Press, pp. 137–61.
Nielsen, H. and N. Nielsen-Westergard. 2001. 'Returns to Schooling in Less Developed Countries: New Evidence from Zambia', *Economic Development and Cultural Change* 49(2): 365–94.
Niezen, R. 1991. 'Hot Literacy in Cold Societies: A Comparative Study of the Sacred Value of Writing', *Comparative Studies in Society and History* 33(2): 225–54.
Noakes, S. 1993. 'Gracious Words: Luke's Jesus and the Reading of Sacred Poetry at the Beginning of the Christian Era', in J. Boyarin (ed.), *The Ethnography of Reading*. Berkeley: University of California Press, pp. 38–57.
O'Brian, D. 1983. 'Chiefs of Rain, Chiefs of Ruling: A Reinterpretation of Pre-Colonial Tonga (Zambia) Social and Political Structure', *Africa* 53(4): 23–41.
Obst, H. 1996. *Neuapostolische Kirche: die exklusive Endzeitkirche?* Neukirchen-Vluyn: Friedrich Bahn Verlag.
Oger, L. 1960. 'Lumpa Church: The Lenshina Movement in Northern Rhodesia', Lusaka: University of Zambia, Special Collection.
Oha, O. 2002. 'Yoruba Christian Video Narrative and Indigenous Imaginations: Dialogue and Duelogue', *Cahiers d'Études Africaines* 42(165): 121–42.
Ong, W. 1967. *The Presence of the Word: Some Prolegomena for Cultural and Religious History*. New Haven: Yale University Press.
———. 1982. *Orality and Literacy: The Technologizing of the Word*. London: Routledge.
Opland, J. 1986. 'The Transition from Oral to Written Literature in Xhosa, 1823–1909', in R. Whitaker and E. Sienaert (eds), *Oral Tradition and Literacy*. Durban: Natal University Oral Documentation and Research Centre, pp. 151–61.
———. 1995. 'The Image of the Book in Xhosa Oral Poetry', *Current Writing* 7(2): 31–47.
Ortner, S. 2001. 'Specifying Agency: The Comaroffs and Their Critics', *Interventions* 3(1): 76–84.
Oxford English Dictionary. 1989. Oxford: Clarendon Press
Parrinder, E. 1953. *Religion in an African City*. London: Oxford University Press.
Pedelty, M. 1995. *War Stories. The Culture of Foreign Correspondents*. New York: Routledge.
Peel, J. 1968. *Aladura: A Religious Movement among the Yoruba*. Oxford: Oxford University Press.
———. 2000. *Religious Encounter and the Making of the Yoruba*. Bloomington: Indiana University Press.
Peirano, M. 2002. '"This Horrible Time of Papers": Documents and National Values', *Série Antropologia* 312: 1–31.
Pels, P. 1997. 'The Anthropology of Colonialism: Culture, History, and the Emergence of Western Governmentality', *Annual Review of Anthropology* 26: 163–83.
Pels, D., K. Hetherington and F. Vandenberghe. 2002. 'The Status of the Object: Performances, Mediations, and Techniques', *Theory, Culture and Society* 19(5/6): 1–21.
Pemberton, J. 1993. 'The History of Simon Kimbangu, Prophet, by the Writers Nfinangani and Nzungu, 1921', *Journal of Religion in Africa* 23(3): 198–231.
Penton, J. 1985. *Apocalypse Delayed: The Story of Jehovah's Witnesses*. Toronto: University of Toronto Press.
Peterson, D. 2004. *Creative Writing: Translation, Bookkeeping, and the Work of Imagination in Colonial Kenya*. Portsmouth: Heinemann.
Phiri, Isabel. 2003. 'President Frederick J.T. Chiluba of Zambia: The Christian Nation and Democracy', *Journal of Religion in Africa* 33(4): 401–28.
Phiri, Isaac. 1999. 'Why African Churches Preach Politics: The Case of Zambia', *Journal of Church and State* 41(2): 323–47.
Posner, D. 2003. The Colonial Origins of Ethnic Cleavages: The Case of Linguistic Divisions in Zambia', *Comparative Politics* 35(2): 127–46.
Postill, J. 2003. 'Knowledge, Literacy and Media among the Iban of Sarawak: A Reply to Maurice Bloch', *Social Anthropology* 11(1): 79–99.

Presler, T. 1999. *Transfigured Night: Mission and Culture in Zimbabwe's Vigil Movement.* Pretoria: UNISA Press.

Price, N. 1995. *The Social and Institutional Context of High Fertility amongst the Gwembe Valley Tonga of Zambia.* Swansea: Centre for Development Studies.

Price, N. and N. Thomas. 1999. 'Continuity and Change in the Gwembe Tonga Family and Their Relevance to Demography's Nucleation Thesis', *Africa* 69(4): 510–34.

Prins, G. 1980. *The Hidden Hippopotamus. Repraisal in African History: The Early Colonial Experience in Western Zambia.* Cambridge: Cambridge University Press.

Prinsloo, M. and M. Breier. 1996. *The Social Uses of Literacy: Theory and Practice in Contemporary South Africa.* Cape Town: Sached Books.

Probst, P. 1989. 'The Letter and the Spirit: Literacy and Religious Authority in the History of the Aladura Movement in Western Nigeria', *Africa* 59(4): 478–95.

———. 1992. *Schrift, Staat und symbolisches Kapital bei den Wimbum: Ein ethnographischer Bericht aus dem Grasland von Kamerun.* Münster: Lit-Verlag.

———. 1999. 'Mchape '95, or, the Sudden Fame of Billy Goodson Chisupe: Healing, Social Memory and the Enigma of the Public Sphere in Post-Banda Malawi', *Africa* 69(1): 108–38.

Quick, G. 1940. 'Some Aspects of the African Watch Tower Movement in Northern Rhodesia', *International Review of Missions* 29(114): 216–26.

Ragsdale, J. 1986. *Protestant Mission Education in Zambia, 1880–1950.* London: Associated University Presses.

Ranger, T. 1965a. 'African Attempts to Control Education in East and Central Africa 1900–1939', *Past and Present* 32: 57–85.

———. 1965b. 'The "Ethiopian" Episode in Barotseland, 1900–1905', *Human Problems in British Central Africa* 37(7/6): 26–41.

———. 1975. 'The Mwana Lesa Movement of 1925', in T. Ranger and J. Weller (eds), *Themes in the Christian History of Central Africa.* London: Heinemann, pp. 45–75.

———. 1986a. 'The Invention of Tradition in Colonial Africa', in E. Hobsbawm and T. Ranger (eds), *The Invention of Tradition.* Cambridge: Cambridge University Press, pp. 211–62.

———. 1986b. 'Religious Movements and Politics in Sub-Saharan Africa', *African Studies Review* 29(2): 1–69.

———. 1993. 'The Local and the Global in Southern African Religious History', in R. Hefner (ed.), *Conversion to Christianity.* Berkeley: University of California Press, pp. 65–98.

Rappaport, J. 1987. 'Mythic Images, Historical Thought, and Printed Texts: The Páez and the Written Word', *Journal of Anthropological Research* 43(1): 43–61.

Rasmussen, A. 1996. *Modern African Spirituality. The Independent Holy Spirit Churches in East Africa, 1902–1976.* London: British Academic Press.

Raymaekers, P. 1971. 'Histoire de Simon Kimbangu, prophète, d'après les écrivains Nfinangani et Nzungu (1921)', *Archives de Sociologie des Religions* 31: 15–42.

Read, G. 1932. *Report on Famine Relief: Gwembe, 1931–1932.* Livingstone: Northern Rhodesia Government Printer.

Richards, A. 1935. 'A Modern Movement of Witch-Finders', *Africa* 8(4): 448–61.

Riesebrodt, M. 1999. 'Charisma in Max Weber's Sociology of Religion', *Religion* 29(1): 1–14.

Roberts, A. 1970. *The Lumpa Church of Alice Lenshina.* Lusaka: Oxford University Press.

Robertson, R. 1995. 'Glocalization: Time-Space and Homogeneity-Heterogeneity', in M. Featherstone, S. Lash, and R. Robertson (eds), *Global Modernities.* London: Sage, pp. 25–44. London: Sage.

Robbins, J. 2004. 'The Globalization of Pentecostal and Charismatic Christianity', *Annual Review of Anthropology* 33: 117–43.

———. 2007. 'Continuity Thinking and the Problem of Christian Culture. Belief, Time, and the Anthropology of Christianity', *Current Anthropology* 48(1): 5–17.

Rockhill, K. 1993. 'Gender, Language and the Politics of Literacy', in B. Street (ed.), *Cross-Cultural Approaches to Literacy.* Cambridge: Cambridge University Press, pp. 156–75.

Rotberg, R. 1965. *Christian Missionaries and the Creation of Northern Rhodesia*. Princeton: Princeton University Press.

Rottenburg, R. 1996. 'When Organizations Travel: On Intercultural Translation', in B. Czarniawska and G. Sevón (eds), *Translating Organizational Change*. Berlin: Walter de Gruyter, pp. 191–240.

Ruel, M. 1982. 'Christians as Believers', in J. Davis (ed.), *Religious Organization and Religious Experience*. London: Academic Press, pp. 9–31.

Scarnecchia, T. 1997. 'Mai Chaza's Guta re Jehova (City of God): Gender, Healing and Urban Identity in an African Independent Church', *Journal of Southern African Studies* 23(1): 87–105.

Schaaf, Y. 1994. *On Their Way Rejoicing. The History and Role of the Bible in Africa*. Carlisle: Paternoster Press.

Schiffauer, W. 2000. *Die Gottesmänner. Türkische Islamisten in Deutschland*. Frankfurt am Main: Suhrkamp.

Schnepel, B. 1987. 'Max Weber's Theory of Charisma and its Applicability to Anthropological Research', *Journal of the Anthropological Society of Oxford* 18(1): 26–48.

Schoffeleers, M. 1978. *Guardians of the Land. Essays on Central African Territorial Cults*. Gwelo: Mambo Press.

———. 1989. 'Folk Christology in Africa: The Dialectics of the Nganga Paradigm', *Journal of Religion in Africa* 19(2): 157–83.

———. 1991. 'Ritual Healing and Political Acquiescence: The Case of the Zionist Churches in Southern Africa', *Africa* 60(1): 1–25.

———. 2002 'Pentecostalism and Neo-Traditionalism: The Religious Polarization of a Rural District in Southern Malawi', in D. Maxwell and I. Lawrie (eds), *Christianity and the African Imagination*. Leiden: Brill, pp. 225–70.

Schulz, D. 2003. '"Charisma and Brotherhood" Revisited: Mass-Mediated Forms of Spirituality in Urban Mali', *Journal of Religion in Africa* 33(2): 146–71.

Scudder, T. 1962. *The Ecology of the Gwembe Tonga*. Manchester: Manchester University Press.

———. 1969. 'The Ecological Hazards of Making a Lake', *Natural History* 78(2): 68–72.

———. 1985. *A History of Development in the Zambian Portion of the Middle Zambezi Valley and the Lake Kariba Basin*. Binghamton: Institute for Development Anthropology.

———. 1993. 'Development-Induced Relocation and Refugee Studies: 37 Years of Change and Continuity among Zambia's Gwembe Tonga', *Journal of Refugee Studies* 6(2): 123–52.

Serpell, R. 1993. *The Significance of Schooling: Life-Journeys in an African Society*. Cambridge: Cambridge University Press.

Shaw, J. 1958. 'The Distribution of Books in Northern Rhodesia', *International Review of Missions* 47(185): 90–5.

Shaw, R. 1990. 'The Invention of "African Traditional Religion"', *Religion* 20(4): 339–53.

Shewmaker, S. 1970. *Tonga Christianity*. South Pasadena: William Carey Library.

Shepperson, G. and T. Price. 1958. *Independent African. John Chilembwe and the Origins, Setting and Significance of the Nyasaland Native Rising of 1915*. Edinburgh: Edinburgh University Press.

Shils, E. 1958. 'The Concentration and Dispersion of Charisma', *World Politics* 11(1): 1–19.

Shuman, A. 1993. 'Collaborative Writing: Appropriating Power or Reproducing Authority?', in B. Street (ed.), *Cross-Cultural Approaches to Literacy*. Cambridge: Cambridge University Press, pp. 247–71.

Simpson, A. 2003. *Half-London in Zambia: Contested Identities in a Catholic Mission School*. Edinburgh: Edinburgh University Press.

Simuchimba, M. 2001. 'Religious Education in a 'Christian Nation': The Case of Zambia', *British Journal of Religious Education* 23(2): 107–16.

Smith, D. 1999. 'Missionaries, Church Movements, and the Shifting Religious Significance of the State in Zambia', *Journal of Church and State* 41(3): 525–50.

Smith, E. and A. Dale. 1920. *The Ila-Speaking Peoples of Northern Rhodesia*, vol. II. New York: University Books.

Smith, J. 1998. 'Njama's Supper: The Consumption and Use of Literary Potency by Mau Mau Insurgents in Colonial Kenya', *Comparative Studies in Society and History* 40(3): 524–48.

Snelson, P. 1974. *Educational Development in Northern Rhodesia, 1883–1945*. Lusaka: National Educational Company of Zambia.

Sökefeld, M. 1999. 'Debating Self, Identity, and Culture in Anthropology', *Current Anthropology* 40(4): 417–431.

Sohm, R. 1892. *Kirchenrecht*. Leipzig: Duncker & Humblot.

Soltow, L. and E. Stevens. 1981. *The Rise of Literacy and the Common School in the United States*. Chicago: University of Chicago Press.

Southwold, M. 1979. 'Religious Belief', *Man* 14(4): 628–44.

Star, S. and J. Griesemer. 1989. 'Institutional Ecology, 'Translations' and Boundary Objects: Amateurs and Professionals in Berkeley's Museum of Vertebrate Zoology, 1907–1939'. *Social Studies of Science* 19(3): 387–420.

Stock, B. 1983. *The Implications of Literacy: Written Language and Models of Interpretation in the Eleventh and Twelfth Centuries*. Princeton: Princeton University Press.

Street, B. 1984. *Literacy in Theory and Practice*. Cambridge: Cambridge University Press.

———. (ed.). 1993. *Cross-Cultural Approaches to Literacy*. Cambridge: Cambridge University Press.

———. 2003. 'What's "New" in New Literacy Studies? Critical Approaches to Literacy in Theory and Practice', *Current Issues in Comparative Education* 5(2): 1–14.

Stromberg, P. 1981. 'Consensus and Variation in the Interpretation of Religious Symbolism: A Swedish Example', *American Ethnologist* 8(3): 544–59.

Summers, C. 2002. *Colonial Lessons: Africans' Education in Southern Rhodesia, 1918–1940*. Portsmouth: Heinemann.

Sundkler, B. 1961a. *Bantu Prophets in South Africa*. London: Oxford University Press.

———. 1961b. 'The Concept of Christianity in the African Independent Churches', *African Studies* 20(4): 203–13.

———. 1976. *Zulu Zion and Some Swazi Zionists*. London: Oxford University Press.

———. 1978. 'Worship and Spirituality', in E. Fasholé-Luke (ed.), *Christianity in Independent Africa*. Bloomington: Indiana University Press, pp. 545–53.

Swedberg, R. 2003. 'The Changing Picture of Max Weber's Sociology', *Annual Review of Sociology* 29: 283–306.

Switzer, L. 1984. 'The African Christian Community and its Press in Victorian South Africa', *Cahiers d'Études Africaines* 96(24): 455–76.

Tambiah, S. 1968. 'The Magical Power of Words', *Man* 3(2): 178–208.

———. 1984. *The Buddhist Saints of the Forest and the Cult of Amulets*. Cambridge: Cambridge University Press.

Tempels, P. 1945. *La philosophie bantoue*. Elizabethville: Lovania.

ter Haar, G. 1992. *Spirit of Africa: The Healing Ministry of Archbishop Milingo in Zambia*. London: C. Hurst.

Torpey, J. 2000. *The Invention of the Passport: Surveillance, Citizenship, and the State*. Cambridge: Cambridge University Press.

Turner, H. 1960. 'Seaching and Syncretism: A West African Documentation', *International Review of Missions* 49(194): 189–94.

———. 1967a. 'A Typology for African Religious Movements', *Journal of Religion in Africa* 1(1): 1–34.

———. 1967b. *African Independent Church: The Church of the Lord (Aladura)*, vol. I. Oxford: Clarendon Press.

———. 1967c. *African Independent Church: The Life and Faith of the Church of the Lord (Aladura)*, vol. II. Oxford: Clarendon Press.

———. 1975. 'African Independent Churches and Education', *Journal of Modern African Studies* 13(2): 295–308.

Bibliography

———. 1979. 'The Hidden Power of the Whites: The Secret Religion Withheld from the Primal Peoples', in H. Turner (ed.), *Religious Innovation in Africa*. Boston: G.K. Hall & Co, pp. 271–288.
Turner, V.1969. *The Ritual Process: Structure and Anti-Structure*. London: Routledge & Kegan Paul.
Tyler, S. 1986. 'On being out of words', *Cultural Anthropology* 1(2): 131–37.
Ukah, A. 2003. 'Advertising God: Nigerian Christian Video-Films and the Power of Consumer Culture', *Journal of Religion in Africa* 33(2): 203–31.
van Binsbergen, W.1993. 'African Independent Churches and the State in Botswana', *Retrieved* 20 August 2007 from http://www.shikanda.net/african_religion/bots0.htm
———. 2004. 'Challenges for the Sociology of Religion in the African Context: Prospects for the Next 50 Years', *Social Compass* 51(1): 85–98.
van Binsbergen, W. and R. van Dijk. (eds). 2004. *Situating Globality: African Agency in the Appropriation of Global Culture*. Leiden: Brill.
van Creveld, M. 1999. *The Rise and Decline of the State*. Cambridge: Cambridge University Press.
van der Kooij, A. and K. van der Toorn. (eds). 1998. *Canonization and Decanonization*. Leiden: Brill.
van Dijk, R. 1999. 'The Pentecostal Gift: Ghanaian Charismatic Churches and the Moral Innocence of the Global Economy', in R. Fardon (ed.), *Modernity on a Shoestring*. London: EIDOS, pp. 71–90.
———. 2002. 'The Soul is the Stranger. Ghanaian Pentecostalism and the Diasporic Contestation of "Flow" and "Individuality"', *Culture and Religion* 3(1): 49–67.
———. 2005. 'Transnational Images of Pentecostal Healing: Comparative Examples from Malawi and Botswana', in T. Luedke and H. West (eds), *Borders and Healers*. Bloomington: Indiana University Press, eds. pp. 101–25.
van Gennep, A. 1922. *The Rites of Passage*. Chicago: Chicago University Press.
Verhoeven, L. 1996. 'Literacy Outside the Mainstream', *International Journal of the Sociology of Language* 119: 1–12.
Vickery, K. 1986. *Black and White in Southern Zambia: The Tonga Plateau Economy and British Imperialism, 1890–1939*. New York: Greenwood Press.
Vincent, D. 2000. *The Rise of Mass Literacy. Reading and writing in modern Europe*. Cambridge: Polity Press.
Volz, C. 1983. *Faith and Practice in the Early Church*. Minneapolis: Augsburg Publishing House.
Wallis, R. 1982. 'The Social Construction of Charisma', *Social Compass* 19(1): 25–39.
Weber, M. 1963. *The Sociology of Religion*. Boston: Beacon Press.
———. 1968a. 'The Nature of Charismatic Authority and its Routinization', in S. Eisenstadt (ed.), *Max Weber: On Charisma and Institution Building*. Chicago: Chicago University Press, pp. 48–65.
———. 1968b. 'The Pure Types of Authority', in S. Eisenstadt (ed.), *Max Weber: On Charisma and Institution Building*. Chicago: Chicago University Press, pp. 46–47.
———. 1968c. 'The Sociology of Charismatic Authority', in S. Eisenstadt (ed.), *Max Weber: On Charisma and Institution Building*. Chicago: Chicago University Press, pp. 18–27.
———. 1968d. 'Bureaucracy', in S. Eisenstadt (ed.), *Max Weber: On Charisma and Institution Building*. Chicago: Chicago University Press, pp. 66–77.
Weick, K. 1979. *The Social Psychology of Organizing*. New York: Random House.
———. 1995. *Sensemaking in Organizations*. Thousand Oaks: Sage.
Weinrich, A. 1977. *The Tonga People on the Southern Shore of Lake Kariba*. Gwelo: Mambo Press.
Wendtland, E. and S. Hachibamba. 2000. '"Do You Understand What You Are Reading [Hearing]?" (Acts 8:30) The Translation and Contextualization of Isaiah 52:13–53–12 in Chitonga', in G. West and M. Dube (eds), *The Bible in Africa*. Leiden: Brill, pp. 538–56.
West, M. 1975. *Bishops and Prophets in a Black City: African Independent Churches in Soweto, Johannesburg*. Cape Town: David Philip.
White, D. and K. White. 1996. 'Charisma, Structure, and Contested Authority: The Social Construction of Authenticity in Mormonism', *Religion and the Social Order* 6: 93–112.

Whyte, S. 1997. *Questioning Misfortune: The Pragmatics of Uncertainty in Eastern Uganda*. Cambridge: Cambridge University Press.
Wogan, P. 2001. 'Imagined Communities Reconsidered: Is Print-Captialism What We Think It Is?', *Anthropological Theory* 1(4): 403–28.
——. 2004. *Magical Writing in Salasaga. Literacy and Power in Highland Ecuador*. Boulder: Westview Press.
Worby, E. 1994. 'Maps, Names, and Ethnic Games: The Epistemology and Iconography of Colonial Power in Northwestern Zimbabwe', *Journal of Southern African Studies* 20(3): 371–92.
Wright, S. 1994. '"Culture" in Anthropology and Organizational Studies', in S. Wright (ed.), *Anthropology of Organizations*. London: Routledge, pp. 1–31.
Yorke, E. 1990. 'The Spectre of a Second Chilembwe: Government, Missions, and Social Control in Wartime Northern Rhodesia, 1914–18', *Journal of African History* 31(3): 373–91.
Zeitlyn, D. 2001. 'Finding Meaning in the Text: The Process of Interpretation in Text-Based Divination', *Journal of the Royal Anthropological Institute* 7(2): 225–40.
Zucker, L. 1977. 'The Role of Institutionalization in Cultural Persistence', *American Sociological Review* 42(5): 726–43.

Institutional Documents and Reports

Annual Report on Native Education. 1931. Lusaka.
Annual Report on International Religious Freedom. 1999. U.S. Department of State.
Report of the Proceedings of the General Missionary Conference of North-West Rhodesia. 1914. Kalomo.
Report of the Proceedings of the General Missionary Conference of North-West Rhodesia. 1919. Livingstone.
Report of the Proceedings of the General Missionary Conference of Northern Rhodesia. 1931. Lovedale.
Report of the Commission Appointed to Enquire into the Disturbances in the Copperbelt. 1935. Lusaka.
Report of the Proceedings of Ninth General Missionary Conference of Northern Rhodesia. 1944. Lovedale.
World Health Report. 1999. World Health Organisation.
Zambia Primary Course; Grade V, Teacher's Handbook; English Language and Reading. 1971. Lusaka.
Zambian Situation Analysis. 1997. Zambian Statistical Office.

Bibliography

Archival Sources

Case Record of Mukusi Division in Luangwa Province, 22 March 1934. NAZ: Sec2/1175.
Case Record of Kapotwe Village in Mumbwa District, 30 March 1935. NAZ: ZA 1/9 /62/1.
Guimbi Sub-District: Annual Report for the Year Ending 31 March 1917. NAZ: KDB 6/2/1.
Gwembe Tour Report No. 3, 1952. NAZ: Sec 2/1016.
Gwembe Tour Report No. 3, 1954. NAZ: Sec 2/1018.
Gwembe Tour Report No. 8, 1954. NAZ: Sec 2/1018.
Letter of Provincial Commissioner (Abercorn) to Chief Secretary of the Northern Rhodesian Government, 22 June 1932. NAZ: Sec 2/337, Vol. 1.
Letter of District Commissioner (Ndola) to Provincial Commissioner (Ndola), 2 September 1932. NAZ: Sec 2/337, Vol. 1.
Letter of Provincial Commissioner (Ndola) to Chief Secretary of the Northern Rhodesian Government, 12 February 1943. NAZ: Sec 2/430.
Letter of Provincial Commissioner (Broken Hill) to Chief Secretary of the Northern Rhodesian Government, 6 April 1943. NAZ: Sec 2/430.
Report on the Conference of Representatives of Missionary Societies, 1919. NAZ: Sec B1/62/2.
Report on Native Affairs for the Quarter Ending 31 March 1932, Batoka Province. NAZ: Sec 2/68, Vol. 4.

Index

Abasiattai, M., 18
Adriaanse, H., 119, 212n1
agency,
    concept of, 8–9, 20, 138, 175
    see also Bible
agendas for church services and meetings
    see church administration
Ahearn, L., 19
ancestral spirits
    see religious pluralism; spirits
Anderson, A., 27n1, 62, 69n14, 70n19
Anderson, B., 28n5, 156
Anderson, D., 28n3
Andersson, E., 13, 14, 29n12, 143n, 212n
Appadurai, A., 157
Aquina, M., 63
Assmann, J., 120–21, 122n5, 135
auralization
    see Bible
Austin, J., 152
authors
    of Christian publications, 12–15, 89, 95–96, 125, 129, 169
    and divine inspiration, 206, 240
    and readers, 129, 135, 244

baptism
    as polyvalent rite of passage, 12, 48, 58, 107, 193, 208–09, 218
    documentation of, *see* church administration
Barber, K., 11
Barnhard, J., 119
Barrett, P., 11
Barton, D., 19, 20
Bauman, R., 144, 147
Baynham, M., 19
Behrend, H., 14, 28n8, 29n11, 103n4
Bendix, R., 143, 152
Berger, P., 9
Besnier, N., 19, 154n1, 154n3
Biakolo, E., 9
Bible
    agency of, 20, 138, 175–76

canonization of books of the Bible, 23, 86, 119, 120–21, 122n5, 155
commentaries, *see* Christian publications
as emblem of Christian identity, 23, 95, 99–102, 103, 108
inerrancy of, 23, 86, 118–20
latency and actualization, 119–21, 122n4, 146, 162
lectio divina, 170–73, 174, 179n4
memorization of verses, 82n6, 96–97, 102, 103n5, 133, 135, 151–52, 171, 176
and missionaries, 10–11, 34–35, 155
ownership of, 91–92
private reading of, 99, 131, 135, 137, 151–52, 161, 163
procurement of, 89–91, 93
quotations from, 95–99, 102, 103n2, 110, 147–48, 154n3, 203
recitation and auralization of, 102, 120–21, 122n5, 135, 145–54, 171, 172, 178
selection and combination of verses, 98–99, 130–31, 132–34, 142, 162, 174
status of, 86–87, 118–20, 125
translations of, 10–11, 24, 34–35, 125–27, 136n1, 136n8, 155, 244
versions of, 15, 24, 125–27, 130, 133–34
Bible studies
    and the use of *Catechisms* according to Martin Luther, 167n5, 176–79, 179n6–7
    in the Spirit Apostolic Church, 134–35, 142–43, 151–52
Bledsoe, C., 138
Bloch, M., 20, 28n9, 29n18, 72
Blot, R., 19, 20, 71
Bond, G., 70n19, 234
booklets
    see Christian publications
Boone, K., 118
Boyarin, J., 143

Breier, M., 28
Brenner, L., 118
Britan, G., 185
Browne, S., 201
Buckland, S., 29n19, 117
bureaucracy
  in Africa, 231–33
  bureaucratic ritualism, 47, 49–50
  and classification, 33, 185, 202, 235
  in colonialism, 45–48
  as founding myth, 188–90, 224, 236
  God as primordial bookkeeper, 13, 206, 241
  and mission societies, 48–50
  neo-institutionalist analyses, 28n4, 186, 237
  officeholders, *see* church offices and officeholders
  in the Pentecostal-charismatic mode, 25–26, 184, 239–41, 245
  as procedure and product, 27, 206, 224–25, 238–39, 240–41
  as protective 'facade', 26–27, 187, 199, 227–30, 233, 242n2, 245–46
  as social practice, 27, 28n4, 184–87, 201–02
  and spirituality, 25–26, 224–25
  and the state, 238–41, 245
  transnational diffusion of, 14–15, 183
  in the Western history of ideas, 5–6, 28n4, 183–87
  see also church administration; church organization

Cahill, S., 201
Callon, M., 25, 29n21, 157, 198
Campbell, J., 51n14
Canieso-Dornonila, M., 82n6
Cannell, F., 2, 10, 137
Caplan, J., 201
Carmody, B., 50n1, 79
certificates for officeholders
  see church administration
charisma
  dispersion of, 190–93, 197–98, 207
  inherited, 193–94
  and institution, 3, 4–8, 9, 16–17, 225, 243
  objectification of, 138
  of the office, 3, 193–94
  routinization of, 7–8, 15–17, 138, 193–94, 225

Christian denominations
  boundaries between, 27n1, 63–68, 128–29, 160, 175, 210, 244
  publications of, *see* Christian publications in area of research, 61–63
  see also religious pluralism
Christian publications
  Bible commentaries, 91–92, 133–34, 135, 178–79
  circulars, 15, 25, 147, 157, 160–65, 167n8, 228
  origin of, 10, 24, 89–91, 125–26, 128–29, 164, 169
  ownership of, 91–92
  pamphlets, tracts, booklets, magazines, 15, 24–25, 36, 40–41, 48, 87–88, 90–91, 92, 128–29, 131–33, 136n2, 155–60, 162–68, 169–70, 228, 244
  printing and distribution of, 33–37, 39–41, 155–66
  private reading of, 131–34
  procurement of, 89–91
  and sermons, 131–33
  see also Bible
Christianity
  in Africa and the state, 26–27, 203, 207–208, 230–35, 236–39, 241, 241n1, 242n5, 242n5–7, 245
  anthropology of, 1–2
  boundaries of, 105–114
  Christian dualities, 1–3, 8–10, 15, 243–46
  as a 'religion of the book', 1–3, 8–10, 23, 102–103, 117–22, 155
  in area of research, 60–64
church administration
  accessibility of administrative documents, 89, 221–22, 224
  agendas for church services and meetings, 26, 183, 188, 198, 206, 213–16, 217, 221–24, 225, 225n1, 228, 230, 236, 238, 240–41
  baptism lists and tickets, 12, 188, 209, 211, 219
  certificates for officeholders, 14, 26, 42, 188, 196, 197, 202–04, 207, 209, 211, 219, 227–28
  church constitutions, 183, 195, 202, 232, 236, 237–38, 240
  letters, 12, 81n3, 89–90, 136n2, 164, 196–97, 228

membership identity cards, 14, 26, 183, 202, 207–08, 209, 211, 212n2, 228
membership registers, *see* church membership
registration form for church meetings, 233, 242n6
reports of services and meetings, 26, 183, 204, 206, 213, 216–24, 225n1, 228–29, 230, 232, 236–37, 238, 240, 241
see also bureaucracy; offices and officeholders; church organization; Holy Spirit
church constitutions
see church administration
church elders
see church offices and officeholders; church organization; Holy Spirit
churches
see Christian denominations
church membership
documentation of, 14, 26, 48–49, 167n3, 167n7, 183, 207–208, 209–11, 212n3–4, 228
flexibility and selectivity in, 62–61, 63–64, 68, 80, 208–11
see also church administration
church offices and officeholders
bishop, 53–57, 63, 64, 65, 108, 142, 188–93, 194, 196–97, 203, 207, 209, 214, 221, 223–24, 225, 229, 236, 240, 241
deacons, 136n6, 191, 195, 196, 222
different types of, 194, 195
pastors, 1, 12, 64, 65–68, 183, 191–92, 195, 196, 197
role complementarity and personal unions, 3, 6, 8, 16–17, 25, 49–50, 184, 193, 194, 244
secretaries, 1, 3, 12, 14–15, 17–18, 25–26, 29n18, 63–64, 73, 115n3, 183, 191, 194, 195, 196, 204–06, 209, 210, 211, 212n1, 213, 217–20, 223–24, 225, 228–29, 239, 241
treasurers, 115n3, 183, 191, 194, 195, 217
vice bishop, 64, 95, 113, 194
see also church administration; church organization
church organization
concept of 'organizing practices', 7, 183–84, 213

formal and informal, 185–86, 187
formal organization, *see* bureaucracy
founding of branches, 56, 188–93, 196–97, 199n1, 202, 203
hierarchies within churches, 21, 74–75, 147–48, 152–53, 161, 162–63, 164, 165, 167n2, 184, 188, 193–99, 202, 211, 227–30, 232, 233
role of mutual ignorance, 195–99, 220, 229–30
see also church administration
church secretaries
see church offices and officeholders
church services
documentation of, *see* church administration
planning of, *see* church administration
circulars
see Christian publications
Clark, S., 69n10
Cliggett, L., 54, 60, 68, 69n5
Cohen, A., 97
Cohen, R., 185
Coleman, J., 145–46
Coleman, S., 62, 69n14, 86, 102
Collins, J., 19, 20, 71
Colson, E., 45, 51n14, 53–55, 58, 62, 68, 68n2–3, 69n8, 69n10–11, 69n13, 69n17, 70n18, 70n20–22, 73, 82, 111, 143n2, 168n10
Comaroff, Jean., 11, 33, 34, 36, 44, 62, 125, 175, 212n2
Comaroff, John., 11, 33, 34, 36, 44, 125, 175
Cook-Gumperz, J., 33, 71
Cooper, F., 33, 49
Cox, H., 27n1
Crapanzano, V., 118
Cross, S., 40, 50n6, 51n12, 58
Crumbley, D., 81n2
Csordas, T., 8
Cunnison, I., 50n6, 167
Czarniawska-Joerges, B., 185

Dagenais, J., 85, 92
Dale, A., 70n20
Daneel, M., 13, 27n1, 29n14, 29n17–18
Davis, J., 6
demons
see spirits
denominational publications
see Christian publications
denominations
see Christian denominations

269

Derrida, J., 29n19
Devisch, R., 62
De Witte, M., 29n10
Dillon-Malone, C., 10, 13, 14, 17, 29n12–14, 148
DiMaggio, P., 186, 231, 237
Dirks, N., 33
divination
　as a feature of Christian practice, 14–15, 61–62, 66, 99, 100–101, 105–106, 108, 110–13, 115n1, 146
　by using the Bible, 12, 98–99, 106, 110–14, 115n1
　non-documentation in administrative documents, 202, 220
　see also Holy Spirit
Draper, J., 11, 13
Droogers, A., 210
Dumont, L., 28n9

Edwards, M., 155
Eisenstadt, S., 5
Eisenstein, E., 155, 175
Elbourne, E., 33
Ellen, R., 92
enablement
　see 'literacy enablement'
Engelke, M., 2, 10, 28n7, 88, 103n1, 138
Englund, H., 69n14
Epstein, L., 50n6, 167n3
Erasmus of Rotterdam, 172–73, 174
Errington, J., 33
Etherington, N., 15, 100

Fabian, J., 4, 15–16, 33, 60, 243
Fernandez, J., 15, 118
fetishization
　of the Bible and other religious objects, 86–87, 138
　of colonial administrative paperwork, 47
　concept of 'fetish' in analyses of sacred books, 121
　non-fetishization, 23, 87, 92, 142
Fields, K., 37, 39, 41, 44, 50n6, 58
Finnegan, R., 95
Firth, R., 6
Fish, S., 7, 165
Flachmann, H., 177–78, 179n8
Foucault, M., 26, 46, 185, 201–2
Fuchs, S., 9

Garvey, B., 49, 50n1, 212n3

Gerth, H., 5
Giddens, A., 186, 201
Gifford, P., 50n6, 62, 69n14, 79, 164, 241n1
glossolalia
　as a feature of Christian practice, 1, 2, 13, 17 28n9, 41, 98–99, 105, 130–31
　non-documentation in administrative documents, 220
　see also Holy Spirit
Goody, J., 6, 9, 18–20, 71, 86, 114, 120, 138, 208
Graff, H., 19–20
Graham, W., 102, 145, 152
Gray, R., 37
Griesemer, J., 29n22, 118
Grimes, R., 21
Gunner, E., 12, 14, 95–96
Guy, J., 95

Hackett, R., 29n10, 62
Halverson, J., 20
Hamilton, M., 20
Hammond-Tooke, W., 62
Handelman, D., 185
Hannerz, U., 167n1
Harding, S., 125
Harré, R., 199
Harries, P., 36
Hastings, A., 10, 44
Hawkins, S., 11
healers ('traditional')
　see healing; religious pluralism
healing
　methods used, 62–63, 69n16, 100, 106–07, 109, 138–40
　polyvalent metaphor of, 62
　therapy management group, 63, 64, 67
　see also Holy Spirit; religious pluralism; spirituality
Heath, S., 19–20, 154n1
Henkel, R., 39, 42, 50n1, 57, 58, 167n7
herbalists ('traditional'); see religious pluralism
hermeneutics,
　principles and practices of, 86, 99, 114, 118–21, 145, 159–60, 162–63, 165, 172–73, 174, 244
　see also Bible; lectio divina
Herzfeld, M., 183
Hetherington, K., 138
Hexham, I., 12, 14, 28n7
Heyman, J., 184, 185

Index

Hinfelaar, H., 50n1
history
   aspects of history in southern Zambia, 53–59
   of Christianity in area of research, 57–59
Hobsbawm, E., 7
Hodgson, J., 13
Hofmeyr, I., 10, 15, 47, 95, 167n1, 168n10, 205, 210
Holy Spirit
   enablement through, 25, 129, 130, 170, 174, 223, 244
   evanescence of, 3, 68, 137–42, 209,
   'gifts of God', 14, 138, 193, 218
   and reading, *see* reading practices
   and writing, *see* writing practices
   see also spirits
Hopgood, C., 70n20, 126
Hoppers, W., 81n3
Howsam, L., 155, 175

inerrancy,
   see Bible
Irvine, J., 61
Iser, W., 7
Ivanič, R., 20

Jackson, M., 12
Janzen, J., 9, 12, 14–15, 29n12, 29n14, 63, 64, 138
Johnson, D., 28n3
Jules-Rosette, B., 64, 102, 147, 148, 150, 196

Kapferer, B., 118
Karp, I., 12
Katulushi, C., 80
Keane, W., 2, 7
Keller, E., 28n2, 87, 159
Keyes, C., 4
Kiernan, J., 6, 16, 122
Kirsch, T., 8, 15, 21, 28n8, 29n11, 60, 63, 106, 122n2, 143n3, 150, 208
Krüger, G., 11, 96
Kubera, U., 58
Kulick, D., 29n2

Leclerq, J., 170
lectio divina
   principles and steps of, 170–73, 174, 179n4

legitimate authority
   charismatic type of authority, 3–10, 15–18, 28n3, 189, 190–94, 197–98, 207, 213, 225, 229–30, 240, 243, 244–45
   different types of, 4–10
   rational-legal type of authority, 4, 7, 184, 185, 202, 202, 211
   'traditional' type of authority, 4, 7
Lehmann, D., 13, 50n6
letters
   see church administration; literacy practices; spirit and letter
'literacy enablement'
   concept of, 25, 173–74
   through denominational publications, 25, 165–66, 169–70, 175–79, 244
   through the Holy Spirit, 25, 125–27, 129–32, 134, 135, 136n4, 169–70, 244
literacy practices
   acquisition of literacy, 71–72, 76–77, 82n6, 204–205
   alternative literacies, 19–20, 22, 71, 80–81
   autonomous model of literacy, 9, 18–19, 20
   in colonialism, 10–12, 20, 22, 28n7, 33–51, 71, 74, 76–77, 212n3–4
   concept of, 3, 18–19
   in historical African Christianity, 10–15
   ideological model of literacy, 19–20
   literacy and social status, 33, 72, 73–74
   literacy events, 19
   multi-literacy, 114, 166
   networks of writing, 26, 41, 149, 155–58, 165–66, 208, 244
   and orality, 3, 9–10, 15, 20, 29n19, 95–96, 145–46, 153, 154n1, 244
   and school education, *see* schools
   skills in reading and writing, 10, 11, 20, 71, 72, 73–74, 76–77, 81n3, 82n6, 148, 204–205
   standardization of, 11, 33, 72, 77
literate cultures
   variations in, 35–37, 49–50, 96, 120–21, 155
Livingstone, D., 10, 57
Lomnitz, L., 185–86
Long, N., 50n6, 167n3
Luckmann, T., 9
Luig, Ulrich., 37, 41, 58, 59

Luig, Ute., xi, 69n5, 69n15, 70n18, 100, 111
Luther, Martin, 119, 122n3, 167n5, 176–79, 179n3–7

MacGaffey, W., 12, 13, 14–15, 29n12, 29n14, 138, 143n4, 205, 235
Malungo, J., 69
materiality
    of healing substances, 107
    and immateriality, 1–2, 7, 28n7
    of religious objects, 23, 138–141
    of texts, 23, 85–88, 92, 102–3, 138, 145–46, 150–53, 154n5, 174, 206, 241, 243
Maxwell, D., 1, 12, 13, 27n1, 28n9, 29n11, 62, 69n14, 241n1
Maxwell, K., 96
Mbiti, J., 13
Mbon, F., 103n5
membership identity cards
    see church administration
membership registers
    see church administration
Meyer, B., 3, 27n1, 28n10, 61, 69n14, 136n1
Meyer, J., 28n4, 186, 237
Mills, C., 5
Moffat, R., 50n2, 86–87, 93n1, 175
Muller, C., 12, 103n1, 146, 210
Murphree, M., 60

Needham, R., 122n2
networks of writing
    see literacy practices
Newell, S., 11
Niezen, R., 28n6
Noakes, S., 154n2

objectification
    and writings, 4, 6, 8, 9–10, 18, 68, 224–25, 240, 241, 243
    see also materiality
O'Brian, D., 69n8
Oha, O., 28n10
Ong, W., 9
Oosthuizen, G., 14
Opland, J., 95, 103n1
orality
    concept of 'aurality', 145–46, 152
    and literacy, *see* literacy practices
    romanticizing ideas about, 3, 95–96
Ortner, S., 20

pamphlets
    see Christian publications
Peel, J., 10, 13, 33
Peirano, M., 202
Pels, P., 33
Pels, D., 138
Pemberton, J., 13
Pentecostal-charismatic Christianity
    characteristics and definition of, 2, 27n1, 62–62
Peterson, D., 11
Phiri, Isaac., 241
Phiri, Isabel., 234
Posner, D., 33
possession cults
    see religious pluralism
Postill, J., 29n20
Powell, W., 186, 231, 237
Price, N., 69n10, 69n17
Price, T., 39
Prins, G., 51n14
Prinsloo, M., 28n8
print globalization
    and denominational publications, 156–57, 165–66, 175
printing press
    and mission societies, 34–36, 50n2, 155, 156, 167n3
Probst, P., 13, 18, 28n8, 103n3
prophecy
    as a feature of Christian practice, 2, 3, 10, 12, 27n1, 61–62, 98–99,102, 106–107, 110, 130, 141, 154n2, 192–93, 205–206, 221, 232, 244, 245
    non-documentation in administrative documents, 220, 228, 238, 245
prophets
    in Africa, 1–2, 10, 13–18, 44, 70n19, 70n21, 102, 103n5, 106, 110, 115n2, 143n3, 149, 154n4, 192–93, 194, 202, 227–28, 234, 245
    lack of offical recognition, 202, 227–28
    and 'priests', 'preachers', 'ministers', 6, 16–17, 28n18, 244
    relationship to bureaucracy, 17–18, 29n18, 232,
Protestant
    concepts of personhood and the self, 11–12, 36–37, 125, 175
    reformation and the print revolution, 155, 175, 179n2

Index

Quick, G., 50n6

Ragsdale, J., 34, 37, 38, 42, 43, 50n9
rain shrines
   see religious pluralism
Ranger, T., 7, 12, 44–45, 46, 50n7, 58, 70n19, 231, 241n1
Rasmussen, A., 29n16
Raymaekers, P., 13
readers
   and authors, 128–29, 135, 244
   during church services, 148–51
reading practices
   and divine inspiration, 24, 125, 127, 128, 129, 130, 134, 135, 137, 138, 169, 174, 244
   private reading, 36, 131–34, 135, 145, 151–52, 159, 161, 163
   recitation and auralization of texts, *see* Bible
   silent reading, 36, 76–77, 131, 170–73, 196
   see also literacy practices
'religions of the book'
   concept of, 2, 8, 23, 102, 117–22, 155–57
   see also Christianity
religious education
   as contemporarily taught in schools, 79–81
   see also Bible studies; schools
religious pluralism
   ancestral spirits, 14, 65, 67–68, 69n17, 70n19–20, 100
   herbalists and ('traditional') healers, 1, 3, 23, 63, 65, 66, 67, 69n16, 99, 100, 105–14, 115n2, 138–40, 183, 189, 192, 194, 202, 227–228, 229, 242n9
   possession cults, 23, 63, 66, 67, 70n19, 108, 110, 111–14, 115n3, 183, 191
   rain shrines, 67–68, 70n19, 70n21, 143n2
   witch-finders, 12, 98–99, 101, 234–35
   see also Christian denominations
religious publications
   see Christian publications
reports of church services and meetings
   see church administration
Richards, A., 58, 103n3
Riesebrodt, M., 28n3
Robbins, J., 1, 27n1, 69n14
Roberts, A., 29n14, 44, 136n, 234

Robertson, R., 1, 156
Robey, K., 138
Rockhill, K., 92
Rotberg, R., 50n1
Rottenburg, R., xi, 29n21, 185–86, 242n4
Rowan, B., 28n4, 186, 237
Ruel, M., 122n2

Scarnecchia, T., 29n16, 212n3
Schiffauer, W., xi, 64
Schnepel, B., 4
Schoffeleers, M., 29n16, 61, 68, 105, 143n2
schools
   coalescence and separation of 'school' and 'church', 41–44
   curricula in Zambia schools, 75–77
   and everyday life, 74–75
   experiences with mission schools, 77–79
   length of schooling, 72–74
   literacy as taught in, 77
   missionary approaches to, 34–39
   religious education, *see* religious education
   student–teacher interactions, 75–77
Schulz, D., 28n10
Scriptures
   see Bible
Scudder, T., 45, 51n14, 53–55, 57, 58, 68, 68n3, 69n8, 70n21, 73, 82n4
secretaries
   see church offices and officeholders; Holy Spirit; writing practices
sermons
   auralization of Bible, *see* Bible
   sequence of interactions, 146–50
Serpell, R., 81n3, 136n2
Shaw, R., 20, 117
Shepperson, G., 39
Sherzer, R., 143
Shils, E., 190
Shuman, A., 77
Simpson, A., 50n1
Simuchimba, M., 80
Smith, D., 241n1
Smith, E., 70n20
Smith, J., 138, 242n3
Snelson, P., 42, 50n5
Sökefeld, M., 28n9
Southwold, M., 122n2
speaking in tongues
   see glossolalia
'spirit and letter'

273

Christian dichotomy, 2–3, 8–9, 15, 18, 20, 96, 246
  see also Christianity
spirits
  evil, 1, 60, 189, 194, 209
  exorcism of, 1, 2, 28n9, 107, 113, 141–42, 191–92, 209
  and the human body, 1, 12, 37, 69n16, 139, 141–42, 151–53
  possession by, 1, 11–12, 61, 62–63, 105, 111–14, 141–42, 183
  possession cults, 23, 63, 66,67, 70n18–19, 108, 110, 111–14, 115n3, 183
  types of, 65–68, 69n17, 70n18–22
  see also Holy Spirit; religious pluralism; spirituality
spirituality
  definition of, 12
  non-documentation in administrative documents, 202, 220, 228, 238, 245
  re-spiritualization of bureaucratic practices, 26, 213, 224–25, 245
  spiritual healing, 2, 3, 12, 28n9, 61–63, 106–108, 115n2, 138–40, 190, 193, 202, 244
Star, S., 29n22, 118
Stoler, A., 33
Street, B., 3, 9, 12, 18–20, 28n6
Stromberg, P., 118
Stroud, C., 29n20
Summers, C., 44
Sunday schools
  see Bible studies
Sundkler, B., 13, 15, 27n1, 29n14, 63, 154n4,199n1
supplementary publications
  see Christian publications
Swedberg, R., 4
Switzer, L., 35

Tambiah, S., 138, 152
Taylor, J., 13, 50n6
ter Haar, G., 29n18
texts
  aural performance of, *see* Bible
  creative re-use, 23, 87–89, 92
  idea of, 29n19, 117–18
Thomas, N., 69n17

Torpey, J., 201
Turner, H., 11, 13, 27n1, 29n13–16, 41, 60, 61, 90, 136n2
Turner, V., 118
Tyler, S., 29n19, 96

Ukah, A., 28n10

van Binsbergen, W., xiii, 27, 186–87, 231–33, 241n2
Vandenberghe, F., 138
van Dijk, R., 27n1, 69n14
van Gennep, A., 209
Verhoeven, L., 19
Vickery, K., 48, 59, 69n11
Vincent, D., 175

Wallis, R., 8, 198
Watt, I., 9
Weber, M., 3–9, 28n3–4, 138, 184, 193
Weick, K., 7, 183–84, 213
Weinrich, A., 69n9
West, M., 6
Whyte, S., 62
witchcraft
  objects used, 98–99, 101
witch-finding
  as a feature of Christian practice, 12, 98–99, 101, 234–35
  see also Holy Spirit; religious pluralism
Wogan, P., 19, 156, 210
Worby, E., 33
Wright, S., 185
writers
  see authors
writing practices
  administrative documents, *see* church administration
  and divine inspiration, 3, 25–26, 205–06, 214, 217–19, 221–23, 228, 240, 241
  collaborative writing, 77, 218–19
  see literacy practices

Yorke, E., 39

Zeitlyn, D., 115n1
Zucker, L., 232, 237